MW00325889

MULTI-COMPUTER ARCHITECTURES FOR ARTIFICIAL INTELLIGENCE

MULTI-COMPUTER ARCHITECTURES FOR ARTIFICIAL INTELLIGENCE

Toward Fast, Robust, Parallel Systems

LEONARD UHR

Computer Sciences Department
University of Wisconsin, Madison

A Wiley-Interscience Publication

John Wiley & Sons

New York   Chichester   Brisbane   Toronto   Singapore

The author greatfully acknowledges the use of the following figures: Figure 1.2 courtesy of C. E. Shannon and J.
McCarthy, eds., *Automata Studies*, Annals of Mathematics Studies No. 34, Copyright © 1956, 1984 renewed by
Princeton University Press; Figure 3, p. 134, reprinted
with permission of Princeton University Press; Figure 6.2
courtesy of Hwang and Briggs, Computer Architecture
and Parallel Processing, 1984, McGraw-Hill, (reproduced
with permission).

Library of Congress Cataloging in Publication Data:

Uhr, Leonard Merrick
    Multi-computer architectures for artificial
    intelligence.

    "A Wiley-Interscience publication."
    Bibliography: p. 30
    Includes index.
        1. Artificial intelligence—Data processing.
2. Parallel processing (Electronic computers)
3. Computer networks. 4. Computer architecture.
I. Title.
Q336.U37 1987   004'.35   86-15746
ISBN 0-471-84979-0

PREFACE

MULTI-COMPUTER ARCHITECTURES FOR ARTIFICIAL INTELLIGENCE

This book is directed toward computer scientists, along with other research scientists and engineers, who are interested in artificial intelligence on the one hand, and/or parallel computer architecture on the other hand. It is also designed to inform the much larger group of people intrigued by the great explosion of possibilities today's phenomenally rapid progress in microelectronic "very large scale integration" (VLSI) opens up, and in the profound potential promise of artificial intelligence. It concentrates on the overall topology of a multi-computer (rather than the design of the individual computer), and on the development of powerful really intelligent systems (rather than programs for specific small problems).

This book has three major purposes:

1. It attempts to give, with a detailed survey and a large number of examples, a clear, concise picture of the great variety of multi-computer architectures already built, already designed, now being designed, and feasible—in the immediate and in the more distant future.

2. It describes the range of problems that confront AI, and sketches out some of the major approaches being taken by AI researchers. Here it focuses on and emphasizes the crucial importance of robust, flexible, extremely fast (hence highly parallel) systems.

v

Such systems are necessary to handle the enormous variability and stringent real-time demands of the real-world problems of perceiving often greatly distorted and poorly sensed objects and concepts, remembering and making inferences in ill-formed domains, and controlling and coordinating an intelligent robot that can do all these things. These entail a number of seemingly simple, mundane problems: for example, to recognize and describe people and objects in a photo; to talk and think about all sorts of "ordinary" things; to navigate the streets and find and get (buy, beg, borrow) things that satisfy one's needs. These are problems that good, general AI systems must handle to achieve real power and real intelligence (as opposed to the simplified and rigid toylike problems for which AI systems are too often developed).

3.   It also presents judgments and opinions as to the most promising multi-computer architectures for AI. It suggests the most promising architectures in terms of (a) meeting AI's ultimate long-term goals of general, fast, robust systems; and (b) the shorter-term development of special-purpose systems that have important practical applications. These architectures include a number of exciting multi-computer structures of which the AI community is largely unaware, and also several suggestions of new and promising structures that appear to be worthy of thorough development and evaluation.

This book examines the present state of parallel multi-computers and of artificial intelligence, but it emphasizes the future. Most AI programs have been designed to handle a specific problem, using serial algorithms for the serial computer. These traditional serial programs are surveyed; but a variety of potentially far faster and more powerful parallel approaches are suggested and explored.

It is almost certainly the case that many of the most interesting and promising parallel architectures (both hardware and software) have not yet been built, or even designed. This book—by examining the variety of feasible multi-computers alongside possible parallel formulations of AI problems—attempts to stimulate an integrated approach to the development of new software/hardware systems, where each is appropriate to the other. The structure of the processes to be executed can, once understood, suggest hardware structures that will execute them with speed and efficiency.

Today's micro-electronic technologies already make possible, and feasible, highly parallel networks with many thousands, or even millions, of computers all working together on the same task. Systems of this size will open up an intriguing range of new possibilities, for physics, chemistry, meteorology, engineering, and computer science. Without computers that are enormously large and highly parallel, true (artificial or natural) intelligence is impossible.

Today we are witnessing the beginnings of a major surge of interest in parallel computing. Very large parallel multi-computer networks appear to many people to offer the only possible way to make today's conventional serial single-CPU (central processing unit) Von Neumann computers substantially more powerful. This is because conventional computers are rapidly reaching the point where they can no longer be made faster; they are approaching the "speed of light barrier." The basic component of a computer—the switch, today realized with transistors—can now be made so incredibly small, hence fast, that the time taken for signals to move along the wire joining two transistors is on the verge of becoming the dominating factor in determining the speed at which computations can be effected.

Artificial intelligence requires very fast and very powerful multi-computer hardware structures for real-world problems where perception, decision making, remembering, inferring, and the other components of intelligence must work within extremely stringent real-time constraints. This will be the case whenever the AI system (e.g., an intelligent robot) must recognize, move to, gain control over, and/or interact with, complex real-world objects as they move about and change.

Therefore AI researchers are increasingly turning to parallel processes. A few have suggested a handful of parallel architectures; but almost nothing has been written that examines, from the point of view of their appropriateness for AI, the many different kinds of multi-computer networks that have been and are increasingly being explored and developed by the larger group of computer architects. This book attempts to fill that gap.

OVERVIEW

The Introduction poses the problem of very fast real-time perception.

Chapter 1 examines the underlying model of a general purpose computer that it embodies.

Chapter 2 describes the traditional single-CPU serial computer, and some of the extensions (many of which are additions of parallel hardware within the single CPU) that have been made to increase its speed and its power.

Chapter 3 presents the great advances in micro-electronics that are beginning to make feasible very much larger, far more parallel, computers.

Chapter 4 introduces the enormous variety of possible topological structures for parallel multi-computers (essentially, all possible graphs), with attempts to put several of these possibilities into a common framework.

Chapter 5 explores the major problems (with which researchers are today just beginning to grapple) in developing fast, efficient, appropriately structured operating systems for highly parallel, closely coupled multi-computers.

Chapters 6-13 examine the great variety of parallel architectures that are running, built, designed, proposed, or possible, including:

a large number of different topologies that are being used or investigated, for both (pseudo-) complete graph connectivity (bus, ring, crossbar, reconfiguring network) and point-to-point connectivity (e.g., line, array, N-cube, pyramid, tree, augmented tree, compounds of clusters, data-flow, heterogeneous structures), along with examples of multi-computers that are based on each;

possibilities for developing more general purpose yet appropriately structured architectures;

two major (overlapping) classes of multi-computer: (a) networks that attempt to be general purpose over a great variety of (or all possible) programs, and (b) more or less specialized algorithm/process/task-structured architectures.

Chapter 14 briefly describes the human brain, both (a) as an existence proof that massively parallel structures can succeed at extremely fast real-world real time processing, and also (b) as a fruitful source for design ideas.

Chapters 15-21 present the major areas of artificial intelligence, and the range of different approaches that researchers are taking—with emphasis on parallel approaches. These include:

pattern perception, computer vision, image processing;

structuring, representing, and accessing information, whether symbolic, linguistic, iconic, or perceptual;

recognizing, analyzing, and understanding speech and language;

thinking: problem solving, theorem proving, decision making, "expert" systems;

robot motor control and coordination;

learning;

integrative systems that combine intelligent processes.

Chapters 15-21 also present the multi-computer network architectures that appear to be the most appropriate for each AI function.

Chapters 22-24 summarize the different architectures examined, evaluate their strengths and weaknesses, and suggest several architectures that appear to be the most promising for a total intelligent system.

The variety of architectures examined in this book is greater than can be found in any other publication of which I am aware. I have tried to choose the most representative, the most interesting, and the most powerful; but these are best considered as examples. The possibilities for the future, both of parallel computers and of artificial intelligence, are so great that today's best understanding will surely be improved upon substantially.

LEONARD UHR

Madison, Wisconsin
February 1987

CONTENTS

PART THREE. ARTIFICIAL INTELLIGENCE: MAJOR APPROACHES; INDICATED ARCHITECTURES

PART FOUR. THE PRESENT STATE; MAJOR PROBLEMS; MOST PROMISING ARCHITECTURES

MULTI-COMPUTER ARCHITECTURES FOR ARTIFICIAL INTELLIGENCE

BACKGROUND INFORMATION
AND BASIC STRUCTURES

KEY ARTIFICIAL INTELLIGENCE PROBLEMS, AND ARCHITECTURES

This book explores three closely related problems, examining the present situation and the range of possibilities for the immediate and especially for the more distant future: A. designing and building highly parallel multi-computers (networks of computers that all work together on the same problem) that can with speed and efficiency execute substantially larger programs than can today's computers; B. developing hardware/ software systems of computers and programs that are truly intelligent; C. designing these computers and programs jointly, so that each is appropriate to the other.

The continuing steady and rapid increase in the potential size of multi-computers that can be built makes feasible a great variety of possible architectures—along with a formidable set of difficult problems that must be solved to use them effectively. For, potentially, a multi-computer can be built using any possible graph topology.

Artificial intelligence is an enormously difficult endeavour. Ultimately it attacks the age-old problem of philosophy and psychology: What is mind/brain, and how does the mind/brain know, understand, and cope with its world? Today we tend to break this problem down into sub-problems: What is perception, cognition, reasoning, concept formation, remembering, motor behavior, learning, discovery, creativity? We tend to choose a particular sub-sub problem to start with—for example, recognizing two-story houses, following stories about restaurants or terrorists, robot assembly, chess—and program in great globs of ad hoc knowledge about these tasks. Each of these functions must be generalized, and all must be integrated, to address the crucial overall question: What is intelligent thinking?

Very flexible, robust, and powerful programs are needed to handle AI problems in a reasonably general way, coping with the enormous range of unanticipated variations. These programs will need highly parallel multi-computers, simply because there are theoretical limits to the power and speed that can ever be achieved with a single conventional computer, even an ultimate super-super version of what today are called "super-computers." And the human mind/brain—which is the only successful intelligent system discovered to date—achieves its great power, robustness, and speed because it is a highly parallel multi-computer.

It is important that the AI community become aware of the many types of highly parallel networks that have already been built or designed, and of the far greater number that are now possible, and develop AI programs that address the fundamental AI goal—the ability to carry out very powerful, general, robust, fast, intelligent thinking in real time. Only then will people be in a position to explain AI's problems and needs, and to ask for multi-computers that fill these needs.

ARTIFICIAL INTELLIGENCE TASKS AND GOALS, AND NEEDED SPEED

The following briefly summarizes key central long-term AI goals for which both highly parallel algorithms and highly parallel multi-computers appear to be absolutely necessary. The human mind/brain's incredible speed sets these levels of performance. It is important to emphasize that the functioning mind/brain also serves as a crucial existence proof that these goals can be achieved.

A. Programs for visual perception must be able to process continuing streams of complex—often severely degraded and distorted—real-world images (each 256 by 256, 512 by 512, 1024 by 1024, or larger, input every 20 to 50 milliseconds), recognizing and describing, and tracking, the salient and significant objects. They must also be able to recognize up to a hundred or so complex objects within a second or less, as when reading a book at the rate of 300 to 1000 words a minute, or when recognizing a complex scene with many complex objects.

B. Systems that, often in situations of ambiguous and/or incomplete information, give "expert" advice, make decisions, choose, diagnose, reason, infer, or solve problems, should (as people do: that is, usually but not always) arrive at appropriate responses within one to five seconds, at most.

C. Speech and language recognition systems must handle casual, often heavily accented and/or poorly enunciated, continuous speech that is spoken by a variety of different speakers, at the rate of 2 to 4 words per second.

D. Semantic memory networks should (often but not always) be able to access correct, or appropriate and cogent, answers or responses to relatively unconstrained, often poorly phrased or ambiguous, natural language sentences, in 1 or 2 seconds or less (the speed that is routinely achieved by human beings engaged in a conversation), or at most (but only when we are in "deep thought") in 5 or 10 seconds.

E. Robot perceptual-motor systems must make use of information perceived through several sensory channels (typically, vision, hearing, and touch) in order to coordinate and control the motions of the robot's various appendages while the robot is moving at realistically fast speeds (ideally, 2 to 100 miles per hour or, for certain applications, even faster, as when, by coordinating hundreds of interacting muscles, a human being crawls, walks, bats a ball, drives a car, flies a plane, or tries to stop a moving bullet or missile).

F. A system that integrates several of the above functions (e.g., a robot that interacts with a dynamic environment, using vision, speech, and touch to guide its behavior, and also deduces appropriate responses) should be capable of appropriate continuing interactions with moving objects and people in its environment in real time (that is, at the speeds with which these real objects and people act).

G. Any of these systems should be able to learn and adapt, as a function of its experiences; the basic experiences from which the system learns must be of the kinds described earlier; the system should learn each specific bit of information in seconds or less; and the learning should achieve good levels of performance fast enough for the system to survive and function effectively.

The human brain achieves these enormous speeds even though its basic "instruction cycle time" is roughly 1-2 milliseconds (the time needed for one neuron to fire another neuron across the synaptic gap between them). That is, the brain's neurons are millisecond devices, in stark contrast to today's computers, whose basic instruction cycle times are on the order of microseconds, or even a few nanoseconds. Thus a computer's electronic circuits are four to eight orders of magnitude faster than the brain's neuronal circuits; yet computers are, when attempting (but not yet succeeding) to handle intelligent processes, roughly four to eight orders of magnitude slower than are brains.

In the 1-2 milliseconds taken to cross a single synapse, the brain accomplishes tremendously impressive feats in both speed and performance—but only because enormous numbers of the brain's neurons are all working in parallel. Even with their much faster basic cycle time, computers cannot possibly work as well or as fast without massive parallelism. For example, the mind/brain recognizes complex objects in a few hundred milliseconds; this means that the serial depth of object recognition is at most a few hundred. But today's first attempts at computer vision programs, when executed on a serial computer, need serial sequences of billions of instructions, and rough estimates suggest that trillions may be needed for successful programs.

THE NECESSITY OF HIGHLY PARALLEL MULTI-COMPUTERS FOR TRUE, ROBUST INTELLIGENCE

The Great Complexity of Real Intelligence, and of Programs Capable of Real Intelligence

This book focuses on artificial intelligence's basic long-term goals: to develop software/hardware systems (they might best be called something like "information processing structures," rather than "programmed computers") that are really intelligent in at least the variety of ways that human beings are intelligent. True intelligence, whether natural or artificial, entails real understanding of the world—of the organisms and objects that inhabit it, of the symbols and ideas that attempt to cope with it and explain it—and of oneself and how to interact purposefully with that world.

This understanding is never complete (indeed it seems likely that there is no such thing as complete 100% understanding); but it is relevant and sufficient, and capable of changing and growing. The perceiver really understands what houses, chairs, and people are. This is a deep understanding that makes possible powerful recognition over extreme distortions and relevant reactions, whether verbal descriptions or complex actions. The language understander really comprehends the meaning of the comment, directive, story, or book. The chess master, master chef, auto mechanic, race car driver, short order cook, mathematician, computer architect, engineer, bartender, brew master, and brewery designer all really understand their own domain, from their own perspective. The "understandings" of a Ferrari by the sales-person, driver, mechanic, mechanical engineer, designer, physicist, psychologist, sociologist, economist, moral philosopher and metaphysician will differ greatly. A truly intelligent AI system need not have all of these levels and perspectives of understanding of all possible things (indeed no single human being does, and that is probably impossible), but it must be capable of achieving (by learning) any of these.

The Great Size of the Hardware Multi-Computer Needed for Intelligence

Parallel algorithms, and very large multi-computer architectures that handle these algorithms efficiently, are absolutely necessary for real time execution of these kinds of large AI systems—to make them work on real-world, as opposed to toy, problems. It seems likely that to perform with the speed and power of the human brain (with its many billions of neurons, each of as yet undetermined complexity) networks of many thousands, and probably millions and possibly billions, of computers will be needed, although each individual computer may be relatively small.

At one extreme, we can contemplate enormously large numbers of very simple processors (e.g., simple boolean logic gates, or threshold logic processors, or idealized neuron-like devices, or simple and basic 1-bit computers). At the other extreme, much smaller numbers of extremely powerful computers may be preferable, especially where massively parallel processes and extremely fast speeds (which are vital for visual perception and robot control) are not so crucial. And a large number of possibilities exist in between.

PARALLEL ARCHITECTURES BEING CONSIDERED BY THE AI COMMUNITY, AND THEIR PROBLEMS

AI researchers interested in problem solving have focused their attention on three major types of hardware multi-computers:

A.1. Specialized computers and small networks to execute expert production systems or/and to do logical inference;

A.2. Larger networks to handle the general AI problem, possibly by assigning different functions to different groups of computers;

A.3. Very large networks to handle semantic memory searches.

The closely related image processing, pattern recognition, and computer vision communities have concentrated on:

B.1. Small networks to do an essentially divide-and-conquer examination of the large image array;
B.2. Very large synchronized arrays of processors to execute in parallel iterated local operations over the entire array of image pixels (picture elements).

It appears, unfortunately, that attempting to parallelize today's "expert" production systems and logical inference systems can give at best only very small amounts of speedup—on the order of 2 or 3, or possibly 10 or 20 at most. These programs, as they are coded today, are almost always designed to execute serial algorithms in a serial manner.

It is exceedingly difficult to develop parallel algorithms. Very possibly this is because our "conscious" thinking is mostly serial; although our not-conscious thinking is mostly parallel—but inaccessible to conscious thought. Another major obstacle to increasing the speed of today's programs is that it is far more difficult, and often impossible, to parallelize a serial algorithm after it has been coded in a serial fashion than to attempt to devise a parallel algorithm in the first place. Parallel formalizations appear to be possible for both production systems and logical inference systems, and there is reason to hope that they can offer greater speedups, possibly as great as two to four orders of magnitude (see Chapter 18).

A large number of networks of completely independent computers have been built with 8 or 16 processors. Several systems have been designed, and a few built, with from 50 to 256. Most of these (described in Chapter 6) link computers via a pseudo-complete graph. (A complete graph has each node linked directly to every other node.) This reflects many people's feelings that complete connectivity is the ideal. A number of structures have been proposed for multi-computers with several thousand, or even more, processors (see Chapters 7-13). Some of these use a tree (a graph with no cycles, e.g., Browning, 1980; Mago, 1980), a tree with some extra links (e.g., Shaw, 1982), or a binary N-dimensional cube—that is, an N-dimensional array with nodes (computers, processors) only at its corners (e.g., Seitz, 1985). However, the topology of such networks too often has no particular relation to the structure of the programs they will execute. And the speedups of such networks are often relatively small. (This is chiefly due to today's operating systems, which introduce enormous overheads and delays in handling communication between processors. It is not clear whether future research will succeed in effecting the substantial improvements needed.)

A very large network of computers to handle a very large semantic memory network appears on the surface to be attractive and straightforward (once—as is rapidly becoming the case—micro-electronic technologies make this feasible). The proposals for actually doing this appear to be either unfinished (e.g., NETL's somewhat magical graph of computers; Fahlman, 1979) or not obviously appropriate (e.g., the Connection Machine's N-cube topology; Hillis, 1981, 1985; anon., 1985; see Chapter 12.)

A small network (e.g., Siegel et al.'s 1981 PASM; see Chapter 13) that can be used to speed up computer vision, by subdividing the large image array into small arrays, all of which are worked on in parallel, would appear to be feasible—except that it is unlikely ever to be fast enough to, e.g., recognize and track moving objects. When multimillion-fold speedups are needed, multiplying the number of computers by a few hundred or thousand is probably not sufficient.

A very large synchronized array (e.g., Duff's 1976 CLIP4; Reddaway's 1978 DAP; Batcher's 1980 MPP) is capable of enormous speedups for a large class of local image processing operations. However, arrays appear to become too slow and inefficient to be practicable when one attempts to use them for the successively more global and higher-level operations needed for pattern recognition and computer vision (see Chapters 8-9.)

A VARIETY OF ARCHITECTURES THAT APPEAR TO BE MORE PROMISING FOR AI

This book sketches out the general picture of the possibilities for multi-computer networks, a far larger set of possibilities than are typically considered today. It concentrates on those architectures that appear to best fit the requirements of artificial intelligence applications—and (of vital importance) are feasible, and reasonably economical. These include several key architectures that appear to be preferable to those that have received the most attention. Several are natural extensions of simpler structures, for example, trees that are augmented with additional links (chiefly at the leaves), and architectures that judiciously combine useful substructures. Briefly:

0.   A serial super-computer can be spec:alized to handle artificial intel-
      ligence as opposed to numerical tasks (Chapters 2, 6).

1.   A system that as closely as possible approximates a logarithmic
      fan-out/fan-in network (where from each node a search to other
      nodes will take only logarithmic steps, and logarithmic numbers of
      nodes converge in to each node) appears to be especially appropri-
      ate for semantic memory networks (Chapter 16).

2.   Logical inference, heuristic search, and "expert" production sys-
      tems can be handled in any (or all) of the following ways, as
      appropriate:

      a.   An augmented tree can be used for the large percent of
            today's production and search systems that, essentially, make
            a diagnosis or find an answer by moving directly down a
            sorting tree (Chapter 18). This is not a parallelization; but it
            can effect an enormous reduction in the number of steps
            needed, to 10 or 20 or so at the most. Substantial additional
            economies can now be gained by streaming a continuing
            batch of such problems through the network in assemblyline
            "pipeline" fashion (Chapters 11-13).

      b.   Completely new kinds of highly parallel structures can be
            implemented to give a process-structured architecture—for
            example to (1) apply a large number of operations at one
            time, in parallel, and then (2) combine their results and make
            choices, again in parallel (these processes can be repeated any
            number of times). Now a parallel network with interspersed
            decision elements can be used to handle parallel sets of oper-
            ations whose results are repeatedly combined and evaluated
            for intermediate decisions (Chapters 13, 18).

      c.   A fan-out/fan-in network can be used, much as for semantic
            memory searches, to make heuristically guided (but probably
            essentially "breadth-first"—that is, "look everywhere")
            searches for solution-paths and valid inferences (Chapters 16,
            18).

3.   Image processing, pattern recognition, and computer vision can be
      handled in a more efficient and better-integrated way than is possi-
      ble with an array alone: First augment the array into a tree/array
      or pyramid. Then augment the pyramid by interfacing and com-
      bining it with an appropriately structured network (Chapters 8-9,
      13, 15).

4.   Robot motor control can be handled with an augmented tree for
      each of the major subassemblies (e.g., each hand, each arm, each

leg). These augmented trees can be combined hierarchically into successively higher-level trees, with appropriate links between them (Chapters 19, 21).

5. The augmented pyramid for perception and the hierarchical augmented tree for motor control can be appropriately linked together and combined into a perceptual-motor system (Chapters 13, 15, 19, 21).

6. Fan-out/fan-in networks used to remember and to infer can similarly be combined into a single structure (Chapters 16, 17, 18, 21).

7. The perceptual-motor system and the inferring-remembering system can be combined into a single perceptual-cognitive system, either by linking their graphs, or by combining their graphs into one (Chapters 13, 21).

8. A general purpose heterogeneous network might be built, one that contained different types of processors or/and different topologies in different regions, as appropriate (Chapter 13).

9. Partial re-configuring capabilities can be added where needed, so that the system can be restructured, as desired, under program control (Chapter 13).

10. An appropriate process-structured information-flow multi-computer topology (possibly one that is reminiscent of the brain) might be built, through which problems are streamed (Chapter 13).

SUMMARY, AND THE STRUCTURE OF THE REST OF THIS BOOK

Artificial intelligence is attempting to attack an extremely difficult set of problems: how a system (whether human being or computer) perceives, makes decisions, solves problems, uses language, remembers, coordinates and controls functional motor behavior, integrates these several processes into an intelligent whole, and learns. Enormously larger and faster parallel multi-computer networks are absolutely necessary if there is to be any hope of handling these problems in their true full-blown real-world complexity (rather than merely demonstrating that carefully chosen simplified and preprogrammed toy examples can be processed correctly).

These issues are developed and examined as follows:

Chapters 1 and 2 briefly describe today's conventional single-CPU serial computers and super-computers, and the closely related theoretical constructs (e.g., Turing machines, Post productions) that they embody. Chapters 3 through 5 examine the technological and design possibilities and constraints that underlie the development of very large multi-computers.

Chapters 6 through 13 describe the great variety of built and proposed multi-computer architectures, describe representative examples of systems being designed or built, and explore the strengths and weaknesses of each.

Then Chapters 14 through 21 describe the basic artificial intelligence problems and the major approaches taken for each, emphasizing parallelizable approaches and suggesting the most suitable multi-computer hardware structures for each.

Finally, Chapters 22 through 24 suggest, examine, explore, and summarize.

Chapter One

UNIVERSAL TURING MACHINES AND THE THEORETICAL BASIS OF COMPUTERS

This chapter briefly describes the theoretical logical systems that underlie today's computers and that give them their great capability. These include universal Turing machines, plus alternative logical systems that have been proved equivalent, and also idealized computers, finite state automata, neuron-like logic elements, and Petri nets. It is valuable to examine these systems because they make clear exactly what a computer is, and they form the basis for a variety of key programming languages, computer structures, and approaches to computing.

THE CONCEPT OF A UNIVERSAL COMPUTER THAT UNDERLIES GENERAL-PURPOSE COMPUTERS

Turing Machines (As Independently Invented by both Post and Turing)

It is illuminating to examine just how simple the basic concept of a general-purpose computer is.

In 1936, Emil Post and Alan Turing independently proposed a very simple kind of computer *that is capable of doing anything that any other computer might conceivably do—given enough time.* This "Turing machine" is a suitably powerful "finite state automaton" (see the following section) to which has been added a "potentially infinite" memory. A number of other independent formulations have also been proved identical, for example, Alonzo Church's 1936 lambda-calculus, Stephen Kleene's 1936 recursive functions, and Post's 1943 productions.

A VERY SIMPLE FORMULATION OF A SIMPLE SERIAL (BUT UNIVERSAL) TURING MACHINE

Figure 1-1 gives Post's formulation of one example of a Turing machine.

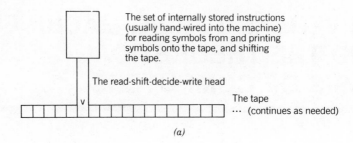

The set of internally stored instructions (usually hand-wired into the machine) for reading symbols from and printing symbols onto the tape, and shifting the tape.

The read-shift-decide-write head

The tape
··· (continues as needed)

(a)

"The worker [i.e., the computer] is assumed to be capable of performing the following primitive acts:

  a. Marking the box he is in (assumed empty),
  a. Erasing the mark in the box he is in (assumed marked),
  b. Moving to the box on his right,
  c. Moving to the box on his left,
  d. Determining whether the box he is in, is or is not marked."

(b)

FIGURE 1-1. Emil Post's 1936 formulation of a Turing Machine. (a) Basic Structure [A "read-shift-decide-write" processor head looks at an arbitrarily long (potentially infinite) tape with symbols]. (b) Emil Post's 1936 formulation of a necessary and sufficient set of primitive instructions.

That is all there is to the concept of the universal general purpose computer! All it need do is have the read-shift-decide-write head execute a sequence of instructions from the simple repertoire:

READ the current symbol;

SHIFT to the next memory/tape location;

WRITE the current symbol onto the current memory/tape location;

IF the current symbol is x, THEN DO instruction i, ELSE DO j;

A simple program can now be put on its tape that will execute any possible program also on its tape.

Information is read from and written onto a "tape"—which serves as the memory of the system. The tape contains all needed information: all the data on which the program must act (including all data that the program generates), *and also the program itself.* [John Von Neumann, 1945, is usually credited with the invention of the stored program concept in the early 1940s; see Randell, 1973. But Von Neumann had many discussions with Turing in the late 1930s and it seems likely that Turing's machine may have given him the idea.]

The processor that executes the sequence of instructions is a simple example of a finite state automaton. The addition of the potentially infinite tape, and the placement of the program on that tape, allow the system to be general purpose, since it can now read, interpret, and execute any program that can be written on that tape (once it is given a short program that executes these functions). One great source of the power of stored-program computers lies in the fact that the program is input to and stored in the same tape/memory that contains all (other) kinds of data.

Note how extremely simple, weak, and low-level the basic instructions are. A program of even a little bit of power will need an enormously long sequence of such instructions, and it will take an intolerably long time to execute. For example, to add two B-bit (binary digit) numbers such a computer must execute the following serial sequence of instructions: Make a sequence of successive shifts to the low-order digit of the first number, and read it. Make a sequence of successive shifts to the low-order digit of the second number, and read it. Make a sequence of successive shifts to find free scratch pad space on the tape. Add the two digits. Shift suitably and write the result. Shift suitably; write the carry. Shift back to get the next digits. Iterate this procedure through all the digits. Before each of these steps the head must shift to the region of the tape that contains the next instruction, which in turn tells it where to shift for the next step and for the next instruction (all this entails additional long sequence of operations).

PARALLEL, MULTI-HEAD, AND MULTI-TAPE TURING MACHINES

Rather than read, process, write, and store everything one bit at a time, a system can be defined to work with B-bit entities (note that these can serve to encode either numbers or symbols). The system can further be extended to use 2, 3, or any number of read-shift-decide-write heads. All might work with one single tape; or each might have its own tape; or several might share the same tape.

All such systems have been proved to be equivalent. That is, the very simplest single-head Turing machine that uses the very simplest 1-

bit processor working on 1-bit pieces of information is capable of executing *any* program that *any other* N-bit Turing machine, with no matter how many processors or tapes, can execute. This is the basis for using a single-CPU serial computer—it is capable of doing anything that any multi-computer, no matter how large, can do (although it may be many orders of magnitude slower). The simplest Turing machine is the most amenable to theoretical analysis, but it is also the slowest. To execute real programs that are nontrivial, more complex systems are absolutely necessary, and they can speed up processing enormously.

The Lambda-Calculus and Recursive Functions

Several other logical systems were developed at Princeton, at roughly the same time that Turing, in Cambridge, England, and Post, at New York University, were developing Turing machines. These include Alonzo Church's 1936 lambda-calculus and Steven Kleene's 1936 recursive functions. All of these, and several later systems, were quickly proved to be equivalent. Marvin Minsky (1967) has suggested that the fact that the universal computer has been independently reinvented so many times is an interesting indication of its importance and generality.

The lambda-calculus and recursive functions led to John McCarthy's 1962 Lisp programming language, which has for many years been the dominant AI language (McCarthy, 1978). Recursive functions have had a profound effect on the style (too often serial to the extreme) of Lisp programming used by most people doing research in artificial intelligence.

Post Productions

Post (1943) developed still another equivalent universal system, Post productions. Essentially, a set of Antecedent-Consequent "IF-THEN" productions can be used to compute and arrive at the results for any computable function. The following gives a very brief description and several very simple examples.

A production system (that is, a logistic system) is a set of axioms and rules of inference.

An axiom is a finite string of symbols from some alphabet.

A rule of inference is a computable function that uses sets of productions of the form (g and h denote constants, $ denote variables; some g, h, or $ can be empty null strings):

$$g_0 \$_1 g_1 \$_2 \cdots \$_n g_n \rightarrow h_0 \$'_1 h_1 \$'_2 \cdots \$'_n h_n$$

Indeed, all such productions can be reduced to systems of productions of the following extremely simple normal form:

$$g\$ \rightarrow \$h$$

Consider the following simple examples (from Minsky, 1967):

**PRODUCTION SYSTEMS THAT GENERATE
ALL EVEN AND ALL ODD NUMBERS:**

	Even Numbers	Odd Numbers
Alphabet:	1	1
Axiom:	11	1
Production:	$\$ \rightarrow \$11$	$\$ \rightarrow 11$

The system for even numbers starts with the axiom "11" and generates 1111, 111111, etc.

The system for odd numbers starts with the axiom "1" and generates 111, 11111, etc.

**A SYSTEM THAT GENERATES PALINDROMES
(STRINGS THAT ARE EXACTLY THE SAME
WHEN READ IN EITHER DIRECTION):**

Alphabet:	a,b,c
Axioms:	a,b,c,aa,bb,cc
Productions:	$\$ \rightarrow a\$a$, $\$ \rightarrow b\$b$, $\$ \rightarrow c\$c$

The development of formal grammars by Harris (1951), Chomsky (1957) and others, and of the programming languages Comit (Yngve, 1957, 1963) and Snobol (Farber et al., 1964) are in the spirit of Post productions.

The much more recent development of artificial intelligence production systems (Waterman, 1970; Newell and Simon, 1973) is also in this tradition, although it is not clear how much these researcher were directly influenced by theoretical developments such as Post's, or languages like Snobol, or whether they simply adapted the IF...THEN... conditional statement that is basic to Turing machines and is an essential ingredient of programming languages.

Models of Computation: RAMs, PRAMs, RASPs, Decision Trees

A variety of ideal computers can be defined (see Aho et al., 1974), including "random access machines," (RAMs), "random access stored program" (RASP) machines, and "decision trees." These have chiefly been used to examine the time and space complexity of different kinds of systems.

A RAM consists of a read-only input tape, a write-only output tape, a program, a memory, and the mechanism to read and execute the program. The model assumes that the memory contains enough individual memory registers to handle the problem being executed, and that each register is large enough to contain the information it is assigned. The program consists of a sequence of instructions; these are not stored in the memory, therefore the program cannot be modified. A few basic instructions (e.g., add, store, and) will suffice; but such a system might be given any desired set of instructions.

Parallel RAMs (PRAMs) have also been defined, but they all assume that a number of processors can simultaneously access a single common memory, with no overhead or conflicts. Although this is useful for exploring parallel algorithms, it is not an appropriate model for an actual hardware system, where only a few processors can be linked to a common memory. As soon as they are, severe contention problems arise.

A RASP is like a RAM, except that the program is stored in its memory. Therefore the program can be modified, as in a Turing machine or an actual stored-program computer. Any n-instruction program that can be executed by a RAM in $T(n)$ time can be executed by a RASP in at most $kT(n)$ time, where k is a small constant for the extra instructions needed to access and fetch an instruction.

A decision tree is a simplified version of a RAM that uses a binary tree (start with a root node; link 2 nodes to it; link two nodes to each new node; continue as long as desired). This is a useful structure for programs that must make decisions, as when sorting or in other ways comparing data. (Note that any n-ary decision can be decomposed into a sequence of binary decisions.)

FINITE STATE MACHINES, MCCULLOCH-PITTS NEURONS, PETRI NETS

No living brain, indeed no actual computer, can have an arbitrarily large potentially infinite memory. The Turing machine is important as a theoretical construct with which to explore the capabilities of computers and prove their generality. But every actual multi-computer that is built, and every program that it executes, will be finite—hence equivalent to a finite-state automaton rather than a universal Turing machine.

FINITE STATE AUTOMATA

A Turing machine's tape memory can be replaced by a set of IF-THEN rules—which can be embedded in a set of processors that actually execute these rules. Figure 1-2 gives an example of a Finite State Automaton.

Present State			Present State Output	
Previous State	Previous Input			
	0	1		
q_1	q_4	q_3	q_1	0
q_2	q_1	q_3	q_2	0
q_3	q_4	q_4	q_3	0
q_4	q_2	q_2	q_4	1

(a)

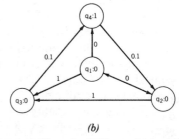

(b)

FIGURE 1-2. An example of a Finite-State Automaton (Moore's 1956 version). (a) Tabled version. (b) Transition-machine diagram.

This builds a particular program into a particular equivalent automaton that embodies it, replacing the Turing machine's memory (which contains the program's instructions and intermediate results). It is no longer a general purpose system, for it does not have a potentially infinite memory. It executes only the program that is embodied in its structure.

MCCULLOCH-PITTS NEURONS, AND BOOLEAN AND THRESHOLD LOGIC ELEMENTS

Warren McCulloch and Walter Pitts (1943, 1965) developed a calculus of networks built from extremely simple neuron-like components. A McCulloch-Pitts neuron either fires a $+1$ or an absolute inhibition across a synapse (whose threshold is a positive integer value) into another neuron. A neuron fires whenever enough neurons fire into it to exceed its threshold, but no inhibitory neurons fire into it.

Kleene (1956) proved that McCulloch-Pitts neurons are equivalent to finite-state automata.

Boolean (2-valued, true-false) logic is typically used for the logic gates with which a computer's processors and memories are built. As

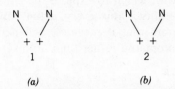

(a)   *(b)*

FIGURE 1-3. McCulloch-Pitts neurons. (a) Threshold = 1, computes disjunction (OR). (b) Threshold = 2, computes conjunction (AND).

Figure 1-3 indicates, McCulloch-Pitts neurons can be used to compute Boolean functions. For example, an "AND" over 7 input neurons will be computed by a neuron onto which all 7 synapse whose threshold is 7. An "OR" will be computed if the threshold is 1.

When threshold values are set higher than the minimum (1) but lower than the maximum (N), a wide variety of additional threshold logic functions are computed.

More efficient variants to McCulloch-Pitts neurons can be defined, by assigning values to firings other than 1 and absolute inhibition (e.g., real or integer numbers, either positive plus inhibition, or positive and negative). These can serve to give simpler and more realistic nets; but an equivalent McCulloch-Pitts net can always be constructed.

PETRI NETS

C. A. Petri (1962, 1969) formulated a system that specifies more about the actual flow of information. A Petri net is a directed bipartite graph built from "places" linked to "transitions." A "token" is put on a place, "filling" it. A transition "fires" as soon as all its input places are full; the result is that one token is removed from each of the transition's input places and one token is put on each of its output places.

(a)   *(b)*

FIGURE 1-4. A Petri Net. (a) At Time 1, both P1 and P2 have fired, placing tokens (X), so T fires. (b) The resulting changed states at time 2.

A token can be interpreted as a piece of information, the result of input or of a previous process. A transition can be interpreted as a process that is executed as soon as all its necessary inputs (tokens) have been received. Thus the Petri net actually specifies how information flows into a process, possibly forming queues, and how the processor actually processes that information. Data-flow graphs (see Chapter 13) are, essentially, Petri nets augmented so they can be used to conveniently specify all the constructs (e.g., iterative "FOR" loops) of a typical program.

SUMMARY

This chapter briefly describes Turing machines and alternate systems, such as Post Productions and RASPs, that have been proved equivalent to Turing machines. These are all universal and general purpose, in the sense that any and all such systems are capable of executing any possible (i.e., any clearly described) program, so long as it has access to enough material (in terms of today's technology this usually means transistors that serve as switches) to store all the information that the program needs. The Turing machine's tape serves as the memory in which this information—all input data and intermediate results, and also the program itself—is stored.

Next, finite-state automata, McCulloch-Pitts neurons, boolean (binary) logic, threshold logic, and Petri nets are briefly introduced. Rather than store information in a potentially infinite memory (the Turing machine's tape), they embody their "knowledge" directly in their processing gates. These are probably better models for systems with intelligence, for all actual systems that exist in the real world are finite. And living brains appear to store all their information in the neurons (probably at the synapses that link neuron to neuron and process information as it flows through) and in the larger structures into which neurons are combined, rather than in a separate randomly accessible memory.

Chapter Two

CONVENTIONAL GENERAL-PURPOSE SINGLE-CPU SERIAL COMPUTERS AND SUPER-COMPUTERS

A conventional single Central Processing Unit (1-CPU) serial computer is, basically, a system that:

1. Inputs information (whether numbers, letters and/or other symbols) and stores it in its memory registers (encoded in any way, but usually in the form of a string of binary digits);
2. Executes a specified serial sequence of operations on that information;
3. Outputs results.

It has much the same structure as a single-head Turing machine. It may look different on the surface, but the differences come chiefly from the need to make Turing machines reasonably fast.

THE BASIC STRUCTURE OF A SINGLE-CPU GENERAL-PURPOSE COMPUTER

At the most schematic level, the conventional computer has three basic parts (see Figure 2-1):

A.   The CPU;

B.   A set of memory storage registers;

C.   Input-and-output (I-O) devices.

FIGURE 2-1. The (idealized) structure of a single-CPU serial computer. [NOTE: CPU = Central Processing Unit; M = Memory Store; I = Input device; O = Output device; |, − = Wires; >, < indicate direction.]

ALL information, including data to be operated on AND ALSO the actual program that specifies the set of operations to be executed, are input to and stored in the memory. All such transfers of information are carried out over wires that link components, often with intermediate switches that can be used to route information in one direction or another, as appropriate.

The CPU typically contains a processing unit that actually executes the program's instructions, and a controller that gets and decodes the program's instructions and, in general, controls and runs the show, telling the computer exactly what to do.

The processing unit (often called the arithmetic-logic unit, or ALU) typically contains one general purpose processor (a processor that can execute any of the computer's instructions, where these include enough operations to give it the general capability of a Turing machine), or a variety of more or less specialized processors, each hard-wired to execute a particular type of instruction as fast as possible.

The controller:

Fetches the next instruction to be executed,

Decodes that instruction,

Fetches data from the locations specified by that instruction,

Ships this information to the ALU (which then executes the instruction),

Stores the results in the location specified by the instruction.

Thus the controller fetches and decodes the next instruction. Then it fetches the data this instruction told it to fetch (by specifying the location where it could be found). The instruction is then executed on the data by the appropriate processor in the ALU and the results stored in the designated location. Then the program goes on to get, decode, and execute the next instruction; and so on.

When information is fetched a copy is made of what is stored in the designated location in memory, and sent to and stored in a high-speed register, to be used by the ALU when it executes an operation on that information. And in general, appropriately linked memory registers, serving as glue holding together the different parts of the system, are used for fast transfer and temporary storage of information.

The availability of a random-access memory (RAM), where any location can be accessed by a single "fetch" or "store" instruction, means that the system does not need to shift one location at a time along a linear tape, as must the basic Turing machine. Any piece of data, and any instruction, can be fetched immediately. The use of an 8-bit, 16-bit, 32-bit, or 64-bit "word" of information that is fetched, stored, and operated on in parallel means that the system need not do everything "bit-serially" (that is, one bit at a time). These are probably the two major improvements and enhancements that turn the excessively slow single-head Turing machines into very fast computing engines.

A computer can be built with any number of CPUs; but almost all computers built to date have been of the very simplest sort, with only one single processor. This kind of "general purpose single-CPU serial stored-program digital computer" executes one instruction at a time, sequentially. It is often called the Von Neumann computer after John Von Neumann, who wrote the first detailed specification of such a system, in 1945, leading to the design and construction of the ENIAC at the University of Pennsylvania. Completed in 1951, ENIAC is usually considered the first general purpose stored program computer.

Almost all computers (see Figure 2-2) actually have several memories—such as very high speed registers and caches, high-speed RAM chips, magnetic disks, optical disks, tape—each successively much slower, larger and cheaper; and several input devices—such as keyboards, tape-drives, television cameras; and output devices—such as video screens, printers, tape-drives. However, all computers have the same basic structure, where both data and program instructions are stored in a memory that the CPU has access to (and can therefore fetch from, store into, and modify), with attendant input and output devices that move information into and out from the computer.

Note that a single device, like a tape or disk, can serve several purposes. Indeed, input and output devices are simply external to and linked to some other device with respect to which they are therefore input and output. Passing information over the wires linking several devices establishes the fact of input into one and output from the other.

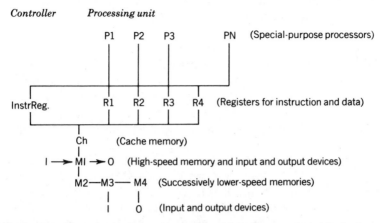

FIGURE 2-2. A typical computer with a hierarchy of memories, I-O devices, and special-purpose processors.

Notice that the memory and the processor within each individual computer similarly serve as input and output devices to one another. "Input," "output," "fetch," "store," "send," "receive," and any other message-passing or data-transferring instructions are all closely related members of the set of operations that move and transfer information.

An attractive and flexible alternative way of combining the several components of a traditional computer is to link them all to a single very high-speed "bus." (A bus is simply a high-bandwidth wire, often augmented with a small, or a large, amount of hardware logic that is added to interface devices, temporarily buffer and store information, and handle other problems, like contention between processors for the same resource). Figure 2-3 shows a simple example.

FIGURE 2-3. A bus-based multi-computer architecture. [C = Controller, I = Input device, O = Output device, P = Processor, M = high-speed Memory, D = Disk, T = Television camera, V = Video monitor.]

PARALLELIZING SOME OF THE PROCESSES WITHIN THE SINGLE CPU, AND SUPER-COMPUTERS

Conventional serial computers can be given more power by increasing the power of the single CPU. Extremely fast special hardware (e.g., parallel adders, floating-point accelerators) can be carefully designed and implemented to execute frequently used instructions. Additional processors (often called coprocessors) are sometimes judiciously added to handle input and output, instruction decoding, and/or other frequently executed tasks.

Possibly the most striking examples of special hardware are found in the "super-computers" like the Cray-1, Cray-XMP, Cray-2, and Cray-3 (Russell, 1978; Chen et al., 1984), Cyber-205 (Kozdrowicki and Thies, 1980), Fujitsu VP-200 and Hitachi S-810/20 (Riganati and Schneck, 1984). These have incorporated into them additional structures of processors, including very powerful pipelines for vector processing (see Chapter 7).

Another step can be taken beyond the conventional single-processor serial computer by adding a second processor, and then, possibly, a third, and a fourth, and so on. [Note that each processor executes a different stream of programs. Processors do not work together in parallel on a single program.] This kind of "multi-processor" system quickly runs into severe memory contention problems: If all processors share a single high-speed memory, several processors will often block one another when trying to access this same memory. It appears that very little if any further increases in power have resulted in systems like those built by IBM (the 360/67) and Univac (the 1100 series) after the first two or three processors (Miller et al., 1970; Patton, 1972). Chapter 6 will examine several newer systems that appear to be more efficient.

Actually the Cray-XMP links two computers together, and the Cray-2 and Cray-3 link up to 16. Often, as with the Cray-2 and Cray-3, a more complex architecture is used, one that includes a whole network of switches through which processors access memory. Specialized to do 64-bit floating point operations (especially multiplication), the super-computers are several orders of magnitude faster than more ordinary computers like the DEC VAX or Motorola 68000. Thus peak floating point multiply rates in millions per second (mflops) are 250 for the Cray-1, 630 for the Cray-XMP, and 1,300 for the Cray-2. (Peak performance is a very misleading figure, but these systems are clearly very fast. The Cray-1 executes a 64-bit floating point multiply in 12.5 nanoseconds, each Cray-XMP CPU in 9.5 nanoseconds, each Cray-2 CPU in 2.5 nanoseconds.) The Fujitsu VP-200 and the Cray-XMP were comparable in a variety of benchmarks (Lubeck et al., 1985) that typify the Los Alamos computing load; the Hitachi S810/20 was roughly 30% slower. The Fujitsu was two or three times as fast in vector mode for large vectors.

The super-computers cost roughly $10,000,000 each. They are usually (but not always—especially when they are not doing floating point operations) more than 100 times faster than more ordinary computers, like the VAXes, that cost roughly $100,000. They are therefore cost effective, especially for the kind of large number crunching problems attacked by physicists, chemists, and engineers. Super-computers of similar power that are specialized for artificial intelligence problems are probably possible—when and if we achieve a firm enough understanding of what is needed. The major attempts of this sort have been developed chiefly for image processing and pattern perception, especially the pipelines examined in Chapter 7 and the large arrays examined in Chapter 8.

Chapter Three

THE PRESENT, IMPENDING, AND FUTURE TECHNOLOGICAL POSSIBILITIES

During the next 5, 10, and 20 years successively more powerful multi-computers will rapidly become feasible at reasonable prices. This is because of the continuing major increases in density of the micro-miniaturized VLSI (very large scale integration) electronic chips from which modern computers are constructed. [Even more exciting, but more speculative and almost certainly farther in the future, are optical components—VLSI chips containing optical gates configured into optical or hybrid computers that are linked via a communication network of lasers, holograms, and photo-diodes. Still other technologies are possible, for example the genetic engineering of proteins or other organic molecules and the growing of networks of polymers. Since it is far from certain that these will be developed soon, they will only be mentioned.]

A multi-computer is built from processors and memories and the connector wires and switches that link them together, plus input transducers, output transducers, and controllers. This basic structure is extremely simple; but it is typically elaborated in a variety of ways, as follows:

Each processor often contains a number of special-purpose circuits for the fast computation of particular frequently executed operations.

Several different types, speeds, and sizes of memories are typically used, from highest-speed individual registers and small caches through the high-speed main memories to successively slower bulk memories, disks and tapes.

Connectors can range in bandwidth from a few hundreds to many billions of bits per second.

Input and output transducers can be thought of as connectors to the outside world (often, as with a tv camera or tv screen, this entails major analog-digital or digital-analog transductions).

Controllers are in charge of a variety of functions, including fetching, decoding and executing instructions, handling input and output, and the general flow of processes.

THE BASIC CHIP FROM WHICH MODERN COMPUTERS ARE BUILT

Today's basic computer component is a rectangular chip (usually made of purified silicon) roughly 4 to 6 millimeters on each side. Today's largest processor chips in commercial production contain 100,000 to 500,000 devices [transistors, (logic) gates; this book, as is commonly done, uses these terms interchangeably]. Computers are used to help design and to draw the intricate chip layouts of transistors linked into logic gates, which in turn are linked together into more complex structures. Typically a half dozen or so enormous floor-plan-like designs will be output, each detailing a different layer of the circuit—much as a number of different master masks are used to make colored silkscreen reproductions.

These are photographed (chiefly using visible light; but, in order to increase resolution, x-rays or electron beams will be used increasingly), and drastically reduced in size. Then several hundred copies are spread out like tiles over a round wafer, and each mask prints and lays down its layer in turn. Finally the wafer is very carefully baked, much like a pot; when done, the separate copies are diced into separate chips.

Chips are designed in terms of a basic unit of measurement, lambda; the minimal distance between transistors or wires is at least 2 lambda. In current commercial technology lambda is typically 2 microns, and even 1 micron. A transistor might be as small as 2 or 3 microns in length or breadth, a wire even narrower. These sizes have been growing steadily smaller, and will continue to grow smaller, at least until lambda = .25 microns. As a result, chips have been doubling in size (i.e., in terms of the number of components) every 12 to 18 months for the past 20 to 30 years. This doubling should continue (possibly at a slightly slower rate) until at least 2,000,000-device and then 10,000,000-device or even larger chips can be fabricated in large quantities and cheaply.

These are actually conservative extrapolations into the future. Individual memory chips (which, because of their extreme micro-modularity, are probably the easiest to design and to pack and miniaturize) with a million bits are already being fabricated and offered commercially. These use about 1.5 million transistors. More complex chips with a million or more transistors have already been fabricated experimentally. It seems likely that chips with several million transistors will be available commercially before 1988, and 10 million transistor chips by the early 1990s. Carver Mead (1985) actually estimates that our current VLSI technologies are capable of achieving billions of devices on a single chip. And new technologies—for example, wafer scale integration, 3-dimensional chips or stacked wafers, optical multi-computers, and chemical and biological computers—may well vault substantially beyond these figures.

Essentially, the designer of the chip's circuit develops a graph whose nodes are devices and whose links are wires. This graph is arranged so that it fills as small as possible a 2-dimensional Euclidean space, and then printed and embedded into the rectangular chip's surface. [Usually the chip is treated as though it is a square grid, with no diagonal wires allowed; this chiefly serves to simplify the design rules and the design process.] Since this embedding entails the printing of a number of layers, it is possible to have wires cross one another occasionally, by burrowing them down into different layers. But such crossings are expensive, and therefore the embedded graph should be "almost-planar."

COMBINING CHIPS INTO THE TOTAL COMPUTER

Design Constraints Within a Chip and Between Chips

Each chip is packaged in a carrier that today contains from 16 to 128 or so pins that link to that chip's outer world. Until different types of technologies mature, it appears unlikely that even 15 or 20 years from now more than 512 or so pins can be accommodated. This means that although the graph realized on each individual chip can have millions of nodes linked to one another via whatever topologies can be embedded sufficiently compactly into its almost-planar space, fewer than 16 to 512 direct links can be achieved from each chip to all the other chips in the multi-computer.

A few dozen chips are plugged into a printed circuit board; a dozen or so boards are mounted in a rack; and one or several racks are built into a chassis. A large system might have several chassis. At each step there are major restrictions in the number and the length of the wires that can be used to link components. Chips must be plugged into boards' pin-holes, and boards into chassis' slots, in a regular fashion. Too many irregularly connected wires can give a spaghetti that is too hard to untangle. As speeds increase, the time taken to traverse a wire becomes critical, so that no wires can be too long, but in general the designer is freer of restrictions than when designing the individual near-planar chip.

Size of the Total Computer

A reasonable rule of thumb is that the feasible limit to the size of a computer is the number of separate basic components (today these are the chips, once the chips have been successfully fabricated) that must be handled individually and wired together. Very roughly, 1 to 100 components gives a micro-computer. One thousand components gives a mini-computer; 10,000 gives a large computer; 100,000 to 300,000 components gives a buildable but extremely large super-computer.

At what is today a much smaller component than the whole chip, a computer is built from only a very small number of:

A.   Processors that transform information (including controllers),
B.   Memories that store information,
C.   Lines linking two components over which information can be passed from one to another,
D.   Switches that join more than two components and can be used to route information in any of several possible directions. These in turn are built from only two primitive components:
    1.   Two-state devices (transistors; basically, switches),
    2.   Wires serving as paths linking devices.

A traditional single-CPU computer needs roughly 50 to 500 devices for a 1-bit processor, 2,000 to 5,000 devices for an 8-bit processor and 10,000 to 100,000 or more devices for a 32-bit processor (Kuck, 1978; Uhr, 1984a). Memory needs 1 to 4 devices for slow dynamic RAMs, and 4 to 12 devices for faster static RAMs. A traditional single-processor serial computer might have 16K to 64,000K words of memory. See Table 1 for a few examples.

Table 1. Examples of Device Counts for Different Kinds of Computers.
(Memory has been minimized for the first two 32-bit computers, to make possible large numbers of computers in toto. But note that the total memory is very large.)

Computer Type	Devices in		Computers in
	Processor	Memory	10^8 to 10^{11} Devices
1-bit	50	50	10^6 to 10^9
1-bit	400	600	10^5 to 10^8
8-bit	2,000	8,000	10^4 to 10^7
32-bit	10,000	90,000	10^3 to 10^6
32-bit	100,000	900,000	10^2 to 10^5
32-bit	100,000	90,000,000	10^{-1} to 10^2
64-bit	500,000	999,500,000	10^{-2} to 10^1
super			

CONTROLLERS AND THE VARIETY OF FUNCTIONS THEY CAN SERVE

The computer's controller can vary greatly in size, depending upon how complex is the total set of jobs it is assigned. In some systems hundreds of thousands of devices are needed. Even the simplest controller that does the basic jobs of fetching, decoding, executing, and synchronizing instructions probably needs at least 2,000 to 5,000 devices (unless it fetches and decodes everything bit-serially, which will slow down the whole system intolerably).

It is important to stress this point because the cost of the controller is much larger than the cost of a small 1-bit processor, and quite large with respect to an 8-bit processor, although it is relatively small with respect to a powerful 32-bit processor. This is one of the overriding factors that have led to the development of today's very large but highly synchronized arrays (see Chapter 8) with one controller for all, or for many, processors. A system with large numbers of processors is possible only when each individual processor is relatively small.

A controller must be linked to all the computer components it controls. This means that it may sometimes be simpler to use several controllers, and thus reduce the numbers and lengths of wires. For example, a controller might be placed at the center of each chip, or each wafer, or each board, linked to the computer components that surround it.

ENORMOUS REQUIREMENTS OF MEMORY IN CONVENTIONAL COMPUTERS

It should be emphasized that no matter how large and how densely packed with devices future chips may be it is very unlikely that a single chip can be fabricated that contains a powerful conventional 32-bit computer plus its entire memory. For although a powerful CPU, with 10^4 or even 10^5 devices, might even today be built on one corner of one 10^5 to 10^6 chip it would need at least 100 or 10 chips for 1 MB of memory. A 10,000,000 device chip will at most hold 1 MB of memory. But a powerful conventional computer needs from 4 MB to 64 MB (or more). [In order to keep a serial computer's single CPU working efficiently, more and more memory is added so that anything that might be needed will be present and immediately available.] Thus several million chips would be needed for a network with a million conventional computers.

Note that this argument holds only for conventional computers with their traditionally large memories. As we shall see, different types of computers can make very large networks feasible without such heroic efforts. For parallel computers it is probably more reasonable to think in terms of the total size of the memory for the whole set of computers that are working on a single problem, and the total amount of memory needed to handle that problem, rather than the size of each computer's memory.

In order to execute a problem faster, a larger amount of processing power must be assigned to work in parallel on that problem. But there does not appear to be any need to also assign a larger amount of memory space. (In fact it may turn out that less memory is needed, since parallel processing may well mean that there is less need to store intermediate results.) Therefore it seems fruitful to explore how parallel multi-computers offer opportunities to increase the percent of devices used in processors that do useful work in comparison to the percent of devices used for memory that stores information the processors will at some moment need (Uhr, 1982).

ALLOCATING BASIC RESOURCES TO A COMPUTER'S DIFFERENT COMPONENTS

It is instructive to examine a computer in terms of the resources expended on its four basic components:

1. Processors (which transform information);
2. Memory (which passively stores information in wait for a processor to use it);
3. Wires (which simply convey information from one device to another);
4. Switches (which merely determine which direction to send information).

Traditional serial computers put virtually all, far more than 99%, of their devices (transistors) into memory. For example, a 32-bit computer whose CPU might contain 10,000 to 100,000 or so transistors will typically have at least 32,000,000 transistors in its high-speed memory. In sharp contrast, several of the multi-computers described below have a far greater percent of their resources in processors. The extreme examples are the massively parallel arrays examined in Chapter 8, where processor gates account for from 10% to more than 50% of the total.

The total cost of the VLSI chip, hence of the whole system, is a function of the area needed for each of its components. Wires, especially when the total topology is irregular or nonplanar, can eat up area, as can large, complex, and nonplanar banks of switches linked by wires. Essentially, a wire (in microelectronic technologies) is simply a very long, skinny transistor. Unless it is kept very short (which will not always be possible), amplifiers will be needed to speed up and relay the signals each wire transmits. So the wires that serve to link components together can use a major part of the total system's resources.

Cost, in terms of money, can also be a useful measure for comparing systems, for total cost integrates all the various aspects of utilizing resources. (Unfortunately the cost of a commercial computer is usually a very poor measure, since the overriding factors are often how much people will pay and the economies of mass production, rather than the computer's true cost.) Here we shall see that several types of linking schemes for networks—the crossbars, rings, and reconfiguring switches examined in Chapter 6—become so costly, as the number of computers in the network grows, that they can potentially dominate. Several relatively small systems have already been built where the communications network costs a third, or a half, of the entire system. If such systems were made substantially larger, the relative costs of communication hardware would quickly rise to almost 100%.

However only the processors are actually doing useful work, and only the subset of gates that actually transform data at any given time. A major unanswered question is whether efficient, flexible systems can be devised that maximize the number of active processor gates, rather than expend excessive amounts of resources on memories, wires, and switches.

WAFER SCALE INTEGRATION (WSI), 3-DIMENSIONAL STRUCTURES, OPTICAL COMPUTERS

It is important to examine the emerging possibilities of wafer scale integration (WSI). Today's 4 to 6 millimeter square chip is diced from a wafer that is typically from 3 to 6 inches in diameter. It is becoming feasible to use the entire wafer, which is the equivalent of several hundred chips, as though it were a super-chip. This can, potentially, give two or three orders of magnitude increases in size. Equally exciting, although more complex and probably farther in the future, is the possibility of 3-dimensional structures, for example of stacked wafers (Etchells et al., 1981; Nudd et al., 1985). These might further increase the size of the basic building block by two or three orders of magnitude.

Wafer scale integration and stacked wafers and other types of 3-dimensional circuits pose formidable new problems:

The yield of properly operating individual VLSI chips is already low, rarely more than 50% and, especially for chips that push the state of the art, often much less. Since the technologies involved in dense packing of devices are being pushed as close as possible to their limits, especially in the state-of-the-art highest density chips, the yield will be lower the larger and more powerful the multi-computer.

Good fault-tolerance techniques will need to be developed to handle this problem. Relatively little work has been done on fault-tolerance for VLSI chips, but without fault-tolerance the yield for a whole wafer of chips will almost certainly be intolerably low. It appears that the costs in terms of the number of redundant components needed will be high even when faults are rare, and likely to reduce the wafer's total count of usable components by a factor of at least two or three.

The near-planar requirements of today's chips extend to wafers. Since wafers are so much larger than chips, they may be too restrictive for many designs.

Wafer scale integration and 3-dimensional structures offer major potential increases in the size of the basic building block. Even more important is the potential elimination of the bottlenecks resulting from the pins that must be used to link chips to one another.

Optical computers (Lohmann, 1985; Nazarathy and Goodman; 1985; Jenkins et al., 1984; Sawchuck and Strand, 1984) may well solve the problems of linking many devices, by using programmable holograms to reconfigure the links between large output arrays of lasers or light emitting diodes, and large input arrays of photo-sensitive diodes. They may also ultimately lessen the problems of heat dissipation, and make possible substantially faster and denser systems. (Heat dissipation becomes the dominant problem when many devices are packed as closely as possible, especially in a 3-dimensional space.)

However, a great deal of research is needed to develop digital optical systems. For example, studies have been made demonstrating that processors can be built from optical gates fabricated on a single chip, and that these gates can be miniaturized and packed in densities comparable to those for today's electronic gates. Major problems remain in reducing the amount of power needed, hence heat dissipated. Arrays of optical emitters and sensors are potentially extremely attractive; but once again major problems remain before large numbers can be successfully fabricated on a single chip. Holograms can today be used to handle large interconnection networks that have many thousands or even millions of links. There are still problems in combining them with the light emitters and sensors, and programmable holograms lie in the future. Thus it is not clear whether optical computers will be available in 5, 10, or 20 years, or ever.

THE ENORMOUS POTENTIAL SIZES THAT VLSI AND WSI TECHNOLOGIES MAKE FEASIBLE

VLSI technologies that will mature during the next 5 to 20 years mean that we can begin to think seriously about the following set of practicable computer topologies: any graph whose nodes are basic devices (transistors, gates) and whose links are wires, that contains 1 to 100,000 or more assemblages (the chips) each of which has 1 to 10,000,000 or more nodes (these probably need to be linked in near-planar fashion), with from 16 to 512 wires linking into each of these assemblages. That is, each chip can contain a structure built from millions of transistors, and the whole multi-computer can contain thousands of chips. Wafer scale integration, 3-dimensional chips and wafers, and optical computers offer much less certain possibilities of further increases of several orders of magnitude.

The design constraints that most stringently reduce the possibilities include the following:

Only hundreds of direct links can be made between each chip and all the other chips.

On-chip topology must be almost planar.

No wires (either on or off the chip) can be excessively long.

Too many spaghetti-tangled wires can make things too messy to handle.

The denser the packing the greater the need to dissipate heat.

Wafer-scale integration, 3-dimensional technologies, and optical computers may overcome these constraints—but they are still in the future and uncertain.

Today's mature, phenomenally successful, and continually improving technologies offer an overwhelming range of possibilities for networks with many thousands, or even millions, of individual computers. Other aspects of the total design, details of the technology, and economic considerations may well make a particular topology unattractive. But it is important to start at and to think in terms of this general level.

Chapter Four

THE BASIC GRAPH TOPOLOGIES FROM WHICH MULTI-COMPUTERS CAN BE CONSTRUCTED

It is helpful, and instructive, to use relatively abstract, and simple, graphs to examine the basic structure of multi-computers. Essentially a multi-computer's topology can be described very succinctly and revealingly by drawing its underlying graph. [A ("connected") "graph" joins nodes via links so that there is a path between every pair of nodes. Its "diameter" is the shortest distance between the most distant pair of nodes. Its "degree" is the largest number of links joined to any node. We use the following notation: Let n {or} o = node, -- {or} - = link, W = whole working computer, P = processor, M = memory, C = controller, R {or} r = register, Ch = Cache, I = input device, O = output device.]

GRAPHS OF COMPONENTS AT DIFFERENT LEVELS OF ABSTRACTION

At the highest level the graph will simply be a set of abstract nodes connected by links, for example:

o--o--o {indicating 3 nodes joined with a minimal number of links}.

At successively lower levels of abstraction, the type of node can be designated, for example:

P--M--P   {indicating a memory linked to two processors}.

Individual nodes can be identified as specific instances of the general type, for example:

P1--M1--P2--M2   {indicating processor1 is linked to memory1 which is linked to processor 2, which is linked to memory 2}.

When information can flow in only one direction over a link, this fact can be indicated with an arrow, for example:

I-->W1-->W2-->O   {indicating Input to computer W1 then W2 then Output}.

GRAPHS FOR TRADITIONAL AND MULTI-PROCESSOR COMPUTERS

Graphs Representing Traditional Single-CPU Serial Computers

A traditional Von Neumann computer can be diagrammed as a single node, as in Figure 4-1(a), although we can blow this up to show successively more detail, as in Figure 4-1(b). Or it can be diagrammed as in Figure 2-3 to indicate input and output devices, special-purpose processors, and memory hierarchies.

W   C—P—r—M

(a)   *(b)*

FIGURE 4-1. A simple traditional single-CPU computer. (a) A single-CPU computer. (b) A single-CPU computer in more detail.

Graphs Representing Single-CPU Multi-Processor Computers

A multi-processor system is diagrammed in Figure 4-2.

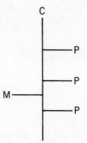

FIGURE 4-2. A Multi-processor computer

GRAPHS FOR MORE THAN ONE COMPUTER (MULTI-COMPUTERS)

Multi-Computers with More than One CPU

To get substantial increases in power we must somehow multiply computers. The simplest method is to add a second computer, as shown in Figure 4-3. The high-level two-node diagram (Figure 4-3(a)) n--n can be interpreted as linking two computers. Or, in more detail (Figure 4-3(b)), the processors can be linked to their memories and to each other via registers. Figures 4-3(c) and 4-3(d) diagram two of the several other variant ways of linking computers.

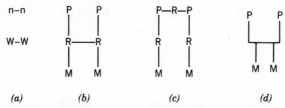

FIGURE 4-3. A Multi-computer with two computers. (a) High-level. (b) Register-register. (c) Processor-processor. (d) Bus-linked.

Figure 4-4 diagrams a variety of basic topologies that are among the simplest (and often, as we shall see, the most widely used and most effective) for linking computers. It is important to emphasize that each diagram pictures only a very simple, small example of each type of topology, but that each type includes arbitrarily large (potentially infinite) graphs. It is also important to emphasize that many of these cannot actually be realized in hardware, or would be completely impractical. For example, only a very small star or complete graph could possibly be built with real computer hardware, because the N-1 number of ports each node needs for all the wires that link it to all the other nodes grows much too rapidly.

NOTE: Usually each node is a separate computer; but it might be a processor, memory, or some other device.

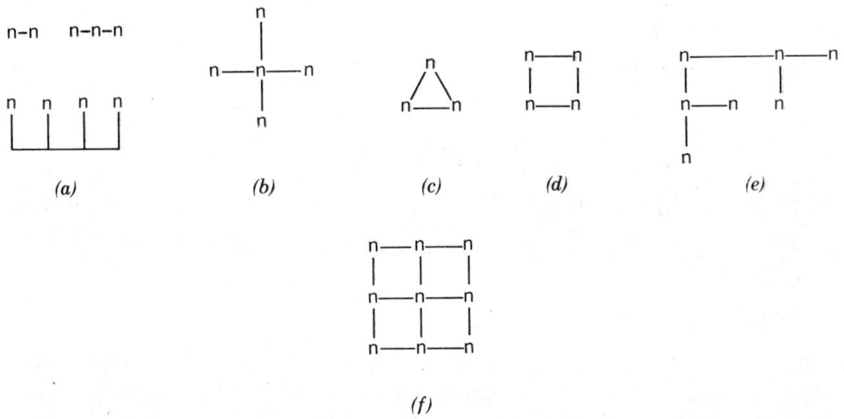

(a)   *(b)*   *(c)*   *(d)*   *(e)*

(f)

FIGURE 4-4. Small Examples of Several Simple Topologies for Multi-Computer Structures. (a) Line (bus). (b) Star. (c) Complete graph. (d) Polygon (ring). (e) Tree. (f) Grid.

LINES AND PIPELINES

The line includes two radically different kinds of structures. The first has a string of nodes linked so that two nodes communicate by passing information through whatever nodes may lie between them. The second links all nodes to a common communication channel. With the first, nodes will have to stop whatever they may be doing in order to receive information and then pass it on. If any node is defective or stops functioning this will break the path on which it lies, and the whole computer will go down.

Very powerful systems can be achieved when intermediate nodes are processors that actually compute functions of the information input to them, and then output results that are passed on to the next processor in the line. Such a system is often called a pipeline, or pipe.

LINES AND BUSES

The second type of line is usually realized by a bus (in the UK sometimes called—more appropriately—a highway). This is a high-bandwidth wire to which a number of computers and other devices are linked, usually with additional hardware (this can be considered another

special-purpose processor) to handle some of the interfacing and contention problems (sometimes called intelligent buses). A high-speed bus is
probably the most widely used technique for linking a few computers—
2, 3, 8, 16, and possibly up to 32 or 64. Since all information passed
between any pair of computers must travel over the single common bus
highway, bandwidth problems can easily arise, and they will grow worse
as N grows.

STARS AND SHARED MEMORIES

A star might in theory have any number of computers linked to the single device at its center. The single central node, however, can quickly
become a bottleneck. Note that this central node might be a computer
like all the others. Often the center node will turn out to be a large
shared memory, or a bus (in the case of a bus Figures 4-4(a) and 4-4(b)
are identical).

COMPLETE GRAPHS

Many people have suggested that a complete graph (a graph where every
node is directly linked to every other node) is the ideal structure for a
multi-computer, since every computer could then talk directly to every
other computer. Since a complete graph needs N-1 links to each node,
only very small structures of this sort can be built with today's technologies.

One crucial problem is that only 2, 3, 4, or up to only 8 or so computers at most, can be directly linked via a complete graph, since the
number of wires and interfaces (ports) quickly becomes excessive.
Another problem is that the operating system overhead (which is typically the overriding bottleneck) for handling communication would be as
great for a complete graph multi-computer as for any other topology.
Therefore people often try to find a graph that appears to be as close as
possible to a complete graph, or one that can be used as though it were
a complete graph.

POLYGONS AND RINGS

A polygon is simply a line with one link added, between the first and
the last nodes (the two nodes with only one link), thus giving a line that
circles back on itself. This minor addition of one extra link can serve
several useful purposes. The diameter of the graph is cut in half.
Information can be made to cycle, for example, from one node through
all the others and back to that node, and again and again. Polygons
are frequently implemented in multi-computers; they are usually called
rings, and sometimes cycles.

Note that the 3-node complete graph drawn in Figure 4-4(c) is also a polygon.

Note also that the 4-node polygon drawn in Figure 4-4(d) is also a 2x2 1-dimensional array.

TREES, AND TREES AUGMENTED WITH EXTRA CYCLE-GIVING LINKS

A tree starts from a root that links to two or more child nodes. These in turn each link to two or more nodes, and so on, ending with a link into each leaf node (a leaf has only one link). The example drawn in Figure 4-4E is commonly known as a binary tree, because each interior node links to 2 child nodes. Note that a binary tree is actually a degree 3 graph, since interior nodes have 3 links. Two types of binary tree exist: those with 2 links to the root and those with 3.

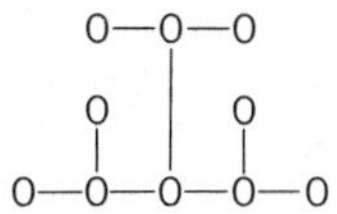

```
      0—0—0
      0   0
      |   |
0—0—0—0—0
```

FIGURE 4-5. A binary tree with three links to the root

More generally, an N-ary tree (with $N+1$ links to each interior node) can have either N or $N+1$ links to the root node.

As defined in graph theory a tree is a graph with only one path between any pair of nodes; that is, it has no cycles that give alternate paths. The term tree is often used loosely to mean a graph that is based on a tree, or has more or less the shape of a tree—but also has additional links that give alternate paths between nodes. This book will often do the same. In particular it will talk about trees with added links (usually these will be added to the leaves—the nodes with only one link). In cases where the properties of an underlying tree are dramatically improved because of a very carefully chosen system for adding links, I will call the resulting graphs augmented trees.

Note that stars are actually trees of minimal depth, that is, trees with one single ply of links that directly connects the root to all of the leaves. Thus stars are extreme examples of what is probably the major failing of trees—the bottleneck when large amounts of information must pass through the root. *All* messages involve the root (the center node) in stars.

GRIDS, ARRAYS, N-DIMENSIONAL ARRAYS, N-CUBES

A grid tesselates (tiles) a simple basic structure over the plane. Figure 4-4(f) shows a small square grid, with links from each node to its 4 square neighbors (often a multi-computer will be given an additional 4 links to the diagonals). The only other primitive structures that can be similarly tiled on the plane are the triangle and the hexagon. [Note that many tilings of artistic interest can be achieved by interlacing two or more primitive structures. None of these have to my knowledge been explored for multi-computers; but it is not clear why the requirement that the tiling contain only one primitive structure is important and should always be met.] The grid is usually called an array, and is often called a matrix or mesh.

N-dimensional arrays can also be constructed. In particular, 3-dimensional arrays appear to be extremely useful for processing information about 3-dimensional spaces that are slices of the real world (just as 2-dimensional arrays are useful for processing 2-dimensional images projected from the real world).

Note that a 1-dimensional array is a line. It is also interesting to note that an N-dimensional array that is only two nodes wide in each dimension (therefore, with nodes only at its vertices) is simply a (binary) N-cube. Therefore the 4-node polygon drawn in Figure 4-4(d) is not only an array, but also a 2-cube (an N-dimensional binary cube where $N = 2$). The 2-node line is a 1-cube; our familiar 8-node cube is a 3-cube; and so on.

FINAL SUMMARIZING COMMENT

A graph can give a very good abstract picture of the basic topology of a computer, and of a multi-computer network. A small number of basic classes of graphs—lines, stars, complete graphs, polygons, trees, and grids (including N-cubes)—account for many if not most of the multi-computer topologies built or designed to date. Very simple examples of these graphs have been shown in this chapter; but each can be made increasingly large, potentially without limit.

Lines (pipelines, see Chapter 7) and grids (arrays, see Chapter 8) are among the most widely used and most useful topologies. Chapters 6 and 9 through 13 examine a large number of systems with more complex topologies.

Chapter Five

THE BASIC HARDWARE AND SOFTWARE COMPONENTS OF MULTI-COMPUTERS

This chapter examines some of the issues involved in combining different types of resources into a total multi-computer system. It focusses on the coordination of the different computers and the transfer of information between processors. Chapters 6 through 13 will then examine the global topologies that underlie the different multi-computers' architectures.

TOWARD A TAXONOMY OF MULTI-COMPUTER NETWORKS

A good taxonomy would help us sort out the different types of multi-computers, contrast and compare them, determine what each is especially suited for, decide which is most cost effective for which problems or mixes of problems, and design and build better ones.

Probably today's most widely used set of distinctions is Flynn's (1972) 4-way categorization, in terms of whether one or several processors execute instructions on one or several structures of data. Thus the conventional single-processor serial computer is "single instruction single data-stream" (SISD), whereas an asynchronous network of many independent computers of the sort examined in chapters 6 and 10 through 13 is "multiple instruction multiple data-stream" (MIMD). The two other in-between possibilities are "multiple instruction single data-stream" (MISD) systems like the pipelines examined in Chapter 7, where all processors work on the same stream of data, in assembly-line fashion, and the "single instruction multiple data-stream" (SIMD) systems

43

like the arrays examined in Chapter 8, where many processors all execute the same instruction, but each on a different set of data.

Flynn's taxonomy is only a first cut at this complex set of possibilities. It is rather like a taxonomy of buildings built on the two variables single inhabitant vs. multi inhabitant and single dwelling vs. multiple dwelling. From this we could distinguish between the single person's houses (SISD), family apartments (MIMD), family houses (MISD), and swinging singles apartments (SIMD). There is much more to be said about buildings than that—and multi-computers are far more complex. It is useful to contrast single-processor SISD conventional computers with pipelines and the other possibilities that all combinations of two variables generate. But this four-way breakdown lumps together too many different possibilities into each single category, especially the MIMD category.

There are a number of ways in which (multi-)computers differ, including the following:

A. The basic over-all aspects:
    1. number;
    2. power, size and cost; and
    3. type

    of each type of component, including:
    a. processors, including type of:
        i.   the main processor,
        ii.   specialized parts, for example, floating point processors,
        iii. co-processors, for example, for input-output and instruction decoding;
    b. memories (possibly shared):
        i.   high-speed registers,
        ii.   caches,
        iii. high-speed memories,
        iv.   auxiliary memories;
    c. wires for linking components and transmitting information;
    d. switches for re-routing information;
    e. controllers;

B. The topological structure of the wires linking components:
1. locally;
2. globally;
C. Information-transmission and control methods used:
1. Operating system and languages;
2. Hardwiring into hardware;
3. The particular combination of hardwired and software control mechanisms;
D. General vs. specialized vs. special-purpose, and the degree and type of each.

Thus in terms of numbers, a conventional computer has one processor and one controller, along with one or more registers and memories.

A multi-processor has more than one processor.

A network with only one controller, but in which each processor works with information stored in its own and nearby memories, is SIMD (see Chapter 8).

A network where each processor has its own controller, and wires between processors serve to pipeline information through all the processors, and the program is loaded into those processors to execute in assemblyline fashion, is MISD (see Chapter 7).

A single multi-processing computer with several processors is typically built so that all processors share memory. A network with all processors linked to a whole bank of main memories (e.g., via a bus or crossbar; see Chapter 6) is similarly often characterized as having a "shared memory," in contrast to a network of computers (where each processor has its own memory) that are linked to one another over some "point-to-point" topology (see Chapters 10-13).

A relatively small number of large and powerful processors gives what is often called "large grain" hardware; a large number of small processors gives "small grain" hardware.

Similarly the time needed to transmit information from one processor to another determines whether programs can be written to execute small grain processes with a large amount of intercommunication between processors, or whether programs must be large grain, with information passed from one processor to another only rarely, or hardly ever.

Today people tend to talk in terms of dichotomies—like large grain vs. small grain, or loosely coupled vs. tightly coupled. Often, as is the case here, there can be many steps between.

Small grain typically means the cheapest cost-effective processor. This might be a 68000, or the less powerful or even cheaper 6800, or the more powerful 68020 or Transputer chip.

Large grain might mean a Cray-1, or the more powerful Cray-2, or a less powerful mini-Cray. And there are many other processors with varying degrees of power. When a processor takes 1 microsecond to execute a typical instruction, .2 to 5 microseconds to communicate between processors might be considered fast enough to allow small grain programs (note that this is a 25-fold range, yet communication will today take even longer). In sharp contrast, a network that takes (as many do) 400 to 40,000 microseconds to pass information between processors is most appropriately characterized as large grain. Unless the system is programmed so that processors rarely must wait such relatively long times before they receive needed information, performance will degrade enormously.

Tightly coupled is often taken to mean having a common shared memory, as in a computer with several processors. Some people extend this to mean having a common shared virtual memory (see Chapter 6), along with enough hardware to handle memory accesses reasonably simply and fast. It probably is better used to mean a multi-computer with good, tight communication between processors, no matter what the underlying combination of hardware and software mechanisms. Processors are always coupled as tightly as possible to their own registers, caches, and main memories, so that information can be fetched and stored as quickly as possible. Multi-computers introduce a new level of coupling—between processors and between computers. Basically, a procesor is still fetching and storing information, but now this can be from and to not only its own memories but another processor. It is similarly important that these transfers of information be as fast as possible.

Synchronized is typically used to indicate complete synchrony, with a single controller handling all processors in exactly the same way. However, different processors might all take the same time, but each execute some variant on the same instruction (e.g., fetching and storing information using different memory locations), or an entirely different instruction, or a different sequence of instructions. Once again, there are many combinations and steps in between.

A good taxonomy should distinguish between the different topologies that underlie different computers, and also between the different amounts of coupling and interaction possible, the different amounts and types of synchrony, and the different types of problems the system is best able to handle. These are not simple matters, and our understanding of multi-computers is probably still too primitive to arrive at a definitive taxonomy.

The attempt to taxonomize is important because it is ultimately the attempt to understand and to express this understanding in a simple, categorical form. Inevitably, it is a simplification and a guide. It reflects our best understanding; it should not be attempted prematurely except in a tentative way, or used as a strait-jacket.

BASIC ELEMENTS OF COMMUNICATION

Probably the biggest problems in today's multi-computer networks are the bottlenecks and delays that occur when two processors communicate information. A processor that finds in its memory all the information needed to execute procedures assigned to it can, if not interrupted, work very efficiently. When several processors are all working on the same program, difficult new problems arise.

The general situation is one where some information, some set of bits, that resides at location A must be copied into location B. At the very least, both locations A and B must be involved.

A classic situation occurs when A is a processor's register and B is a location in that processor's memory. Copying the information from register to memory is effected by a store instruction; copying it from memory to register is effected be a fetch instruction. These are two of the simplest and most basic instructions for any computer. They are usually among the fastest—a small computer typically takes a few hundred nanoseconds to fetch or store a word of information, and a microsecond or more to add or multiply. The CPU is in control of the processor and the memory. The hardware connections between memory and processor have been wired to handle fetches and stores with maximum speed. Since there is only one processor that can execute only one instruction at a time, it is guaranteed that there will be no contention for memory.

But there are a variety of problems that can arise when a system has more than one processor. The communication path must be set up between processors when one needs to send and the other to receive information, and the actual communication effected in a secure and reliable manner. Several processors might clash, because they contend for the same common resource (e.g., a shared memory, an output device, or information that is stored in still another processor's memory). When one processor makes a change to information, all processors must from that instant on use the correct new information. When several processors attempt to make such changes, an unambiguous procedure must adjudicate. One processor might need information from a second processor or its memory when it is not convenient for that second processor to send it. It might even be desirable for a processor to stop what it is presently doing and turn to a more important task that has been requested by another processor, or by the operating system. An act of communication between two processors might also need to interrupt still other resources.

Therefore a multi-computer almost always (with a few important exceptions) has one other entity involved, the operating system's set of procedures that handle communications (often called the message-passing protocol). Point-to-point networks must also involve the entities that lie between A and B, since the information must pass through the whole sequence of computer nodes that intervene on the path used to transmit information between the two nodes involved.

Each node that must be involved in communication might be in any of several different states: (1) waiting to serve (as is a memory node); (2) working on something else, but interruptable (as might be the operating system, or the processor that is the target of a request for information); (3) working but not interruptable (as when a high priority task is being executed).

When the operating system is involved, it can be a very busy resource. With a large multi-computer it will often have a long queue of requests to process; these today's serial operating systems can handle only one at a time, serially. Therefore the operating system can easily become a severe serial bottleneck. The system can periodically interrupt itself, as when an operating system periodically stops what it is doing to see whether anything else needs doing, or a processor moves among a whole set of procedures it is executing in time-shared mode. But it takes time and hardware to interrupt, save contextual information, and abandon one job and move back to another.

There are indeed a number of ways that this situation can be handled so that communication is reasonably fast and efficient. Unfortunately most networks that link completely independent computers via a bus or ring (see Chapter 6), or via a point-to-point topology (see Chapters 10-13) today use message-passing protocols that take literally thousands of times longer for one computer to fetch information from another than to fetch it from its own memory. It is not at all clear why this is the case, and nobody has ever proved that it is necessary. The problem may well lie in the present relatively primitive state of multi-computer operating systems and specially designed communications hardware. Most of today's multi-computer operating systems are extensions of operating systems that were developed to handle multi-programming on a single conventional single-CPU computer. Virtually nobody has attempted to start afresh, to rethink the problems of control and coordination for multi-computers, to pass information as quickly as possible.

THE PROBLEMS IN COORDINATING INDEPENDENT COMPUTERS

In most of the multi-computer systems that have been built or designed to date each computer is a conventional Von Neumann machine. Each works independently, executing whatever procedures have been input to it. Each computer has its own controller; each goes its own way. Whenever it becomes necessary, one computer passes information to another, or requests information from another, which is a passing of information in order to instigate a second passing of information.

The necessary coordination of communications is up to the programmer, the operating system, the programming language, additional built-in hardware, the way that the total system is designed, or some combination of all of these. These systems typically assume random mappings of program into architecture. They do not ask the programmer to give any specifications about the flow of data through the program, or how the program might best be mapped into and executed by a network. Therefore the programmer cannot appropriately structure code for efficient execution.

Synchronized and Pipelined Systems Send-Receive as Fast as They Fetch-Store

Systems that have only one controller (e.g., the arrays like the CLIP, DAP, and MPP examined in Chapter 8), so that each computer executes the same instruction in SIMD mode, handle communication between computers with great efficiency and speed. Typically they take virtually the same time to send information from one computer to any of its directly linked near neighbors as to fetch (i.e., send) information from memory. This is accomplished by having each processor fetch information (which means that this information is loaded into the processor's register), and immediately pass that information on to the register of the designated processor (these parallel array computers are typically linked via these registers).

Pipelines (see Chapter 7) and the closely related systolic systems (see Chapters 6, 13) synchronize the flow of information through the successive processors of the pipe, and thus handle this local passing of information with great efficiency.

But both arrays and pipelines can become very slow when they must pass information over long distances.

Some Partially Synchronized and Shared-Memory Systems Are Almost as Fast

Several MIMD multi-computer systems have been developed where information can be passed from one computer to another almost as fast as each computer can fetch information from its own memory. These include systems where several computers share the same memory registers, either directly via dual-port memories, via a common bus, or via a network of switches. Unless care is taken, this kind of system can be plagued by several major problems. For example, two processors might contend at the same moment for the same memory. Or more than one processor might try to change the information in the same memory. Several techniques have been developed to handle these problems, including the following:

The processors can be synchronized just enough so that they don't contend (as in the dual-port memories, which actually buffer one of the requests and process it immediately after the other).

Systems where processors share memory can use intelligent caches to anticipate what information a processor will need, and to handle updating efficiently.

Hardware that computes and follows the path to the required memory information can be used to give virtual shared memory.

Still other systems use partial synchronizations to achieve relatively fast sending-receiving of information between different computers that do not share the same memory. For example, some systems that use crossbars or shuffle-based reconfiguring networks of switches (see Chapter 6) to link computers have additional hardware that delays and buffers otherwise competing messages. The passing of information will often still be slow. To keep from degrading performance excessively this must be kept as rare as possible. Networks linked via reconfiguring networks (e.g., the NYU Ultracomputer and BBN Butterfly examined in Chapter 6, and the Purdue PASM examined in Chapter 13) are good examples of such systems. The MIT Connection Machine examined in Chapter 12 is an example of a synchronized SIMD array that will handle message-passing between distant nodes in this way.

Under certain circumstances message-passing can take place at the same time that processors are working. The Maryland ZMOB (see Chapter 6) and the NASA-Goodyear MPP (see Chapter 8) work this way.

Shared memory and partially synchronized systems typically take 3 to 5, or even 10, times as long to send information between processors as for a processor to fetch information from its own memory. Sometimes they take as little as twice as long, or even less. Usually (but not in the case of ZMOB) they take longer as the path the information must take becomes longer.

These are appreciable degradations, and it will be interesting to see how much they can be reduced. But they can be lived with, and they are trivial in comparison with the completely asynchronous MIMD systems with operating systems that use today's message-passing protocols.

Systems with Languages that Specify Program Flow and Mappings into Hardware

A programming language/software system of the sort that has been developed in the Occam language to go along with Transputer systems (see Chapter 10) can ask the programmer, and help the programmer, to give enough information about the path of computers through which a message should be passed, and to coordinate message-passing to the point where it can be handled efficiently.

Such a system can potentially pass information from one computer to another with great efficiency. The time needed will be a function of the distance between the two computers. This means that the program should be coded, and then mapped into the network, so as to minimize distances over which information should be passed. That is in striking contrast to message-passing operating systems that assume random mappings of program into architecture.

Asynchronous Message-Passing Systems Take Thousands of Times Longer

Asynchronous MIMD networks that do not have shared memory raise extremely difficult and as yet little understood problems, problems that revolve around the transmission of information from one computer to another. To indicate the severity of the problem, in most of the asynchronous multi-computers examined in Chapters 6 and 10 through 13, the operating system executes many thousands of instructions whenever it sends a message (i.e., transmits a packet of information), where each message is typically on the order of 1, 80, or occasionally up to 2000 bytes (Wulf et al., 1974; Wittie, 1976, 1978; Wittie and Van Tilborg, 1980; Finkel and Solomon, 1980a, Finkel et al., 1983; DeWitt et al., 1984). Thus it takes thousands of times longer to transmit information than to operate on that information.

In striking contrast, in a synchronous array (see Chapter 8) each computer can receive information from one (or in the case of the CLIP array any subset) of its 4, 6 or 8 nearest neighbors in one instruction cycle. Pyramids (see Chapter 9) should be equally fast at passing information to and from all of a processor's siblings, children, and parents. Pipelines and systolic systems (see Chapter 7) are even faster, since they flow information directly from processor to processor. True hardware data-flow structures (see Chapter 13) should be equally fast. Essentially what is often called message-passing is handled at the same speed, and with virtually the same operation as, a fetch.

The message-passing protocol consists of a complex program (see Finkel and Solomon, 1980a, for an example) that typically executes on the order of 5,000 to 15,000 or more instructions in order to complete sending information from one computer to another (and often from one process to another even though they might both be time-sharing and executed on the same processor).

For example, a typical message-passing operating system will do the following: Copy and temporarily store the message to be sent; check the priority for this message; check whether the buffer for waiting messages has room; put the message on the waiting buffer if its priority is high enough and there is room; check whether the potential recipient of the message is busy; alert the recipient about the message; ask the recipient to decide what to do about the message; ... ; if all has gone well, get the message from the buffer; send it to the recipient; get the recipient's acknowledgment; tell the sender that the message has been received; if the sender desires, repeat the message back, so that it can be tested for accuracy; erase the message from the buffer.

There appears to be some hope of shortening this protocol, and of dedicating additional hardware to handle some of it. The programmer might be asked to handle aspects of communication, and given options to use fewer services. To estimate roughly, possibly the time can be reduced to 400, giving a range from 400 to 40,000 instructions to fetch—as opposed to one instruction to process. But the degradation of such systems, from the overheads needed when passing messages to make them reliable, avoid contention problems, and give the user a variety of other (some essential, some not essential) services is so severe that unless relatively large numbers of computers are linked together but rarely exchange messages their increases in speed and power can easily be negligible.

It is suggestive to compare a multi-computer that combines a number of separate individual computers with the sociology of small groups of individuals (Uhr, 1984a). How do we get 4, 8, or 16 or so human beings to work together effectively on a common task? Unfortunately the separate computers, and the subprograms that each executes, have none of the intelligence of a human being, and they have no a priori concept of cooperation (unless we program in such a concept—which is a major, far-from-solved, AI problem that would eat up large amounts of additional computer hardware and time). They do not even have the most basic understanding of the jobs they are to carry out, how to do them, or how to communicate. All aspects of coordination and cooperation, and all aspects of their behavior, must be worked out and programmed in, or else wired into the hardware. For fast, efficient real-time processing, multi-computers must be organized and regimented in simple, rigid ways.

The Need to Develop Appropriate Operating Systems for Parallel Multi-Computers

Multi-computer networks are being developed for at least three major purposes:

1. To communicate between computers, as when one sends mail to another;
2. To allow different computers to make use of shared resources, for example, printers or disks containing large databases;
3. To achieve more power and speed when executing a single program, for example, to execute in real time the large AI programs that are the focus of this book.

The operating systems that have been developed to run the networks of type (3) that this book examines usually handle networks of the first two types as well. In fact, they are typically developed as extensions of the traditional operating systems for conventional single-CPU computers: first, to multiprocess several users on a time-shared system; then, to handle several processes in a single program, all running on the same computer, that must be coordinated; and finally, to run several processes in a single program but possibly on different computers.

This appears to have resulted in systems where speed and efficiency are treated as relatively secondary when compared to the importance of absolute security, transparency of the system, and ease of programming.

Many systems programmers, especially those developing operating systems and programming languages, appear to feel that traditional approaches for conventional serial computers should be extended to multi-computers. This means that the programmer should not be asked to think about the hardware, or to worry about how to map the program into, and execute the program on, that hardware. The result in most systems is that the operating system does not try to consider the program's structure. This means that the operating system must assume that processes might be randomly related.

Operating systems are developed with the assumption that the programmer does not want to be bothered about any issues of the topology or details of the (multi-)computer on which the program will execute. That would be very nice, but not if it results in the development of programs that are more serial than they might have been, mappings of programs into architectures that destroy the program's topology, and operating systems that therefore must assume there is no useful topology. It seems reasonable to try to develop entirely new kinds of operating systems and programming languages that will allow the programmer to specify, simply and naturally, how the program should be mapped into the multi-computer, and also how it should pass information, so that processing can be efficient and message-passing can be fast. An attractive possibility is interactive graphical languages that help the programmer build the actual software/hardware structure of processes, and actually see called-for details of these displayed as desired on monitors, and displayed while actually executing in emulations.

This is especially attractive when, as seems highly desirable, process-structured architectures are used (see Chapters 7-13), and the system maps the program's data-flow graph into the multi-computer graph in order to allow information to flow smoothly through the computer's physical processors. This means that processors that pass information to one another should be as physically close together as possible. The programmer should be encouraged and helped to think and to program in terms of these process-structured graphs. The programmer might be asked, or given the option, to help the operating system map the program structure into the hardware structure of the multi-computer that will actually be used. By asking the programmer to do this, the system is helping the programmer think in terms of parallel processing, and getting from the programmer a great deal of help in figuring out how to execute these processes with efficiency and speed. The Occam-Transputer system is one of the most promising steps in this direction.

SUMMARY COMMENTS AND COMPARISONS

Completely synchronized systems that have a single controller driving all processors avoid the message-passing problems of MIMD networks where each processor has its own controller, hence processors can, if not handled with great care, contend, clash, and do a variety of conflicting or incompatible acts. Although they raise major new problems with respect to message passing, independent processors can, potentially, execute processes with much greater flexibility, and therefore efficiency, and thus do a greater variety of things. When all goes well they need not wait around doing nothing if what the controller commands is not appropriate for them. Indeed, it will often be the case that many or most of the processors, when working in lockstep synchronized fashion, cannot be used fruitfully at each and every step. For example, an SIMD array may be looking for a feature, such as an edge, angle, or window everywhere, even though the program has already gathered enough information to infer that in many parts of the scene there is no point in doing that.

Systems can be partially synchronized by introducing periodic message-passing periods between processing periods. The programmer can have all processors work for a while, then all processors send information. Hardware can be added so that messages can be passed at the same time that processors are working. But these devices are of little help if message-passing takes far longer than processing, in which case the system cannot execute programs with great speed and efficiency unless communication between processors is made extremely rare.

Each computer can be allowed to work independently. In theory this makes possible far more flexible and powerful processing. In practice, at least today, it raises major new problems. It is substantially more expensive, since each processor must have its own controller, and additional hardware and software resources must be used to handle the much more complex interactions between processors. Passing information between processors becomes appreciably (roughly 2 to 10 times) more expensive when shared memory systems are used, and extremely (roughly 400 to 40,000 times) more expensive when message-passing protocols are used. One of the most promising alternatives is to use an integrated programming language/operating system that allows the programmer to specify how information should flow through the system, and that makes use of this to map the program into the architecture and to execute the program.

PARALLEL AND PROCESS-STRUCTURED MULTI-COMPUTER ARCHITECTURES

Chapter Six

LINKING SMALL NUMBERS OF COMPUTERS INTO PSEUDO-COMPLETE GRAPHS

This chapter begins the examination of multi-computers, starting with the smallest and simplest designs, and moving toward topologies whose global and local properties offer promise of larger, more powerful, often process-structured, architectures. Structures with a few dozen, a few hundred, or even a few thousand, computers can be built in the form of a complete graph (where every node is directly linked to every other node) or more precisely a pseudo-complete graph—that is, giving the appearance to the outside world of a complete graph but in fact having some other physical structure. Pseudo-complete graphs include the bus, ring, crossbar, and shuffle network-based systems to be examined in this chapter. [Any connected graph can be made to appear to the programmer as a complete graph, but these are the only topologies that will do so with reasonable efficiency.]

The Major Problems in Directly Linking Every Computer to Every Other Computer

A number of researchers have suggested that the ideal topology for a multi-computer network would physically link every computer directly to every other computer, in effect forming a complete graph.

However, there is a basic limitation on the number of direct links (wires) that can be ported (interfaced) to a single computer. A true complete graph means that each computer in an N-node network must have N-1 interfaces, to link it to the N-1 other computers. Interfaces are expensive, fragile, and fault-prone. Many people argue that three or four direct links are all that the technologies of pins linking to chips and buses linking to computers, realistically allow. Most computer architects agree that more than 8 direct links, or possibly 16 or so, are not feasible. Therefore, as we move to networks with hundreds, thousands, or millions of computers, systems with point-to-point links—that is, with each node linking directly only to an increasingly small percent of the other nodes—become absolutely necessary.

That seems fine, since there appear to be many potentially very powerful point-to-point topologies. They pose new problems, since the system must find and follow good paths; but there is no reason to think that these cannot be solved. Point-to-point linked multi-computers will be examined starting in Chapter 7.

The complete graph is an ideal only in an ideal world that has nothing to do with the real world's constraints. [Note that this is the same unreal world that would immediately solve all of our AI problems. Since each human brain is finite and the period since birth, during which all learning has occurred, is finite, all AI problems are at worst simply large but finite combinatorially explosive NP-complete problems (needing exponential time unless executed on a nondeterministic computer, which needs polynomial time). For example, we can trivially code a program that plays perfect chess simply by having it look ahead along the enormously large number of paths to all possible game endings. We can code a program to find any piece of information in an arbitrarily large semantic memory network by having it search everywhere. We can code a vision program that stores and matches a complete template for each possible configuration of an input image. None of these are plausible, because the size of the computer needed and/or the amount of time needed are impossibly large (though finite, hence programmable and in theory executable). The practical constraints on designing computers are that only a few billion, or a few trillion, transistors can be used, and results must be got in a few seconds, or hours or months at the most.]

There are several ways to build reasonably efficient multi-computers that on the surface look like complete graphs, or that can be made to look like complete graphs by the operating system and the programming language. These "pseudo" complete graphs are examined in this chapter.

Some of the Techniques that Can be Used to Pass Information

Processors in synchronized SIMD systems can send and receive information to near-neighbor processors at the same very fast speeds with which they fetch and store information from and into their own memories (see Chapter 8).

When they must pass information at greater distances they can be given additional hardware that allows this to be done at the same time that processors are working. But these systems are able to pass information only in very synchronized, limited ways.

When processors work more independently, with asynchronous MIMD aspects, the new problems that arise suggest several possible approaches.

They can pass information directly from one to another, as in a pipeline (see Chapter 7).

They can be partially synchronized, so that all processors pass information at the same time.

They can be structured to share memories and therefore pass information by having one processor store it into a memory and a second processor fetch it.

They can communicate under the control of a message-passing operating system (see Chapter 5), but with major delays.

They can be coordinated by a higher-level language/operating system, as in the INMOS Occam-Transputer structures (see Chapter 10).

ATTEMPTS TO BUILD MULTI-COMPUTERS DIRECTLY LINKED VIA A TRUE COMPLETE GRAPH

It seems unlikely that anyone has actually directly linked several computers together, to form a true complete graph. Since this could only be done conveniently with four or five computers at most, a shared bus would be simpler and would probably work at least as well. One possibility for a true complete graph architecture would be to take five INMOS Transputers (Whitby-Stevens, 1985; see Chapter 10) and link them together. This would be relatively simple, because the basic Transputer module is a complete computer on a single chip, with four relatively powerful high-speed 10 Mbit per second buses available to link each Transputer to other Transputers. (The Transputer has been specially designed to form a primitive component in a large multi-computer.)

If one tried to link still more computers, not only would the number of links and interfaces quickly grow beyond any reasonable numbers, but also one would have to introduce intermediate registers, a whole network of switches, and additional larger buffer memories; this means that the system would form a pseudo, rather than a true, complete graph. Almost certainly, wires would have to be multiplexed, each serving more than one link, to live within the technology's physical constraints. So it is more exact to call such a system an approximate, or a pseudo, complete graph.

PSEUDO-COMPLETE CONNECTIVITY: BUS, RING, STAR, CROSSBAR

Most of the small prototype networks built to date have linked their separate computers via either a common bus or ring (i.e., a line or a polygon of big high-bandwidth wires, e.g., Bell, 1985; Farber and Larson, 1972); a shared memory (one version is a star whose center is a memory, e.g., Wulf et al., 1972; another version is a common bus to which all processors and all memories are interfaced, e.g., Bell, 1985); or (as diagrammed in Figure 6-1) a crossbar grid of switches (e.g., Widdoes, 1980; Maples, 1981).

Bus, ring, star, and crossbar are probably the simplest ways to connect computers. They are feasible only for very small networks, of 4, 8, 16, 32, or, possibly in special cases (as when special caches are used), up to a hundred or so.

A Single Common Bus or Ring to Link Computers

Buses and rings give the appearance of linking each node directly to any other node. Hence they appear to behave like a complete graph. The actual details of such an implementation are more complex. Each node is linked to the common bus or ring; thus a message passes from a node to and then along the bus or ring, and then to another node. (Alternately the processors might actually be on the ring, so that information passes from one to the next.) Therefore the complexity of the hardware interfaces, and the time needed to move information from sender to receiver, are greater than might be needed with a direct link between the two processors.

BUS-LINKED MULTI-COMPUTERS

A convenient, flexible, and commonly used architecture for a single-CPU computer is one that employs a high-speed bus to link its various resources, including its CPU, several banks of memory, and input and output devices. Several multi-computer systems also add more CPUs to the bus—up to 2 (Cray-XMP), up to 4 (the HP-9000), or up to 10

(ELXSI). Aliant, Concept, Denelcor, Encore, and several other companies have built systems of this kind. Intel, Motorola, National Semi-Conductor, and other companies are now selling relatively powerful several-MIP processor chips for relatively cheap, and continually decreasing, prices. AMD, TRW, Weitek and other companies have fabricated new 10 MFlop processor chips that, when linked via a bus, will make for unusually powerful multi-computers. NEC has developed a high-density chip specially designed for image processing data-flow. Although any desired topology might be used to link these chips, buses and pipelines, being the simplest, are usually used.

CACHE-BASED PROCESSORS WITH SHARED MEMORIES ON A COMMON BUS

The use of a cache associated with each processor, and in particular an intelligent snooping cache of the sort proposed by Goodman (1983), appears to make possible significantly larger numbers of processors in a shared memory system. Bell (1985) points out that a cache can reduce memory accesses by 95%. The snooping cache handles the updating problem when several processors may be using and modifying the same piece of memory, and thus makes the use of caches possible in a multi-processor shared memory system.

Bell uses the term "multis" to refer to such systems when all processors and all memories are linked via a common high-speed bus. Although the largest such systems built to date have roughly 16 or 32 processors, Bell suggests that systems with several hundred processors are possible, and that these can be cost-effective competitors to Cray-type super-computers.

THE ELXSI MULTI-CPU MULTI-PROCESS SYSTEM

The ELXSI (anon., 1984) is an interesting example of a system that is designed for parallelism. It can have up to 192 MB of memory, 4 input-output processors, and 10 CPUs (each with a 16KB cache), all on a very high-speed 320 MB bus. Each CPU can execute a 64-bit floating point multiply in 300 nanoseconds. Each CPU has 16 sets of registers, which allow it to time-share among 16 different processes. Therefore a 10-CPU system can be used to simulate a 160-processor multi-computer (albeit with only at most a 10-fold increase in speed over a single ELXSI processor).

RING-LINKED MULTI-COMPUTERS

The ring was proposed by Farber and Larson (1972) as a technique for securely handling messages between a small number of up to 30 or so devices (computers, disks, printers, etc.), but without much thought to having several computers working under real time constraints on the same problem. The ring is usually structured so that messages pass through (the interface to) each computer node in turn. This means that when the message arrives back at the sender node the sender knows that all other nodes have had the opportunity to look at and use it, and, possibly, other nodes' responses will be appended.

THE WISCONSIN CRYSTAL SOFTWARE PARTITIONABLE RING

The University of Wisconsin's Crystal multi-computer (DeWitt et al., 1984) was originally proposed as a ring with 100 VAX-750s, where the goal was to have all 100, or a smaller subset, of the computers work on the same problem, each with its own controller, in MIMD, asynchronous mode. This original proposal included a ring with a bandwidth of several hundred thousand MB, anticipating future replacement by a fiber optic ring with a multi-gigabit (billions of bits per second) bandwidth whose development DARPA was funding. But Crystal funding was received to buy only 40 VAX-750s, and the highest-bandwidth bus that turned out to be commercially available and feasible was 10 Mbits.

The 1985 running Crystal system had 20 VAX-750s, to be upgraded to 40 nodes (including microvax-2s) and a 10 MByte ring. Crystal is probably pushing the limit in terms of the number of computers linked over a ring (or a bus).

Multi-Computers Linked into a Star (E.g., Via a Single Shared Memory)

A single memory cannot really be shared in the sense that two or more processors can fetch data from or store data to different locations at exactly the same time. Rather, a network of switches is needed to han dle simultaneous access of several processors to what, at the basic hardware level, turns out to be a whole bank of separate memories. Additional hardware is also needed to adjudicate simultaneous attempts to access a single memory, with buffer stores for the delayed instructions. Devices called dual-port memories are available commercially, but they are simply memories that buffer one of the two fetch or store instructions and then slip it in right after the first.

Similar problems arise if one tries to link many computers to a single computer, forming a star (actually a tree with all leaves linked directly to the root). A tree-shaped switching network would be needed, and the bottleneck would be severe.

Crossbar-Based Multi-Computers

A crossbar is a 2-dimensional array of wires linked where they cross via switches. Each of N computers might be linked to one row and to one column. Or, alternately, a different set of nodes, for example, memories, or/and input-output devices, might be linked at the columns. Thus a crossbar linking N computers has NxN switches. A crossbar linking N computers to M memories or other resources has NxM switches. (See Hwang and Briggs, 1984, for details).

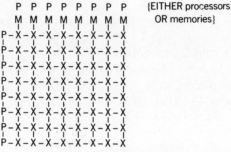

FIGURE 6-1. The array topology of the crossbar switch. An 8-by-8 crossbar links 8 processors to 8 memories, or to 8 processors (usually the same).

Crossbar switches allow each node at the left (of a row of switches) to access any node at the top (of a column of switches). The crossbar, when it provides separate paths between any pairs of nodes (one heading a row, the other heading a column), probably comes closest to simulating a complete graph.

CROSSBARS LINKING SMALL NUMBERS OF COMPUTERS

Crossbars have been used in a variety of systems where small numbers of computers are linked. One of the earliest, and one of the very first multi-computers, was the Carnegie-Mellon C.mmp (Wulf and Bell, 1972; Wulf et al., 1980), which linked about 8 DEC PDP-11s via a crossbar to a shared memory. The potentially very powerful S-1 system, designed and partially built at Lawrence Livermore (Widdoes, 1980), is planned to have up to 64 very powerful Cray-class 64-bit floating point computers linked via a crossbar.

AQUARIUS: THE BERKELEY CROSSBAR-BASED PROLOG MACHINE

Aquarius, a very powerful single-CPU machine, is being developed at the University of California, Berkeley (Despain, 1985; Dobry et al., 1985) to execute programs coded in Prolog, a language that uses logic for symbolic programming that can also include numerical code. [Prolog is the language that the Japanese have designated as the basis for their fifth generation symbolic computers. It is, basically, a language that allows one to program in first order predicate calculus logic. It also appears to be one of the most promising languages for a variety of AI problems.] A prototype version built from off-the-shelf TTL logic is now running. It has been benchmarked as executing up to 300K LIPS (logic instructions per second). This compares very favorably with its competitors, including the fastest built-and-running Japanese fifth generation system (30K LIPS), the Symbolics 3600 (53K LIPS), which is the probably faster than the other commercial symbol/list processors (e.g., Texas Instruments, Xerox), and the very powerful IBM 3081 (200K LIPS).

Aquarius consists of a single CPU (built from about 500 chips) that is designed for logic processing, linked via a bus to memory. The processor is specialized, in order to increase its speed, with a variety of carefully designed resources, including a large number of high-speed registers, specialized caches, and a vector processor. The next step planned is a system built with a VLSI processor chip (now being designed) that will use a crossbar to link 16 Prolog processors to 32 large memory modules.

The Problems with Bus, Ring, Star, and Crossbar-Based Multi-Computers

THE VIRTUES AND SHORTCOMINGS OF COMMON COMMUNICATION CHANNELS IN BUSES AND RINGS

Forcing every processor to send messages via a common channel can to some extent take advantage of the law of large numbers in smoothing out the load. Many computer programs will have frequent and necessary communication peaks when large numbers of processors must all send large messages. To keep from degrading system performance at such times, either the programmer must be asked to load-balance messages, or the bus or ring must be designed to handle peak loads without significant delays. Most of the time—except when there are peak bursts of message-passing—large amounts of capacity will sit idle. Unless the bandwidth of the single common communication channel (the bus or ring) equals the maximum possible total of simultaneous messages, bus- and ring-based systems will experience at least occasional bottlenecks and delays.

CONTENTION AND BOTTLENECKS IN STARS AND OTHER SHARED MEMORY SYSTEMS

Shared memory invites contention problems, which can only be handled by having, at the lowest levels, separate physical memories that give the superficial appearance of being a single shared memory, but that actually have a whole intermediate network of switches and registers through which each of several separate memories is accessed.

A star of more than 3 or 4 processors or computers would have severe contention and bottleneck problems.

THE NEED TO DISCOVER ALGORITHMS COMPATIBLE WITH THE SYSTEM'S CONSTRAINTS

To use a limited communications channel effectively, one must:

Develop algorithms with a suitably large grain (i.e., with processes that execute as big a hunk of code as possible before they must send information to other processes).

Keep all messages as short as possible.

Try to space messages smoothly, to avoid large bursts.

Try to anticipate when information will be needed, and send it far enough in advance so that the recipient processor will not be forced to wait.

DEGRADATION OF PERFORMANCE DUE TO OPERATING SYSTEM OVERHEADS

Actually, long before the limited bandwidth of a common bus or ring bottlenecks the system, today's programs will be slowed down, far more than by communications bottlenecks, by the operating system's overhead. Consider Crystal's Charlotte operating system (Finkel et al., 1983), which takes roughly 15 milliseconds to initiate one or a stream of messages (messages can be from one to 2000 words long), and a similar amount of time to complete each message.

For example, a vision program that might execute a short sequence of one to 20 instructions, taking only a few microseconds in toto, would then need thousands of times as much time to transmit the results to another process that needs these results. This will be a common occurrence, as when a large array is processed by computing a local window function (e.g., to average, or to look for an edge or an angle). To do this, the programmer must map subarrays of the large array into separate Crystal processors. To compute the local window function at the interior border row (or column) of these subarrays, the processor must first be sent the results from the processor that is processing the next adjacent row (or column). Therefore unless the programmer can anticipate that information will be needed many milliseconds—that is, thousands of instructions—in the future, and can produce that information at least that far ahead of time, message-passing can lead to severe delays.

The single bus, ring, or shared memory experiences increasing problems of contention and overload as the number of computers linked to it increases. [The even greater delays produced by today's operating systems are a problem not just for bus- or ring-based topologies, but for all multi-computers that use today's message-passing operating systems. The problem arises whenever the operating system treats information as messages, and must therefore step through a long and elaborate message-passing protocol (e.g., Finkel and Solomon, 1980a, Wittie and van Tilborg, 1980). But there is reason to hope that this is a temporary problem. Better operating systems, languages and algorithm-structured architectures, along with hardware and programming languages that handle some of the operating system functions, may well substantially reduce operating system overheads.]

THE CROSSBAR'S GOOD INFORMATION TRANSMISSION CAPABILITIES AND GREAT COST

The crossbar is most naturally used in a relatively synchronized manner, with all or many of the processors fetching or storing information at the same time. That is, all, or most, of the processors pass information most of the time. This can largely avoid the need for a traditional message-passing protocol. But the crossbar's complexity is $O(N^2)$, and therefore its cost is too great for any multi-computer with more than at most a few dozen nodes.

The crossbar, which needs NxM B-bit switches (where B is usually 32), rapidly becomes too expensive. The largest crossbar-based system proposed is the very powerful and very expensive S-1 multi-computer under development at Lawrence Livermore Laboratories (Widdoes, 1980). Each of the 64 Cray-equivalent 64-bit computers in a full S-1 system will itself be so powerful and so expensive that the costs of the expensive crossbar may not be relatively excessive. But 64, and even 32, are probably already beyond the reasonable limit from an economic point of view, since they would need 4,096, or 1,024, 64-bit switches.

ATTEMPTS TO EXTEND THE SIZE OF BUS-, RING-, STAR-, AND CROSSBAR-BASED MULTI-COMPUTERS

The basic problem with bus-, ring-, crossbar-, or star-linked systems is that they cannot be built with enough processors to achieve very significant speedups. A good rule of thumb appears to be to use processors that are as powerful as possible. But these processors will normally also have larger input and output capabilities and needs, so they can well end up with the same bottlenecks unless the programmer is asked, or told, not to overload the shared communication channel.

The Maryland ZMOB of Asynchronous Computers with a Synchronizing Message Ring

The University of Maryland's ZMOB (Rieger et al., 1980) is to some extent a clever exception to the limited size of rings. It was originally designed to have 256 Z-80 processors, all linked in a ring via a 256-stage shift register that is 256 times as fast as the relatively slow Z-80s, and hence needs only one Z-80 cycle to shift information once all the way around the ring. [The actual running ZMOB is using only 124 processors, to avoid problems from heat dissipation.]

To describe it more generally, the ZMOB concept links an N-node polygon of computers to an N-stage shift register that shifts information N times faster than each computer executes an instruction.

The incommensurately faster speed of ZMOB's ring means that each processor can send two 8-bit words of information, and receive two 8-bit words of information, at each cycle. Thus the ZMOB's ring is roughly equivalent functionally to a crossbar switch that would have to have 256x256 16-bit switches. In ways it is even better than a typical crossbar, since all simultaneous mappings from all processors to all processors, where each processor sends and receives up to one 16-bit message, are possible.

The restriction that each computer can send and receive only a very small message, must break longer messages up into time-consuming short messages, and must synchronize messages, may well be a burden of unknown proportions on the programmer. It will probably mean that only a small fraction of the ring's bandwidth will actually be used (but that will be true of many other systems). And the cost of ZMOB's shift register ring is roughly half the network's total cost (Rieger, personal communication). This seems too high a fraction for wires that merely transmit messages as opposed to computers that compute.

Probably the chief, almost paradoxical, drawback of ZMOB is that an N-computer ZMOB works efficiently only when processors N times slower than its shift register are used. This guarantees that a traditional single-processor computer could be fabricated, using the shift register's faster technology, that would be at least as powerful as the entire ZMOB. To put this another way, the ZMOB concept forces one to build and use processors that are much slower than technology allows, just to make it possible to implement this kind of message-passing using state-of-the-art technology. For adequate message-handling with state-of-the-art technology, processing must use obsolescent technology!

Fiber Optical Buses and Rings, and Optical Computers

It appears that fiber optics will soon make feasible and economical buses and rings that transmit in the multi-gigabit range.

ENORMOUSLY HIGH BANDWIDTH OPTICAL BUSES AND RINGS

Some researchers feel that therefore buses and rings will be the most attractive topology even for linking hundreds or thousands of computers. However, a system with thousands of computers sharing the same single communication channel will inevitably have bottlenecks unless computers rarely communicate, or unless each computer is kept suitably small and slow (the ZMOB philosophy). The basic problem remains: Unless the communication channel is relatively large in comparison to the system's average total communication load, and even to its occasional near-peak loads, the system's behavior will degrade enormously.

THE CONCOMMITANT POSSIBILITY OF SIMILARLY MORE POWERFUL OPTICAL COMPUTERS

In any case, it seems likely that commensurately faster and more powerful highly parallel optical computers will similarly become feasible (see, e.g., Sawchuck and Strand, 1984). [Researchers developing optics for processors argue that optical technology would advance at a much faster rate if as much research funding were allocated to optical computing as to optical transmission of information; e.g., Lohmann, 1985.] Therefore any increased bandwidth from fiber optic buses would probably best be used to handle computers of similarly increased power, rather than substantially larger numbers of much slower computers on a single bus. The situation is much the same as for the ZMOB: Unless each processor is kept much slower than the state of technology allows, inadequate communication bandwidth will degrade performance. If very fast and very powerful optical computers are developed, large numbers of them could overload fiber optic buses.

But if and when the technologies are developed for chips with large arrays of lasers linked via mirrors and programmable holograms to arrays of photodetectors, the possibilities for both massive processing and massive communications will improve substantially.

Local Pseudo-Complete Graph Clusters as Part of a Larger Point-to-Point Linked Topology

A bus, ring, or crossbar is an attractive candidate to link a small number of computers together into a local cluster of a larger multi-computer built from a number of such local clusters. But this raises the question of how to link the local clusters together into the overall structure—a question that the architectures examined in subsequent chapters are designed to address.

RECONFIGURING SWITCHING NETWORKS FOR PSEUDO-COMPLETE CONNECTIVITY

The crossbar linkage can be approximated with a Benes reconfiguring network (e.g., Lawrie, 1975; Batcher, 1976; Pease, 1977; Siegel, 1979, 1984; see Benes, 1965) that is built from several banks of "shuffle exchanges" (Stone, 1971). Probably the first multi-computer built with reconfiguring networks is Batcher's 1973 STARAN array of 1-bit processors, which will be described in Chapter 8. A reconfiguring network (see Figure 6-2) links N nodes to N (either the same or different) nodes using $\log_M N$ banks, each with N MxM switches (each receives M inputs and has M output links). Usually 2x2 switches, with 2 inputs and 2 outputs, and occasionally 4x4 switches, are used. Probably the general rule of thumb is to make M as large as economically feasible in the available VLSI technologies.

A large number of almost equivalent constructions of this sort have been described in the literature. They have the property that many remappings of N pieces of information can be made in one logN pass through the switching network; and all additional mappings can be made in two passes. Briggs et al., 1979, compared a crossbar with Patel's (1978) delta reconfiguring network. They found that a crossbar built to link 256 nodes would cost roughly 20 times as much as a delta network, but the crossbar has only roughly twice the bandwidth, being able to handle on the average 162 vs. 77 messages per cycle.

Reconfiguring networks can be used in several ways. They might link a set of N computers to one another, or a set of processors to a set of memories (often called "dance-hall" fashion); or a set of computers, each with its own memory, to a set of additional memories; or a set of computers to a set containing one or more other types of resources. When they link processors to memories they might serve to fetch permuted sets of data, as when executing a fast Fourier transform. Or

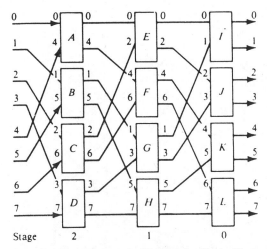

Stage 2 1 0

FIGURE 6-2. A Reconfiguring network built from logN shuffle-exchanges. Information shuffles left to right through 3 banks of 2x2 switches (Lawrie's 1965 Omega network).

they might fetch and store more or less randomly spread out data. Or they might serve to pass messages among processors via their shared memories.

Reconfiguring might be done only at the start of a particular job, or occasionally or periodically during a job. Or the reconfiguring network might serve (when given the necessary additional hardware to handle routing and adjudicate conflicts) as a very high bandwidth global communication link, much like a common bus.

Thus these networks can be used to structure and re-structure the network's topology, or to effect N-way remappings of data, or to route information between nodes in such a way that the multi-computer is perceived by the programmer as one where all processors share and have immediate access to the entire memory.

One particular reconfiguring network construction may be better for a certain set of programs that make use of a specific set of remappings, while another may be better for some other set of programs. It appears, however, that only a very small number of regular N-way remappings of this sort are actually used. These include the fast Fourier transform, for which these systems were originally developed, and also array operations—which allow the reconfiguring network-based STARAN and ASPRO multi-computers (see Chapter 8) to handle array operations efficiently. In addition, when the reconfiguring network is used as the communication channel for an asynchronous multi-computer, many more or less random remappings of information can be handled.

It is instructive to build this kind of reconfiguring network in several steps, as follows: First link a single node in a set of N nodes to all N nodes, by using an M-ary tree $\log_M(N)$ plies deep, whose root is the single node. For example, a binary tree needs $\log_2 N$ steps (Figure 6-3).

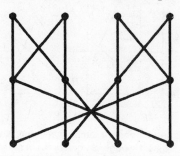

FIGURE 6-3. Each bottom node links via a binary tree to all top nodes.

Now do this for each of the N nodes. Rather than use a separate tree from each node to all the other nodes, all the trees can be combined so that each interior node has two links going into it and two links going out from it (Figures 6-3, 6-4).

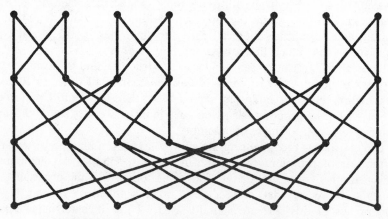

FIGURE 6-4. A reconfiguring network built from trees.

Multi-Computers Linked Via Reconfiguring Networks

A reconfiguring network reduces the NxN switches needed in a crossbar to NlogN switches. For example, whereas the impossibly large number of 1,000,000 switches would be needed to link 1,000 computers using a crossbar, only (sic) 10,000 would be needed using a reconfiguring network. This kind of system has been designed by a number of people, including Jack Lipovsky and co-workers (1977; Lipovsky and Tripathi, 1977; Sejnowski et al., 1980; Deshpande et al., 1985) at Texas; H. J. Siegel (1979, 1981), and Faye Briggs et al. (1979) at Purdue; and Jacob Schwartz (1980) and Allen Gottlieb et al. (1983) at NYU.

THE BBN BUTTERFLY MACHINE, A RECONFIGURABLE NETWORK OF M68000 COMPUTERS

The Butterfly machine, which was designed and built by BBN (Bolt Beranek and Newman) under funding from DARPA (Department of Defense Advanced Research Projects Agency) is now commercially available, with 16, 32, 64, 128, or 256 processors. [Systems with as many as 8,192 processors are being considered (Crowther, personal communication).] Both the hardware (Crowther et al., 1985) and the Butterfly's Chrysalis operating system (Rettberg et al., 1983) were originally developed to collect and concentrate digitized speech. Each node has a 16-bit M68000 processor with up to 4MB of memory, plus a coprocessor built with AMD2901 bit-slice hardware that serves as node controller. New models are being built with 32-bit M68020 processors and hardware floating-point multiply. Apparently the largest system ordered and built to date is a 128-processor machine for the University of Rochester's computer vision research group (Brown et al., 1985).

A program can address any memory location in any node. The reconfiguring network handles access and contention. The node controller decides whether a location is local, or whether it must be accessed via the switching network. Local access takes .625 microseconds, remote access takes 3.75 microseconds Each of the 4x4 switches used in the reconfiguring network delays message transmission 125 nanoseconds. Each processor has an I/O bus with which to communicate to disks or other computers, for example, via an Ethernet. Software is developed on a separate host. At present (at Rochester) a VAX-11/750 running under UNIX is used to develop C programs for the 68000. These are loaded into the Butterfly over a very low bandwidth serial RS232 link. Researchers at Rochester plan to develop a new set of interactive debugging tools and a distributed operating system.

THE NYU AND TWO IBM (ONE DANCE-HALL) RECONFIGURABLE COMPUTERS

The goal for the Ultracomputer being designed at NYU (Schwartz, 1980; Gottlieb et al., 1983) is 4,096 (or possibly even 8,192) processors (each with a small cache-like memory) linked in "dance-hall" fashion over a reconfiguring network to 4,096 large memory banks, so that programs can be coded and executed as though each processor has direct access to all these memories. All processors access information in what is now effectively a shared global memory via this network. The reconfiguring network is augmented with hardware buffers and processors, including special circuitry to execute "fetch-add" instructions, to handle contention and iteration. A full 4,096-processor design would need 49,152 32-bit or 64-bit switches—a really large number, but one that the NYU group has carefully designed and feels would be feasible.

A small prototype with 8 68000s (actually linked via a crossbar, but programmable as though via a reconfiguring network) is now running at NYU. There are tentative plans to build a 64-node system, using 68000s for processors and, possibly, using Transputer chips for the intelligent switches.

A somewhat larger 512 processor variant system, RP3, is being planned by IBM Yorktown (Pfister et al., 1985). A 64 processor prototype is now being built. The IBM design has been changed, to link computers (that is, processor plus memory) to computers, as well as to link computers to memories, using two separate reconfiguring networks. This makes the IBM system much more like the BBN Butterfly. In both cases, information can be accessed appreciably faster from the processor's own memory, even though each processor treats all processors' memories as though they belong to a single global memory. It seems likely that very different programs would be coded for the RP3 variant, as opposed to the original NYU Ultracomputer. The original NYU design would typically have large numbers of processors fetching and storing information over the reconfiguring network. The RP3 can work in a similar mode, but it should also be able to improve efficiency by having each processor use its own memory as much as possible.

IBM Yorktown is building a second system, the GF11 (Beetem et al., 1985) that will have 576 processors, each capable of executing up to 20MFlops, or 11.5GFlops in toto. It will be an SIMD machine, with all processors executing the same instruction. Apparently this system will typically be run using 512 processors, the rest acting as spares. Each computer will have 64KBytes of high speed static RAM and 256KBytes of dynamic RAM, plus 256 12.5 nanosecond registers. Computers are linked via a 3-stage reconfiguring network (each stage has 24 24x24 crossbars). These are used to re-structure the topology rather than to give the programmer a global memory. The GF11 has been designed for problems in quantum chromodynamics, where it is estimated it should be able to sustain 10GFlop performance; but its designers feel it should be suitable for a wide range of physical problems. It would appear that, when completed, this will be one of the very most powerful networks.

PURDUE'S PASM, A MULTILEVEL RECONFIGURABLE SYSTEM

Purdue University's PASM (Siegel, 1979, 1981; Siegel et al., 1981), which has a much more complex design, with several levels of controllers and several reconfiguring networks, will be described in Chapter 13 below. Siegel contemplates a full-blown system with 1,024 computers.

Software and Hardware Sources of Slowdowns in Reconfiguring Networks

Reconfiguring networks introduce several new types of overheads.

First, the program must actually reset the network's physical switches every time a new remapping is to be effected. This can be time consuming, and/or need extra hardware, since NlogN switches are involved. When it effects remappings, the program must compute the compatible switch settings for all desired paths between sender nodes and receiver nodes, and it must then open all these paths. Typically (when the system is given additional hardware) a whole bank of switches can be reset in parallel, so that the whole set of switches can be thrown in order NlogN time. A system like the Butterfly, Ultracomputer, and RP3 that links pairs of nodes over individual paths whenever they are needed must be given additional hardware to find and establish routings that are not blocked.

Second, the information sent along each path must pass through logN switches. Here there is a small amount of time, the gate delays, involved at each stage. Typically this is relatively small in comparison to the basic instruction cycle time of the hardware involved, but as the reconfiguring network grows larger and logN becomes appreciable the series of gate delays can become significant. For example, a computer that fetches data from memory in 100 nanoseconds might have gate delays of 5 to 10 nanoseconds. Therefore a reconfiguring network for 1,024 processors would slow every fetch of data by 50 to 100 nanoseconds. The timings for the BBN Butterfly given previously are a good example of the total amount of the resulting delays.

COMPARING ALTERNATIVE POSSIBILITIES FOR COMPLETE AND PSEUDO-COMPLETE GRAPHS

As mentioned earlier, a true complete graph can be built from only at most 4, or a few more, nodes. The Transputer, with its 4 built-in high-speed buses for linking to other Transputers, might be used to realize a 5-node complete graph with little trouble, but that may well be the practicable limit.

An NxM crossbar can be used to link N nodes to M (same or different) nodes. But the hardware for switches quickly grows as N and M grow.

Buses and rings simulate a complete graph, but at the price of delays for the message to go from a node to the bus, along the common bus, and from the bus to the recipient node. In addition, unless the bus or ring has more bandwidth than the largest possible burst of messages, and also has some way of handling simultaneous messages, there will be further delays from contention, and major delays from the operating system protocol used to coordinate message-passing. However, buses and rings are simple and popular approaches for small systems where only 4 to 16, or possibly 32 or even more, computers are to be linked together.

The reconfiguring networks reduce the amount of hardware needed for a crossbar from NxN to NlogN, with relatively minor decreases in the number of simultaneous permutations possible. They avoid the contention and bottleneck problems of buses and rings, without excessive increases in costs (until they become quite large). The time needed to reset switches and the gate delays from signals passing through logN switches may slow message-passing down by a factor of 2 to 10 or so; but this is far less than the operating system delays for message-passing systems that use buses or rings. Reconfiguring networks make possible multi-computers with several hundred, or even several thousand, nodes—in contrast to the several dozen that can be combined using a bus, ring, or crossbar.

Point-to-point linked topologies might also be used to give the programmer the impression of working with a (pseudo-)complete graph global memory (see Moore graphs, de Bruijn networks, Connection machines, and other systems examined in Chapters 10-13). They can be used to pass several, or many, pieces of information between different pairs of nodes. And they can be used to broadcast sets of information.

Reconfiguring Networks, ZMOB Rings, and Broadcast Schemes Compared

It is of interest to juxtapose the reconfiguring networks with the ZMOB scheme for using a very fast ring. In both cases each node is a traditional computer, with its own controller. Thus both types of system can execute in true asynchronous MIMD mode. Each has a special kind of synchrony imposed on it in terms of communicating information.

ZMOB has each processor send (up to) two words of information at each instruction cycle, and receive (up to) two words. This is handled by having each processor place its quota of information onto the shift register (along with information identifying the recipient), and each processor look for and input its quota of received information. (The operating system must adjudicate conflicts.)

A reconfiguring network similarly has each processor send and receive (up to) one piece of information.

Actually the ZMOB communication is more general in that any node can send a message to any other node in one cycle, whereas each reconfiguring network allows only some combinations.

The ZMOB is appreciably slower, since it takes N steps, whereas the reconfiguring network takes logN steps. The time for each ZMOB step depends on the speed of the shift register that is used. To eliminate delays, this must be N times the speed of a single processor instruction.

ZMOB needs a very fast shift register that is N stages long, while a reconfiguring system needs $Nlog_M N$ MxM switches.

Basically, ZMOB has each processor broadcast a message to every other processor. Each processor serially receives and has the opportunity to examine each message. This scheme could be used for any graph topology where a path could be drawn through all nodes (retraversing one or a few nodes would merely introduce small additional delays). Such a serial reception of a broadcast is inherently slow; it can work only when the broadcast channel is made commensurately fast.

Basically, a reconfiguring network has many nodes send information in parallel, each piece routed to its intended recipient only.

THE NEED FOR POINT-TO-POINT TOPOLOGIES IN LARGE MULTI-COMPUTERS, AND SUMMARIZING COMMENTS

The topology of a parallel multi-computer network can be any possible graph. However, there is a mind-boggling number of possible graphs, even with only a few hundred or a few dozen nodes, much less thousands or millions.

Although many people have suggested that a complete graph (where each node links directly to every other node) would be the ideal, since every processor could communicate directly with any others, a true complete graph can be built only when the number of computers is kept so small that at best only trivial speedups can be achieved. Since today it is the operating system, rather than the hardware communication links, that is the overriding factor toward slowing down and blocking communications, an MIMD network linked via a complete graph would (in common with most other topologies) be bottlenecked by the operating system long before the hardware bottlenecks were reached.

A complete graph can be emulated by linking all computers to a single common bus or ring, or via a crossbar array of switches. But the crossbar, which needs NxN switches for an N-processor network, becomes too expensive to handle more than 8, 16, or 32 or a few more processors, and wasteful to the extent that all processors are not sending messages. And the bus or ring cannot possibly have great enough channel capacity to handle more than similar numbers—unless the processors are kept deliberately slow, or the programmer is forced to spread out the load, or send information between processes only rarely.

A shuffle exchange-based reconfiguring network can reduce the NxN switches needed by the crossbar to NlogN switches. Therefore it can be used for networks with 64 to 1,024, or possibly even 2,048, 4,096 or 8,192 processors. A price must be paid to compute paths and reset switches, and in the gate delays as the signal passes through the logN switches. Fewer permutations can be effected than with the crossbar. Reconfiguring networks appear to be a promising way to increase the size of multi-computers from a few dozen to hundreds, or, possibly, even thousands.

The pseudo-complete graph systems are typically designed so that the programmer can think in terms of a single giant computer where any processor can fetch and manipulate any pieces of data. This means that the programmer can think in traditional ways, as though a super-giant conventional single-CPU computer were being used. It also means, depending on one's point of view, that the programmer can avoid and ignore many of the problems of developing parallel algorithms (although at a largely unknown cost in efficiency), or can evade, and suffer from the loss of, an understanding of the parallel aspects of the problem.

The only way that larger networks can be constructed is with point-to-point topologies. Chapters 7 through 9 examine relatively highly structured topologies that are suggested by the structure of the programs and processes they are designed to execute. Chapters 10 through 13 examine a variety of other promising point-to-point topologies.

Chapter Seven

PIPELINES AND ASSEMBLY LINES

Rather than establish an anarchy of independent computers, as is essentially the case when several conventional computers, each with a complete controller, are linked together via a crossbar, bus, ring, or complete graph, various kinds of overall coordination and control can be superimposed. ZMOB rings and some reconfiguring networks (e.g., STARAN and PASM) begin to introduce some coordination—since they usually assume that all processors send messages at the same time, and that these messages are spread out to different destinations in such a way that they don't contend with one another. [This assumption is not crucial; to the extent it is violated only (possibly extreme) degradation, but not absolute disaster, results.] But each of the computers linked together with a reconfiguring network or ZMOB ring is (typically, with the exception of STARAN) still an entirely independent entity, with its own master controller.

THE STRUCTURE OF A PIPELINE MULTI-COMPUTER

Possibly the simplest structure that begins to coordinate the different computers is a small linear pipeline (see Figure 7-1). It is also among the most powerful and the most successful.

$$I \longrightarrow C-r \longrightarrow C-r \longrightarrow C-r \longrightarrow C-r \longrightarrow C-r \longrightarrow C-r \longrightarrow C-r \longrightarrow C-r \longrightarrow O \longrightarrow$$

FIGURE 7-1. A pipeline multi-Computer. [I = Input, C = Computer, r = register, O = Output.]

Now information is input to the first computer, which processes it and sends its output (via intermediate registers) to the second, and so on, until the pipe is filled. At this point, the final results are output. Each computer in the pipeline is still independent in the sense that each has its own controller and executes a different instruction. However, processing is most efficient when each computer repeatedly executes the same instruction, and the pipeline's sequence of instructions is executed on many pieces of data as these data stream through. Therefore Flynn (1972) calls pipelines multiple instruction single data-stream (MISD) networks. [Note that each computer can also execute a sequence of instructions. In the simplest case the same process is repeatedly applied. This is an extremely useful case for repetitive assemblyline-like processing of the sort frequently needed in image processing and other areas of AI.]

To achieve maximum efficiency, all computers in the pipeline should spend exactly the same time executing their instruction(s). Hardware can be built so that this requirement is imposed on the programmer, by having each instruction take a standard amount of time and by limiting each computer to execute only one instruction. Or the programmer or the operating system can be asked to balance the load among processors.

Short pipelines (called vector processors) of very powerful processors that contain a large number of special high-speed vector registers are what give the Cray-type super-computers much of their power in number-crunching vectors and arrays of numerical information, for example, for solving large matrices of partial differential equations. Similar pipelines can be bought separately and interfaced to one of the high-speed buses of a conventional computer. These add-on vector processors, manufactured and sold by Floating Point Systems and a number of other companies, will be described below.

Pipelines are also extremely useful, as we shall see, whenever information input continuously (as by a tv camera, or iteration through an array) can fruitfully be transformed as that information streams by. For example, the local region surrounding each pixel can be averaged or differenced; specks of noise can be eliminated; and local gradients or edges can be detected. Pipelines have therefore been used in a number of systems (to be described below), both commercial and experimental, for image processing and pattern perception.

Figure 7-2 rings a sequence of changes on the basic pipeline:

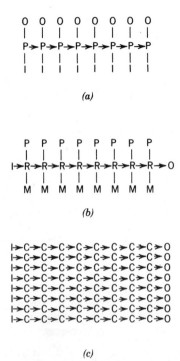

(a)

(b)

(c)

FIGURE 7-2. Linking a line of computer components. (a) Information is Input to and Output from a Computer; many computers (possibly linked) work side-by-side. (b) Information is Input to and Output from a line of Registers that also serve to link each Computer's Processor and Memory. (c) Information is streamed through a 1-dimensional array of 1-dimensional pipelines.

7-2(a): The pipeline can in effect be turned over onto its side and made into a 1-dimensional array.

7-2(b): Now this 1-dimensional array can be used as a 2-dimensional pipeline with only one computer in each pipe, simply by streaming information through each single-processor pipeline, and storing intermediate results in a register or memory cell as appropriate.

7-2(c): Or a 2-dimensional pipeline can be constructed so that a different computer executes each process.

A pipeline reduces the time, P, needed for a single computer to execute the whole sequence of processes to $(P/C)+C$ (since all of the C computers are working together in parallel, and it also takes C steps to fill and empty the pipe). More generally, a D-dimensional array can be

used to pipeline-process an N-dimensional array of information
(D< = N). For example, a 1-dimensional array (what is today typically
used as a pipeline) can process arrays of data of 2, 3, or N dimensions.
It can be used to stream data moving from processor to processor
through the pipe; or it can be used as a 1-dimensional array where each
processor handles a different set of data from the data array. A 2-
dimensional array can be used to process a 3, 4, or N dimensional array
of data. A 0-dimensional array (that is, a single-CPU serial computer)
can be used to process a 1, 2, ... or N dimensional array of data.

Several pipelines of processors or computers have been built. These
are much in the spirit of an assemblyline of workers, with the major
simplification and restriction that, at least in the 1-dimensional systems
built to date, all processors link in a single line. That is, each processor
inputs information from only one other processor, and outputs to only
one other processor. Typically each processor in the pipe repeatedly
executes the same instruction on a sequence of data flowing through
that pipe.

Consider situations when the same sequence of instructions is to be
executed on a large number of different pieces of data. This is the case
whenever the data stored in an array are to be operated on in parallel,
for example, in a (possibly nested) FOR-loop. A pipeline as long as the
sequence of instructions can be built, and information (e.g., information
from a tv camera, or information stored in the cells of an array) flowed
through the pipeline's processors. Figure 7-3 explains in more detail the
actual step-by-step processing carried out by such a pipeline.

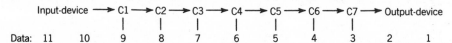

Input-device ⟶ C1 ⟶ C2 ⟶ C3 ⟶ C4 ⟶ C5 ⟶ C6 ⟶ C7 ⟶ Output-device

Data: 11   10   9   8   7   6   5   4   3   2   1

FIGURE 7-3. A pipeline of N computers through which data flow.

At Time 1, C1 will execute the 1st instruction on the 1st piece of
data; at Time 2, C2 will execute the 2d instruction on the 1st piece of
data, and C1 will execute the 1st instruction on the 2d piece of data,
and so on. The data row shows the state of the system at time 9: C7
(the last stage in a 7-stage pipeline) is executing the 7th process on
data-job 3; C1 is executing the first process on job 9, which is just starting; jobs 1 and 2 are finished, and have been output (probably to some
memory storage device).

If the pipeline has N processors, then (once the pipe is full) the program will execute up to approximately dN times as fast as a 1-processor
computer (d is the often appreciable additional saving from not having

to fetch and decode the next instruction, when each processor fetches code only once, and keeps executing the same instruction). Each processor will repeatedly execute the same instruction, or sequence of instructions, each time on a different set of data, but different processors will be executing different instructions. The processor that needs the longest time will determine the system's speed, since all the other processors must wait for it to finish. Therefore the ideal mapping of a program into a pipeline would have each processor do exactly the same amount of work (in terms of time taken).

EXAMPLES OF THE MOST POWERFUL AND THE LARGEST PIPELINES

The Cray, Cyber, Fujitsu, and Hitachi Vector Processing Super-Computers

The fastest of today's super-computers (see Chapter 1), Seymour Cray's Cray, Cray-XMP, Cray-2, and Cray-3 (Russell, 1978; Chen et al., 1984), the Control Data Cyber-205 (Kozdrowicki and Thies, 1980), the Hitachi S810/20 and the Fujitsu VP-200 (see Riganati and Schneck, 1984), use one or more pipelines of this sort, with very powerful and expensive processors and a large number of very fast vector registers in each, to execute vector operations on arrays of data for number crunching (including 64-bit floating-point multiplies). The pipelines are typically relatively short, with a dozen or so processors. The Fujitsu VP-200 has a substantially longer pipeline, giving substantially greater speed in processing large vectors.

Linkoping's PICAP Pipelined Image Processor

Bjorn Kruse's (1973, 1976, 1978, 1980; Antonsson et al., 1982) PICAP, built at the University of Linkoping, uses a pipeline of processors specially designed to effect local 3-by-3 window functions. These compute any 1-bit boolean logic operation—where each cell contains either a 1 (used to signify "black," or "figure") or a 0 (signifying "white," or "background")—or 8-bit arithmetic operation, whose operands are the center cell of the window plus whichever of the 1 to 8 neighbor cells the programmer chooses to use. The window operation is computed everywhere. That is, each cell in the large array being processed is in turn centered under the 3-by-3 window array.

PICAP-I linked a system that scanned a 64-by-64 image array in this manner to a conventional computer so that each time the window function succeeded the location of that success was stored in a table in the serial computer's memory. This information could then be analyzed by the serial computer, and also used to direct further processing by the scanning array. Thus, for example, a typical manner of using PICAP was to examine the entire 256-by-256 tv image originally input to its buffer memory in 64-by-64 averaged form (this averaging was done in hardware), search this averaged image for regions of interest, and then zoom into these regions to examine them in more detail, moving back and forth among them as suggested by what was found so far. Thus a parallel-serial, top-down + bottom-up search could be effected.

PICAP-II combined a number of different carefully tailored special-purpose processors with several scanning arrays of this sort. It might best be thought of as an example of a heterogeneous system examined in Chapter 13, but specialized within the special-purpose domain of image processing. The result was a version that was 10 to 50 times faster than PICAP-I on most problems.

COULTER'S DIFF4 SYSTEM FOR BLOOD CELL RECOGNITION

An especially interesting example of a completely integrated commercial image processing system is the diff4 (Graham, 1983). It was developed at Perkin-Elmer and then at Coulter, to scan blood smears for defective cells (this is one of the most widely used clinical medical tests). It includes a microscope under computer control, as well as several image processing modules. The basic image processing operation used is a hexagonal near-neighbor transform (Golay, 1969, Preston, 1971) that is executed at the rate of 25 nanoseconds per pixel plus its surrounding hexagon.

The diff4 was developed and marketed as a turnkey clinical tool for the particular blood cell application. However, it was designed as a general system that, potentially, is capable of handling a variety of image processing operations.

ERIM'S POWERFUL CYTOCOMPUTER PIPELINES

Among the longest pipelines built to date is Stanley Sternberg's (1978, 1980) Cytocomputer-I (built at ERIM, the Environmental Research Institute of Michigan), a multi-computer specialized to execute image processing operations. The Cytocomputer has two types of processors. One computes boolean functions over the center cell and its 8 neighbors, and the second computes 3-bit arithmetic, which is useful in perception programs for handling grey-scale images and weights. [Note that a 1-bit processor is completely general purpose, and can compute N-bit functions, but only bit-serially. This means it needs at least N times as much time.] Each processor is much simpler and smaller than those found in a Cray-type super-computer; but this first ERIM Cytocomputer, and still one of the largest, has 113 processors in toto.

Cytocomputers with Long, Short, and Reconfigurable Pipes

Several newer systems that are variations on the Cytocomputer concept have been built.

IBM Yorktown has built MITE, a new 256 processor Cytocomputer (Kimmel et al., 1985). It is the longest Cytocomputer pipeline built to date, and may well be the longest pipeline of any sort. It can be reconfigured under program control; hence it is potentially significantly more powerful and more flexible than a strictly linear pipeline. The full MITE system (see Figure 7-4) is built from 8 cages, each containing 8 groups of 8 processors and 1 enumerator (which lists the locations of features found by the processors).

The 8 processors in a group are effectively reconfigurable, since they are linked via a common bus. This means that information can be passed using a wide variety of data-flow graph topologies. For example, a processor can link to two or three other processors; each can pipe information through additional processors; then this information can be input for further processing to a single processor; and then it can be passed onward through the system. MITE systems with 512 or even more processors are being planned.

The newer Cytocomputers use only one type of processor, an 8-bit processor with 8 bits of memory, that does both the nonlinear logical operations and also the 8-bit numerical operations. ERIM's latest system, the Cyto-HSS, also handles subarrays and scattered arrays as well as full arrays, examining whatever points the program specifies at the speed of 10 million 3-by-3 window operations per second (Lougheed and McCubbrey, 1985). It can therefore be used to simulate other structures, including pyramids (see Chapter 9). With the exception of the IBM MITE, the newer Cytocomputers use relatively small pipelines of 10 or so processors.

Purdue's Algorithm-Structured Pipeline for Speech Recognition

Bronson and Jamieson (1985) are designing a specialized pipeline of computers to recognize spoken speech in real time. Different groups of processors in the pipe will handle different stages of processing: for example, acoustic processing, labeling, segmentation. It is estimated that 43 M68000 processors will be needed for real-time recognition of spoken speech.

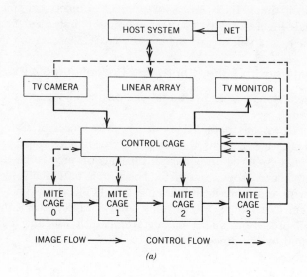

IMAGE FLOW ———→   CONTROL FLOW – – – – →

(a)

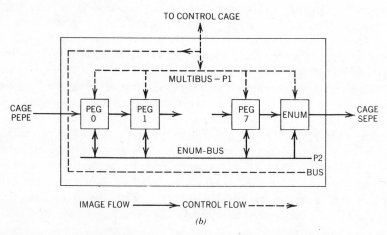

IMAGE FLOW ————→ CONTROL FLOW – – – – ➤

(b)

FIGURE 7-4. The IBM MITE system. (a) System architecture. (b) MITE cage— eight PE groups and one enumerator group.
(*Source*:   Kimmel, Jaffe, Mandeveille, and Lavin, 1985.)

Some Problems with Pipelines

There appear to be several reasons for keeping the pipeline short:

- It is difficult to keep a longer pipeline full. Not all problems can be formulated as a suitably long string of iterated operations. It is hard to formulate procedures where the intermediate results can be kept small enough so that they can all be passed through the inevitably small number of memory registers available in the pipe. It is also expensive to allocate extra memory hardware for that purpose.
- It can be difficult to load-balance over all stages of the pipe.
- The start-up and wind-down times become increasingly long as the pipeline increases in size (it is illuminating to think of these as input and output times).

For numerical problems, where iteration is common but the size of the matrix to be processed is variable and often small, the Cray-type supercomputers' short pipes seem reasonable (especially considering the size, power, and cost of each processor). When large image arrays with many thousands or millions of cells must be processed, and great speed is the most important criterion, much longer pipelines appear to be desirable—if their attendant problems can be worked out.

COMMERCIAL PIPELINE ARRAY PROCESSORS THAT SIMULATE PARALLEL PROCESSING

The term array processor is commonly used for a number of commercially available pipelines. These systems have been developed in two different varieties, each specialized for a different problem domain.

Array Processors for Numerical Problems (E.g., Floating Point Systems)

The first, exemplified by the Floating Point Systems (FPS) processors, are usually built and sold as add-on devices to be interfaced to a conventional computer's high-speed processor bus. They process vectors or arrays of numerical data by rapidly streaming those data through one carefully specialized processor, or a small pipe of processors. Typically, therefore, each processor is optimized to compute 32-bit or 64-bit floating point operations. These short pipelines are in the family of and similar to (but usually less powerful than, less well integrated to the host computer, and cheaper than) the Cray-type super-computers' vector processors.

Array Processors for Image Processing (E.g., deAnza, Vicom)

The second, built by Vicom, deAnza, and a number of other manufacturers, is specialized for image processing. Whereas the numerical processors execute powerful floating point operations over a set of numbers that might be of any size, the image processors stream a fixed size array (usually 512 by 512 or 1,024 by 1,024) of 8-bit numbers (indicating grey-scale or primary color intensities) or 1-bit values (indicating object-vs.-background, or true-vs.-false, or yes-vs.-no) through a specialized processor or short pipe that computes 8-bit fixed point arithmetic or 1-bit logical and matching operations at tv scan rates (roughly 30 milliseconds for the whole array, which means roughly 100 or 25 nanoseconds to operate on each pixel). Often special-purpose boards with built-in hardware can be purchased as add-ons for fast computation of histograms, 3-by-3 mask operations (usually convolutions), or other commonly used image processing functions. (Boards have been developed to handle larger windows in a single scan, e.g., a 16-by-16 convolution.)

These systems can be thought of as simulating arrays. But whereas a true parallel hardware array of the sort examined in Chapter 8 will take one microsecond or less to execute an operation everywhere on the entire array of information, the simulated arrays will take 30 milliseconds. (PICAP and the Cytocomputer are roughly similar to these image processing arrays, but they are appreciably faster because of longer pipelines, additional hardware, and/or more powerful hardware.)

SPECIAL-PURPOSE CHIPS THAT PARALLELIZE FREQUENTLY COMPUTED FUNCTIONS

Custom chips can be designed and fabricated to speed up key, frequently computed, processes. Typically (but not always) these will be used to iteratively compute the same function over a large set of data streamed through them in MISD pipeline or assemblyline mode. Several chips of this sort have been designed or proposed. They include custom-made chips for specific frequently executed operations, and systolic chips, which attempt to use pipeline-like data-flow operations built into the hardware structure.

Special-Purpose Custom Chips for Specific Operations

A single chip that computes a relatively large convolution, e.g., 7 by 7, 11 by 11, 17 by 17, 64 by 64, or even larger, can speed up processing enormously (if and where convolutions of that size are frequently used). This kind of chip might execute the entire convolution at a particular location in 100 nanoseconds, or even faster—fast enough so that when the chip is incorporated into a larger system that appropriately streams the image through that chip a convolution can be computed over the entire image array at tv scan rates. Several such chips have been fabricated.

One chip of special interest computes the convolution and zero-crossing (i.e., thresholding at zero) used by David Marr and his associates (1982) as a key step in turning the raw image input by a tv camera into a primal sketch (something roughly like a very redundant and tentative edge/line drawing of the image).

Special-Purpose Systolic Chips

A more elegant version of such a chip can be achieved by carefully designing a systolic system (Kung, 1980, 1982, Kung and Lam, 1984), where the whole structure of gates has been custom crafted to execute iterated processes as data are pumped through in true pipeline, assemblyline fashion. These structures are more complex than linear pipelines; they typically have several inputs to each processor. Each processor is usually very small—simply the minimal set of transistors needed to compute that processor's step in the total function being computed. For example, H.T. Kung has developed a very fast special-purpose systolic convolution chip (Kung and Song, 1982).

The special-purpose systolic chips are similar to custom circuits carefully designed to handle particular heavily used processes. They are probably most appropriately interfaced, much as are the vector processors, to the CPU's high-speed bus, in order to make available fast and efficient processors for frequently used processes.

MORE GENERAL-PURPOSE AND FLEXIBLE PIPELINES AND SYSTOLIC SYSTEMS

Rather than hardwire the systolic process into a special-purpose chip that, in effect, is a (sometimes quite elaborate and elegant) finite-state automaton, a network of general purpose processors can be constructed, and used to compute whatever specific systolic processes are specified by the program. More traditional pipelines can be extended so that they can be reconfigured in a variety of ways. We have already seen one example of this in the IBM MITE Cytocomputer, and several more general purpose systems of this sort will be described in Chapter 13.

The Bureau of Standards' PIPE System

Kent et al. (1985) have designed and built a pipeline that can, in addition to passing information forward through the pipe, cycle processes through the same stage, and back to previous stages, as desired by the programmer.

Each stage can compute one to five operations over an entire 256-by-256 array in 16 milliseconds, including one or two 3x3 neighborhood operations.

This system has several unusual and potentially powerful features, including the following:

- Information can be combined and stored into smaller arrays, making possible pyramid operations and pyramid convergence (Kent and Tanimoto, 1985; see Chapter 9).
- A region-of-interest operator can direct processing as the result of extracted features.
- Up to 256 different operations can be executed at the same time, in MIMD mode, by using one of each stage's two 8-bit memories for table lookup of the operation to be executed at that location.
- The fact that images can be transformed in the forward or backward directions, or successively in the same stage, gives, when the programmer desires this, an important top-down component to processing.

PIPE can also be linked directly to a conventional computer like a VAX. Information can be transferred from its final stage to the conventional computer's memory at the same video frame rate it is transferred from one stage to another within it.

Carnegie-Mellon's Programmable Systolic Processors, and the Warp Array

H.T. Kung and his associates (Dohi et al., 1985; Fisher et al., 1984) have designed a general purpose programmable systolic chip that contains a large and powerful 10MFlop programmable processor, with the intention of building arrays (1 or 2 dimensional) of large numbers of

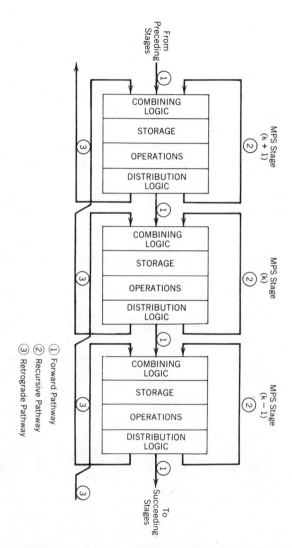

FIGURE 7-5 The PIPE processor consists of multiple modular processing stages connected by concurrent interacting, image-flow pipelines. Results of independent operations on images in each stage are output over forward, recursive, and retrograde pathways. The input to each stage may be obtained from any algebraic or Boolean combination of the images arriving on the three pathways.

these chips, and using them as general purpose MIMD systolic networks to execute the particular systolic processes specified by the programs. The first such system, called Warp (Kung and Menzilcioglu, 1984), is being developed for low-level vision and robotics. A prototype with two processors is now running, and systems with 10 processors configured into a 1-dimensional array are to be delivered by CMU's partners in this project, GE and Honeywell.

USC's Systolic Wavefront Array Processor (WAP) Systems

S.Y. Kung and his associates, working with Hughes Aerospace, have designed a systolic chip to be used in wavefront array processing (WAP) systems for signal processing (Kung and Gal-Ezer, 1985). The WAP is similar to programmable MIMD systolic arrays, and to data flow systems that actually pipeline programs through the physical hardware. Because it makes use of wavefront principles, such that two wavefronts can never intersect, it can handle a variety of asynchronous delays.

PIPELINES, RINGS, AND PIPELINE-SIMULATED ARRAYS

It is illuminating to compare pipelines, which operate on and transform data at each stage, with rings, ZMOBs, and shift registers, all of which simply shift data along through each stage, unchanged. Each can be thought of as having a processor at each stage; but all, except for the pipeline, have processors that execute only the null operation. That is, they do nothing except shift the data on (input and then output the data), hence they leave all the information unchanged. That is not quite true, since the processors in a conventional ring or ZMOB ring examine data passing through and, when appropriate, make a copy and deposit a message notifying the sender that some datum was received. When a system is already using a shift register to transfer a stream of data (e.g., to input a tv image), each simple shifter can be replaced by a full-blown processor.

This is one of the things that make the pipeline-simulated arrays like the deAnza and Vicom so attractive. A tv image is routinely stored into today's computers by serially streaming in its pixels so that all are input within the 30 milliseconds or so taken for a single frame. The processors in these simulated arrays simply replace some of the shift registers used to input the image by the pipeline of processors that executes image processing operations.

Pipelines appear to be limited to a few dozen, or at most a few hundred, computers. This is not because of any inherent problems in building longer pipelines, or even in conceptualizing how they might be used. Rather the crucial factors appear to be the practical limitations of formulating problems in ways that can make good use of a very long pipeline. A pipeline achieves its parallel speedups by imposing an extreme serialization on the program. The longer the pipeline the longer the serial sequence of operations that must be executed in order to use that pipeline efficiently. The pipeline speeds things up because there is an even longer stream of data to which this long stream of operations can be applied.

When and if these requirements can be met, a pipeline becomes a very fast, powerful, and efficient tool.

Chapter Eight

VERY LARGE NETWORKS STRUCTURED INTO ARRAYS

This chapter examines the multi-computers that today have by far the largest number of processors—the massively parallel 2-dimensional arrays.

Very large and highly parallel arrays of computers can be built, potentially without any theoretical limit with respect to size, simply by increasing the size of the array to whatever total desired. Indeed, 2-dimensional arrays with many thousands of computers have already been built. These arrays can be used to process large 2-dimensional sets of data (images, or arrays of numbers or other kinds of information) by having the pixels (picture elements) in an image or the entries in a matrix spread uniformly throughout the memories of the computers in the array. This means that the entire array of processors can process many individual regions of an image array, all at the same time. Assume an N-by-N grid of computers, and an nxn image array. If $n = N$, each computer can be assigned a single pixel of the large image. If $n = kN$ (k is a small integer), a kxk subarray of the image can be stored in each computer's memory.

An array multi-computer will execute instructions, and sequences of instructions, in parallel everywhere (i.e., simultaneously at each processor). Such a system can execute local operations over a window of any shape, or any set of nearby cells, with extreme speed and power. For example, it can compute linear and non-linear functions of 2 by 2, 3 by 1, 3 by 3, 5 by 3, 5 by 5, or even larger windows, or of other sets of neighbor cells, to average, difference, convolve, get gradients and edges, look for textures and colors, and get a variety of other local features, or to combine simple local features.

Depending on the details of how much has been hard-wired into the processor, the entire operation might be executed in a single instruction. Or it might need several instructions—but only a few, because information can be shifted and fetched very rapidly among near-neighbors.

Arrays are among the most promising candidates for a component of a vision system that is fast enough to execute in real time. More generally they are capable of handling a variety of numerical, nonnumerical, and associative problems when arrays of information are involved. So it is important to examine this kind of system in some detail.

TODAY'S VERY LARGE 2-DIMENSIONAL PARALLEL ARRAYS

Several very large 2-dimensional arrays have been built in recent years. These include the 64-by-64 DAP (Distributed Array Processor) designed by Stewart Reddaway (1978, 1980) at ICL; the 96-by-96 CLIP4 (Cellular Logic Information Processor) designed by Michael Duff (1976, 1978, 1982) at University College London; and the 128-by-128 MPP (Massively Parallel Processor), designed by Kenneth Batcher (1980, 1982) along with David Schaefer (Schaefer et al., 1982) and others at Goodyear-Aerospace and NASA Goddard.

All of these systems' thousands of computers are synchronized to execute the same instruction, but each will execute it on a different set of data, in SIMD (single instruction multiple data stream; Flynn, 1972) fashion. The data to be processed are input to a large array. The simplest and in most cases the fastest mode of operation is to have the image array be the same size as the array of computers, so that each computer has one pixel from the total image in its memory. Then each computer operates on data stored in its own memory, and also on near-neighbor data (see Figure 8-1).

The only ways, in addition to:

a.   the square array (shown in Figure 8-1), to tile out ("tesselate") a single near-neighbor linking scheme on the 2-dimensional plane are to:

b.   link each node to six neighbors, forming a hexagonal array,

c.   link each node to two neighbors, forming an array of equilateral triangles,

d.   add additional links (e.g., to the 4 diagonal neighbors in a square array).

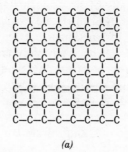

(a)

P P P P P P P P
Input→ r – r – r – r – r – r – r – r→Output
M M M M M M M M

(b)

FIGURE 8-1. Arrays of computers. (a) A 2-dimensional 8-by-8 array of computers, viewed from above. Each computer's processor links via registers to that computer's memory (not shown in this view), and also, via the links shown, to the memories of its 4 square neighbors. (b) A 1-by-8 array, each processor linked to its own memory, and to input, output, and other processors, via registers. Input of images and output of results take place by successively shifting information through the linked registers, using the same operation that fetches information from a neighbor. (Alternately, this figure diagrams the above 8-by-8 array viewed from one side, showing how each computer's processor in a 1-by-8 1-dimensional subarray of that 8-by-8 2-dimensional array links to its memory and to input-output via registers.)

A SHORT HISTORY OF ARRAY MULTI-COMPUTERS

Both CLIP and the MPP were designed for image processing and pattern recognition. They are quite similar to two earlier 32-by-32 arrays of 1-bit processors: the almost-completed Illiac-III (McCormick, 1963), which was destroyed by fire, and Solomon 1 (Slotnick et al., 1962; Gregory and McReynolds, 1963), which was the precursor of the Illiac-IV super-computer, an 8-by-8 array of very powerful 64-bit floating-point processors (Barnes et al., 1968).

Unger (1958, 1959) appears to be the first person to propose a parallel array of this sort (for pattern recognition). He also specified the design of an individual one-bit processor, and a number of simple algorithms for basic feature-detecting operations.

The Theoretical Development of Cellular Automata

The development of cellular automata by Von Neumann, Burks, Thatcher, Codd, and others (see Burks, 1966; Codd, 1968) was a major influence on the CLIP design. In sharp contrast, Reddaway (personal communication) designed the DAP as a number-crunching super-computer, and was unaware of any of the other array computers, or of the theoretical development of cellular automata.

GOODYEAR-AEROSPACE'S RECONFIGURABLE STARAN AND ASPRO ARRAYS

An important, but somewhat smaller, precursor was Kenneth Batcher's STARAN (1973, 1974). STARAN was designed to be built using from 1 to 12 modules. Each module has 256 processors linked to a bank of memories via an 8-by-256 reconfiguring network of 2-by-2 switches (the flip network, Batcher, 1976).

Roughly STARAN's gates are equally divided, one third devoted to processors, one third to memory, and one third to the switching network.

Among the many remappings of data that STARAN's flip network can effect are a 2-dimensional array and the butterfly shuffle permutations needed to compute fast Fourier transforms (FFTs). Thus the STARAN is a very interesting precursor of both the massively parallel arrays (like the CLIP, DAP, and MPP) and the reconfiguring networks (like the BBN Butterfly, PASM, and Ultracomputer). Indeed STARAN can handle any of the tasks that either type of system can handle—within the limits of its smaller array size (1,024 by 1 is a large STARAN, in contrast to 64 by 64, 96 by 96, or 128 by 128) on the one hand and its weaker and simpler processor (1 bit fixed-point vs—at least in some cases—32-bit or 64-bit floating-point).

ASPRO (anon., 1979), a VLSI version of STARAN, was built to fit in a .6 cubic foot box in the nose of a radar surveillance airplane. ASPRO is constructed with 32 processors plus their memories and a 5-by-32 flip network on each chip. ASPRO configurations have over a thousand processors in toto. A number of ASPRO systems are being built for Grumman.

ILLINOIS' ILLIAC-III ARRAY AND HETEROGENEOUS SYSTEM

Bruce McCormick, 1963, designed and almost completed the very interesting Illiac-III, a heterogeneous system (to be described in Chapter 13) that was to contain a 32-by-32 array of 1-bit computers, to be used for pattern recognition (primarily of particle events in bubble chamber photos).

ILLINOIS' SOLOMON COMPUTERS, AND ILLIAC-IV

Daniel Slotnick (Slotnick et al., 1962) designed a similar 32-by-32 array of 1-bit processors for number crunching. Following a successively diverging line of development, Slotnick's Solomon-1 array of 1-bit processors evolved into Solomon-2, an array of 24-bit processors, and, finally, Illiac-IV, which was originally designed to contain a 2-by-2 array of 8-by-8 arrays of very powerful 64-bit processors. Only one of the four 8-by-8 arrays was finally built. Illiac-IV was judged to be the most powerful computer running during the late 1970s—and also (at over $60,000,000) the most expensive computer ever built.

CUSTOM CHIPS FOR ARRAY PROCESSORS

CLIP4 uses CMOS custom chips designed to be driven by a 2.5 mherz clock. Each chip has a 2-by-4 array of 8 computers, each consisting of the processor, additional logic for the parallel fetch and processing of the 8 neighbor values needed in a window operation, and 32 bits of memory (plus several 1-bit registers, including a carry register to expedite bit-serial arithmetic). A 4K off-chip RAM, which only became available after the original CLIP4 was designed, has been added for additional, slightly slower, memory.

The DAPs that are actually running have been built from off-the-shelf TTL ICs driven by a 10 mherz clock (each processor links to a 4K or 16K off-chip commercial 200 nanosecond RAM memory). New chips, each with several processors plus registers, have been fabricated. It appears that future DAPs will use these chips, plus commercial RAMs for memory.

The MPP uses NMOS custom chips designed to be driven by a 10 mherz clock. Each chip has 8 processors, each with several registers plus a 32-bit shift register, and each linked to 1K 80 nanosecond off-chip RAM.

A VLSI chip (containing roughly 100,000 devices) with an 8-by-8 array of processors has been fabricated by the Japanese Telephone Company. A 256-by-256 array using these chips is under construction (Kondo et al., 1983). Martin Marietta (Pemberton, 1985) is using a 6-by-12 72-processor chip built by NCR to build GAPP array processors of several different sizes. The largest to date is 108 by 388 (Pemberton, personal communication). (NCR is developing several small arrays to be used as add-ons for IBM PCs, VAXes, and other computers.)

Both of these highly packed arrays are limited to only 128 bits of (on-chip) memory for each processor. The limited number of pins available on each chip necessitated designs that use very small on-chip memories rather than substantially larger RAM memories. Access to off-chip memories would be extremely slow, since pins would have to be shared among processors.

SOME DETAILS AS TO HOW THE LARGE CLIP, DAP, AND MPP ARRAYS OPERATE

Basic Operations, Using the Array's Links to Neighbor Computers

Information can be fetched from a computer's own memory, or from the memory of any of the neighbor computers to which that computer is directly linked. Thus the sequence of machine language instructions:

fetch_east 117
fetch_or_self 117
fetch_or_west 117
store 118

will have each and every one of the N-by-N
computers in the array fetch the information stored in location 117
of the computer directly to its East, fetch and or the
information stored in location 117 of that computer, fetch and
or the information stored in location 117 directly to the west,
and store the result in location 118.

The DAP and MPP link each computer to its 4 square neighbors. CLIP links each computer to its 8 square and diagonal neighbors. CLIP also (under program control) can be reconfigured to be a hexagonal array, with each computer linked to its 6 surrounding neighbors.

A basic CLIP4 machine-language instruction has (in 11 microseconds) every computer fetch (in parallel) and operate upon information from its own memory and also from any or all of the 8 immediately surrounding near-neighbor computers' memories—that is, from the 3-by-3 window that surrounds and includes it. This instruction is quite similar to the window operations executed by the PICAP and the Cytocomputer pipelines that serially simulate arrays. It is important to emphasize that the actual hardware embodiment is radically different, since CLIP *executes the ENTIRE window operation EVERYWHERE in the array SIMULTANEOUSLY, in ONE PARALLEL instruction.* In sharp contrast, the pipeline systems must serially flow each pixel and its surrounding window through the sequence of processors that execute this instruction.

The DAP and MPP do not have built-in window operations. Their basic instructions consist of "fetch," "store," "fetch_add," "fetch_or," or some other sequence of one fetch followed by an arithmetic or logic operation on that (1-bit) piece of data and a second piece of data presently in an accumulator register. This means that the DAP and MPP must use a sequence of up to 12 machine instructions (including several instructions to shift the values stored in the window's diagonal cells into square directly-linked cells from which they can then be fetched) to execute a single window operation. A basic instruction takes 250 nanoseconds on the DAP, and 100 nanoseconds on the MPP. So a window operation that needs 4, 8, or even 12 instructions will be executed very fast, in only a microsecond or two. It is important to emphasize that this operation will be executed in parallel by THOUSANDS OF DIFFERENT processors during that SAME microsecond or two.

These arrays have from 4,000 to 16,000 computers. But well within current technology and current economics are much larger arrays, with 256 by 256, 512 by 512, 1,024 by 1,024, or even more computers. Indeed, such larger arrays are now underway, at the Japanese Telephone Company, Martin Marietta, and the University of Massachussetts (see Chapter 13), and one has been completed at Thinking Machines as part of the Connection Machine (see Chapter 12).

The Larger Architecture Surrounding the Array

The CLIP, DAP, and MPP arrays are all part of a larger system that includes a conventional serial computer and large disks in which images can be stored. All three both input and output images (or any other type of information) by shifting them into, through, and out of, the rows of the array. This means that an array with N rows and M columns will have N input channels, one to each row, and will need M shifts to input an N-by-M image so that it is entirely inside the array.

TV INPUT OF IMAGES AND FAST PROPOGATION OF INFORMATION IN CLIP

CLIP is linked to a tv camera plus hardware that can be used to take a picture, digitize, and store it in a buffer image memory, and then when instructed shift that picture into the CLIP array's memory. CLIP can then execute an arbitrarily long sequence of programmed operations on that image. It can also output the image to the buffer image memory, from which it can be displayed, or input to the conventional computer, or stored on a disk. CLIP takes roughly 8 milliseconds to input or output a 1-bit black-white image, or 1 bit-plane of an 8-bit or N-bit image.

In order to pass information over long distances, CLIP also has an unclocked propagate instruction that is roughly 10 times as fast as a sequence of shift instructions.

PARALLEL INPUT, OUTPUT, AND PROCESSING IN THE MPP

The MPP has extra registers and grid links for input and output that allow it to shift an image 128 steps along all 128 rows in 128 100 nanosecond "fetch_from_east" (i.e., "shift_from_east") instructions. Therefore after a sequence of 128 instructions, taking 12.8 microseconds, an entire 128-by-128-by-1-bit image will have been shifted into the array's input-output registers. (At the same time the MPP's computers can be shifting a second image out and also executing a sequence of 128 instructions on information already stored in their memories.) Then the entire image is stored with one "store" instruction. To output, a bit-plane is first fetched (taking one instruction), and then the image is similarly shifted out, in 128 instructions. Since at the same time, processors can be executing a sequence of 128 instructions on data stored in their memories. So the entire process of input or output of information takes only one instruction away from other processing.

THE DAP'S LINK TO ITS CONVENTIONAL SINGLE-CPU HOST, VIA SHARED MEMORIES

The DAP has an additional, potentially very interesting, link between the actual array and the host serial computer. A 64-by-64-by-4K DAP memory of 1-bit stores also serves as the host serial computer's 512K memory of 32-bit stores. That is, the DAP shares its memory with its serial host. From this point of view we can describe a DAP as an array of processors that have been set above and added to a memory bank of the conventional computer.

In theory, this means that the DAP array and the serial computer can work on the same information, via the shared memory, with no delays! In practice, an unfortunate and unnecessary part of the total design makes it impossible to make use of this potentially very powerful capability. For the serial computer to which the DAP is coupled is a very large and expensive several-million-dollar mainframe that, to be used in a cost-effective manner, must be multiprogrammed. Therefore the only way for a DAP program to have the serial computer execute an instruction on information stored by the DAP processors is to interrupt the operating system. This is a process that takes several milliseconds, and is incommensurately slow with respect to the DAP's 200 nanosecond instruction cycle. The DAP group (Reddaway, personal communication) has long been interested in using a suitably smaller and cheaper serial host. There have been suggestions that such a system might be developed, possibly in conjunction with a PERQ workstation.

LINKS JOINING OPPOSITE EDGES OF THE ARRAY

DAP has links between the left-most columns and the right-most columns, and the top-most rows and the bottom-most rows. Normally this would convert the array into a torus (i.e., a donut, bagel, or inner tube). To expedite some of the shifts needed for numerical problems, an N-by-N DAP links (modulo N) cell 1,j to N,j + 1 and cell i,1 to i + 1,N. That is, it links each leftmost cell in a row to the rightmost cell in the next row, and each topmost cell in a column to the bottommost cell in the next column. (Neither the CLIP nor the MPP arrays has such wraparound links. They would be easy to add, but since both these systems were developed for image processing there appeared to be no reason to do so.)

ADDITIONAL DAP AND MPP HARDWARE FOR FAST REMAPPING OF DATA

DAP also has additional "row and column highway" hardware that was incorporated to carry out the remappings of data needed for numerical computations (e.g., matrix inversions, fast Fourier transforms). This hardware will in one instruction fetch an entire row or column of data, then store it in any or all of the rows or/and columns of the array. With this hardware, the 64-by-64 DAP has been shown (Reddaway, 1978, 1980), on a variety of benchmarks, to do substantially better than any of the traditional super-computers (including the Cray-1).

The MPP has buffer memories that can be used to effect remappings, by shifting data out to them (in 12.8 microseconds), then permuting and shifting the data back (in 12.8 microseconds). This technique was chosen by Batcher, who was the architect of all three systems, as a cost effective alternative to the reconfiguring networks used in STARAN and ASPRO.

PASSING INFORMATION GLOBAL DISTANCES IN ARRAYS

Linking the edges of an array to form a torus or other improved topology is obviously a good idea, but this only reduces the array's O(N) diameter by one half. This leaves the array still much too large for convenient shifting together of distant pieces of information. For example, an 8-connected 128-by-128 toroidal array will still need up to 63 shifts; a 1,024-by-1,024 array will still need up to 511 shifts. Therefore to handle global computations—for example, the solution of matrices of partial differential equations, fast Fourier transforms, or the recognition of large and complex objects—arrays need additional hardware.

CLIP propagation, DAP's row and column highways, the MPP's buffer staging memories, and the TMI Connection Machine's N-cube linking scheme (see Chapter 12) are all designed to help with this problem. It would be interesting to see good space/time cost analyses and benchmark comparisons of these different aproaches.

Processing Image Arrays that are Larger than the Hardware Array

Picture arrays that are larger than the array of computers can easily be processed, in either of two ways (see Figure 8-2):

1. A subarray of the picture array is stored in each computer's memory. For example, a different 8-by-8 subarray of a 1,024-by-1,024 array might be stored in the memory of each computer in a 128-by-128 computer array.
2. A subarray of the picture array that is the same size as the computer array is input to the computer array, storing one cell of the picture array in each computer's memory. This process is repeated until the entire picture array has been processed.

Each of these alternatives has its problems:

Of crucial importance for real time processing, both of course need more time, since they must use the smaller computer array to iterate through the larger picture array.

The first also needs additional time (or/and hardware) to index through the subarray and test for the borders, and additional memory to store the entire subimage and all resulting transformations.

The second must handle windows at the interior borders, where cells adjacent to but outside the subarray being processed must be examined as part of the window. This means that either:

1. The system must constantly reinput needed border rows and columns,
2. Overlapping subarrays must be used, with commensurate additional slow-downs (this only cuts down but doesn't eliminate the need to re-input borders),

```
1a  1b    2a  2b    3a  3b    4a  4b
1c  1d    2c  2d    3c  3d    4c  4d

5a  5b    6a  6b    7a  7b    8a  8b
5c  5d    6c  6d    7c  7d    8c  8d

9a  9b   10a 10b   11a 11b   12a 12b
9c  9d   10c 10d   11c 11d   12c 12d

13a 13b  14a 14b   15a 15b   16a 16b
13c 13d  14c 14d   15c 15d   16c 16d
```

(a)

```
1 1 1 1    2 2 2 2
1 1 1 1    2 2 2 2
1 1 1 1    2 2 2 2
1 1 1 1    2 2 2 2

3 3 3 3    4 4 4 4
3 3 3 3    4 4 4 4
3 3 3 3    4 4 4 4
3 3 3 3    4 4 4 4
```

(b)

FIGURE 8-2. Processing image arrays larger than the computer array. (a) A subarray of the image is stored in each computer's memory. All cells with the same number are stored in the same computer's memory. The example pictured in this figure indicates how a 16-by-16 picture array is mapped and stored into a 4-by-4 array of 16 computers (numbered 1 through 16). Each computer's memory stores a 2-by-2 subarray of the image (lettered a through d). (b) Sub-arrays of the image array, each the same size as the array of computers, are processed in turn. The example pictured in this figure decomposes a 16-by-16 picture array into four 4-by-4 subimages that are input into and processed, one at a time, by a 4-by-4 array of computers.

3. Additional hardware must be added, to make the borders accessible by storing and updating overlapping columns of the image in memories that can be treated as either the left-border or the right-border, and overlapping rows that can be treated as either the top-border or the bottom-border.

Stout (1985) and Miller and Stout (1985) have shown that asymptotically the most efficient size of the array for global operations (e.g., finding connected components or convex hulls) is $N^{1/3}$ by $N^{1/3}$. This reduces the number of shifts between computers, by substituting fetches within each computer.

It is not clear how large the image array must be before this mixed scheme, with its additional constant overhead, would actually become more efficient and more practical for a real computer. This will also depend heavily on the mix of relatively local vs. relatively global operations required. Much more experience is needed to gain an understanding of how array programs will combine these. As programs improve, as arrays grow larger, and as problems that are attacked increase in complexity, the percent of relatively global operations can be expected to increase, and this mixed scheme should become more attractive.

The Suitability and Generality of (General-Purpose) Arrays' 1-Bit Computers

These very large arrays of many thousands of computers have become feasible largely because each computer has been made as simple as possible, and all execute the same instruction (which means that only one controller is needed for the entire system).

Today's large arrays use processors that compute one bit at a time. This is entirely appropriate and efficient for logical operations. Logic operations include at least three very important classes of operations—

1. Those where two things (images, models, graphs, strings, etc.) are matched;
2. Those where several features are examined together and combined, and the likelihood of the resulting characteristic (often called a "label" or a "symbol") being either "present" or "absent" is assessed and stored for each cell;
3. Those used with binary (black-white) images, or images that have been histogramed and thresholded, and thus converted into, binary images.

Arithmetic and string-matching operations that must be executed on pieces of data longer than 1 bit are quite straightforwardly carried out by 1-bit processors, but only serially, 1 bit at a time, in what is called bit-serial mode. This means that, for example, when 8-bit, 21-bit, 32-bit, 47-bit, 64-bit or 89-bit arithmetic or comparison operations must be executed they will take 8k, 21k, 32k, 47k, 64k or 89k times as long as the 1-bit operation that must be iterated (k is a small constant, roughly on the order of 1 to 5, for any overheads due to the iterations). Thus, at the price of occasional roughly 8-fold, 64-fold or greater slowdowns when large numbers and strings must be handled serially, today's actual running arrays gain 4,000 to 64,000-fold increases in speed whenever large arrays of numbers or symbols are handled in parallel.

Note that one can tailor such a bit-serial operation to exactly the precision desired, rather than use arbitrary conventional sizes like 32 or 64. This makes for an interesting reversal from the traditional computer, which has a fixed 32-, 64-, 16-, or 8-bit parallel fetch, store, and operate mode, but handles sets of data of any size. In sharp contrast, the array has a fixed N-by-M format for its data but can tailor operations to any number of bits.

THE NEW GENERATION OF ARRAYS

The University College London CLIP7 Array

CLIP7 (Fountain, 1983, 1985), which is now being completed, promises to make several important steps toward increasing the power of today's parallel arrays. It will use 8-bit rather than 1-bit processors, and therefore will be able to handle numerical calculations with the same speed and efficiency that the 1-bit processors exhibit for logical operations. It will do a certain amount of serial scanning, from which it will gain a good amount of power and flexibility in moving information long distances. It will introduce some capabilities for having each processor execute processes on a different set of data, and thus, although still benefiting from largely synchronized behavior, begin to move in the direction of the MIMD world.

The original plans were for CLIP7 to scan a smaller array of processors (probably 512 by 4) over a 512-by-512 image array fast enough to execute a typical mix of 8-bit operations and 1-bit operations everywhere over the entire 512-by-512 array at microsecond speeds. This is the same amount of time CLIP4 now takes to execute this mix of 1-bit and 6-bit (truncated from 8 bits because CLIP4 inputs a 6-bit image) operations over the much smaller 96-by-96 array. For example, to get the maximum in a 3-by-3 window of 8-bit numbers will take 1.2 milliseconds; a 3-by-3 1-bit logical operation will take .2 milliseconds. It appears (Duff, personal communication) that a modified system will be built first, one that scans a 256-by-1 array over the 512-by-512 array (taking about 8 times longer). Two processor chips will be used for each of these processors, with one of them handling the addresses of information fetched and stored. This means that the system will be able to take a major step in the direction of introducing MIMD processing into the system.

The fact that CLIP7 serially scans the image will also allow it to move information about in the image array without always shifting that information through near neighbors. For example, it will be able to simulate pyramid structures (see Chapter 9) far more efficiently than can a completely parallel array, which must shift information long distances to move it as though from one level of a pyramid to the next, much smaller, level.

CLIP7 will thus be in a position to take advantage of both the massively parallel aspects of the array and the serial aspects of the sequential scan. It will be straightforward to increase the size of CLIP7 when and if that is needed in order to increase its speed for real-time applications. For example, a 512-by-64 CLIP7 would be 16 times faster than the 512-by-4.

1-Dimensional Scanning Arrays, and Arrays Combined with Other Resources

Steve Wilson, 1985, at Applied Intelligent Systems, has built PIXIE-5000, a 1-dimensional array of up to 1,024 1-bit processors, which scans (much like CLIP7 and the Cytocomputer and Pipe scanning arrays) over the larger 2-dimensional image. It can execute neighborhood operations over a full 1,024-by-1,024 array at the rate of 3.5 billion operations per second. The array is part of a total image processing system, as shown in Figure 8-3.

University of Massachusetts researchers plan to combine a large SIMD array with a network of more independent processors (see Chapter 13). The TMI Connection Machine embeds an array in an N-cube. Several researchers are designing and beginning to build pyramids of arrays (see Chapter 9).

THE PROSPECT OF INCREASINGLY LARGE, CHEAP, MICRO-MODULAR ARRAYS

Possibly the most important feature of the array, a feature that will become increasingly compelling over the next 10 to 20 years, is the fact that its total size and thus degree of parallelness can be increased with relative ease. Its basic computer module is iterated in very large numbers, in a very simple and regular design that is almost ideal for fabricating small subarrays on VLSI chips and then combining chips into larger arrays. A 512-by-512 array is simply 16 128-by-128 arrays array-linked into one single array. A 1,024-by-1,024 array is simply 4 512-by-512 arrays. Along with larger sizes come major economies of scale, since mass production savings are achieved as larger numbers of

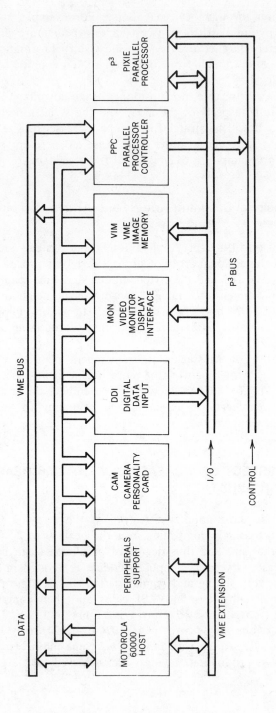

FIGURE 8-3. PIXIE-5000 1-dimensional array.
(*Source*: Wilson, 1985.)

identical chips are fabricated, and as larger numbers of identical boards and other modules are tied together.

It appears that the computers in this kind of array can be built far more cheaply than traditional serial computers, because each computer has been made relatively much simpler and the whole micromodular structure of the array makes design and fabrication quite straightforward and far more appropriate for VLSI.

Roughly it appears that a 32-by-32 array of 1,024 of this kind of simple 1-bit computer may well cost less than a single traditional 32-bit computer (Uhr, 1984a). This is so chiefly because although the CPU of a conventional serial computer can fit easily on a single VLSI chip, the many millions of bits of memory that it must be given to keep it busy will need at least a small handful of additional chips. In sharp contrast, a 100 to 800-device processor with a 400 to 4000-device memory of several hundred or several thousand bits (these are typical sizes for 1-bit computers), should, because of its highly micromodular and simple design, pack more and more densely into future VLSI chips. So single chips with one to several million transistors containing a 16-by-16 array of 256 such computers, or a 32-by-32 array of 1,024, appear to be reasonably conservative goals. Additional off-chip memory chips might be used or, especially if pin limits dictate, more memory and fewer processors might be put on each chip.

With future VLSI technologies these parallel arrays will almost certainly become increasingly attractive. Their simple micromodular and highly iterated structure makes them, along with memory chips, especially easy to design and to fabricate. By the 1990s, when ten million or more devices can be fabricated on a single chip, it should become possible to put a 64-by-64 or even larger array on each chip, and to use only a small number of such chips to build a really large array (or, as we shall see in Chapter 9, a pyramid of arrays).

Several important further parallelizations can be built into array hardware:

The entire window or other region surrounding the cell that each computer processes can be fetched and examined in parallel. This is done by CLIP for the surrounding 3-by-3 window. In future systems the window could be extended to any desired size or shape.

An entire production rule-like image processing or transforming procedure can in many cases be further parallelized with additional hardware (e.g., to, in parallel, evaluate the several parts in a compound and then in parallel imply several consequences).

N processors can be placed in each cell, so that N transforming procedures can be executed in parallel.

More powerful 4-bit, 8-bit, 16-bit, 32-bit, or other-sized processors can be used (when costs decrease sufficiently to justify this) to replace the 1-bit processors in today's arrays.

Rectangular, rather than square, arrays might be used. For example, a cinemascope-like shape might be more suited for images of several objects (e.g., a city block of houses) spread out laterally on the ground.

More than one controller might be used. For example, a C-by-D array of controllers might be scattered uniformly through an N-by-M array of computers, each controller responsible for an N/C-by-M/D subarray.

In stark contrast, very little more can be done to make today's single-CPU serial computers more powerful. They are rapidly reaching the point where they cannot possibly be made faster (except by introducing special-purpose parallel processors into the single CPU), because they will have reached the ultimate speed-of-light barrier.

A SHORT SUMMARY OF SOME VIRTUES OF ARRAYS

Tomorrow's arrays, each with hundreds of thousands or millions of computers, will achieve 5, 6, or even more orders of magnitude increases in speed. These arrays are capable of effecting a wide variety of very powerful local operations. At the cost of extra time to shift information together through the array, they can execute any possible operation, no matter how global. It is important to emphasize that these massively parallel sizes and enormous increases in power and speed can be achieved only because:

The size of each processor is reduced to the minimum; but this does not diminish generality. When it is justified, or required, more powerful processors can be used. (This will become increasingly feasible as VLSI costs go down.)

The links between processors are kept short and simple, and therefore in a near-neighbor grid. This also is dictated by simplicity and economy, not necessity. More links could be used, and these could reach out to more distant processors. However, the near-neighbor linkage allows for information to be shifted when necessary from more distant processors, by shifting over a path from neighbor to neighbor.

The design of each processor, and of the total system, is kept very simple. Here again, more complex and costly designs can be used where indicated.

The size of each processor's memory is kept small (however the total memory of the system is very large, and the ratio of processor transistors to memory transistors is therefore substantially greater than that found in conventional serial computers). More memory can be used, if desired. However, it seems likely that the optimal size of memory is a function of the size and complexity of the problem (which for image perception is in turn a function of the size of the image), rather than of the number of computers used to solve the problem.

The number of controllers is minimized. (In today's systems it is one; more generally the number of controllers will be far smaller than the number of processors, to the extent that complex controllers are relatively more expensive than simple processors.)

The number of computers that can be fabricated onto each single chip is therefore large. (From 8 to 72 have been put on a single chip today, and hundreds or thousands should be feasible within 5 or 10 years.)

The highly iterated micromodular structure of an array means that it is relatively easy to design a chip of high density, and relatively easy to combine a number of chips into the total system.

A conventional serial computer must serially execute kNxM instructions to apply a local window operation at all locations in a large array. In striking contrast, a parallel array needs one instruction. The pipeline scanning arrays, with built-in hardware to increment locations and test for borders, need $(NxM/P) + P$ instructions (for a P-processor pipe, including the time to fill and empty the pipe). Thus, for example, to execute one 3-by-3 window operation that takes 10 instructions (plus 5 instructions to increment locations and test for borders) at all locations in a 1,000-by-1,000 array, a dedicated serial computer with a 1 microsecond instruction time will need 15,000,000 microseconds (15 seconds). A pipeline scanning array like the deAnza will need 30 milliseconds (30 nanoseconds for each location, assuming that its hardware is built fast enough to handle video scan rates). A 1,000-by-1,000 parallel array with 3-by-3 window operations built into its hardware will need 1 microsecond, or 30 nanoseconds, or (if such further speedups are needed) even less.

Chapter Nine

AUGMENTED ARRAYS; PYRAMIDS; TOWARD AUGMENTED PYRAMIDS

An array of computers can be extremely fast and powerful when attacking problems where local operations can fruitfully be applied everywhere to an array of information. This is frequently the case in image processing and the lower levels of pattern perception and computer vision, when (as is inevitably true for a general perceiver) the system has no *a priori* knowledge of what to look for or where to look. It is also the case for several other operations. For example, one can multiply many thousands of pairs of 100-bit numbers in a few hundred microseconds. One can match thousands of pairs of 100-bit or 1000-bit strings (as in firing rules in an "expert" production system) in a few hundred or a few thousand microseconds.

Although they are general purpose and therefore in theory can do anything, the highly synchronized arrays that have been built can become relatively inefficient, slow, and wasteful of resources. When something that is being looked for everywhere actually occurs in only a few regions, most of an array's processors will either be masked out and doing nothing, or else spinning their gears. If a perception system has been preprogrammed to know where to look and what to look for (this will occasionally be the case, but usually only with simple, highly constrained environments and toy problems), or, more interestingly, has gathered and absorbed information about where to look, then more flexibility is needed than today's single-controller, completely synchronized SIMD arrays can muster.

This chapter examines several promising ways to keep the virtues and powers of arrays, at the same time eliminating their faults.

AUGMENTING ARRAYS INTERNALLY AND BY COMBINING THEM WITH OTHER COMPUTERS

Today's arrays are highly synchronized SIMD systems, with every processor executing the same instruction stream, albeit each on a different structure of data. They also use very cheap and simple 1-bit processors and near-neighbor connections between computers. They need not be this way; but the economics of building a very large array strongly suggests these choices—at least today. Without these simplifications, systems with 10,000 and more computers could not have been built.

Some of the Problems and Inefficiencies of Arrays

As a result, arrays can be inefficient, and even slow, in executing processes that are relevant only to subregions of the array of information, or where different relatively distant parts of the array need to communicate with one another, or where different processors need to execute different instructions.

In an array, to communicate between two nodes a piece of information must be shifted through a path of intervening computers one step at a time, across the grid. Unless the programmer is extremely careful, these paths can become excessively long, up to the diameter of the array. That is, hundreds or thousands of shifts are needed in a large array. Unless almost all of the processors need information that can be got via exactly the same patterned sequence of shifts, most processors will be wasting their time while information is being shifted in this way. Unless the program has been very carefully written to make as much use as possible of common passings of information, it will be common that information is passed between only one pair of nodes at a time, which means that all but two of the processors are sitting idle and wasting their time.

To have different processors execute different instructions, the array must effectively turn off all the computers that shouldn't be executing instruction 1 (this is usually handled with built-in masking hardware, but it can be effected by fetching a bit-plane that contains a 0 for each processor to be turned off, and logical-anding that bit-plane with the final results of the operation), then turn off all the computers that shouldn't be executing instruction 2, and so on. This means that the different instructions are executed one at a time, serially, and that all the computers that are turned off are simply being wasted.

Modifying and Augmenting Arrays

There are a number of ways in which SIMD arrays might be augmented to at least partially overcome their problems. All of these need additional resources, hence cost money; therefore they must be justified as cost effective.

ADDING CONTROLLERS; INCREASING PROCESSING POWER; CHANGING LINKS

An array might be improved on by adding controllers (e.g., for the n-by-n subarray on each chip of an N-by-N array), by using N-bit processors (as in CLIP7), by changing the local linking scheme, or/and by adding links between distant processors. Here there are a great variety of possibilities, only a few of which have been explored.

Links between processors at the opposite borders, to form a torus or a spiral, are the most widely used augmentation. There have been several proposals for handling near-neighbor array operations using different internal linking schemes (e.g., Sequin's, 1981, twisted torus networks, Fiat and Shamir's, 1984, polymorphic arrays, and Batcher's, 1973 flip network for the STARAN array). These offer a wider variety of efficient embeddings of arrays of processes into the hardware array, although at the price of more hardware and/or less efficiency in nearest neighbor processing.

There have also been several proposals for adding links to expedite global processing (e.g., Rosenfeld, 1983, for "powers of 2" links to processors 2, 4, 8, or more away, and also Kumar and Raghavendra, 1985, and Kumar and Tsai, 1985, for links that move arrays toward trees and pyramids).

ADDING A CONVENTIONAL COMPUTER, OR A NETWORK OF COMPUTERS

Alternately, or additionally, the array might be combined with one or more augmenting computers. Probably the most straightforward augmentation simply links an array to one conventional single-CPU serial computer.

Today's arrays are actually linked to a conventional serial computer that serves as the "host" on which programs are coded and debugged, and then compiled into the array's machine language. But the serial computer cannot actually be used to execute those parts of the program for which it might be more appropriate. Today's systems have simply not been designed to allow for efficient use of both array and conventional serial computer in executing the same program.

PROBLEMS IN INTERFACING LARGE ARRAYS TO A CONVENTIONAL COMPUTER

That kind of integrated design poses severe problems, because the gross mismatch between these two systems—the highly parallel array with its very large number of processors and the host serial computer with its single processor—makes it extremely cumbersome to pass information from one to the other. Traditionally arrays shift information in to and out from their rows starting at one edge. This is too slow from the point of view of the very fast parallel array and can make the system severely input-bound and (when, for example, simply enhancing images rather than recognizing objects) even output-bound. Data might instead be input and output every Cth column (e.g., to every board, or to every chip) in order to speed up input-output.

Shifting only into the edges is already far too fast for, and would overwhelm, a conventional serial computer, if one attempted to link it directly. For example, the 128-by-128 MPP shifts 128 bits of information into one edge and out the opposite edge every 100 nanoseconds. It thus needs 12.8 microseconds to input or/and output an entire 128-by-128 image of 16K 1-bit pixels. Its input-output bandwidth is therefore extremely large by conventional standards—1.28 billion bits per second. A conventional serial computer does not have interfaces fast enough and appropriate for such a flow of data. To have any hope of keeping the array busy the serial computer would need something like a whole bank of disks that can be used to input in parallel to the array (this is being considered as a way of augmenting the MPP). A nontrivial network of switches and memory registers is needed to buffer input-output between an array and a serial computer. This might be combined with, or replaced by, some kind of mechanism that simply reduces the amount of data—for example, eliminating 0 entries, compressing, or transforming (Pfeiffer, 1985).

USING MORE THAN ONE CONVENTIONAL COMPUTER TO AUGMENT THE ARRAY

Rather than use one single conventional serial computer to augment a large array, it may well be preferable to use one computer for each of the large array's subarrays. Each subarray can now be made small enough to eliminate the data-transfer bottlenecks. These augmenting computers might be linked into a network with any desired topology, for example, a line (bus), polygon, N-cube, tree, or array, or in one of the more powerful topologies described in Chapters 10 through 13.

This kind of extension would be very helpful, if only to handle the input-output mismatch between a large parallel array and a conventional serial computer. If the array can input N times faster than the conventional computer can output information to it, N conventional computers can be linked to it, and each used to store and transmit 1/Nth of the total array. Even more important, the network of conventional computers can now execute processes for which an array is inappropriate, and can execute different processes on different regions of the image and on different aspects of the problem.

CONVERGING/DIVERGING PYRAMID MULTI-COMPUTERS

An attractive alternative is to extend the array so that the very structure of the extended system serves these input-output purposes (among other potentially even more important purposes). This can be accomplished in a rather simple and elegant manner, by combining the original array with successively smaller arrays, to form a pyramid.

This appears to be an especially appropriate structure for image processing, pattern perception, and other areas of AI where information should be simultaneously transformed and converged (or, moving in the other direction, broadcast and diverged). For example, an image can be input to and processed by the array that forms the base of the pyramid. Then, whenever the programmer chooses, the resulting arrays of information can be merged (using whatever function desired) and moved into the next, smaller array. This process can be repeated, converging upward toward the pyramid's apex, or/and diverging back down toward the base.

Two different types of pyramids are being designed and built. One, directed toward numerical problems, uses a small number of relatively powerful independent mini-computers (Handler and associates: Fritsch et al., 1983; Bode et al., 1985) or super-computers (Maples, 1985). This type will be examined in Chapter 11. The other, directed toward vision, uses thousands of very small processors—much like those found in the arrays—to build massively parallel systems.

Massively parallel pyramid architectures have been examined and designed by Dyer (1981, 1982), Schaefer (1985), Cantoni et al. (1985), Stout (1983, 1985a, 1985b, 1985c), Miller and Stout (1984), Tanimoto (1981, 1982, 1983a, 1984), and Uhr (1981, 1984a). Tanimoto, Schaefer, and Cantoni et al. are now building such structures.

Pyramids, along with pipes, arrays, and systolic systems, are among the best examples of process-structured architectures that have been designed to date. It is therefor important to examine them from the point of view of the processes they will execute.

The Basic Pyramid Structure, and Variations

All the pyramids designed or proposed to date have been 3-dimensional structures that are imposed over, and include, a 2-dimensional array at the base.

PYRAMIDS DESCRIBED

A pyramid can be built from a set of successively smaller arrays, as follows: Each processor links to its near-neighbors in its own array (i.e., the 4 square neighbors, or 8 square-and-diagonal neighbors, or 6 hexagonal neighbors), exactly as in an array like CLIP, DAP or the MPP. Each processor also links to nearby offspring in the next-larger array below it (usually a 2-by-2 subarray of 4 offspring) and to one, or to several, parent nodes in the next-smaller array above (with the exception of the top array, which has no parents, and the bottom array, which has no children).

A pyramid can also be built, or viewed, as a tree linked at its buds to an array and (probably) with its interior nodes linked to nearest-neighbor siblings, thus forming interior arrays at any or all levels (often called plies).

VARIATIONS ON THE PYRAMID THEME

A number of variations on this converging hierarchical local-neighborhood pyramid architecture are possible (some of these will be examined below, and in Chapter 13):

Each processor can be linked to 4 or 8 neighbors in a square array, or to 6 neighbors in a hexagonal array (or, if more wires can be handled, to any desired number of other processors in a more complex topology).

Processors can be given more than one parent; this results in "overlap."

Each layer, each subarray at each layer, each subpyramid, or any other desired substructure of computers, can be broadcast a different instruction to execute, or given its own controller.

Each processor can be given its own controller.

Each processor, or some of the processors, can be made more powerful. For example, 8-, 16- or 32-bit processors can be used.

As the arrays become smaller the individual processors all can be made more powerful. For example, 4-, 8-, 16-, 32-, and finally 64-bit processors can be used.

Different kinds of interconnection topologies can be added to the array/tree linkages, or can replace them. This seems especially

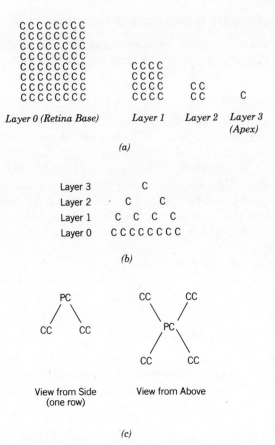

FIGURE 9-1. Building a pyramid from successively smaller arrays: A 4-layer pyramid with an 8-by-8 "retinal" base and 2-by-2 convergence from each layer to the next, until a 1-by-1 "apex" is achieved. (a) Four arrays of computers are first constructed, forming the layers of the pyramid. (b) These array/layers are stacked, each successively smaller layer above the last (side views are given, showing only one row of each layer). (c) Computers are linked from layer to layer so that each parent (PC) has enough children (CC) so all children have parents.

appropriate at the higher levels; for example, reconfiguring networks might replace the mesh.

A layer of processors can be sandwiched between two layers of memories, each processor linked to a 2-by-2 subarray of 4 (or some other local window, for example, a 3-by-3 subarray of 9) offspring memories and to 1 parent memory, or (to give overlap) 4 or more parent memories.

A network of traditional computers (of the sort examined in Chapters 6 and 10 through 13) can be linked, each to a set of pyramid nodes. These links might most appropriately be effected at higher layers. They might also be used for feedback to, and interaction with, lower-level processing at lower layers. For example, each 32-bit processor might be linked to 32 1-bit pyramid processors, either at a higher layer or interspersed as desired over several layers. These links might either be direct, or via a common dual-ported memory, or via a reconfiguring network.

Some Examples of How a Pyramid Multi-Computer Can Be Used

An image array is input to the memory stores in the large "retinal" array at the base of the pyramid. A variety of different types of operations and different strategies can now be used (see Chapter 15). For example, array window operations can be executed to transform this raw image, with each result stored into one of the memory locations of the same array, or merged into the next array's memory.

Then, successively higher-level operations can be executed, as the successively abstracted and transformed image is processed, compacted and merged, and passed up through the pyramid. This whole process might consist of a complex structure of successively more global feature-detectors and characterizers that serve to model and hence recognize a number of different complex objects.

At the other extreme, the program might simply average at each level, to give a sequence of images of different resolutions.

The Pyramid's Drastic Logarithmic Reduction of Message-Passing Distances

A pyramid architecture allows information to be converged and merged as the image is successively transformed. It also effects a crucially important reduction in the distances over which information is transferred and messages are passed. For example, a 1,024-by-1,024 4-square-connected array needs 2,046 shifts to send data or any other kind of message from one of its corners to the opposite corner. When a 1,024-by-1,024 array is used as the base array of a pyramid only 20 operations are needed, since the message can be passed up to the pyramid's apex and then back down. To state this more generally, whereas the diameter (i.e., the worst-case message-passing distance) of an N-by-N array is O(N), the diameter of a pyramid that includes that array is O(logN).

It is important to emphasize that although a pyramid can give the impression of being a much more imposing, complex and expensive multi-computer than an array, it is at most only one-third bigger. For example, a 64-by-64 array (with 4,096 nodes) forms the base of a $log_4 4,096$ pyramid that, with 2-by-2 convergence (the SMALLEST convenient convergence scheme, hence the scheme that results in a pyramid with the LARGEST number of nodes) adds only the much smaller 32-by-32, 16-by-16, 8-by-8, 4-by-4, 2-by-2 and 1-by-1 arrays (with 1,024 + 256 + 64 + 16 + 4 + 1, totaling 1,365, additional nodes). A 243-by-243 array (with 59,049 nodes) forms the base of a 3-by-3 converging $log_9 59,049$ pyramid with 81-by-81, 27-by-27, 9-by-9, 3-by-3 and 1-by-1 arrays (with 6,561 + 729 + 81 + 9 + 1, totaling 7,381, additional nodes).

MULTI-ROOTED PYRAMIDS, EXPANDED PYRAMIDS, AND LINEAR PYRAMIDS

This section examines several variant types of pyramids, and several ways for expanding pyramids into multi-pyramids. Chapter 13 will examine a variety of additional ways augment pyramids.

Combining a Number of Trees or Pyramids into Larger Systems

Several pyramids can be linked at their base, to form a multi-rooted system. For example, start with an L-ary tree, where each internal node has L links and each leaf node has 1 link. Now link L such trees together at their leaves (Storwick, 1970). Note that this multiplies the number of nodes in the network by L, but without increasing either diameter or degree (the maximum number of joins to links at any node). We might similarly combine a number of pyramids. For example, in a pyramid where each node links to 4 children, 3 additional pyramids might be linked to the lowest layer without using any more joining ports than are needed at the higher layers. Additional pyramids might be added, at the relatively small cost of extra ports (raising the degree, but not the diameter).

Narendra Ahuja and his associates (Ahuja and Swami, 1984; Sharma et al., 1985) have designed NETRA, a set of tree/pyramid cluster modules that can be constructed, using reconfiguring switches, into a variety of pyramid-like structures.

Another alternative would link only some of the cells in the pyramid's base. For example a tree might be superimposed over each row and/or each column in the base, or over subarrays of the base. Now additional links might be used to tie these separate trees together. [Note that a conventional pyramid ties together 2-by-2 or n-by-n subpyramids at successively higher levels.] All these apexes might then be linked by, for example, a tree or a pyramid or (if there are only a few) a crossbar or bus.

N-by-N-by-Log(N) Arrays

A pyramid can be expanded into a 3-dimensional solid that may continue to have the pyramid's good converging properties, as well as the good local properties within each array-layer, but tends toward a more rectangular shape. This might be called a logarithmic lattice. This kind of log-lattice of arrays has logN arrays, just as a pyramid of arrays has logN arrays. In the log-lattice, however, all arrays are the same size, giving an N-by-N-by-logN solid. Note that a log-lattice is far larger than a pyramid, with N^2 apexes and almost logN times as many processors; but it is far smaller than a cube, which would have almost N times as many processors.

Reconfiguring Benes networks can be built by successively superimposing trees, as shown in Chapter 6, and used for this construction—except that now we must use a computer rather than a switch for each node. For a large pyramid this probably gives too many apexes, as well as costing too much in terms of added hardware. Rather than build the entire network, we might have only half the number of apex nodes, or, more realistically, only N nodes or even fewer (e.g., $logN^2$ or logN). That is, any number of trees might be drawn from the N^2 nodes in the pyramid's base, from 1 (which gives the basic pyramid) to N^2 (which gives the full reconfiguring network).

Rosenfeld (1986) has proposed stacking logN N-by-N arrays into a "prism"—where cell (i,j) in array k of a 2^n by 2^n prism is linked, with wraparound, to cells (i,j), $(i+2^k,j)$, $(i,j+2^k)$ in array $k+1$. Local operations on fine details are executed using the array links, and the results then passed from one layer to the next (e.g., for continuing linear pipeline-like processing) using the (i,j) links. The two other links can be used to pass information over greater distances. Note that prisms no longer have the pyramids' tree-like links for converging information into successively more global structures.

N-by-N-by-N Arrays, Linear Pyramids, and Logarithmic/Linear Pyramids

A more straightforward O(N) 3-dimensional array can be built with diagonal links moving upward through the third dimension exactly like the diagonal links moving through the two dimensions of a 2-dimensional array. This gives an N-by-N-by-N cube. Such a structure has N^3 computers, and diameter N. Thus both its total size and its diameter are probably too large for most jobs.

A linear O(N) pyramid can similarly be built, simply by carving the pyramid from the center of the 3-dimensional array. It will converge from an N-by-N array at its base to a 1-by-1 apex array in N/2 layers. Like the O(N) array, its size ($N^3/4$) and diameter (N) are probably too large. A useful type of structure would sandwich one or several layers of an O(N) array or pyramid between adjacent layers of an O(logN) pyramid structure. This would allow one to construct a pyramid with any desired height and speed of convergence.

Consider N-by-N-based pyramids. If N = 1,024, a logarithmic O(logN) pyramid will have only 10 layers, which may well be too shallow. An O(N) (linear) pyramid will have 512 layers, which would almost certainly be too many. A desirable in-between depth could be achieved by using logN layers—or log(N/L) (L = Layer) or any other suitable number—of the O(N) pyramid between every pair of the O(logN) pyramid's layers. Alternately, every second, third, or nth layer from the O(N) pyramid might be sandwiched between each pair of layers in the O(logN) pyramid, using just enough to converge from the larger to the smaller. The same number of layers might be inserted at each level (in which case, because of the smaller convergence at higher levels, several layers of the same size might be used); or different numbers of layers might be inserted at different levels. A suitably sized section of an O(N) pyramid might be inserted between successive layers of the O(logN) pyramid. For example, between the 8-by-8 and the 4-by-4 layers of an O(logN) pyramid might be inserted the 7-by-7, 6-by-6, and 5-by-5 layers of the O(N) pyramid. Insertions are probably most appropriately done at the higher, smaller layers, since it seems likely that more processing will be needed there. In general, however, they allow one to program processes that only gradually coarsen the grain of detail at which they work.

From one simple aspect, a pyramid can be thought of as a lens that can zoom images into finer or coarser detail. A logarithmic pyramid has only logN possible zoom settings; but a linear pyramid has N. Wherever it might be useful to have a finer range of settings with smaller differences between each, an appropriate section from a linear pyramid or array can be inserted into the logarithmic pyramid. Note that since a logarithmic pyramid can either execute a sequence of operations at the same layer or pass information to an adjacent layer, a sandwiched structure that has the same number, K, of O(N) layers between each pair of O(logN) layers will be equivalent to the O(logN) pyramid—except for the important difference that the sandwiched system (when fully used) will be K times as fast.

THE GENERALITY OF PYRAMIDS (WHICH INCLUDE ARRAYS AND SERIAL COMPUTERS)

Remember that at least three-fourths of an unaugmented logarithmic pyramid consists of the array at its base. Obviously, then, a pyramid of arrays can do everything that an array can do, if only by never using any of its computers that are not part of the base array. Each array-layer of a pyramid can be made to act like a self-contained pure array, simply by having it execute only code that stores the results of operations back into that array's processors' own memories. However, in a pyramid the processors can also execute instructions to gather information from, or pass information to, their children's memories whenever desired. Information can thereby be passed up the pyramid, and thus moved together, combined, transformed, and converged. Or it can be passed down the pyramid, and thereby broadcast, or sent as messages to designated recipients (e.g., to adjust thresholds or give contextual global information).

Similarly a pyramid, array, or any other kind of multi-computer network can, trivially, do anything that a traditional single-CPU serial computer can do, since it can use any of its many individual computers exactly as a traditional computer is used. Such multi-computer systems are therefore general purpose in the sense of Turing machine generality. Indeed, each computer is general purpose (but usually memory bound and input-output bound because of its own relatively small memory and the fact that much of the data it may need to work on is stored in the memory of, and must be fetched and shifted from, other more or less nearby computers).

THE PROBABLE NEED TO AUGMENT PYRAMIDS

Pyramids can efficiently handle the wide variety of local processes typically applied at every cell in an image that array multi-computers like CLIP, DAP, and the MPP can handle so well—if only because pyramids are built from sets of successively smaller arrays. Pyramids can also handle a wide variety of other important processes, where information must be gathered together, coalesced, abstracted, or in other ways transformed, and where information must be broadcast, passed to distant nodes, or in other ways disseminated.

But there are a number of processes—especially those that appear to be useful at the higher, more cognitive levels of perception—that probably should be executed more independently of one another, or may be inherently serial. For example, the program might be trying to recognize different objects in different regions of an image. Thus there might be tentative indications that must be explored further, for example, of a bird below a cloud to the upper left, a house in the middle, a car to the lower left, several trees to the right, and bicycles below toward the right. Or the set of operations needed to process different regions of the scene, or to explore different possibilities, might be markedly different in size. This would mean that in a relatively synchronized pyramid (or array), more and more processors would complete their tasks, and then remain idle until the longest task was finally completed.

These situations can be handled in one or more of the following ways:

Execute the different processes one at a time, serially. This can be very inefficient and slow; it probably would not succeed within the real time constraints imposed by dynamic environments and moving images.

Reformulate serial procedures into equivalent, or near-equivalent, parallel-serial pyramid procedures of appropriate power. The brain is an existence proof that this is possible; but it is very difficult. Very few people are working on these problems; and progress is slow.

Augment the pyramid with additional appropriate internal hardware—for example, more controllers, or more, or more powerful, processors, probably interspersed throughout the higher layers.

Augment the pyramid with additional appropriate external hardware, for example, a network of appropriately configured, more independent and more powerful computers.

There appears to be a large variety of attractive externally augmented pyramids. Basic pyramid or tree modules might be linked together via reconfiguring networks. A number of different topologies might be used for the augmenting MIMD network. The pyramid and the network might be linked together in a number of different ways. For examinations of pyramid augmentations, see Pfeiffer (1985), Tanimoto (1985), and Uhr (1983a, 1983b, 1984a, 1984b). Since these can best be viewed as heterogeneous systems, pyramids linked to and augmented by MIMD networks will be examined in Chapter 13.

Chapter Ten

POINT-TO-POINT LINKED TOPOLOGIES FOR LARGE MIMD MULTI-COMPUTERS

The simple basic topologies examined up to this point already account for most of the multi-computers that have actually been built to date. Until very recently, virtually all the completed systems have used buses, rings, crossbars, or reconfiguring networks, giving a pseudo-complete graph. The major exceptions are the MISD pipelines for processing vectors and arrays, and the large SIMD arrays of thousands of 1-bit computers.

THE NECESSITY OF POINT-TO-POINT TOPOLOGIES

However, a large number of additional topologies have been proposed, and a very large number are possible. A few are now being built, both for general purpose architectures and also for a variety of specialized applications. As we have seen, the problems of linking and interfacing computers dictate that the only feasible topologies for large multi-computers link each node directly to a very small number of the other nodes in the total graph. In terms of current technologies for linking chips via the limited number of available pins, and computers via complex and error-prone interfaces, no more than 4, 8 or (possibly) 16 or so direct links are feasible.

Such structures, where each computer is linked to a relatively small number of other computers in the total system, are commonly said to have "point-to-point connectivity." Only rarely can they send information directly from one computer to another. Rather, information must typically go through a whole path of intervening nodes. (Note that pipelines, arrays, and pyramids can be made very large, in principle to any size, because they are point-to-point structures with a relatively small number of links to each node.)

Some of the Problems and Opportunities of Point-to-Point Topologies

Point-to-point topologies pose several new and difficult problems:

Should the program be formulated and coded with the topology of the multi-computer that will execute it in mind, so that the program fits that topology as well as possible?

Should the program be mapped into the computer graph so that message-passing distances are minimized, and if so how?

How can the system efficiently find the best path for transmitting a message?

How can the system find an alternate path when necessary (e.g., because a node has crashed and is not working, or is busy transmitting a competing message, or refuses to interrupt whatever it is doing)?

How many of these burdens should be placed on the programmer's shoulders, as opposed to the operating system or/and the language?

Whether there are correct, or best, answers to these questions is today not at all clear. With the major exception of Occam (see below), operating systems for asynchronous networks have not been designed to take advantage of the program's actual structure of processes, and are extremely slow in transferring information between computers (see Chapter 5). The development of new integrated operating systems-languages-design tools that are appropriate for parallel multi-computers may well be the key to achieving programs that can be executed with speed and efficiency.

Point-to-Point Topologies Actually Built

Only a few of the point-to-point topologies have been examined and developed to the stage where one can judge that they have, potentially, the size and the power needed for large AI problems. These include chiefly N-cubes, trees, and trees with a few extra links. There appear to be a number of potentially more promising topologies waiting to be explored. These include augmented trees (e.g., where all leaf nodes are given as many links as the interior nodes), compounds of clusters, heterogeneous structures, and a variety of process-structured architectures.

THE NEED FOR MORE THAN A FEW DOZEN COMPUTERS IN THE NETWORK

Only a small handful of networks of any type have actually been built with more than 50 computers. The somewhat arbitrary number 50 was chosen for two reasons. First, given the difficulty in using an MIMD network efficiently, at least with today's operating systems and parallel algorithms, fewer than 50 computers will not give substantial increases in power and speed. Rarely, at least today, will 50 computers give 50-fold speedups. Indeed, what has become known as Minsky's conjecture (from Minsky and Papert, 1971) suggests that only logarithmic speedups can be obtained by a parallel computer.

This conjecture is clearly false, since there are many algorithms that, when properly mapped into and executed by an appropriate multi-computer, give linear speedups. These include local iterated operations (as when effected by a massively parallel array for image processing and computer vision), and also parallel converging/diverging operations (as when effected by a suitably structured pyramid or augmented tree). Many algorithms need global processing - which means that at least logarithmic time is needed to gather information. Appropriate process-structured hardware and multiprogramming can be used to meet that bound and to minimize the number of nonfunctional computers.

Inappropriate topologies can indeed give problems. A story about an MIT multi-computer that ignored the issue of mapping the program's structure appropriately into an appropriate hardware structure is that people were predicting that when 50 computers were finally achieved it would reach its break-even point. This term is used for a nuclear fusion reactor that reaches the point where it generates more fuel than it consumes. In this case, it meant the point where the 50 computers would finally have the throughput of one single computer!

With today's still primitive understanding of how to develop parallel algorithms and use them effectively, N computers will rarely give N-fold speedups. Therefore even a multi-computer with 50 nodes may well give only 20, 10, or 5 - or less than 1 - times the speedup of one node serving as a traditional single-CPU serial computer. Many thousands of nodes may well give only the power of a few hundred, or less.

If 50 processors give 10- or 20-fold improvements, 25 or 16 will not give improvements so large that they could not be accomplished on a somewhat more powerful single-CPU system (e.g., one Cray rather than a network of mini-Crays; one ELXSI rather than a network of 68000s), or with a not intolerable increase in time using just one node of the multi-computer. Anything much smaller than 50 will probably not give substantially more insight than can be got with 8 or 16, or with a simulation.

SYSTEMS WITH AT LEAST 50 COMPUTERS

The following briefly summarizes the large systems already built or nearing completion:

The partially synchronized systems include two pipelines (Sternberg's 1978 113 processor Cytocomputer; and Kimmel et al.'s 1985 256 processor MITE, an extended Cytocomputer), and one network with 128 or 256 independent processors but synchronized communication (Rieger et al.'s 1980 ZMOB).

By far the largest networks are the single-controller synchronized arrays (Duff's 1976 CLIP, Reddaway's 1978 DAP, Batcher's 1980 MPP, Pembrobe's 1984 GAPP, Hillis' 1985 Connection Machine) of 4,096 to 65,456 very simple (albeit general purpose) computers.

Several large systems have been built that attempt to give the programmer a pseudo-complete graph. These include the highly synchronized STARAN (Batcher, 1973) and ASPRO (anon., 1979) arrays, with 256 to 2,048 1-bit processors, and the shuffle-exchange based BBN Butterfly MIMD multi-computers (Crowther et al., 1985) with 32, 64, 128, or 256 computers (the largest actually built—for the Computer Vision group at the University of Rochester—has 128 computers). Other still larger systems are now being planned or are under construction; these will be described in the following chapters.

A few point-to-point linked MIMD systems have also been built. These will be examined later in this chapter. They include the 50 node Cm* cluster of clusters (Swan et al., 1977), the 45 and 65 node EMMA networks (Manara and Stringa, 1981), and the Cal Tech 64-computer Cosmic Cube (Seitz, 1985) - along with INTEL's commercial version (Warner, 1985), which is now being sold with 16, 32, 64, or 128 computers, and NCUBE's commercial version, which can be bought with up to 1,024 processors.

The possibilities for still other, completely new topologies are enormous, and intriguing. A variety of topologies have recently been identified as worthy of further exploration. So little is known about large graphs with thousands or millions of nodes that many more graphs with interesting sets of properties are almost certain to be discovered. This large variety of promising architectures with point-to-point topologies already designed, being designed, or feasible, will be examined in this and the next three chapters.

THE ENORMOUS VARIETY OF POSSIBLE ASYNCHRONOUS NETWORK STRUCTURES

It was only because of several simplifications made to the massively parallel arrays that it was economically feasible and possible to build them at all. These include their 1-bit processors, the single controller, and the near-neighbor connectivity between processors. Many of the specialized aspects of other more or less synchronized designs, like pipelines, systolic systems, and pyramids, are also to a great extent a function of cost - what is feasible, economical, and sensible.

If money and material resources were made available for multi-million dollar AI-oriented experimental multi-computers (actually, costing no more than the physical sciences-oriented super-computers, and only a small fraction of the "big science" expenditures of the sort made in physics) one could today build, for example, very large arrays or pyramids using a full-blown 32-bit computer, complete with its own controller, at each node. One could also build very large more or less asynchronous networks.

The power and economy that result from appropriately used specialized architectures usually also narrow their capabilities, and many people feel that the asynchronous MIMD networks are, potentially, substantially more general and more powerful. This they certainly are in theory, since each processor is much more powerful and independent, and entirely under its own control. However, some topologies appear to be far more powerful and/or more general purpose than others. It is important to consider MIMD networks' substantial extra hardware costs (which will continue to decrease as VLSI technologies improve) and the appreciable and often crushing delays from communications overheads (although these should lessen as systems improve).

A Brief Overview of Point-to-Point Topologies that Have Been Suggested

We have already looked at MIMD systems linked into a complete or pseudo-complete graph via a bus, crossbar, ring, star, or reconfiguring shuffle network. A large number of other MIMD networks have been described or designed, and proposed for possible implementation. These include variations on different kinds of clusters, linked clusters, snowflakes, lenses, N-cubes, arrays, trees, X-trees, Hyper-trees, and a variety of other graph structures (see Thurber, 1976; Stone, 1980; Hwang and Briggs, 1984; Uhr, 1984a).

Trees have been suggested by several researchers (e.g., Handler, 1975, 1977; Handler et al., 1979; Bentley and Kung, 1979; Browning, 1980; Mago, 1980; Stolfo and Shaw, 1982). Trees to which have been added additional links (usually at the leaves but often at a middle interior level) that really turn them into graphs with cycles have been investigated by a number of people (e.g., Despain and Patterson, 1978; Goodman and Sequin, 1981; Gemmar, 1982; Shaw, 1982, 1984).

N-cubes have been examined by Wittie, 1976, 1978; Sullivan et al., 1977; Preparata and Vuillemin, 1979; and Fox and Otto, 1984.

We will examine the most interesting of these in the next several chapters.

Asynchronous Point-to-Point Topologies Actually Built to Date

As summarized above, very few such networks have actually been built. This section describes those with at least 50 nodes whose construction has been completed and that have been running for some time.

THE CARNEGIE-MELLON CM•

Cm* was one of the earliest multi-computer actually constructed and evaluated. It was built using off-the-shelf computers (PDP-11/32s). These were linked via a bus into 10 clusters of 5, and these clusters were linked via a second global bus. The operating system handled communication relatively quickly among processors on the same primary bus, but quite slowly from cluster to cluster. Communication overhead was therefore so great that unless the programmer very carefully eliminated almost all message-passing, and tried to keep what remained as much as possible within the single cluster, degradations were severe. Apparently people have found Cm* so difficult to program and to use that it is no longer being used.

THE EMMA PROCESS-STRUCTURED NETWORKS

The EMMA system was developed by ELSAG in Genova, Italy (Manara and Stringa, 1981) in several versions, each specialized to the particular problem posed. The first system, built from about 45 microprocessors, was designed for the Italian Post Office, to handle the part of the address on an envelope that gives the city, province, and ZIP code, either typed or hand-printed. The second system, designed for the French Post Office to recognize the city district and street name as well as the city, province, and ZIP code, has 65 processors. The overall structures of both networks is similar: Local bus-linked clusters are organized into a hierarchical structure, much like Cm* (apparently each was designed without knowledge of the other). The image is processed in what is to some extent an assemblyline process-structured data-flow manner.

THE CAL TECH COSMIC CUBE, INTEL'S IPSC, AND OTHER N-CUBES

The hypercube multi-computers are of much higher dimensionality than the familiar 2-cube (square) and 3-cube (cube) - as Fig 10-1 begins to indicate.

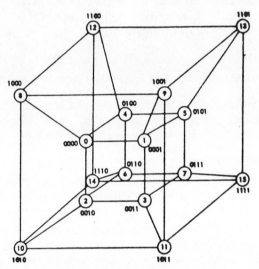

FIGURE 10-1. A hypercube (4-cube).
(*Source*: Tuazan, Peterson, Prill, and Liberman, 1985.)

INTEL is now marketing the iPSC (Warner, 1985), its commercial version of the California Institute of Technology's Cosmic Cube (Fox and Otto, 1984; Seitz, 1985). INTEL advertises that this is "the first commercial realization of computers employing concurrent processing on a large scale."

Systems with either 32, 64 or 128 processors are being offered, at prices ranging from $150,000 to $520,000. Peak performance estimates are 2.5 to 10 MFlops (million floating-point operations per second). In addition to the N-cube links, each processor is connected to a host that manages the system. Each computer has an INTEL 80286 CPU and 80287 floating-point processor plus 512KBytes of RAM memory. An INTEL 82586 local area network coprocessor controls each link, and passes messages via direct memory access communications channels. INTEL estimates that a 128-node iPSC costing $520,000 is 24 times as powerful as a $225,000 DEC VAX-11/780.

A new 32-node version of a hypercube is being built at the Jet Propulsion Lab (Peterson et al., 1985; Tuazan et al., 1985) using more powerful node processors capable of 2 MFlops and fiber optic devices for communication. They estimate that, on problems they have identified where they predict it can run with 80% efficiency, it will be the equivalent of a Cray-1. This system will be expandable to 1,024 nodes.

Several other companies are in the process of announcing and marketing commercial N-cubes. The NCUBE Corporation (see Mudge, 1985), has delivered systems that can be bought in 16, 32, 64, 128, 256, 512, and 1,024 computer versions. Each processor is capable of more than 1 MFLop. The smaller configurations can at any time be expanded to the full 1,024 size. Floating Point Systems is building a very powerful hypercube that uses Weitek processor chips in vector processors at each node. Host transputer chips and the OCCAM operating system are used to handle communications. INTEL is building a 15 MFlop vector processor board that can be added to each node of its N-cube.

A System for Building Multi-Computers: INMOS' Transputer Chip and Occam Language

The INMOS transputer chip (May and Shepherd, 1984; Whitby-Stevens, 1985) was developed to be a general purpose component in large multi-computers of a variety of different designs. [The name transputer was chosen to indicate that they are meant to serve as the primitive components of tomorrow's multi-computers in much the same way that transistors serve as primitive components of today's single-CPU computers.]

THE TRANSPUTER CHIP AS A BUILDING BLOCK FOR MULTI-COMPUTERS

Each transputer chip has a 32-bit computer capable of executing 10 million instructions per second, plus 2KBytes of memory, four 10Mbit per second buses for linking to other computers, and one 25MByte bus for linking to high speed memories and other resources. More powerful chips are planned for the future. Thus transputer chips should be very attractive components for building large multi-computer networks.

Each chip's 2KByte memory can be treated much like a high-speed on-chip cache, and its 25MBytes per second bus linked to a much larger main memory. Its four 10Mbit buses can be directly linked to four other transputers. This can be iterated out indefinitely - for example forming a 2-dimensional array. Transputer chips can be directly linked into any desired degree 4 graph. To build a multi-computer that is represented by a graph with nodes whose degree is greater than 4, simply fan out to the larger degree, either using transputer chips that can perform intermediate computations during the fan-in or fan-out process, or using much simpler trees of switches.

THE OCCAM LANGUAGE FOR DESIGNING AND PROGRAMMING TRANSPUTER NETWORKS

A vital part of the INMOS system is the Occam language (INMOS, 1984) for concurrent parallel processing. Occam serves several purposes: It can first be used as the language within which the design of a desired multi-computer is specified. After this computer has been built, by interlinking a set of transputer chips as specified, Occam can be used as the language for writing programs. (It will also be possible to write programs in C or in Pascal.)

Occam asks the programmer to handle message-passing as part of a generalized input-output statement, and to be aware of the structure of the program, and to map the program properly into the network's structure. This is almost certainly desirable. In several respects Occam asks programmers to do more work, but it also gives programmers tools that can help them develop more parallel algorithms, uncover and make use of parallel structures, and think in terms of parallel processes.

The net result is extremely efficient message-passing, on the order of a few microseconds - that is, literally three orders of magnitude faster than typical operating systems of the sort used in today's pseudo-complete graph and point-to-point linked MIMD networks with conventional message-passing operating systems. Thus Occam handles operating system and language functions together, in a well integrated manner.

TOWARD MORE POWERFUL ARCHITECTURES

An interesting bestiary is coming into being, of both structures built and structures proposed. Large amounts of study and simulation are needed to evaluate such systems, to determine how well they are likely to work. It is very time consuming and expensive to actually design one in detail and drum up funding to build even a 4 to 16 processor prototype, much less a system large enough to give a firm idea how well one much larger still, with many thousands or millions of processors, would work.

There appear to be two major types of networks that most researchers have been striving toward. The first are the networks that are structured to reflect the tasks/processes/algorithms they are designed to execute. These tend to be more or less specialized, if not special-purpose. (However, Chapter 13 will examine possibilities for general purpose architectures that can be used efficiently in a task/process/algorithm-structured way). The second are networks that attempt to be generally usable.

Rather than simply propose a topology, there are several criteria that might be used to decide what are good topologies and why, and to help direct the search to discover good new topologies. A great deal needs to be done to improve our understanding of how best to search for, discover, and evaluate possible topologies. We will examine some of these issues now.

Chapter Eleven

GOOD (AND A FEW OPTIMAL) TOPOLOGIES FOR MULTI-COMPUTERS

The possibilities for multi-computer topologies are potentially infinite, since they include all conceivable interconnections among (as technology continues to improve and grow cheaper) a continually growing number of processor components—that is, all possible finite graphs. But the problems are enormous. Today, people are just beginning to attack the very difficult problems of designing such multi-computers, developing parallel algorithms, programming and mapping these algorithms properly into the network, and coordinating the many different processors that are executing the same program so that they work with reasonable efficiency (see Uhr, 1984a, for an examination of these interrelated aspects of the problem).

CRITERIA FOR EVALUATING TOPOLOGIES

Not only the relatively small handful of graphs that have been built or proposed so far, but ANY N-node graph, can form the basis of an N-node multi-computer. It is not at all clear how to evaluate and choose from this enormous set of possible topologies.

Probably the most common criterion that researchers have suggested (see, for example, Wittie, 1976; Finkel and Solomon, 1977) is the minimization of the total graph's diameter (the longest shortest distance between processors) for a given degree (the maximum number of links to any node). A variant on this is the minimization of the average distance (Despain and Patterson, 1978; Goodman and Sequin, 1981). This gives graphs that are as "dense" as possible, in the sense that they pack more nodes within a given diameter and degree. Other criteria that have been suggested include the existence of simple algorithms for finding distant processors' addresses and alternate paths to them, connectivity (the minimum number of vertices that can be eliminated before the graph is disconnected), edge-connectivity (the minimum number of edges that can be eliminated before the graph is disconnected), and various symmetries.

Density will be used as the major criterion for evaluating topologies, because it is probably the most widely suggested and agreed on by computer architects, and because it has been the most widely used by graph theorists in directing the search for good topologies. Density is only one possible criterion; it is used here to point out that once we have chosen a set of desirable criteria we can use those criteria to search for and evaluate topologies. A whole set of good criteria should be used to guide the search, and much work needs to be done to arrive at a good set.

Topologies are often judged chiefly on the basis of the global density measure of diameter distance (possibly simply because that is the most common measure, and a good bit is known about it). Average distance is almost certainly preferable, or even a weighted average that emphasizes nearby distances, on the assumption that most interactions in a well structured program that is properly mapped into an appropriately structured network (Bokhari, 1981; Uhr, 1984a) will be between near neighbors, if not nearest neighbors. Table 11-1 gives a range of examples of different topologies of different sizes, showing their densities in terms of the number of processors for a given diameter and degree.

N-cubes are often characterized as dense and desirable from this point of view of packing nodes close together; the comment is typically made that the worst-case (diameter) distances are O(logN). As Table 11-1 demonstrates, N-cubes are actually rather poor. This may not be surprising when we consider that an N-cube is simply a 2^N array, that is, an N-dimensional array with 2 nodes in each dimension. An array with more than 2 nodes in each dimension is even poorer in terms of global density; but it is linked more usefully for local operations, and it does not need more and more interfaces.

In contrast, trees are, rather surprisingly, among the denser known topologies. Some augmented trees (e.g., Moore graphs, De Bruijn networks) are among the very densest known.

The diameter of arrays is O(N). The diameter of N-cubes is $O(\log_2 N)$. But the diameter of a large variety of other graphs is $O(\log_d N)$, where d might be 4, 8, 16, or any other realizable number of

Table 11-1. Example topologies: number of nodes at a given diameter and degree.

Topology	Degree	Diameter	Nodes
N-Cubes			
6-cube	6	6	64
8-cube	8	8	256
10-cube	10	10	1,024
11-cube	11	11	2,048
15-cube	15	15	32,768
20-cube	20	20	1,048,576
Arrays			
8x8 array	4	14	64
8x8 array	8	7	64
8x8x8 array	6	21	512
8x8x8 array	26	7	512
32x32 array	8	31	1,024
1024x1024 array	8	1,023	1,048,576
32x32x32x32 array	8	124	1,048,576
32x32x32x32 array	80	31	1,048,576
5x5x5x5x5	10	20	3,125
Toroidal Arrays			
8x8 array	4	6	64
8x8 array	8	3	64
8x8x8 array	6	9	512
8x8x8 array	26	3	512
32x32 array	8	15	1,024
1024x1024 array	8	511	1,048,576
32x32x32x32 array	8	60	1,048,576
32x32x32x32 array	80	15	1,048,576
5x5x5x5x5	10	10	3,125
Trees			
6-tree	6	6	156
10-tree	10	10	73,811
11-tree	11	10	122,222
11-tree	11	20	12,222,222,222

Augmented Trees
(? = Least possible reductions in diameter)

6-tree	6	?4	156
10-tree	10	?6	73,811
11-tree	11	?6	122,222
11-tree	11	?12	12,222,222,222

Reconfiguring Nets

lens	4	6	64
lens	4	9	384

Dense Topologies

Petersen (optimal)	3	2	10
Singleton (optimal)	7	2	50
N + 1 Singleton compound	8	5	2,550
DeBruijn augmented tree	8	8	65,536
DeBruijn augmented tree 10	10	9,765,625	
Bermond	compound	4	6
Bermond	compound	8	8
Bermond	compound	10	10
Bermond	compound	15	10

links to each node. As Table 11-1 indicates, the differences between $\log_2 N$ and $\log_d N$ $(2 < d < 15)$ can be enormous.

The lens (Finkel and Solomon, 1980b) is of interest for comparative purposes because it actually turns out to have the same topology as a reconfiguring network; it differs only in that each of the NlogN nodes is a computer rather than a switch. It is certainly not one of the best topologies from the point of view of density. It is interesting to note, however, that the reconfiguring nets are optimized to pass N pieces of information in parallel among N nodes, whereas density optimizes the network to pass one single piece of information between the most distant nodes. A lens is therefore optimized to send N messages in logN time-steps between two sets of N processors that are logN distance apart in the NlogN set of processors that form that lens. But note that the most distant pairs of processors in a lens built from computers—in contrast to a reconfiguring network built from switches—will be in two layers that are less than logN distances apart, and will define paths with more than logN steps (to move up, and then down, the tree that joins them).

Thus, a reconfiguring network is not especially good from the point of view of worst message-passing distances for single messages (density), and a lens is even poorer.

Possibly the most appropriate measure would optimize for passing the expected amount of information (number of messages) over the expected range of distances. Rather than pass information at either extreme, of one message or N messages, far more commonly a system will need to pass some number in between. The expected number of simultaneous messages will typically be small—usually greater than one, but far less than N.

OPTIMALLY DENSE GRAPHS, AND GRAPHS THAT APPROACH THE OPTIMAL

There is actually an upper bound, known as the Moore bound (Hoffman and Singleton, 1960; see Bondy and Murty, 1976), after E.F. Moore, who pointed out to Hoffman the minimum diameter of a graph with a given number of nodes and a given degree:

$$N_{(d,k)} = \frac{d(d-1)^2 - 2}{(d-2)} \quad (d > 2)$$

$$[N = \text{nodes}, \ d = \text{degree}, \ k = \text{diameter}]$$

This bound is probably most simply visualized by starting with a tree with d links from each and every node (except the leaves, which have 1 link, and the root, which can have either d or d-1 links), and with all leaves equi-distant from the root. The distance from any leaf to the root is the tree's radius. The diameter of such a tree is twice the radius, since for some pairs of leaves the only path goes through the root. The Moore bound states that if we add links until all leaves have d rather than 1 link, at best the diameter can be reduced to the radius. This is obviously the case: The distance between a leaf and the root must remain the same, since no new links can be added to interior nonleaf nodes.

Optimally Dense and Optimally Symmetric Moore Graphs

Hoffman and Singleton proved that only three nontrivial graphs can possibly achieve this Moore bound: one with 10 nodes, degree 3 and diameter 2, one with 50 nodes, degree 7, diameter 2, and one that may exist but has not yet been discovered, with 3250 nodes, degree 57, diameter 2. [The complete graphs and polygons are also Moore graphs. They are trivial and useless for our purposes, because they are the extreme cases. The complete graph guarantees the minimum diameter of 1 (and therefore increasingly and unrealizably high degree); the polygon guarantees the minimum degree of 2 (and therefore increasingly and unnavigatably high diameter). Therefore they pack relatively very few nodes within reasonably well balanced, buildable degree-diameter specifications. For example, a degree 10 complete graph has 11 nodes (but diameter 1); a diameter 10 ring has 19 nodes (but degree 2).]

THE OPTIMALLY DENSE 10-NODE PETERSEN GRAPH

Figure 11-1 shows the optimally dense Moore graph first discovered by Petersen (1891), with 10 nodes, degree 3, diameter 2. Note that there is only one graph shown in Figure 11-1, in a number of different guises. Each of the diagrams is an isomorphic redrawing of the same abstract graph. It seems of interest to show these alternate drawings because

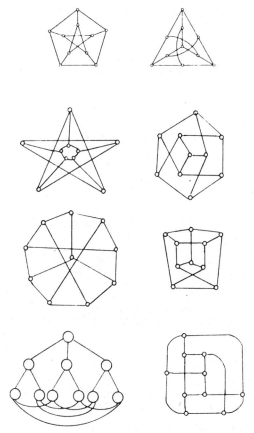

FIGURE 11-1. The 10(3,2) optimally dense and symmetric Petersen graph

they throw light on the graph's properties, and they also illustrate how difficult it is to know what even a very small graph really is like, and when two drawings of graphs are isomorphic. Indeed, a large number of additional very different looking drawings are possible.

A revealing way to look at a complex graph is to build it out of pipecleaners, or toothpicks and marshmallows. [Stretchable slinky-toy-like toothpicks would be useful, since one could then examine many non-linear transformations. Until such analog slinky-toothpicks are invented, it might be instructive to use computer displays that handle rotatable, deformable 3-dimensional graphics models.] A 3-dimensional construction exhibits the Petersen graph's ball-like character.

THE OPTIMALLY DENSE 50-NODE SINGLETON GRAPH

Figure 11-2 presents the only other known non-trivial Moore graph, the Singleton graph with 50 nodes, degree 7, diameter 2.

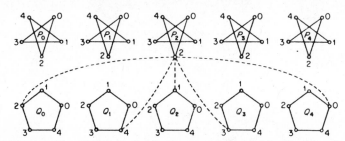

FIGURE 11-2. The 50(7,2) Optimally Dense and Symmetric Singleton Graph

POSSIBLE USES OF PETERSEN AND SINGLETON GRAPHS IN MULTI-COMPUTERS

Although 10(3,2) and 50(7,2) are relatively small, they are attractive candidates for several purposes.

Each might be used for a small network, treated either as a pseudo-complete graph or with its point-to-point topology actually taken advantage of.

Each might be used as a local cluster treated as a pseudo-complete graph in a larger network.

Each might be used to augment some other type of network (e.g., a pyramid or an array), or as part of a larger heterogeneous network.

Each might be compounded into a larger compound-of-compounds topology. For example, 51 copies of (7,2) will compound into a graph with 2550 nodes, degree 8 and diameter 5.

RELATIVELY DENSE GRAPHS

A number of other new, relatively dense graphs have been discovered in the past few years. Bermond et al. (1982, 1983, 1986) summarize recent results, and periodically updated results can be obtained directly from them.

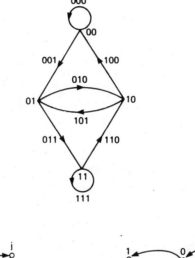

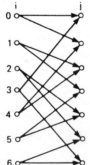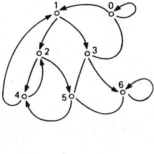

FIGURE 11-3. De Bruijn networks (shift registers), drawn in different ways.

The densest known graphs for more than a few thousand nodes were, until recently, the De Bruijn (1946) networks (Imase and Itoh, 1981; Samatham and Pradhan, 1984). De Bruijn graphs of degree 4 are widely used by Electrical Engineers and known as binary shift registers. Imase and Itoh in Japan independently rediscovered them and proved them to be denser than any previously discovered graphs.

Still denser graphs have recently been discovered by Bermond and his associates in France (Bermond et al., 1986).

As soon as the graph has more than a few hundred, or even a few dozen, nodes, the densest graphs discovered to date achieve only a small fraction of the Moore bound. There has been steady progress during the past few years in discovering interesting, and often densest-found-so-far, new graphs. It seems likely that these discoveries of still denser graphs will continue.

Density is certainly not the only, or even the best, criterion to use for networks. It would probably be most useful to examine not only the densest known graphs but also the much larger number of relatively dense graphs. The most important point is that whenever a criterion is agreed upon, or a set of criteria, graph theory can be a very powerful tool with which to search for good instances. The very rare Moore graphs, plus a few small graphs that come fairly close to the Moore bound, optimize connectivity, edge-connectivity, and symmetries as well as density. This suggests that trying to find improved graphs with respect to the Moore bound may also give graphs that are improved with respect to other criteria as well—although this whole gamut of improvements is not likely to be achieved until the graph is far closer to the Moore bound than are those discovered to date.

Since density is typically given as the primary criterion for choosing point-to-point linked networks, it is illuminating to compare some of the topologies that people have chosen with density in mind. It is interesting to note that even topologies that have been chosen because they were thought to be dense (e.g., N-cubes) are not nearly so dense as other topologies, including some that people wrongly think are much poorer (e.g., pure trees).

CLUSTERS, AND COMPOUNDS OF CLUSTERS

It will often be the case that a program can be coded and mapped into a topology so that each node needs to send information to and receive information from only a few other nodes. This might well be one of the primary goals for a "well structured" parallel program. In such cases multi-computers with small local clusters of processors that are compounded (possibly several times) into much larger total structures appear to be especially desirable.

Possibly the simplest structure of this sort uses a bus to link local clusters together, as done in Cm*, (Swan et al., 1977) and planned in Cedar (Kuck et al., 1983; see Chapter 13).

Arrays, Trees, and N-Cubes as Compounded Clusters

Probably the most widely used compounding operations are those that build arrays, N-cubes, and trees:

Arrays are built by taking a basic array (e.g., four nodes linked as a square) and tesselating it (joining it with other arrays, by appropriate linkings from one to the next).

Trees are built by taking a star (a root directly linked to leaves, for example, 2, 4, or 8) and replacing each leaf by the root of another star.

N-cubes are built by taking two N-1-cubes and linking corrresponding nodes.

These build compounds using many copies of one single structure. The result is a homogeneous total system that can be made increasingly large. That can be done by incrementing the size of the basic array, the number of leaves in the basic tree, or by compounding 2 N-1-cube used to form the N-cube. Therefore arrays and trees can be grown gradually; but N-cubes can only be successively doubled in size.

LAWRENCE BERKELEY PYRAMIDS OF CROSSBAR-LINKED CLUSTERS

Maples' 1985 MIDAS was designed to link 16 relatively large computers via a crossbar, and then link a number of these clusters at successively higher levels. In effect this builds a pyramid of independent processors. A one-cluster prototype has been built using processors roughly equivalent to a VAX/780. A proposed two-level system would have 128 processors at its base. A full 3-level system (see Figure 11-4) would have 1,024 processors at its base, or 1,097 in toto.

Large Classes of Potentially Interesting Compounded Structures

A number of graph theory operations have been found, some quite recently, that give interesting and potentially useful denser new compounds that should be explored. The following constructions give simply structured, relatively dense graphs.

Embed graphs (call them N-node clusters) of whatever structure with degree d and diameter k into a degree N, diameter j, M node graph, as follows:

Make $N + 1$ copies (including the original) of an N-node graph; embed one of these in each node of an $N + 1$-node complete graph

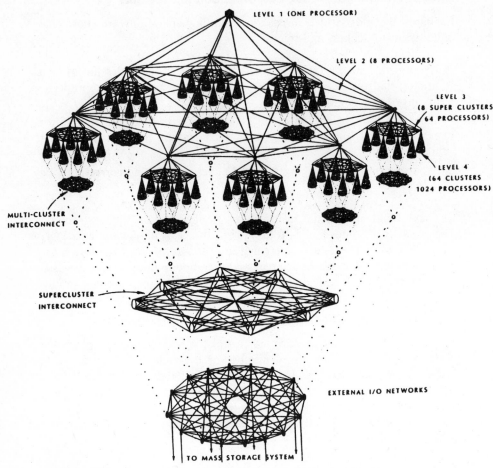

FIGURE 11-4.
(*Source*:   Maples, 1985.)

(which has degree N, diameter 1—hence has N links at each node); join each of the N nodes in the N-node graph to a different link coming into the complete graph node in which it is embedded. This results in a new graph with N(N + 1) nodes, degree d + 1, diameter 2k + 1, since one extra link has been added to each node and the diameter distance is the diameter within both of two copies plus 1, to move from one copy to the other.

Similarly, 2N copies can be made of an N-node graph, and each copy embedded in a different node of a complete bipartite graph with N nodes linked to N nodes, each copy using a different node to link to each of the N copies.

Embed any desired N node graph into each node of the M-node graph, joining each node of the N-node graph to a different link coming into that node.

There are a number of reasons why different graphs might be appropriate for different parts of the total structure. For example, the bipartite graph construction might link each embedded graph to graphs of a different type. This might be useful for programs that successively execute two different types of operations, for example, trying to match and fire a parallel set of productions or feature-detectors and then evaluating and combining results. P-partite graphs might be used as large parallel sets of P-stage pipelines, where each stage can compute a structure of N processes. Different types of resources can be scattered throughout any of these constructions, or/and concentrated in different regions.

There appears to be a great deal of freedom and plasticity in building compounds. One can use formal operations like compounding good structures with complete graphs or complete P-partite graphs, guided by formal criteria such as density. Or one can build good relatively small structures for particular types of processes, and then combine these into successively larger structures. Or one can use a judicious mixture of both, in an attempt to build process-structured but formally guided systems. Such procedures appear to offer new tools that may well lead to more powerful, general, efficient structures.

INCREASING, OR DECREASING, THE RATIO OF PROCESSOR TO MEMORY GATES

A widely accepted rule of thumb for conventional, single-CPU computers is that whatever amount of memory is provided, more would be better. Enough memory should be present so that the processor will always find what it needs, rather than be stopped and forced to wait while information is input from some very much slower store (e.g., a disk or tape). Today's massively parallel systems have moved in the direction of increasing the ratio of processor power to memory size. At the other extreme, a group of researchers at Princeton are exploring computers with a tremendously augmented memory.

Increasing the Ratio of Processor Gates to Memory Gates

In sharp contrast to conventional computers' many millions of bits of high-speed memory, the synchronous arrays like CLIP, MPP, and DAP have individual processors that each have very little memory and are in addition severely memory bound by the computers that surround them. Since processors do the work, whereas memory serves only to keep ready and waiting information that at some point will need to be worked on, in theory the higher the percentage of transistors used in processors as opposed to memory the more work the computer can do. Note that this will be true only if the transistors in the processors are themselves actually working, rather than sitting idle—as is the case with a CPU that contains a number of highly optimized special-purpose processors but that uses them only one at a time.

There appear to be two general points of view among people developing asynchronous networks. Some feel that each computer should be as powerful as possible. They argue that this will allow for more efficient linkings and operating systems, and takes advantage of the powerful designs of today's conventional supercomputers. Others feel that systems should be designed so that in a few years very large numbers of computers can be used. They argue that this takes advantage of the modular properties of VLSI technologies. The first group tends to use the traditional ratio of memory to processor gates. The second group tends, though not nearly so radically as the designers of the synchronous arrays, to use a smaller memory for each computer than would be found in a traditional design.

It seems likely that the amount of memory needed is primarily a function of the problem (i.e., the amount of information that must be processed, and the complexity of the processes in the sense of the amount of intermediate information they generate) rather than of the size, speed, and power of the processor. Therefore to the extent that a multi-computer distributes the load of processing relatively equally among its many processors, each processor's memory demands might well go down commensurately.

Princeton's Potentially Infinite Massive Memory Machine

The Princeton machine is a deliberate attempt to explore the remaining extreme. Rather than work toward designs that make effective use of a larger percent of gates in processors, Richard Lipton and associates (Garcia-Molina et al., 1984) are investigating what might be gained by drastically increasing the size of main memory, to 10^{10} or more bytes for a 1 to 10 MIP processor. Rather than put 99.99% of the computer's gates into memory, as in today's conventional computers, they are suggesting that 99.999999. . .% of the gates be in memory. They point out that memory is very cheap, and is rapidly getting cheaper (although they tend to ignore that this is also the case for processors). They also point out that when a lot of information is needed, as is frequently the case for an artificial intelligence program, things become much simpler and much faster if all that information can be stored in the main memory to which the processor has direct and fast access.

A program that must deal with a semantic memory network is an especially appropriate example. Today's programs can handle only small, toy networks, and even these may well be stored on auxilliary disks and are constantly rolled into and out of main memory, a small piece at a time. A great deal of hardware is typically devoted to this process, in the form of dedicated input-output processors. There are also major problems with the operating system and programming language, which must offer the programmer simple ways to deal with a large enough virtual memory to contain the whole net. The operating system must constantly worry about rolling the needed parts in and out. Often the operating system will do rather poorly, with increasing amounts of time spent in swapping and waiting. Sometimes, the system will thrash about with little if any useful work done. All this would be eliminated if the entire body of information could simply be put into main memory, once and for all.

This the Princeton group is beginning to explore.

Chapter Twelve

TOWARD VERY LARGE MIMD NETWORKS WITH POTENTIALLY MILLIONS OF COMPUTERS

To achieve massively parallel speedups on very large problems, massive numbers of computers are almost certainly needed. This is especially true to the extent that the multi-computer is neither task/process/algorithm-structured nor synchronized. It seems unlikely that N computers will give anything close to N times the speed or power of one computer unless hardware architecture and task/process/algorithm are highly compatible with one another. The major speedups needed for real time execution of powerful nontoy AI programs may well come only when systems are achieved with at least many thousands, or millions, of very powerful nodes. The processes that an intelligent system must execute are indeed large, as is the human brain—our one and only existence proof that they can be accomplished.

This chapter focuses on architectures with, potentially, extremely large numbers of independent computers.

N-CUBE BASED SYSTEMS

Several researchers have proposed building "mega-micro networks" (Wittie, 1976) containing millions of computers each.

SUNY and Columbia N-Cube Networks

Wittie (1976, 1978) and Sullivan et al. (1977) were among the first to point out that such enormous sizes were soon to become technologically feasible, and are desirable for a variety of important applications (e.g., weather prediction, wind tunnel modeling, simulations of neural networks, artificial intelligence, pattern perception). Both proposed what are essentially N-cube designs. Wittie's Micronet is a 20-cube; Sullivan's system is a 17-cube with each node a cluster of 8 computers. Wittie designed and built a 16-computer prototype system; Sullivan's CHoPP has, apparently, not yet been started.

More recently, Wittie has lowered his sights. He feels (personal communication) that at most a few thousand computers will be realistically feasible. This is chiefly because of the complexity of each of the traditional computers he would use were he to build a very large system, and of a second computer (that handles message-passing functions) with which each is paired. For Wittie anticipates that no matter how high the density one can achieve on a single chip, at most only one processor plus message-passing coprocessor and memory could be placed on each chip. A million chips would make too large a system to build.

NEWER, AND OLDER, N-CUBES

Several newer and potentially larger systems have recently been completed. One, called a "Connection Machine," built at Thinking Machines Corp., an MIT spin-off, will be described in a later section, since it is a hybrid system whose architecture is a good bit more complex than just (sic!) a simple N-cube. Others are the Cal Tech Cosmic Cube and the related commercial systems described in Chapter 10.

It is interesting, and curious, to note that one of the first microcomputer companies, IMSAI (now bankrupt) announced around 1979, in a number of full-page ads, an N-cube built with their 8080-class 8-bit computer that could be bought in 16, 64, and 256 processor versions for roughly $1,000 per computer. It appears that none of these were ever sold. It is not clear what type of operating system or programming language was used, or planned, or what types of programs could be run.

N-Cubes Compared with Other Topologies in Terms of Density

Since N-cubes have logarithmic diameters, they are often characterized as dense. But there are major differences, as indicated in Table 11-1 above, among different structures with logarithmic diameters. Consider the following:

A 10-cube has 1,024 nodes, degree 10 and diameter 10. [A 5^5 toroidal array has 3,125 nodes, degree 10, diameter 10.] In contrast, a pure tree of degree 10 and diameter 10 has 10x9x9x9x9 = 65,610 nodes in its leaves, and 73,711 nodes in toto! This means that the tree with only one link to each of its leaves (and most of the nodes in a tree are leaves) has over 70 times as many nodes as an N-cube. People often comment that reducing diameter to O(logN) is the best one can hope to do; hence some particular O(logN) graph (e.g., the N-cube) is optimal. These comparisons make clear how great the differences can be, depending on whether $\log_N$ is, say, $\log_2$ or $\log_9$. The differences continue to grow as the number of nodes in the multi-computer network is increased, hence the diameter grows.

Even more striking, the Moore bound for a degree 10 diameter 10 graph is 4,358,480,501.

It seems likely that with good augmentations to the leaves of a tree the diameter can be reduced to the radius plus 1 or 2 or a few. If we assume, conservatively, that an augmented tree of diameter 10 has 7 plies, rather than the 5 plies in a pure tree, this degree 10, diameter 10 augmented tree will have 10x9x9x9x9x9x9 = 65,610x81 = 5,314,410 nodes in its leaves alone! And the degree 10 diameter 10 Bermond, Delorme, and Quisquater (1983) graph (possibly the densest diameter 10 degree 10 graph discovered to date) has 14,981,200 nodes. It is interesting to note that until Imase and Itoh discovered the De Bruijn graphs' good densities the densest known degree 10 diameter 10 graph had only 170,685 nodes (Storwick, 1970)—little more than twice as many as a pure tree!

Consider a second comparison of interest: A degree 8 diameter 8 8-cube has 256 nodes. The compound got by linking 51 copies of the degree 7 diameter 2 50-node Singleton graph has 2550 nodes, degree 8, diameter 5. It thus has roughly 10 times as many nodes, the same degree, and only 5/8ths the diameter. In addition, it is a highly symmetric compound of highly symmetric structures, and therefore an attractive candidate for mapping modularized programs into local structures.

It does not appear that repeated compounding is a good idea from the point of view of density. One compounding of a carefully chosen good graph can give good results, but the resulting compound is not as good as the original. Each successive compounding appears to further degrade the resulting graph. Therefore, an N-cube, which is actually the result of N compounds—and a redundant compounding operation at that—is not likely to be very dense.

It is important to point out that N-cubes have several virtues of a different sort: It is very easy to compute paths between pairs of nodes, and to compute a new alternate path when a barrier is reached. But many other graphs have simple routing schemes, and table lookup will often be the fastest and most efficient procedure. Many (but not all) arrays can be mapped efficiently into an N-cube.

ARRAY-BASED SYSTEMS

David Schaefer and James Strong (1977) proposed an optical computer made from fiber optics with 10,000 processors in each of 10,000 bundles. This proved to be technologically unfeasible for the state of the art at that time; but it led to the design and construction of the MPP. More recently Schaefer (1979) proposed that a next generation super-MPP might be built using microelectronics that contained a large MPP array of 1-bit computers on a single wafer, and a whole stack of wafers forming a 3-dimensional multi-computer. Thus, for example, 100 wafers might be used to pipeline images through successive 128-by-128 or larger arrays.

Etchells et al., 1981, are developing a very interesting system that will use 3-Dimensional stacked wafers. Each wafer will have an array of processor, input-output hardware, or memory modules. An array of complete computers is built by stacking 5 or 10 of these modules.

N-Dimensional Arrays and Density

The parallel arrays that have been built to date have generally been 2 dimensional, but arrays can be built of any dimensionality. In particular, a 3-dimensional array might well be an appropriate design for handling 3-dimensional near-neighbor operations, as when modeling a 3-dimensional section of the environment—for example, to predict the weather, design airplanes and boats, or simulate an environment as a space of objects with which an AI program might interact. A very interesting design of this sort was developed by Cyre et al., 1977. But unfortunately it was never funded.

An array might well have each dimension a different size. For example, a 600-by-1000 array would conveniently handle rectangular images of the sort usually taken by cameras; a 10,000-by-50-by-50 array might be used to model a basin of fluid through which a simulated boat might move. However, almost all arrays built or designed to date have been N^D arrays, where each of the D dimensions has the same N (number of processors—that is, the same length).

Arrays are especially rich in links to nearby nodes, and especially good at local operations. Each internal node has 2^D square, or (when D > 1) $3^D - 1$ square + diagonal links. [Unless nodes on the surface are linked to nodes on the opposite surface they have fewer links, down to the minimum of D links for corner nodes.] A regular 2-dimensional toroidal array (where all nodes have been made interior, by linking nodes at opposite edges, and diameter has been cut in half) links each cell to its 4 square or its 8 square + diagonal neighbors. A 3-dimensional array links each cell to its 6 square or its 26 square + diagonal neighbors.

Global distances (diameter) and global density are poor in arrays. The diameter of a square-linked array is DN-1. Thus the greater the length of each dimension, the greater the diameter. The diameter of a square + diagonal-linked array is N-1; but its degree quickly grows much greater.

For example, a 10^6-array (with 10 nodes in each of its 6 dimensions) will have a million nodes, and a diameter of 54 and a degree of 12. Alternately diameter can be kept down, but at the heavy price of adding dimensions and diagonal links in every dimension. For example, 729 square + diagonal links will reduce the diameter of the 10^6-array from 59 to 9. Diameter could be reduced even further, but at the heavy price of adding still more links to more distant nodes.

Space (Number of Processors) vs. Time (Sequence of Instructions) Trade-Offs

Consider situations when it is possible and desirable to execute a whole array (or other graph structure) of processes at the same time.

A 2-dimensional array of processors can always simulate a 3-dimensional array, by iterating serially, handling one of the third dimension's 2-dimensional planes at a time, to process a 3-dimensional array of information stored in its memories. Thus processors can be eliminated, at the cost of using the same processors over and over again—that is, at the cost of converting an N-way parallel operation into a serial operation that takes O(N) more time. However, enough memory will still be needed to store the entire 3-dimensional array (or else time must be taken to input each piece of the array when it is needed). Now an operation that takes one instruction cycle for a 3-dimensional L by M by N array of processors will take kL instruction cycles for an M by N array of processors (k is a small constant for indexing memory and testing for the end of loops).

Similarly a 1-dimensional N-processor array can be used to scan iteratively over the 3-dimensional array in kLM instruction cycles. And the familiar single-CPU (0-dimension array) Von Neumann computer will take kLMN instruction cycles. In general, an

$$N_1 \text{ by } N_2 \ \cdots \ \text{by} \ \cdots \ N_i$$

array can be scanned over by the subarray

$$N_1 \text{ by } N_2 \cdots \text{ by } \cdots N_i \quad \{j \leq i\}$$

in $O(N^{i-j})$ time.

More generally, any array can be simulated by any subarray that scans over it. This is most efficiently done when each dimension in the large array can be factored into integers, each of which is a different dimension of the subarray. Otherwise some of the nodes in the scanning graph will be idle with no nodes to simulate.

Most generally, any graph can be scanned over by any subgraph(s) into which the large graph can be decomposed.

The two extreme cases are the most familiar. When the multi-computer that scans is an array or arbitrary graph that is isomorphic to the array (or arbitrary graph) being scanned, the operation will take one instruction cycle. This is the case of a hardware array exactly the size of the array of information it processes. At the other extreme, when only one single node is used to scan over the entire array or arbitrary graph, a sequence of $O(N)$ (N is the total number of nodes) instructions is needed. This is the case of the conventional single-CPU computer.

An in-between case will be efficient only when the array (or graph) to be scanned can be decomposed so that the scanning array (or graph) can be successively matched to it with no (or little) waste. Thus the 1-node Von Neumann computer is guaranteed to be efficient with space (i.e., computer hardware)—ignoring the often appreciable and important overheads in indexing and testing for boundaries. And it is also therefore guaranteed to be the slowest. The more nodes in the scanning graph the more possibilities for speedups. But the scanning graph must be able to decompose the large graph with reasonably little waste. Otherwise the speedups will be less than optimal.

This appears to be feasible for the many situations where arrays are used to process arrays, and the exact size of the array is unimportant so long as the body of information being processed contains sufficient detail (for perception, this means that it resolves all the features needed to recognize objects). It is not clear whether arbitrary graphs (e.g., for semantic memory networks) can be made regular enough so that structures of computers that decompose them can fruitfully be used to process them.

Note that the fixed word-size of a 16-bit, 32-bit, 36-bit, or 64-bit computer presents a similar dilemma. These are arbitrary, rigidifying numbers, but they have been chosen to be as compatible as possible with the sizes of sets of information to be processed; and, circularly, the sizes of sets of information are similarly chosen to fit these numbers. A

1-bit processor that did everything in bit-serial mode would be the most efficient in hardware/space but the most inefficient and slowest in time.

TREE-BASED SYSTEMS

Trees—that is, pure trees in the graph theory sense, with no cycles— have several major advantages, and disadvantages. They are reasonably dense—far from the densest, but far better than, for example, N-cubes. They have a simple planar topology that packs reasonably well onto a VLSI chip. They are very good for converging and combining information, moving up the tree, and for diverging and broadcasting information, moving down the tree. However, the tree's single root node can be a fatal bottleneck when information is re-arranged rather than reduced, as in sorting. When information is to be sent between random pairs of nodes, each step moving up the tree brings increasingly heavy traffic.

Fat-Trees to Eliminate Tree Bottlenecks

Leiserson (1985) points out that this can be overcome by using "fat-trees," where successively more message-passing bandwidth is used moving toward the tree's root.

More generally, wherever the load is greater (whether of messages, items to be stored in memory, or processes to be executed) greater bandwidth can be introduced by enlarging the relevant resource. On the other hand, it is probably true that trees should be used in such a way that communication is usually as local as possible.

Leiserson further proves that an N-node fat-tree (but not 2-dimensional arrays or ordinary trees) can simulate any other N-node structure of the same volume in, at worst, $O(\log_3 N)$ time. This proof follows from the fact that a graph can be successively cut and decomposed, thus giving a binary tree. It seems likely that to speed up message-passing the pieces of the decomposed graph could then be rearranged into other, more efficient structures, and the fat-tree could be augmented with additional links.

The Columbia Dado and Non-Von Trees

David Shaw (1982, 1984, 1986) has described the ultimate version of his Non-Von multi-computer as consisting of millions of computers. The general architecture of the Non-Von is an SIMD binary tree whose size will be determined by the number of computers (each with an 8-bit processor and a relatively small amount, a few hundred bits, of memory) that can be fabricated onto a single chip. Nodes at an intermediate ply of the tree are linked laterally to a control processor. A prototype system with 63 processors has been built out of off-the-shelf components. Input-output to and from the chip will be through the root of each of several local trees. Thus, for example, if a binary tree of $1 + 2 + 4 + 8 + 16 + 32$ computers were put on a single chip, one piece of information could be broadcast to any one, two, or all, of the processors in 6 cycles, while different pieces of information could be sent to each of the 63 processors in 63 cycles.

The original motivation for the Non-Von was to handle very large databases, but it is now being developed as a general purpose AI system. Estimated timings on a variety of simple basic algorithms for image processing (Ibrahim, 1984), access to large databases (Hillyer, Shaw and Nigam, 1984), and production systems (Hillyer and Shaw, 1986), indicate (Shaw, 1985) that Non-Von should perform better, in terms of speed and cost, than either a traditional computer like a VAX or a multi-computer that has been specialized for a particular task.

Note that the Non-Von's binary tree can to some extent be used for pyramid processes, by inputing the image to the appropriate set of leaves (taking care that each 2-by-2 set of grandchildren of a single grandparent contains the pixel from the appropriate cell in a 2-by-2 subarray) and then processing and converging in two steps, first to two parents, then to one grandparent. This appears to have a major, and probably fatal, drawback in that there is no overlap. This means that information can fall between the cracks, and, because of trivially small displacements from one image to another, simple regions can be assessed only by moving information all the way up to the pyramid's apex.

A new Non-Von is planned (Shaw, personal communication) with a 64-by-64 array of processors at the base of an array-augmented tree that should alleviate some of these problems. Each of the processors will be linked via a 1-bit line to its nearest neighbors.

Salvatore Stolfo, also at Columbia, is designing and building a similar structure, but one that is a pure binary tree, called DADO (Stolfo and Shaw, 1982; Ishida and Stolfo, 1985). DADO is being designed as a special-purpose computer to handle expert production systems. Each DADO processor is planned to be a good deal more powerful than the Non-Von processor. A module of 63 processors is fabricated on an individual board that can be used to build larger systems. Arrangements have been made to produce and sell DADO systems commercially.

NETL, AUGMENTED TREES, SEMANTIC MEMORY NETWORKS, AND CONNECTION MACHINES

Danny Hillis (1981) has proposed "Connection Machines" with millions of computers. These systems appear to have originally been conceived as an attempt to handle a wide range of problems, including image processing, computer vision, and especially semantic memory searches of the sort Fahlman's (1979, 1980) NETL is designed to handle.

NETL, a Hardware Embodiment of a Semantic Memory Network

Fahlman's conception of NETL is basically a direct embodiment of a semantic memory network like Quillian's (1968) much earlier system. Each node is linked to several neighbor nodes, which in turn are linked to several neighbor nodes, and so on.

Therefore a system's effective distances between pairs of nodes will depend on the number of links from each node and on the ability of the system to find the shortest path between nodes. To the extent that the system has local cycles (alternate paths between pairs of nearby nodes) density decreases and distances will grow greater, as in an array. If there were no cycles (i.e., if each pair of nodes had only one path between them), the system would fan out like a tree.

Augmented Trees, to Realize Semantic Memory Nets

Consider a tree. If, for example, each node had 11 links, then 1,222,222 nodes could be linked together, with the greatest distance between any pair of them (the diameter of the tree) only 12. If each node had 101 links the diameter would be reduced to 6; if each node had 10,001 links (a typical number for the dendrites linking a single neuron to its environment) a system of diameter 6 would have 1,222,222,222,222 nodes.

However, when leaves are judiciously linked, with the purpose of reducing the distances between most distant nodes, hence reducing diameter, a tree can be markedly improved upon, so that its diameter is reduced to its radius (in the rare case of the Moore Graphs, see Chapter 11), or to radius + k (where k is often 1 or 2). Therefore extra links can be used to draw together a tree's leaves, giving augmented trees (e.g., the fan-out/fan-in graphs of the sort to be described in Chapters 16-18). This, as we shall see, gives one of the most attractive topologies for a variety of semantic memory and problem-solving tasks.

SUGGESTED HARDWARE NETWORK REALIZATIONS OF NETL

Fahlman suggested possible hardware implementations for NETL. To create links he suggested one might use a miniaturized robot-like wire-wrap device, or develop new technologies that would use "some sort of electrolytic solution by establishing a current between the two terminals to be connected. . . a long thin 'whisker' will grow along the path of least resistance."(Fahlman, 1979). He realized that such solutions are unlikely to be feasible in the foreseeable future, and instead suggested using a very large crossbar or, possibly, clusters of those processors that must interact, linked as appropriate to other clusters. Thus when it comes to the problem of an actual hardware implementation, NETL appears to point vaguely in the direction of an unrealizably large crossbar or nerve-network-like topology.

The Heterogeneous Connection Machines

The Connection Machine (Hillis, 1981) was apparently originally motivated by a desire to implement a system capable of handling NETL-like semantic memory networks. Two versions of the Connection Machine concept are presently being developed—one at MIT (Kahle, 1982; Flynn, 1982; Christman, 1984), the other at Thinking Machines Corp., (Hillis, 1985; anon., 1985).

THE THINKING MACHINE CORP. (TMC) N-CUBE-LINKED CONNECTION MACHINE

The TMC version of a full Connection Machine (anon., 1985) is intended to be a 1,024 by 1,024 array (much like an MPP) that is also linked into a 14-cube. Each chip contains 64 1-bit processors, with each chip forming one node of the 14-cube. Processors on each chip are linked into a 6-cube, completing the full 20-cube. Processors are also linked to 4 neighbor processors, forming a directly linked array, much like the MPP or DAP systems. Note that smaller systems can be designed, with 8, 16 or 32 processors on each chip and an N-cube where N might be any small integer up to 14.

The system that has actually been built for sale commercially (anon., 1985; Hillis, 1985) has 64K synchronized SIMD 1-bit processors, each with 4K bits of memory. The paper points out that it can be reconfigured to full size, 1,000K, in the standard software manner, by assigning 64 "virtual processors" to each actual hardware processor (i.e., having each processor iterate through 64 sets of data). That would reduce memory for each virtual processor to 64 bits. All processors are linked into a 4-connected array and also into a 12-cube over which a "router" sends messages of potentially any length. Each chip has 16 processors plus one router processor that handles communication via the N-cube links.

"The communications network represents most of the cost of the machine, . . . and most of the performance limitations." (Hillis, 1985, p. 54). Each router can receive up to 12 messages, and also send up to 12 messages, during one "routing cycle" that serially steps through the 12 links to each node. This appears to mean that the system takes at least 144 serial information-passing steps during its message-passing phase. When more than one message is sent over a single wire, up to 7 can be buffered, to be sent in subsequent routing cycles. A store instruction sends a message. When more than one message is to be stored into the same location a "store-with-add" instruction sums them.

A good amount of hardware appears to be dedicated to handling possible contention among messages. For example (anon., 1985), "if there is too much traffic along a particular path, however, some messages will take their routing steps in a different order, thus guiding them along alternate paths . . . . If the chip's buffer space still fills, it refers messages to neighboring chips." As a result, "router throughput has been measured at 3 gigabits per second under heavy load" (when all 64K processors repeatedly sent 32-bit messages to random destinations).

The paper claims that the system "reconfigures itself to match the natural structure of applications exactly, while providing computing power in excess of 1000 MIPS. Unique among parallel architectures, the system allows the connections among its processors to be altered at will." The paper claims: "FFT's and trees: two more problem topologies that can be matched exactly to the Connection Machine system. . . . Artificial intelligence, natural language processing, and knowledge representation . . . accommodated with equal ease, because all linkages are software controlled."

These are strong claims for N-cube linkage; and if they apply to the Connection Machine they also apply to other N-cube-based systems, such as Cal Tech/Intel's and NCUBE's. Even more important, any connected graph can be reconfigured in the manner described to match any other structure. The crucial question is whether this can be done quickly and efficiently. Very little is known about what graphs programmers might want to map into architectures in this way, and what topologies can accept them most efficiently.

COMBINING ARRAYS WITH N-CUBES OR OTHER TOPOLOGIES

The one type of graph that maps best into an N-Cube is an array (including a 1-dimensional pipelining array), but not all arrays will map efficiently. For example, consider mapping a 15x9x13 array into a 12-

cube. In the case of the Connection Machine, the N-Cube links combined with the array connectivity may well be redundant for these purposes. N-cubes can indeed handle many arrays—although it seems likely that the simpler array design is substantially cheaper. Arrays indeed need to be augmented, as indicated in Chapter 9—but why use an N-cube? Polymorphic arrays (Fiat and Shamir, 1984), fat-trees (Leiserson, 1985), reconfiguring networks, trees, pyramids, De Bruijn graphs (Imase and Itoh, 1981) and other augmented trees, and good compounds of good compounds all appear to be attractive alternatives in terms of both embedding a wide variety of structures of processes into the hardware array and global message-passing.

The N-Cube is attractive in its ability to route and reroute messages in relatively straightforward ways, but it is rather poor in terms of density—that is, the distances over which messages must be sent. The routing algorithm and attendant hardware enhancements may well give major speedups, but they have not been well enough described or benchmarked to judge. In any case, they can probably better be used with other, denser topologies.

THE MiT RECONFIGURING NETWORK-LINKED CONNECTION MACHINE

In contrast to the TMC Connection Machine, the MIT design links chips via an NlogN reconfiguring network rather than an N-cube. [A system with 256K processors has been planned, but it is not clear whether this design will actually be implemented in hardware.] This more general topology may well be an improvement, since it is not at all clear whether the key AI problems map efficiently into an N-cube.

An N-cube can be used to permute data, with one pass through the N-cube serving as the equivalent to one of the logN stages in a reconfiguring network (see Siegel, 1984). However the TMC Connection Machine would need 144 cycles to move once through the N-Cube and effect one shuffle exchange, and several such cycles to complete more complex permutations. The NlogN reconfiguring network needs more switches, but fewer links to each switch. It would be very instructive to see analyses and comparisons of these and other structures. Hillis' book mentions a variety of other possibilities (crossbars, rings, trees, fat-trees, De Bruijn networks, Moore graphs, random nets); but it does not explain why the N-Cube was chosen.

Closely Related Systems

Several earlier systems bear a striking resemblance to the Connection Machines.

SULLIVAN'S CHOPP, AN N-CUBE WITH LOCAL CLUSTERS

It is interesting to note the similarity between the Connection Machine and Sullivan's 1977 proposal for a 17-cube with a cluster of 8 computers at each node. Sullivan envisioned substantially more powerful, completely independent computers in an MIMD system.

CUBE-CONNECTED CYCLES

Another similar design is Preparata and Vuillemin's 1979 cube-connected cycle. This embeds an N-node cycle (i.e., a polygon, or ring) into an N-cube, with each node in the cycle joined to a different one of the N links going into the original node in the cube. Thus, it is a specific instance of embedding N-node graphs into an N-degree graph, as described in Chapter 11. The cycle can be linked very effectively as a pipeline or vector processor, but in terms of density almost any other embedded graph would be an improvement.

EMBEDDING OTHER POSSIBLE GRAPHS INTO THE N-CUBE'S NODES

Rather than a cycle, one might use any small graph with at least N nodes, joining a different one to each of the N links to other nodes in the N-cube. For example, the 10-node Petersen graph reduces worst-case distances in a 10-cube connected 10-cycle from 28 to 14.

Using Connection Machines as Arrays for Vision or Trees for Memory Search

The intention appears to be to use Connection Machines to handle semantic memory nets and, also, language understanding, computer vision, and the general AI problem.

The Connection Machine designers expect to use the system as a large 1,024-by-1,024 array of 1-bit processors for computer vision and image processing. When used in this way, a Connection Machine will be almost identical to a large CLIP, DAP or MPP. The additional N-cube links reduce global distances to some extent; but trees, pyramids, and a variety of other networks appear to be more appropriate for that task. The DAP row and column highways and the MPP's buffer memories and parallel I-O may well be faster and more cost-effective.

For language understanding and semantic memory searches the Connection Machine designers appear to contemplate using tree-like processes to spread and search out into the large memory. But it is not clear how well such tree-like processing could be mapped into the N-cube. Although a tree can be embedded into any connected graph (trivially: simply break links until all cycles are eliminated, but never eliminate all paths to a node; more powerfully: do this in a way that results in the minimal spanning tree, that is, the tree with the fewest edges), the N-cube embedded tree is not very well balanced.

Chapter Thirteen

TOWARD MORE GENERALLY USABLE AND/OR MORE ALGORITHM-STRUCTURED ARCHITECTURES

This chapter examines several possibilities for massively parallel multi-computers that appear to be especially promising, yet to date have been explored relatively little:

A. Partial reconfiguring might be effected by relatively small and limited sets of switches, so that the hardware can be re-structured, under program control, from one desirable topology to another.

B. True data-flow networks might be constructed, and problems flowed through them—much as information appears to flow through and be transformed by the brain of intelligent living systems.

C. A variety of new heterogeneous systems might be designed and built, where different regions of the total network have different topologies, each appropriate for different purposes.

These several rather disparate approaches are examined in the same chapter for two reasons:

1. They can fruitfully be combined together, to further improve the system.

2. They are all relatively speculative. Very little is known about each, and virtually no research has been done on each.

A fourth major possibility for powerful new designs lies in the discovery of good new topologies, such as the graphs examined in Chapter 11, which more closely approach the general purpose and optimal with respect to whatever set of criteria are deemed important. This in turn entails the development of a good set of criteria.

All of these issues could benefit substantially from much larger amounts of good research.

RECONFIGURING SWITCHES TO ENRICH STRUCTURES

Reconfiguring switches can potentially play a number of very important purposes, in addition to shuffling data between two sets of nodes.

Local, Partial Reconfiguring

Reconfiguring networks have primarily been used in NlogN banks of switches, to allow N pieces of information to be shuffled around among N major components (computers, processors, memories), as described in Chapter 6. Much smaller sets of switches can also be interspersed, at a variety of levels, to effect some partial reconfiguration.

RECONFIGURING AN ARRAY TO BE EITHER SQUARE OR HEXAGONAL

A simple example is the CLIP array, which can be reconfigured, under programmer control, so that each cell is directly linked to either 8 square + diagonal neighbors or 6 hexagonal neighbors. This turns out to be very easy to do, since a square array becomes a hexagonal array if the odd rows are shifted by half a column, as shown in Figure 13-2(a).

RECONFIGURING ONE TOPOLOGY TO ANOTHER

There are several possibilities for using relatively small numbers of switches to reconfigure from one desirable topology to another. For example, Sandon (1985) has proposed an implementation of a 3-dimensional pyramid by configuring and reconfiguring a 2-dimensional array.

Another interesting example is a tree that can be reconfigured into an array, as shown in Figure 13-2(b). (Note that in VLSI chips trees are often embedded into square arrays, using a simpler, more regular but more space-consuming design.)

It is of great interest to find larger sets of important topologies that can be embedded into one another with minimal reconfiguring.

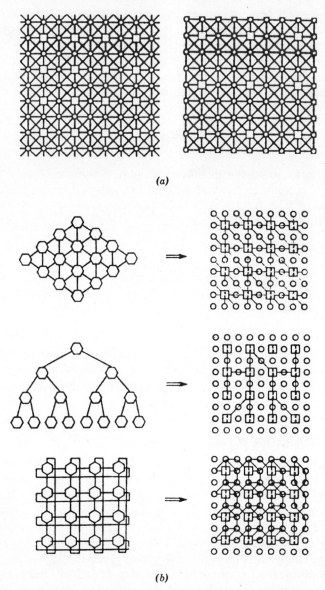

FIGURE 13-1. Examples of blue chip reconfigurable arrays. Small round nodes are switches; large square nodes are processors. (a) 2-dimensional square arrays. (b) Examples of other topologies embedded in arrays.

(*Source*: Kapauan, Field, and Gannon, 1984.)

ARRAYS OF SWITCHES TO RECONFIGURE ARRAYS OF PROCESSORS

The Blue Chip system (Snyder, 1982, 1984; Kapauan et al., 1984) reconfigures at still another level. Here an array of computers much like CLIP, DAP, or the MPP has one or several rows of linked switches between each of its rows, and a column of switches between each of its columns (in toto forming an array of switches), as shown in Figure 13-1 and 13-2(c). This kind of reconfiguring should be very useful in building fault tolerant computers. For example, Leighton and Leiserson (1985) show how 2-dimensional arrays with defective processors can be reconfigured into smaller arrays where minimal length wires link only the good processors. Yalamanchili and Aggarwal, 1985, examine a variety of reconfiguring techniques of this sort.

```
C C C C C C C        5 4-5 6-5      x - C - x - C - x
C C C C C C C        |  |  |   |    x - x - x - x - x
C C C C C C C        4-3 4-3-4      x - C - x - C - x
C C C C C C C         |    |        x - x - x - x - x
C C C C C C C        5-2-1-2 5      x - C - x - C - x
C C C C C C C        |  |   |  |    x - x - x - x - x
C C C C C C C        4-3 4-3-4      x - C - x - C - x
C C C C C C C        |  |  |  |  |  x - x - x - x - x
C C C C C C C        5 4 5 6-5      x - C - x - C - x

     (a)                (b)              (c)
```

FIGURE 13-2. Examples of local switches for partial reconfiguring. (a) Square-Hexagonal Array: Links between computers are not shown. (b) Array-Tree: | and -- indicate tree links (array links are not shown). (c) Blue Chip grid: x indicates switches, where an array of switches surrounds an array of computers (vertical links are not shown).

RECONFIGURING PROCESSORS TO B/K-BIT INSTRUCTIONS

Still another type of local reconfiguring is found in the Illiac-IV (Slotnick, 1967; Barnes et al., 1968), where each processor can be reconfigured to serve as either one 64-bit processor, two 32-bit processors, or eight 8-bit processors.

More generally, a B-bit processor might be reconfigurable into k B/k-bit processors (where B can be factored into B/k strings without remainder). Snyder (1985) has begun to investigate "multigauge" processors of this sort.

Most generally, the processor might be reconfigurable into processors of different sizes, the sum of whose bit-sizes is B.

RECONFIGURING PYRAMID PROCESSORS TO MIX TOP-DOWN AND BOTTOM-UP FLOW

An interesting construction in a process-structured system is a pyramid whose 64-bit processors (possibly arranged in an 8-by-8 array; possibly each with its own controller) could be reconfigured to 2 32-bit, 4 16-bit, 8 8-bit, 16 4-bit, 32 2-bit or 64 1-bit processors. Now, one subset of these processors could be assigned to work on bottom-up processes (computing functions on data stored in their childrens' and their siblings' memories, and passing results up to their parents), while the other subset could execute top-down processes (passing results of functions, and also commands and information, down to their children).

USING ANY D-LINKED NODE (WHETHER SWITCH OR COMPUTER) AS A RECONFIGURING SWITCH

Whenever there is a node with several 2-way links to it, information can be input or output over any of those links. That node might be a simple switch, or it might be an arbitrarily complex computer. Any node in any multi-computer topology can serve such a switching function.

If a node is only to be used for switching, it would be a great waste of resources to put a whole computer there in addition to the simple switch (which would have to be there as a part of the computer in order to switch information to the proper link). If the node is a computer and is often used for switching, a little more hardware (essentially, an extra switch) will allow it to input information from another node, and switch to and output it over the proper link, but at the same time continue processing other information—that is, both passing information and computing in parallel.

Partial Reconfiguring at More Global Levels

Partial reconfiguring can be introduced at any level, from the most local to the most global. A number of interesting designs have been proposed for partial reconfiguring at more global levels.

PURDUE'S PASM, A MULTILEVEL RECONFIGURABLE SYSTEM

H. J. Siegel's PASM (Siegel et al., 1979, 1981; Kuehn et al., 1985) makes very interesting uses of reconfiguring at several levels. The full 1,024 processor PASM is designed to have each node be a conventional serial computer with its own controller. In addition, PASM has 64 global controllers, plus a capability to reconfigure the linkages between global controllers and processors so that a variety of different groupings can be made. (The prototype under construction will have 16 Motorola 68010 computers and 4 global controllers.) In addition, the basic linkages between all the individual computers are also effected via a global reconfiguring network.

This means that a variety of different topologies and data-flows can be achieved. For example, PASM can emulate an array, by assigning different subarrays of a large image to different processors, and passing data from one to another as needed over the reconfiguring network. It can emulate a pyramid, simply by passing information originally processed by four different computers to a single computer (simultaneously reducing or/and transforming this information, as desired, along the way).

In general, PASM appears to combine many of the virtues of the synchronized, specialized structures like arrays and pyramids with those of asynchronous systems, such as Cm*, Crystal, and the Cosmic Cube. It appears to minimize the message-passing problems and delays of the asynchronous systems. Whether these important virtues justify the additional costs is not clear. The reconfiguring networks will be large (although smaller than those in the Ultracomputer), but they will do a number of extremely important jobs.

It will be very interesting to see how this kind of system compares with arrays, pyramids, and augmented pyramids, in terms of costs, generality, flexibility, programmability, power, and speed.

PASM's projected goal of 1,024 computers all linked by a reconfiguring network, and the Ultracomputer's projected goal of 4,096 computers all linked by a 4,096-by-12 reconfiguring network, are probably at, or even beyond, the limits of feasibility in terms of the number of switches used. Larger numbers of computers can be handled by starting with a reconfiguring network, crossbar, or bus of a suitable size (e.g., 32 or 64 processors), and then using a reconfiguring network to compound a number of these (e.g., 32 or 512) together.

Several such systems have been partially designed, as described in the following.

RECONFIGURABLE PIPELINES AND ARRAYS

The vector processing pipelines that have proved so useful on Cray-type supercomputers can be made more flexible by adding reconfiguring capabilities. This is already being done in the Fujitsu VP-200 (anon., 1982; see Lubeck et al., 1985). Wah et al. (1985) have examined how information can be reformated as it moves from one such pipeline of processors to another.

Hwang and Xu (1985) are designing Remps, a multilevel network that links processors to processors via a reconfiguring network, and also links processors to shared memories via a second reconfiguring network. It is intended that among the processors to be linked in this way will be a variety of special-purpose systolic arrays. In addition, each processor is itself a set of processors that can be reconfigured into a pipeline or some other topology. Remps is reminiscent of the earlier PM4 design

(Briggs et al., 1979), which linked scalar processors to processors via a reconfiguring network, and also linked processors to shared memories via a second network.

THE UNIVERSITY OF ILLINOIS' CEDAR, A HIERARCHICAL RECONFIGURING NETWORK

Cedar (Kuck et al., 1983; Abu-Sufah and Kwok, 1985) links a local cluster of 8 computers to a 32 megabyte cluster memory via a crossbar. The commercially available 4-CPU Aliant serves as this basic cluster node. Each processor is capable of delivering a 6 megaflop peak load, or 48 megaflop peak for the total cluster.

Cedar links a number of these clusters via a reconfiguring network to a very large high-speed memory. To accomplish this, the Illinois group is adding a global interface board to each Aliant cluster, plus global interconnection networks and global memory. The system has two uni-directional interconnection networks built from a stage of 8x8 crossbars, one linked to each cluster, that are linked via a shuffle to a second stage of crossbars. A 64-bit word can be fetched from or stored into global memory in about 1.5 microseconds. Blocks can be transferred at a stream rate of 85 nanoseconds per word.

Cedar thus uses two levels of pseudo-complete graphs, as though a pseudo-complete graph were embedded in each node of a pseudo-complete graph. This gives rich interconnectivity, both within each local cluster, and also for accessing information from the global memory. Clusters communicate with one another via the global memory only.

Plans are to double the number of clusters each year, until a 16-cluster system is brought up, originally planned for around December, 1988.

A POLYMORPHIC SYSTEM THAT RECONFIGURES AMONG BASIC MODULES

Hungwen Li (Li et al, 1985) is beginning to investigate hardware designs similar to polymorphic arrays (toruses with four diagonally linked helixes that efficiently map systolic arrays of processes into processors; Fiat and Shamir, 1984). Li's planned design will include several arrays of 1-bit computers that serve to link a 1-dimensional array of conventional computers to a large memory. He is also developing a language to be used both for specifying and designing such a system and for programming it. Partial reconfiguring, using switches at the local level of the 1-bit computers' mesh interconnects, will serve to reconfigure among the basic modules. It is expected that realizable reconfigurations will include 1-dimensional (pipe)lines, 2-dimensional arrays, trees, and pyramids (Li, personal communication).

INFORMATION FLOWED THROUGH APPROPRIATELY STRUCTURED AND RE-STRUCTURED NETWORKS

A potentially very attractive concept is the following: Use a data-flow programming language to build a "data-flow graph" that shows exactly how processes will operate on it, and will transmit data.

The Data-Flow Concept

A data-flow graph gives a clear and direct picture of how information flows through the structure of processes that make up a program. Instead of specifying a sequence of operations that entail fetching data, computing transformations, storing results, and so on, the data-flow graph specifies both the structure of processes and the way data flow through that structure. Essentially it is a variant of a Petri net, extended to handle as efficiently as possible a full set of commonly used constructs (e.g., iteration loops, arrays).

The Nondata-Flow Hardware Used Today to Handle Data-Flow Programs

One can conceive of a multi-computer that was built directly from the data-flow graph for a particular program. It would look almost exactly like that program: It would have a processor (either special-purpose or general purpose) at each node, and wires linking into each node from the processors that send it its input operands, plus wires linking out to the processors that receive its output. Such a system would be overly rigid and special-purpose, capable of executing only programs that have exactly that program's structure. As we shall see, several practical examples of such systems, which might be named "true data-flow hardware," already exist, and there is some hope that more can be achieved.

The actual data-flow computers being designed and built today handle things in a completely different manner. Each instruction sits in the computer's memory, waiting to receive its operands. As soon as an instruction has all its operands, it is ready for execution. At that point the typical data-flow computer sends the instruction with its operands over a bus to a processor that will then execute it. If the processor is busy, the instruction will wait in a queue.

From the point of view of the processor this is an extremely efficient procedure. It can keep working all the time so long as its queue is not empty. One of the major virtues of the data-flow approach is that it increases CPU utilization from the typical 20 to 50% to almost 100%. A processor will not be stopped because it cannot fetch data. The program does not need to keep track of which instruction to execute next. Rather, whenever an instruction has been input its operands, that instruction is ready to be executed (this is easier said than handled; a great deal of research has gone into how to make sure the correct operands have arrived).

The actual data-flow computers completely destroy the data-flow topology. The typical data-flow computer will have one, or possibly a few, CPUs. Extra large memories are needed to store the program, since additional storage is needed for each instruction's operands. Buses with extra bandwidth are needed to handle the traffic of operands to memory and of instructions ready to be executed to processors. For systems with more than one processor, buses, crossbars, or reconfiguring networks are planned.

True Data-Flow Hardware

A data-flow program would be executed with great speed by flowing a continuing stream of information through a multi-computer with an isomorphic topology. Unfortunately today that can be done in only a few very simple situations.

SIMPLE REALIZATIONS OF TRUE DATA-FLOW IN LIMITED SITUATIONS

A pipeline can effect this kind of process, but only when the stream of information and transformations forms a simple line. Other examples are arrays that carry out sequences of local operations, and pyramids that pipe and transform a sequence of images—for example, the successive frames in a moving picture.

A good traditional example is a structure of gates that has been carefully designed for fast execution of some basic function (e.g., a parallel adder). Good examples in the world of VLSI are the special-purpose systolic chips (Kung, 1980, 1982; Kung and Song, 1982; Kung and Lam, 1984), where data are pumped into an appropriate structure of gates that computes the results and from which answers are output.

TOWARD GENERAL STRUCTURES OF POSSIBLY RECONFIGURABLE BASIC MODULES

All these examples require carefully and appropriately structured, if not special-purpose, hardware. They assume that this hardware will be dedicated to a steady, continuing stream of appropriately structured information. Especially attractive would be a topology for the hardware that was general enough so that most, if not all, of the programs' data-flow topologies could easily be embedded in it. A fan-out/fan-in network (see

Chapter 16) might be appropriate, since it might be possible to map a variety of data-flow graphs into it.

Complete generality would not be necessary. The network might contain local reconfiguring switches that could change the hardware topology as needed. If perfect mappings cannot be achieved such a system would still work, albeit at the cost of lower efficiency.

It would appear to be extremely difficult to achieve efficient and general structures of this sort. In the general case, the operating system would have to figure out how to efficiently embed any graph into any other graph, using reconfiguring switches that someone had previously determined should be added so that the operating system could change any graph to any other graph.

It seems possible that a relatively small number of basic structures can be used to compose the much larger and more complex structures needed for most programs. At the moment only a surprisingly small number of structures appear to have special virtues (e.g., arrays for local operations, trees and pyramids for broadcasting and converging information, reconfiguring networks for shuffling, Moore graphs for optimal density and symmetries, systems based on lines and polygons for piping and circulating information). However, virtually nothing has been done to date to try to find a full set of good basic topologies, techniques for combining them into larger data-flow structures, guidelines for coding appropriately structured data-flow programs, procedures for mapping such programs into appropriately structured multi-computer hardware, and techniques for partially reconfiguring one hardware topology into another.

THE POSSIBILITY OF A RECONFIGURABLE GENERAL DATA-FLOW SCANNER

Another virtually unexplored possibility might be a much smaller network that is used, essentially, to scan down and immediately execute the active nodes in the data-flow graph of the program. Ideally, such a network would be reconfigurable to whatever structure of operations the data-flow graph demanded at each and every step. It would also need a buffer memory to store results that could not be used immediately, and an efficient network (possibly a reconfiguring network) to bring this information, as needed, to the processing structure. A small number of processors linked via a crossbar or reconfiguring network to a very large shared memory might be a simple and adequate approximation to such a system. Such a system would also need additional highly parallel modules, such as large arrays and pipelines. It would probably be appreciably slower than a network where processors could pass information directly to the next appropriate processors.

DIFFERENT KINDS OF GRADIENTED AND HETEROGENEOUS SYSTEMS; POSSIBLY RECONFIGURABLE

To the extent that different kinds of specialized architectures are indicated for different perceptual or cognitive functions, it would appear that a total hardware system capable of computing these several different functions might best be specialized in one way in one region of the multi-computer and in a different way in another. Several such systems have been designed, including the following.

Systems that Augment Arrays with Other Structures

ILLIAC-III AS AN EARLY EXAMPLE OF A HETEROGENEOUS SYSTEM

Bruce McCormick's 1963 Illiac-III was planned to combine three different types of computer: (a) the 2-dimensional array described in Chapter 8 (for local image processing operations); and also (b) a conventional CPU (designed to handle statistical and numerical tasks); and (c) a list-processing computer (designed to manipulate symbolic information structured into graphs). Unfortunately this extremely interesting and for its time very ambitious design was never completed, because of fire.

THE WISCONSIN ARRAY/NET

The array/net (Uhr, Thompson and Lackey 1981) was designed as a single system capable of serving as (a) a 16 by 16 SIMD array of synchronized 8-bit processors, (b) a 4 by 4 array of 4 by 4 SIMD arrays of 8-bit processors, or (c) an asynchronous MIMD network of 32-bit processors linked both by the array and via a bus. The design has a controller centered in each of the system's 16 boards. Each can serve either to control a powerful 32-bit processor, or to control, in SIMD mode, a 4 by 4 array of 8-bit processors. That is, the hardware surrounding the controller can be reconfigured between these two types of processor.

Thus the array/net can conveniently alternate between working as an asynchronous MIMD network of 16 32-bit processors, or as a synchronous SIMD network of 256 8-bit processors, or 16 separate synchronous SIMD 8-bit processors, each set in a 4 by 4 array. Since all of these possibilities use the same memory, they can share and work on the same data.

More generally, this type of system might be designed, by making its processors appropriately reconfigurable, to use an N by M array of B-bit computers, or an N/j by M/k array of jkB-bit computers.

THE MASSACHUSSETTS 4-LEVEL SIMD-1-BIT ARRAY PLUS MIMD ARRAYS

Caxton Foster, Steven Levitan, Chip Weems, Allen Hanson, and Edward Riseman at the University of Massachussets are designing CAAPP, a system that will combine an SIMD array of 1-bit processors with two successively smaller MIMD arrays, of 16-bit and 32-bit processors (see Figure 13-3). It is being designed to handle a particular 3-level approach to image processing and computer vision, but it should be a powerful system for a number of different problems and approaches.

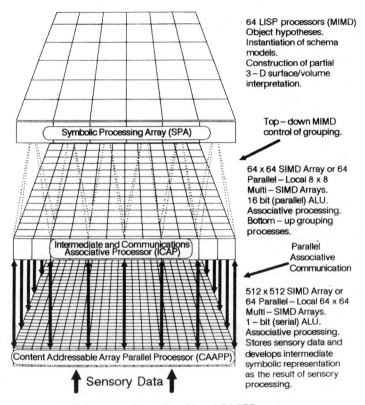

64 LISP processors (MIMD) Object hypotheses. Instantiation of schema models. Construction of partial 3 – D surface/volume interpretation.

Symbolic Processing Array (SPA)

Top – down MIMD control of grouping.

64 x 64 SIMD Array or 64 Parallel – Local 8 x 8 Multi – SIMD Arrays. 16 bit (parallel) ALU. Associative processing. Bottom – up grouping processes.

Parallel Associative Communication

Intermediate and Communications Associative Processor (ICAP)

512 x 512 SIMD Array or 64 Parallel – Local 64 x 64 Multi – SIMD Arrays. 1 – bit (serial) ALU. Associative processing. Stores sensory data and develops intermediate symbolic representation as the result of sensory processing.

Content Addressable Array Parallel Processor (CAAPP)

↑ Sensory Data ↑

FIGURE 13-3. The several-level CAAPP system.

Each chip will contain both a small subarray of 1-bit CAAPP (content-addressable array parallel processor), processors, all linked to one 16-bit processor in a smaller second-level array. Each of these 16-bit processors will have its own controller. A third level of processors will be an array of 32-bit computers (probably Lisp processor chips). Finally the total system will link to a single host.

The plan is to have each of the three levels handle a different level and type of image processing operation. The first layer of 1-bit SIMD processors will be used for "low-level" operations over local regions—for example, to average, detect gradients, extract short edges and detect simple features. The second layer of 16-bit MIMD processors will do "middle-level" operations, such as region growing, contour finding, and segmentation. The third layer of 32-bit MIMD processors will do "high-level" operations involved in recognition of objects, and handle top-down processing. For example, it will tell the lower-level processors what kinds of things to look for.

Present plans are to fabricate a chip that contains an 8 by 8 array of 1-bit CAAPP computers, each with 128 bits of memory, and also one 16-bit processor to which they are all linked. A prototype system will be built on one board that contains an 8 by 8 array of these chips, giving a 64 by 64 array of 1-bit processors at the first level and an 8 by 8 array of 16-bit processors at the second (Levitan, personal communication). The full CAAPP system that is planned will have a 512 by 512 SIMD array of 1-bit processors, a 64 by 64 MIMD array of 16-bit processors, a 16 by 16 MIMD array of 32-bit processors, and a single host. It might be viewed as an array augmented with an MIMD network of two arrays, or as a pyramid that has 8 by 8 rather than the more typical 2 by 2 convergence, and that is internally augmented with more powerful processors and additional controllers.

Systems that Augment Pyramids

There are a variety of ways in which pyramids might be extended.

GRADIENTED PYRAMID SYSTEMS

An attractive example of a gradiented system is a design for a pyramid that is some variant on the following: At the lowest retinal layer there is a large array of 1-bit processors, all synchronized to execute the same instruction stream. (Since nothing is yet known about the sensed image, the system must begin to process the image everywhere and look for information everywhere. There is no reason to execute different processes in different regions.) Moving up through the layers of the pyramid, computers can gradually be made more and more powerful, for example, by using 4-bit, 8-bit, 16-bit, 32-bit and 64-bit processors. And the number of controllers per layer can go up, with each controller responsible for a smaller and smaller subarray, subpyramid, or other substructure, until each processor has its own separate controller.

AUGMENTING AND MODIFYING THE PYRAMID'S INTERNAL LINKING TOPOLOGY

Leiserson's (1985) fat-tree augmentations to the bandwidth of the communication channels moving upward toward the root can be used within a pyramid, moving upward toward the apex, as well as within a tree.

The actual topology of internal links can be modified as well. One attractive scheme is to use an NlogN reconfiguring network to link together local subarrays at a higher level—for example, an 8 by 8 array of 4 by 4 arrays of computers at the 32 by 32 layer. This would greatly reduce the root bottleneck problem inherent in trees and pyramids and make possible fast and efficient sorting and shuffling of information (Stout, 1983; Miller, 1984; Miller and Stout, 1984). A reconfiguring network might also be used instead of array links for communication among all nodes, as in STARAN and ASPRO (Batcher, 1973; anon., 1979).

HETEROGENEOUS NETWORK-AUGMENTED PYRAMIDS

Pfeiffer (1985) has designed and simulated a system that shifts information stored at the base of a pyramid out in 4 directions into separate and much more powerful serial computers that will continue processing. Additional hardware is used to compress this information as it is shifted out, for example into a Freeman chain code of edges.

Tanimoto (1985) is designing a system that links specially designed "hetero-ported" memories in the base array of the pyramid to both the pyramid processors and a set of independent computers. A special "schizo chip" is being designed to handle the necessary transfers and remappings of data. Thus this system will allow information to be fetched in the traditional manner, an entire bit-plane at a time, by the array of processors in the pyramid's base, and also fetched a word at a time by the serial computer linked to the memory.

Pyramids augmented with networks of more powerful and more independent computers (Uhr, 1983a, 1983b, 1985a, 1985b) are still another good example of heterogeneous systems. There are a number of networks that might be appropriate, including a Petersen or Singleton graph, N-cube, good compound, or small pyramid. The two subnetworks might be linked directly to one another, or via an NlogN reconfiguring network. A variety of different linking schemes might be used. For example, an 8 by 8 array of 16-bit Von Neumann computers at the base of an $8x8 + 4x4 + 2x2 + 1x1$ asynchronous pyramid might be linked to all the computers at the 32 by 32 layer of the pyramid, or to every 4th computer at the 64 by 64 layer, or to every computer at the 16 by 16 layer and also to a scattered 32 by 32 array of computers in a very large low-level layer, for example, the 128 by 128 or the 512 by 512.

Heterogeneous Combinations of Special-Purpose Systolic Chips

A number of special-purpose systolic chips might be combined into a general purpose total system, in any of the following ways:

> Add the systolic chips to a conventional computer's high-speed bus. Such a system would be much like PICAP II (Kruse et al., 1980), and also like traditional CPUs with specialized processors added for extra speed on important frequently computed processes, and like vector processing super-computers.

> Build a network whose nodes are systolic chips, each type scattered uniformly throughout. Such a system would need a topology and an operating system that could flow streams of data through the appropriate processor. A cluster of clusters, where each cluster was a bus-based set of different systolic processors, appears to be an appropriate topology.

> Build a network whose nodes are specialized sets of systolic chips; send information to be processed to a chip in the appropriate node. Such a system might similarly be built as a cluster of clusters, but now each cluster's systolic processors would all be of the same type.

Compounds of (Structured or Unstructured) Clusters

An attractive type of architecture starts with relatively small local structures chosen for good local properties, and then compounds or in other ways combines these into larger structures. Possibly compounding operations can fruitfully be applied several times, each time multiplying the size of the total system.

The structures that compound several different types of structures (e.g., CHoPP, Cm*, Cube-Connected Cycles, Connection Machines, etc.) that have already been described are good examples of heterogeneous systems of this sort. The compounding operations described in Chapter 11 that have been used to achieve relatively dense graphs offer a variety of additional promising candidates.

Possibly the most powerful structure would be one where the topologies of the local clusters reflected the topologies of the information flowing through them, and the topologies of the more global interconnection scheme similarly reflected the more global flows of information. For example, small converging tree-like networks can be used by the programmer to combine information gathered about a particular problem (e.g., a region in a picture, a burst of speech); these can feed into a region containing processors that choose the maximum from among a competing set of possibilities; the chosen information can then be passed to another region, for further processing.

Different Structures in Different Regions, as in AI Architectures

An attractive architecture for an integrated AI system would be one that combined the most appropriate structures for each of its subsystems. These will be examined in the sections of Chapters 15 through 21, on AI processes, that describe the architectures that appear to be most suited to each. Briefly, we might combine an augmented pyramid for vision with additional (probably much smaller) augmented pyramids for hearing and for touch, a fan-out/fan-in graph for remembering and problem solving, and a tree of trees ... of trees ... for hierarchical motor coordination and control. The pyramid's highly parallel arrays can locally process the massive amount of information input from the external environment; the tree and fan-in links in all parts of the system serve to combine and communicate information globally.

An opposing ideal and goal to this kind of heterogeneous system would be a single general structure that would handle all these different, more or less specialized functions. To a great extent the particular choices made for this heterogeneous structure already embody a good bit of generalization (pyramids for vision, hearing, and touch; fan-out/fan-in graphs for memory searches and for problem solving). They offer real promise for further generalizations, since pyramids and fan-out/fan-in structures are both rather similar to trees.

SUMMARY OF MULTI-COMPUTER ARCHITECTURES (CHAPTERS 6 THROUGH 13)

The following briefly recapitulates the basic overall structures used, or suggested, to date for multi-computer architectures, and also the basic modules from which larger structures can be composed.

The Small Number of Good Basic Modules Identified to Date

It seems curious that so few basic topologies with obviously good properties are known that might form the primitive building-blocks for constructing larger systems.

Lines and polygons are cleary powerful in pipelining vector processors.

Meshes are clearly good for local operations.

Trees are clearly good for broadcasting (moving down the tree), and for fan-in operations (moving up the tree) where information is converged, transformed, and reduced at rates commensurate with the trees' similarly converging structure.

Reconfiguring Benes networks can handle the efficient passing of information greater distances among a somewhat larger number of nodes than can lines, polygons, meshes, and trees.

Optimal Moore graphs, and other carefully chosen small graphs, appear to have a number of good properties, both when used by themselves and when compounded or combined into larger structures.

It is worth noting that the rather simple lines, polygons, meshes, and trees have all evolved in natural systems; but, so far as I am aware (and one would expect), Benes networks, Moore graphs, and some of the more complex overall topologies, such as N-cubes and De Bruijn graphs, have not. But nature appears to build complex and powerful fan-out/fan-in architectures, stitching together simple local array and tree components, and also using a significant number of links between distant substructures.

The Major Overall Topologies Used for Multi-Computers

Crossbars (meshes), buses (lines), rings (polygons), and stars (diameter 2 trees) can handle at most only a few dozen nodes.

Reconfiguring (Benes) networks can handle up to a few hundred or a few thousand, but at increasingly substantial costs in hardware and in time.

Pipelines (lines, polygons), arrays (meshes), and pyramids (arrays combined with trees) all offer the possibility of building very large systems (potentially unlimited in size) with many thousands or millions of computers. These systems can potentially give striking speedups on large classes of algorithms for which they are appropriate.

N-cubes (N-dimensional binary arrays) can, potentially, be built with millions of computers. They have several desirable properties (easy addressability, ability to handle many arrays) that have made them unusually attractive to a large number of people. However, they need too many ports, are poor in density, and would probably be difficult to use efficiently for many AI problems.

Trees can be very useful for what trees are good at: computing functions of, and combining, information moving up the tree, and broadcasting and dispersing information moving down the tree. But they can be very bad for processes that might be bottlenecked by the decreasing number of processors moving up to the root, for example, sorting, and large amounts of global message-passing.

De Bruijn graphs and other judiciously augmented trees can eliminate many, and sometimes all, of these bottleneck problems. Although relatively little explored, they, along with compounds of good basic structures, appear to offer especially attractive potential topologies.

Compounds of structures offer real possibilities of using appropriate process-structured local topologies within a larger global topology similarly optimized for good global properties (e.g., high density, to expedite message-passing).

Reconfiguring networks used to compound structures linked via reconfiguring networks (and this might be repeated indefinitely) appear to give the richest linkages, but at a potentially heavy price in hardware. They are attractive when N pieces of information, or close to N pieces, are moved about within each structure, and also between structures, at each step.

But that will be an unusual occurrence. More appropriate would appear to be heterogeneous architectures with good local densities within appropriately configured local structures large enough to handle most of the information-passing interactions among the processes executed, along with a similarly adequate number of links to the other structures of processors in the network.

True data-flow hardwares would, if feasible, offer potentially very fast and efficient possibilities.

There are almost certainly a large number of as yet undiscovered topologies that are worthy of exploration for multi-computer architectures. It seems quite possible that some may well turn out to be substantially better than any known today.

Toward Designs that Allocate Resources in Order to Maximize Useful Work

Processors can be given a common controller when enough are doing the same thing so that synchrony is desirable. When such sharing is not efficient, separate controllers can be used. Extra links and switches can be added to a bank of controllers, so that controllers can be reconfigured in and out, as desirable, under program control; but controllers, links and switches can eat up valuable resources.

Processors can be made of any size, from 1-bit to 64-bit, or even bigger. Processors can be parallelized and specialized to specific functions. Memories can be made larger, and additional faster caches and registers added. Processors, and whole structures of computers, can be made reconfigurable. All of these options are a matter of tradeoffs of the basic resources—the transistors and wires that take up area on the computer's chips and boards.

SIMD systems should be kept from having too many processors idle too much of the time. Conventional computers should be kept from having too small a percentage of their resources committed to active processors. Flexible and reconfigurable networks should be kept from investing too many resources in switches. Message-passing costs should be acknowledged, understood, and minimized. The total hardware-software system should be designed to make the passing of information as fast and as efficient as possible.

The design of massively parallel and very large multi-computer networks may well be the most complex and the most difficult architectural problem that human beings have ever tried to handle. A total system must appropriately structure all levels of detail—from individual memory cell and special-purpose processor through chip and board level designs to overall topology—into a powerful and efficient overall architecture. It has taken 40 years to evolve today's relatively well designed single-CPU serial computer. Multi-computers are far more complex, with far more promising different alternative possibilities to be explored.

There are today only a small number of good basic building blocks at our disposal with which to develop good overall topologies, and a relatively small number of different architectures that appear to be promising. This offers the opportunity—a venture that has scarcely begun—to explore them more fully than might otherwise be possible, and also to search for even better new ones.

ARTIFICIAL INTELLIGENCE: MAJOR APPROACHES; INDICATED ARCHITECTURES

Chapter Fourteen

THE HUMAN MIND/BRAIN, AND POSSIBILITIES OF PARALLELISM IN EACH AI FUNCTION

We now begin to examine the different intelligent processes, and the ways that living beings and computer hardware/software systems appear to carry them out. We will focus on those processes that we human beings execute almost constantly, as we conduct our daily lives, with special emphasis on perception, remembering, language, everyday reasoning, perceptual-motor skills, and learning.

The performance of human beings and of other higher animals is a compelling existence proof not only that intelligent entities are possible, but also that nature's intelligent entities perceive, think, and act enormously faster than can any existing artificial intelligence system. Of vital importance from the perspective of this book, they are also substantially faster than any conceivable system that could ever actually execute on any theoretically constructible single-CPU serial computer. The living mind/brain proves that extremely fast, massively parallel multi-computers are possible and, at least from the criteria of natural evolution, efficient.

This is in striking contrast to traditional artificial intelligence's highly serial programs. A typical AI program will examine a bit of information, apply a set of procedures (e.g., heuristics, inferences) to decide what to do and what information to examine next, and continue in this kind of serial loop until its job is done. But to be fast enough for real-time problems, the system must do many more things in parallel.

The human mind/brain is closely embedded within the larger environment, with which it intimately interacts via the body's complex transducing mechanisms (e.g., eye's lens and photon sensors, skin's touch and pain receptors; and, on the output side, arm's, hand's, mouth's, tongue's muscles). Organism and environment interact continuously, the organism receiving (sensing, perceiving) a continuing stream of experience. From this (along with internally stored information, both learned and built-in) the organism achieves an understanding of what is there, what is relevant, what is happening, and what is happening because of what it did. Perception and cognition recognize, appreciate, and carve out from the enormous stream of experience the small structures of information that are relevant.

If we want intelligent software/hardware systems to help and interact with human beings, and even to take over complex tasks that today require human intelligence, these new kinds of intelligent entities must work at least as fast as humans. Otherwise they will not be able to interact and cooperate with human beings and the rich environment within which human beings exist. They will not be able to get their jobs done in time (at least without driving crazy the poor humans who must wait for them to respond). Of equal importance, good computer hardware/software models can play a vital role in the development of a firm theoretical understanding of the human mind/brain.

This chapter will sketch out some of the major structures and a few of the highlights of the brain that appear to be most relevant. Visual perception will be emphasized, since far more is known about it than about any other major intelligent function. The brain is far from being completely understood, but it is illuminating to examine what is known about how it works.

THE AMAZINGLY SMALL SERIAL DEPTH OF HIGHLY PARALLEL HUMAN THOUGHT

The human brain is a highly parallel multi-computer built from many billions of active components (the neurons) linked to one another (over the synaptic junctions) into a massively parallel structure, an extremely large and complex graph. The visual system includes the eye's retinal array of sensing elements (rods to detect changes and cones to detect color and intensity) and neurons, the optic nerve that conducts information from the retina to the primary visual area of the cerebral cortex, and a number of secondary visual areas and polysensory and perceptual-motor association areas.

Synapsing Neurons

The synapse is a tiny region where one of a neuron's axons comes close to another neuron's bush-of-fine-wire-like dendrites. When one neuron is charged with an electrical impulse a complex process diffuses neurotransmitters out from that neuron into the synaptic gap, across it and into tiny openings in the membrane of the dendrite being fired into.

It takes roughly $1-2$ milliseconds to fire a neuron (i.e., to fire into and bridge the gap across a synapse, building up excitation in the neuron fired into so that, when its threshold is finally exceeded, that neuron fires). A relatively small amount of additional time (which depends on the length and the thickness of the neuron's fibers) is needed to transmit the resulting impulses to the synapses into which this neuron in turn fires.

Some neurons also interact more directly, by spreading their charges without first having to exceed a minimum threshold of excitation. This is the case for the several layers of retinal neurons in the eye. This type of interaction is finer grained, smoother, and more continuous, compared to the discretizing effect when a charge must be built up until it exceeds a threshold. It can be modeled by threshold elements whose thresholds are set very low, at zero, or close to zero.

These are the major ways that the nervous system transforms and passes information from one neuron to the next. A neuron's neighbor neurons send and tend to spread their charges to that neuron. The level of excitation needed to fire a neuron serve as a threshold. The neuron's synapses thus serve to integrate the various signals that impinge upon it from neighbor neurons. It appears possible (although this is conjectural) that a whole structure of synapses effects a complex nonlinear integration of signals from many dozens, hundreds, or even thousands of the other neurons firing into each single neuron.

The brain appears to compute its basic functions via these mechanisms, using complex structures of synapse-computed integrating and thresholding operations.

The Extremely Slow Brain and Extremely Fast Computer Basic Components

The brain's cycle time for a basic operation is $1-2$ milliseconds!

This contrasts sharply with the microsecond and nanosecond cycle times of today's computers. For example, a minicomputer like a VAX takes roughly 1 microsecond to add two 32-bit numbers; a Cray-XMP takes 12.5 nanoseconds to add, or to do a floating-point multiply, on two 64-bit numbers. A simple thresholding operation that entails combining two to five, or even several hundred or thousand, weights, and then testing whether they exceeded a threshold, might take roughly four to ten to hundreds or thousands of times as long. But the computer would still be several orders of magnitude faster than are the living brain's synapses. And it could be given specialized threshold-operation processor hardware that parallelized this long sequence of instructions. That is, if a neuron into which thousands of other neurons input computes complex integrating and thresholding operations over all these inputs, similar parallel operations could be hard-wired into a neuron-like processor that could execute its basic thresholding-integrating instruction at microsecond or nanosecond speeds. For example, rather than link a pyramid processor to 4 or 9 children, it is (in theory, using a switching network and ignoring costs) possible to link it to thousands.

THE EXTREMELY FAST (BECAUSE MASSIVELY PARALLEL) BRAIN'S GLOBAL PROCESSES

We human beings carry out a wide variety of extremely complex cognitive tasks within .1 to 10 seconds. We can recognize and describe complex objects in complex scenes, make deductions, solve problems, think about things, "figure things out," engage in conversations, access and remember pertinent information, manipulate tools—all in a few seconds, and often in split-seconds.

Of course there are many intelligent processes that take us many seconds, minutes, hours, days, months, years, or centuries. For example, solving a maze, putting together a jigsaw puzzle, formulating a computer program, predicting the weather, proving a theorem, perfecting a spitball, learning to dance, designing an airplane, finding the next prime number, developing a theory of evolution, putting colonies in outer space, building intelligent robots, explaining the physical universe, understanding the mind.

The Enormous Speed of Most Intelligent Everyday Activity

However, much (and likely most) intelligent behavior takes but a second or two. Consider the enormously fast and complex key accomplishments described in Chapter 0, emphasizing the following:

We perceive large, complex scenes of complex moving objects in a few hundred milliseconds. Here we immediately recognize and subjectively focus on those objects (e.g., the people we know best, the attractive chair), and the subtle relations among them (e.g., the way the person or the chair looks) that are most relevant to our expectations, needs, and goals.

We intelligently converse and interact with people and things. We think, consider, and generate facts, ideas, and inferences, in a second or two. These are typically complex mixtures of remembered specific pieces of information; analogies, concepts, and generalizations; and computed, deduced, or more or less loosely induced, thoughts.

We figure out what to do next—for example, whether to get dressed, and how (e.g., put on that shirt, pull that sock this way with these fingers), and what to do then (e.g., go to that movie, solve that problem), and how to do it (e.g., drive, walk, daydream, calculate), and start doing it—usually in a few seconds.

We coordinate dozens or hundreds of muscles, to smoothly execute complex slow or rapid motions, as when gesturing, walking, running, throwing a curve, threading a needle, playing an organ, dancing.

We continue to learn and to adapt. Some things (e.g., a new face, or the plot and atmosphere of a book as we read it) are learned immediately; other things (e.g., how to walk or dance, a foreign language) are learned in many, each immediate, successive steps—but over the months or years.

The Extremely Shallow Serial Depth Possible in Such Short Times

The serial depth (i.e., the number of serial steps that must be taken from start to finish) of these kinds of subjectively instantaneous cognitive processes is at most 1,000 to 10,000.

Almost certainly it is far less, since the brain's basic cycle time is a millisecond or two. When each frame in a scene of moving objects is processed in 30 milliseconds by the human nervous system, the maximum possible serial depth is 15 to 30. When the many objects in a complex scene are perceived in substantially less than one second, the maximum serial depth is a few hundred. When a piece of information is accessed or a simple question is answered within one second, the serial depth is 500 to 1,000 at the very most. When fine perceptual-motor interaction controls split-second coordination, it seems very unlikely that the serial depth could possibly be greater than a few hundred, or a few dozen.

These are astoundingly small numbers; they document a serial depth that is so shallow that only massively parallel systems can possibly achieve it. They can be taken as empirical existence proofs of the enormous speedups that are possible—with appropriate parallelizations.

The Massively Parallel, Shallowly Serial, Structure Necessitated

But it is important to emphasize that the brain is not entirely parallel. The serial depth is absolutely crucial, whether it is only a few thousand, or even a few hundred or a few dozen. In a multi-computer, or an abstract graph, it serves to give a hierarchical structure that allows nodes to converge in and diverge out, and thus communicate and interact with one another. When nodes are linked as in a tree or an augmented tree, this process is made logarithmic; this means that even billions of nodes, for example, the billions of neurons in the brain, can easily be traversed by such structures in a few dozen steps.

THE MASSIVELY PARALLEL (BUT ALSO SERIAL-HIERARCHICAL) LIVING BRAIN

The anatomy of the brain gives strong empirical evidence that human thinking is massively parallel, but shallowly serial (see for example Kuffler and Nicholls, 1976; Stone et al., 1979; Kandel and Schwartz, 1981). The retina, and all the areas of the cerebral cortex, are constructed from several layers of massively iterated neurons. Occasionally (as in the bipolar cells that are fired into by sensor cones) a neuron will have only one, or a few, links. But more typically, each neuron has roughly 1,000 to 30,000 links to other neurons (synapses to dendrites that receive information, from axons that send information). In the retina and within the perceptual areas of the cortex, along with many other areas, most of these links send information to nearby neurons. Links are crowded together, so that many links synapse onto the same neuron. In the association areas that handle higher-level cognitive processes it appears that links are often far more diverse, with many neurons each linking to thousands of other neurons.

The Retina and the Lateral Geniculate

The retina contains several layers of neurons, which do the following: Each of the millions of neurons that are fired into, by the hundred million rod and ten million cone sensors in each eye, sends (via laterally projecting horizontal and amacrine cells) excitatory signals to the neurons lying directly behind it, and inhibitory signals to neurons nearby but not directly behind—or the opposite. This serves to enhance differences, and thus emphasize gradiented spots.. Essentially, this computes a second order difference apparently similar to a difference of Gaussians, or a Laplacian.

The simplest possible discrete Laplacian can be computed in a 3-by-3 window, by assigning a high positive weight (8 is often used) to the center cell, and a low negative weight (-1 is often used) to each of the 8 surrounding cells. The living retina computes a much more sensitive function, over a whole region of surrounding cells.

Note that this could all be realized using micro-electronic technology. Just as CLIP is hardwired to compute in parallel a function over 9 cells in a window, so additional links could be added (using a fan-in tree) to compute functions over hundreds or thousands of neighbors. In a sense a pyramid already does this, by using several layers to compute functions over larger neighborhoods.

The well known blind spot is a large region where no signals occur, because the optic nerve (for evolutionary reasons) links to the retina at its front (toward the eye's lens), and therefore actually forms a sensorless blind region where it must pass back through the retina. Every human being also has a number of defective rods, cones, and larger regions of sensors. These become more numerous with aging; but they are rarely noticed and, subjectively, have no effect on recognition or on the precision of vision. (These defects can be seen relatively easily; simply look at a fairly bright milky white field, for example a hazy sky.)

The optic nerve is a cable of roughly 1,000,000 neurons. It carries signals from the retina to the cerebral cortex, but via one intermediate synaptic step—that is, one layer of processing elements—at the lateral geniculate.

The Cerebral Cortex

The cerebral cortex is a thin, crumpled, essentially 2-dimensional sheet containing six layers of neurons. The signals from the lateral geniculate project into the primary visual cortex at the back of the brain, resulting in a representation that continues to be topographically localized, much like the original image.

Complex columnar structures, each with a hundred or so interlinked neurons, rise side-by-side through all six layers of this sheet (Mountcastle, 1978; Szentagothai, 1978). These columns appear to be the major functional units, where it is likely that features, and successively more complex and more abstract features, are assessed. Each has rich connections laterally to other columns, and also to different parts of the cortex and the rest of the brain. Information flows through the layers of the columns, and from column to column—possibly once, possibly cycling. Krueger (1985), using multi-electrode recordings from a 5-by-6 array of 30 electrodes to examine the firing pattern of a column, has found different but stable patterns for different stimuli. Many different stimuli appear to fire each neuron; but the pattern of firing over a whole set of neurons differs from stimulus to stimulus. (Gerstein, 1985, has found similar stable patterns of activity in the auditory system, resulting from 3-note sound patterns.)

From the primary visual cortex information flows through at least 20 other visual areas, and also nonvisual areas. The total process of perception appears to involve a shallow hierarchy of operations that arrive at successively more complex sets of information. Possibly the most striking examples are found in vision. First, gradients are enhanced in the retina. Next, neurons sensitive to simple oriented moving edges, first located in a particular region, then located anywhere in the visual field, are found in the cortex, possibly followed by more complex features (Hubel and Wiesel, 1959, 1962, 1965, 1977), and even (as described below) extremely complex high-level features, like hands and faces (Gross et al., 1967; Bruce et al., 1981; Perrett et al., 1984).

A great wealth of suggestive new information has been accumulated during the past few years about the higher levels of perceptual processing. The results of the primary visual cortex's processing of the abstract image input to it are transmitted to a number of secondary visual sites (Allman and Kass, 1974; Von Essen, 1985). It appears that some of these handle special types of features, for example, color, motion, or shape (Zeki, 1978; Woolsey, 1981). As information moves up through these areas it appears to become successively more general and more complex with respect to shape and location.

Mishkin et al., 1983, conclude from a large amount of anatomical and physiological evidence that there are two major pathways through the subsequent visual areas after the primary visual cortex. These pathways diverge in the prestriate cortex. The one that processes color and shape, leading to the recognition of objects, moves into inferior temporal areas. The second, which moves into inferior parietal areas, is involved with the spatial interrelations among objects, and with how objects move about and change these spatial relations.

Thus there seem to be at least two major parallel (and shallowly serial) types of processing—those involved with the recognition of objects using shape and color, and those involved with relations among entities, and with change (motion). (Obviously, these two kinds of information must later be combined, since the system is able to recognize and also locate objects—just as information from eyes, ears, and skin are combined. Information gathered at earlier stages, before these two paths diverge, about shape on the one hand and about motion on the other, can also be used together, each process helping the other.)

At least 20 visual areas have already been identified (in the macaque monkey). Van Essen and Maunsell (1983; Von Essen, 1985) have shown anatomically how these are wired together by at least 80 pathways of neurons between pairs of the 20 visual areas. The overall structure appears to be a parallel-serial hierarchy with each area richly linked to other areas. Note that this is far from complete connectivity, which would link each of the 20 areas to all 19 others. Each area links to two or three other areas on the average (several link to one, several link to seven or eight). There are also links into the association areas that combine vision, hearing, and touch. Those paths that have been examined sufficiently have been shown to be reciprocal, with a set of neurons carrying information in each direction. Since there are still unexplored nearby regions of the cortex it is likely that a number of additional visual areas and pathways exist.

In general, moving up through these visual areas, it seems likely that more and more abstract features are responded to by individual neurons. At the same time, each neuron appears to behave as a feature-detector that is sensitive to a more and more complex feature found in a larger and larger region of the retinal field. Those links that move into the temporal lobe and the frontal lobe make possible the association of visual information about objects with information from the other sense modalities, and also with emotions and motor behavior.

Gross and his associates (Gross et al., 1967; Gross, 1973; Bruce et al., 1981) recording from single neurons in a superior temporal polysensory area, have found neurons that appear to be very selectively tuned and sensitive to complex objects, such as face or hand. These neurons appear to exhibit the culminating step of the most complex structure of processes found to date. These high-level neurons have been found, first by Gross and his associates and more recently in a number of other laboratories (e.g., Benevento et al., 1977; Perrett et al., 1979, 1984; Pigarev et al., 1979), to fire in a very specific manner to extremely complex stimuli.

For example, a single neuron fires when the stimulus is a hand, no matter where it is presented in the visual field, but not to a face or to a variety of other stimuli. A second type of neuron responds to a face, but not to a hand or to a picture that contains all the parts of a face, but jumbled around. Thus Bruce et al. found that 59 neurons of 199 examined responded most strongly to particular stimuli. Seven of these responded strongly to human and monkey faces, but not to simple stimuli like bars, spots, or edges, or to complex stimuli like hands or brushes. Perrett et al., 1984, found neurons that responded to a particular person's face. The response decreased when the eyes were eliminated from the picture, and also when the picture was chopped into 16 pieces and rearranged—which suggests that the response is to the complex whole. [These are striking and controversial results, and it appears that many biologists are skeptical. One problem that bothers many people is that these results appear to identify "grandmother cells"—that is, one individual neuron that is responsible for recognizing each possible object. Actually a large number of cells (3.5%) respond to faces. Each of these cells is simply the last step in a complex network of transformations, and is probably part of a larger structure that fires to that object. Thus it does not appear to be the single cell that recognizes faces, but rather the whole structure.]

There is also evidence that the more complex the object the longer it takes to recognize it. For example, the neurons that respond to simple stimuli, like bars, take roughly 45 milliseconds, but those that respond to complex stimuli like faces take roughly 150 milliseconds.

Still other neurons have been found that respond only when stimuli enter through several sense modalities. For example, the sight of a hammer shattering a piece of glass, when accompanied by the sound, will evoke a strong response; but there will be no response to either sight or sound taken separately.

A BRIEF SUMMARY OVERVIEW, AND SOME COMMENTS

What are the brain's overall design principles? Billions of neurons, each typically with thousands of synapse links, fire volleys of information to one another, apparently serving as discrete, but to some extent analog, thresholding elements. The sheet-like brain is organized into layers, each containing large numbers of simultaneously firing neurons. There are typically large numbers of connections laterally within a layer, and also to adjacent layers, and often to more distant layers. Smaller structures of neurons are organized into iterated columns that rise through several layers. The general overall structure is rich in both converging and diverging pathways, as well as cycles of links that appear to serve for rich feedback loops.

This chapter has concentrated on the system for visual perception, because far more is known about it at a relatively firm anatomical/physiological level than about any of the other intelligent processes. Roughly half of the brain's many billions of neurons are involved with perception, predominantly with vision.

The overall structure of the visual system is relatively clear: The sensory interface, where information impinges upon the system from the outside environment is, with its millions of input devices, massively parallel. Relatively local near-neighbor operations successively transform sensed information, at the same time converging and diverging it, as it flows through the several layers of neurons in the retina and in the primary and a number of secondary visual cortexes.

The brain's basic mechanism is the neuron. Each neuron appears to compute a threshold function over the information transmitted to it by the large number of other neurons that synapse onto and therefore link to it. This threshold operation takes roughly $1-2$ milliseconds; yet the mind/brain handles extremely complex problems, like recognizing and describing scenes of objects, remembering facts and ideas, conversing, and making inferences, in a few seconds or less. Visual recognition takes roughly $30-200$ msec. Therefore the serial depth of processing is extremely shallow, possibly only a few dozen, or a few hundred at most.

There is a serial depth of two or three transformations in the retina, followed by one transformation in the lateral geniculate and possibly three to five in the primary visual cortex. The perceptual process continues with transformations effected as information flows through a hierarchy of at least 20 visual areas. Since this is a parallel-serial hierarchy, the depth in terms of secondary visual areas is roughly 6. Therefore, if three to five transformations are effected in each layer, the total depth of transformations would appear to be roughly 30 or 40. In addition, the richness of interconnections and feedback loops from layer to layer within each area suggests that information may well cycle more than once through an area.

This suggests that processing proceeds in a massively parallel but to some extent serial manner moving through these perceptual areas.

A number of separate areas are involved in processing. In general, within each area, processes are massively parallel and also to a small but essential extent serial. Rich interconnectivity, with each neuron linked to large numbers of others, effectively gives rich convergence and divergence of information—that is, a fan-out/fan-in network. It is also common for different areas to be linked to one another. Most areas that are connected appear to be connected with two-way links, but each area is typically linked to only a few other areas (1 to 8 in the analysis of the visual areas described previously). Sometimes the visual system appears to examine different components of the total process in separate parts of the brain. However, then this information must be merged together, as is information from the different sense modalities.

People developing connectionist models of the brain (e.g., Kohonen, 1982; Hopfield, 1982; Ballard, 1984) appear to interpret the brain's rich connectivity, especially between major areas, as indicating a completely connected graph, or something close; but the brain is clearly far from completely connected. Each neuron may have thousands of links, and many neurons may link to thousands of different neurons; but most of these are quite nearby, and a few thousand is a miniscule percent of billions. Even the functional areas are linked in what may well be a data-flow manner, rather than as a complete graph. Each of dozens, or hundreds, of areas links to only a handful (2 or 3 or up to 8 in the visual areas), not to all the others. Thus the brain has a point-to-point, and not a complete graph, topology.

Moving up through the visual system, more and more abstract aspects of the scene are recognized. This culminates in what appear to be neurons that fire selectively to complex objects like faces and hands, and to complex multimodality stimuli, like the sound and the sight of a hammer striking a windowpane. There appear to be enough of these neurons to give fault-tolerant redundancy. Each of these neurons is not the recognizer of the complex object, but simply a member of the team of speakers for a whole complex structure of neurons that have accumulated, transformed, and assessed the information in the image.

Chapter Fifteen

PERCEPTION: IMAGE PROCESSING, PATTERN RECOGNITION, COMPUTER VISION

Of all the intellectual processes, image processing and the perception of real-world patterned objects may well be the most complex. Indeed, more than half of the brain is involved in perception. Perceptual processes are certainly among the fastest, and the most parallel. Anatomical evidence indicates clearly that they are extremely parallel at the level of the retina, which contains a massively parallel 2-dimensional array of hundreds of millions of sensors. The anatomical structure of the entire visual system, and the astounding speed of perception, also strongly suggest massive parallelism throughout.

THE PROBLEM OF PERCEPTION POSED

A good general perception program should be able to recognize and describe any complex real-world scene that contains a few dozen, or even a few hundred, different objects. It must further be able to do this in real time, while some of these objects are moving about, by processing the stream of images input continuously to it via a tv camera or similar transducing device. Researchers have not yet come close to achieving such systems—although once sufficiently large and suitably configured multi-computers are made available, rapid progress may become possible.

Perception is an extremely complex and difficult problem. There are thousands, or millions, of different objects. Each object can vary in a countless number of unknown and wildly nonlinear ways: Consider all the different kinds of chairs, houses, or dogs, or how a face can blossom into a smile or dissolve in pain.

Dozens of more or less specific perception problems have been posed, such as printed letters, polyhedra, living-room scenes, house-street scenes, aerial photos, blood cells, lung x-rays, faces. Each such domain, or even the recognition of a single complex class of objects (e.g., chair, Versailles, neuron) in each one of these domains may well be equivalent in difficulty to a separate game, like tic-tac-toe, checkers, chess, GO. The general perception problem is at least equivalent to the goal of developing a general problem solver-game player—another tremendously difficult problem on which very little progress has been made. Specialized vision systems can and should be developed for particular problems of practical importance, as for medical images of blood cells, neurons, tumors. However, a general system is not only the crucial long-term goal; it is almost certainly necessary for reasonably good performance with relatively unknown and unsimplified natural real-world images of any specific sort.

A single complex object—like an apple, typewriter, chair, house, neuron, bike, airplane or face—must, to be recognizable, be digitized and resolved into (roughly) at least a 64-by-64 or 128-by 128-array. A whole scene, of 5, 10, 100, or more such objects, needs an array at least 256 by 256, 512 by 512, or 1024 by 1024 in size.

Each of a human being's eyes contains a roughly circular array of roughly 10,000,000 cones (the receptors for color and shape), plus an array of roughly 100,000,000 rods (the receptors for the detection of change, in both space or time). These massively parallel arrays of input transducing devices set the specifications for the very large amount of information that must be input to a program, and its format in a 2-dimensional array. A television camera is today the most convenient and most widely used transducer capable of approaching these specifications to a reasonable degree. Very large arrays of memory cells are needed to store the resulting images.

Far more important than the very large amount of data that must be processed is the extremely complex set of processes that must be effected. Objects must be recognized under severely distorting conditions (e.g., fog, camouflage, occlusion, inadequate or uneven lighting, the linear transformations of translation, rotation, and magnification, and—by far the most difficult—the potentially infinite number of different particular non-linear transforming states, as rock crumbles, wood rots, muscles move and sag, skin ages, emotions distort).

A large amount of semantic, contextual information must be used. The perceptual system must have in some form or other good, general, working models of each object it is capable of recognizing, and it must be able to apply and use these models in an extremely short interval of time.

INPUT TRANSDUCTION AND THE PRELIMINARY PROCESSING OF IMAGES

All vision programs for the digital computer do the following: The image is transduced and input to an array of "pixels" (picture elements), and then examined for information of interest. Occasionally—as with an extremely well controlled and error-free industrial assemblyline, or a standardized envelop with properly placed address, return address, and stamp—the system need only examine specific locations. However, except for very specific problems the system might find virtually anything virtually anywhere; so a general system must examine the entire image.

The first operations typically attempt to assess local gradients, edges, textures, shadings in the 2-dimensional image that can be used to infer 3-dimensional shapes, and optical flow (Rosenfeld and Kak, 1976; Marr, 1983; Horn and Sjoberg, 1978; Ullman, 1979). It would appear that all of these are amenable to the massively parallel application of relatively local processes.

Alternative Approaches to Early Preprocessing, and Appropriate Hardware

PARALLEL ASSESSMENTS EVERYWHERE, USING PARALLEL ARRAYS

This first examination of the raw transduced array of pixels can be made parallel, hence very fast, by having an array of processors like the CLIP, DAP, or MPP (see Chapter 8) apply one or more simple local operations: for example, 2- or 4-cell gradient detectors, 3-by-3 windows to extract short edges, and possibly V-by-W windows for other larger features like angles, curves, rectangles, squares. (V and W must be kept small or else processing can grow costly in either extra hardware for parallel execution, or in time.) An N-by-M array of processors can examine an N-by-M image array using a k-instruction sequence of processes (e.g., gradient, edge, and other local feature detectors) in k instruction cycles when the window is built into hardware, or 9k instructions when it must shift and fetch information in a 3-by-3 window one piece at a time. For larger windows that are not built into the hardware, still more shifting operations are needed, to move each pixel along the path to the center cell, where it is processed.)

STREAMING THE SENSED IMAGE ARRAY SERIALLY THROUGH A PIPELINE

Alternately the scan for simple local features like gradients and edges can be carried out by serially streaming the tv image through a pipeline like the PICAP, Cytocomputer, Pipe, or deAnza (see Chapter 7). When the tv image is input serially (as is universally the case today; even when input via a parallel solid state sensor like a CCD array, the image is then shifted serially into the computer) the image can at the same time be streamed through the pipeline with virtually no additional time needed. [This is the case only because what could and should be a parallel process—the input of the parallel image—has been serialized by today's techniques for interfacing tv cameras to computers, with the resulting much too slow millisecond speeds.] Since a k-stage pipeline can execute a k-instruction process over an N-by-M image in $NM + k$ instruction cycles, it is inevitably far slower than the single instruction cycle needed by a parallel array.

SERIAL SCANNING, ATTEMPTING TO LOOK ONLY AT REGIONS OF INTEREST

Finally the scan can be made serial and placed under the control of a program that periodically assesses the information it has gathered so far, and decides where to look and/or what to look for next. This is the simplest approach when using a conventional serial computer, and probably the approach most commonly taken today. A small MIMD network (see Chapters 6, and 10-13) may, when a divide-and-conquer approach can be taken, be used to speed up the process.

In theory, such a system need not look at all the parts of the image; it need look only at those subregions that previously gathered information suggests are likely to contain useful information. It needs $kS + jA$ instructions to examine S spots with a k-instruction process, and make A assessments with a j instruction process. How frequent and how time consuming these conditional pauses to re-assess the situation are, how much of the image can safely be ignored, and how often these decisions are correct, will depend heavily upon the image's complexity. Therefore, to the extent that (as is the case in real-world scenes) individual instances of an object vary more widely, and images are rich with detail, and distorted and obscured in a wider variety of ways, more regions must be examined and more intermediate decisions must be made.

Unfortunately, this kind of approach invites careful preparation of simplified images—for example, with strongly contrasting, unbroken contours and simple, rigid objects. With such carefully simplified toy images this approach, since it need not look everywhere in the N-by-M array, might be faster than the NM + k pipeline scan. But in the general case, there is always the important possibility that any spot in the image will contain crucial information—the crooked nose, freckle, smoking gun, or telltale sign. Therefore not only might it need kNM instructions (or even more, since it might decide it needs to look at the same spot several times), but to this must be added the jA assesments and decisions (j might grow very large, and endless loops are possible).

QUANTITATIVE-QUALITATIVE AND ICONIC-SEMANTIC ENCODINGS

This section attempts to put the first stages of image processing in the same framework as all the subsequent stages of object perception (to be examined next), and language understanding and associative semantic memory networks (to be examined in Chapters 16 and 17). Because each of these tasks is typically formulated using a radically different memory representation, major problems arise when one tries to integrate these separate parts into a total program. Yet there is real hope that they can all be formulated using the same basic structures.

As soon as information is input to a digital computer it has, by definition, been digitized and discretized. The raw transduced image array typically contains either one integer for each cell, indicating its grey-scale intensity, or three integers, indicating intensity on each of three primary colors (usually red, green, blue). When gradients, oriented edges, textures, angles, or other simple features are computed, the results are usually output into arrays where each cell contains an integer that indicates the strength, or certainty, or probability that this feature has been found at this location.

Each array in which a (transformed, abstracted) image is stored implicitly "labels" or names that image. That is, the program's pointer to that array (the name used to identify that array when it is to be processed) serves as its symbolic component. Alternately, the symbol can be made explicit, by storing (in either an array or a list) name-value pairs (e.g., 'red-3', 'green-5', 'blue-8', 'vertical-7', 'L-angle-3', 'bark-4', 'square-21').

Thus there are always two components to a piece of information: the symbol labeling it, and the number showing its strength. Even the raw input image has an array of name-value pairs like 'red-3'. This is true even when only one grey-scale value is stored, since these values are actually arrays of name-value pairs of the form 'intensity-5'.

Researchers often talk about the "numerical," "iconic" (probably better called "pictorial") quality of the raw image and "pixel-pushing" the "low-level" transformations like gradients and edges. At some point—certainly by the time such entities as house, penguin, Nixon, and possibly even window or square are implied—the image is considered to be converted into a "high-level" "symbolic" domain. But this appears to be a subjective (and vague) judgment on the part of the researcher, based upon the meaning of these concepts to an intelligent human being. 'House-17','window-9','vertical-7','red-23' all specify exactly the same kind of name-value structure.

There is a tendency to think of the symbolic semantic levels as deterministic (either it is a house or it isn't), and of the iconic numerical levels as analog—reflecting the analog energies input to the computer, and their spatial interrelations. The real difference lies in the fact that a 2-valued logic is often used at the higher levels—either it is a house or it isn't. There is no need to store either 'house-0' or 'house-1', The name 'house' will suffice, since it need not be mentioned if its value is '0' ('false').

Thus at every level of perception, language processing and remembering information always has both a symbolic and a numerical component (although one or the other may be of more importance depending on the circumstances). This suggests that programs can be formulated that move gradually from iconic to symbolic.

THE TRANSITION TO SUBSEQUENT HIGHER-LEVEL PROCESSING

The information extracted from the array's parallel scan is most simply stored in the array's memory, ready for further parallel array processing. Or, if the array is linked as in a pyramid, it can be merged into a suitably smaller array. To be handled in a serial manner it must be sent to a conventional computer, or to a suitably asynchronous multi-computer. To accomplish this, today's arrays need N instructions, to shift all N columns out through the rows. Better input-output networks linking the array to a serial computer or MIMD network (see Chapter 13) could eliminate this bottleneck.

The result of a pipeline's serial scan can be stored in one or more conventional computers, but now each computer will work serially. C computers can give up to C-fold speedups; but they can be severely degraded (as is almost always the case today) by message-passing delays and unanticipated waits for needed information.

The following sections examine what different types of vision programs do once the image has been input and any preliminary processing has been completed.

APPROACHES TO THE PERCEPTION OF COMPLEX SCENES OF PATTERNED OBJECTS

Several different kinds of computer programs have been coded to attempt to process real-world images, and to recognize and describe the objects that they contain.

Systems that Use Structures of Feature-Detectors

A large number of programs have been developed that make use of structures of features (e.g., Doyle, 1960; Marill et al., 1963; Levine, 1969; Shirai, 1978). A very large number of feature-detectors have been formulated and coded. Programs of this sort tend to be a collection of such feature-detectors chosen to handle the specific or general set of images being processed.

Some of these features are global (e.g., the area, perimeter, center of gravity, convex hull, or moments of a bounded region). Many are more or less local (e.g., edges, angles, curves, enclosures, textures, spikes, legs, noses, ears).

Some programs use a very carefully chosen set that is clearly ad hoc to the type of image to be processed. Others use a more general, usually larger, set of more general features in the hope of being able to handle a wider range of pictures.

Some programs apply all feature-detectors in parallel, and then combine their implications. Others use a serial discrimination tree to apply features. Still others use both parallel and serial control mechanisms— for example, applying several features, then assessing the results and deciding which to apply next, and where, continually looping through this process.

Some programs use only one level of features (although often the different features differ markedly in complexity and globality). Others compound or in other ways combine features, building up successively higher levels.

Several different approaches can be taken in terms of the amount of certainty the system demands before it makes decisions. At one extreme, all features must be matched precisely, but in order to handle real-world images each feature must be made a disjunction that will succeed as a result of any of a wide range of possibilities. At the other extreme, the system can make a set of imprecise probabilistic assessments, assign a number (e.g., a probability, fuzzy value, certainty, or weight) to each implied possibility, combine the numbers with which each possibility is implied, and choose the most highly implied.

There are several other dimensions along which these programs can range. Possibly the crucial issue is simply how good are the particular features and the total combination.

This approach is inevitably weak, since it cannot examine relations among features. For example, it might find a seat, and several legs— but it would not be able to tell whether the legs were below and supporting the seat. (This is not entirely true, since a more complex feature-detector might be coded to look in one fell swoop for "legs supporting seat." But that means that a separate, monolithic, feature-detector would be needed for every possible instance of every possible object and subobject, leading to an impossibly large and slow program.)

Prototype and Frame/Schema-Based Vision Systems

A "prototype" based system usually makes use of one global feature-detector (or occasionally several) for each object to be recognized. It attempts to match the prototype with some region of the image.

Often the prototype is a simple template, and the match an exact and completely rigid template-match, or, alternately, a looser correlation (Unger, 1959; Kazmierczak, 1960; Sebestyen, 1961; Rabinow, 1968; see Duda and Hart, 1973). The prototype can be much more sophisticated, for example a 3-dimensional graph that attempts to model the object in all its variations (Sakai et al., 1976; Brooks, 1981).

Probably the kind of prototype structure most widely proposed today (although complete working programs have not yet been written except to handle one or two perfectly crafted simple line drawings) are "frame/schema-driven" systems, which essentially attempt to match a graph that has been abstracted from the raw input image with the appropriate object-graph stored in the program's memory. The "frame" (Minsky, 1975) is an attempt to make precise and programable what the British psychologist Bartlett described in 1932 as a "schema"—which in its turn is an age-old concept that is probably earliest described by the Indian philosophers as an active flame-like stuff that continually re-constructs itself to take the shape of the object being recognized (see, for example, Zimmer, 1951).

Essentially a frame is a Pascal record extended to contain (a) components that are procedures as well as variables, and (b) default values to be used when information cannot be found. The record often contains other records as components; these records contain other records; and so on. Therefore the frame structure can be used to represent a complex graph. Figure 15-1 gives a few simple examples of small fragments of graphs.

```
((roof,above-touching,wall)&
    (wall,contains,([window,window,door]:window,left-of,door)&
            (window,right-of,door)))
                                        (a)
```

```
(((frame,built-from,(crossbar,dropbar,frontfork)) &
    (crossbar,back-joined-to,dropbar)&
    (crossbar,front-joined-to,(frontfork,handlebars))&
    (dropbar,top-joined-to,crossbar)&(dropbar,bottom-joined-to,wheel)&
    (frontfork,top-joined-to,crossbar)&(frontfork,bottom-join-to,wheel)&
    (handlebars,center-joined-to,crossbar))
                                        (b)
```

FIGURE 15-1. Fragments of graphs for 'house' and for 'cycle'. (a) Part of the highest levels of the graph for 'house.' Window, door, and so forth will subsequently be defined. Strings like 'left-of' and 'contains' call appropriate procedures that in effect are the system's interpretations of these terms. (b) A part of the high level graph for 'cycle' (with some but not all the needed detail of the relative positions of subparts and their joins specified). Complex, well-tuned procedures are needed to interpret and look for things like "crossbar" and "wheel" and relations like "built-from" and "top-joined-to."

Converting a photograph or tv image into a perfect abstract graph of high-level features that a graph-matching program can then use to recognize the scene is a somewhat magical (if not impossible) task. This is because in many cases (except for very simple or carefully prepared images) the often highly defective and distorted real-world objects must first be recognized before they can be converted into a perfect line drawing and then into a perfect graph.

The scheme that most researchers appear to have in mind is to find either contours or regions (or, occasionally, both) from which to construct the line drawing. Serial algorithms are typically used to trace contours, and to grow regions and then piece them together into larger regions. However, one can destroy virtually all contour information (simply take a large artgum and make random, drunken erasings), or region information (simply take brushes and paint in random textures or abstract squiggles), and still have scenes that human beings recognize with no trouble at all.

The typical frame-based system takes the abstract graph into which the raw image has been converted and attempts to match it, serially, against each of the graphs of the different objects that the system has been preprogrammed to contain. Since nobody has come close to achieving programs that transform complex real-world tv images into good line drawings, researchers begin with carefully human-drawn images, or with tv images of very simple scenes (e.g., well lit polyhedra, or highly contrasting satellite images of rectangular buildings, grass and concrete).

Only a few object-models are used: It is very difficult and time-consuming to construct them. More than a few will take the computer too long and lead to errors, since matching is a time-consuming and fallible process.

Syntactic Recognition Systems

Another possible approach is to use a 2-dimensional picture grammar to parse the scene and recognize objects (Grimsdale et al., 1960; Narasimhan, 1966; Miller and Shaw, 1968; Fu, 1974).

There are several reasons why this is by no means a straightforward extension of the linguistic grammars that have been powerfully developed for programming languages and partially developed for natural languages:

> The perception system must start with the raw pixels of the image as its primitives; there are no high-level built-in primitives such as the letters of the alphabet and the words that are used in language.

> The 1-dimensional language string always has each word linked to at most only two other words—the single word immediately to its left and the single word immediately to its right—whereas the 2-dimensionality of the scene allows each pictorial entity to be linked to a potentially infinite number of other entities.

> The system must cope with a potentially infinite variety of different representations of the same object, whereas language systems always insist that everything be spelled perfectly and be properly bounded by spaces.

> The system must cope with arbitrarily large amounts of distortion and noise, and of missing parts.

> A 2-dimensional grammar must be constructed, and it must be able to handle the far greater variability in relative placement of objects and of groups of objects, including touching, occlusion, and arbitrarily large gaps and spaces between objects.

As a result, linguistic systems must also start with simple, perfect line drawings rather than with raw real-world tv images. The system then tries to parse the scene, by applying the grammar's production-like rewrite rules until a root node is achieved. Almost always this parse is a serial procedure, as it is for linguistic parsing (although parallelizations would appear to be possible).

Cone- and Pyramid-Based Systems

A number of researchers have been developing computer vision systems that have multi-layer converging structures of the sort that map naturally into pyramid multi-computers (e.g., Hanson and Riseman, 1974, 1976, 1978, 1981; Neveu, Chin, and Dyer, 1984; Tanimoto, 1976, 1978, 1983b; Uhr, 1972, 1976, 1978; see Tanimoto and Klinger, 1981; Rosenfeld, 1984). Indeed, these systems have been the primary impetus toward the specification and development of hardware pyramids.

A variety of different algorithms, programs, and general approaches have been developed for pyramids. Some researchers (e.g., Burt, 1984) compute simple Gaussian averages and Laplacian gradients at each level of resolution. Others (e.g., Levine, 1978, 1980) move "bottom-up" from the raw input image to extract features at each level. Others (e.g., Pietikainen and Rosenfeld, 1981; Cibulskis and Dyer, 1984) move up and down through the pyramid to attempt to link different features at different levels. Others (e.g., Kelly, 1971) have the higher levels direct processing in a "top-down" manner, for example, zooming in to regions of interest, and glancing about (PICAP—see Kruse, 1980—was designed and used in this way). Others (e.g., Uhr, 1972, 1978; Uhr and Douglass, 1979; Li and Uhr, 1986) attempt to successively transform the raw image's information into successively more abstract representations, of successively more complex features, characteristics, subobjects, and objects, and to use this higher-level information to help direct lower-level processing, thus combining bottom-up and top-down processing. Transformations are effected by micromodular operations that examine a relatively local region of the image being transformed, but with each operation applied everywhere, in parallel. They are thus best executed by an array (or other local ensemble) of processors—for example, a bundle of neurons. They are reminiscent of IF-THEN productions, except that they make use of the implicit spatial information in the image arrays, they typically use weights (or probabilities or fuzzy values) and thresholds, and the overall parallel-serial pyramid structure determines how they imply and combine their results, by merging them into spatially related locations of neighboring layers of the pyramid.

To take a simple example, the raw image is transduced and input to the array (call it the "retina") at the base of the pyramid. Now a great variety of processes can be applied to the raw image and to the abstracted images generated by previous processes, as indicated by the following simple example: First, local averaging and differencing operations can be used to eliminate tiny specks of noise and to get gradients. Next might come local edge, color and simple texture detectors; then detectors for longer edges, simple curves and angles, and more complex textures; then detectors for simple enclosures (e.g., square, rectangle, loop) and simple subobjects (e.g., windowpane, brick); then for more complex shapes and objects; and on and on, moving up through the layers of the pyramid as determined by the program.

Figure 15-2 gives a few very simple examples. Typically the transform would look for many more things and for several things at the same location, weights and thresholds would be carefully adjusted (possibly by learning), and large numbers of transforms would be used to imply each possibility; and contextual information would frequently be used.

There are a number of alternative ways in which such a pyramid system of micromodular transforms can be organized. For example, each detector can examine whatever region of information the programmer chooses. (It is probably preferable to use several layers of the pyramid to examine large regions; for example, a 9-by-9 region might be processed using a 3-by-3 window that examines the information implied by a 3 by 3 of 9 3-by-3 windows at the next-lower level.) A large number of detectors will typically be used; each might imply a number of different possibilities; each might be as complex as the programmer chooses. Each possible alternative will typically be implied by a large number of detectors.

Features can be applied at any and every level of the pyramid deemed appropriate, and not only (as in an array) at a single level. This means that successively more abstract entities can be implied, moving up the pyramid, and successively more abstract and more global features can be assessed. Complex structures of a number of features from several different levels can be combined into each individual decision. Numbers (e.g., weights) can be associated with features and their implications, and used to make choices.

It seems likely that dozens, or even hundreds, of such image processing, feature-detecting, compounding, and characterizing transforms would be needed at each layer of such a pyramid—but not thousands or millions. Separate pyramids might be used for different hierarchies (e.g., one for texture, another for contours, another for shape, another for region growing). However, it seems preferable to have all the information implied by all processes stored in a single pyramid (so long as it

```
-1 -1 -1 -1                          1  1  1  1  1
 1  1  1  1  ≥ 3 →  UP-HOR, H       -1 -1 -1 -1 -1  ≥3 →  DOWN-HOR, H
```

           (a)   *(b)*

```
  2 -1 -2           -1  1 -1          3  1  0 -1 -3
 -1  4 -1           -1  1 -1          3  1  0 -1 -3
 -2 -1  2           -1  1 -1          3  1  0 -1 -3
  ≥2 NWDIAG          ≥0 THINVERT, V    ≥ 8→RIGHT-VERT, V
```

        (c)   *(d)*   *(e)*

```
V=2    H=-3            NW-ANGLE =5    NE-ANGLE =5
V=3    H=-2
V=4,                  SW-ANGLE =5    SE-ANGLE =5
H=4    H=3   H=2
       ≥ 10→SW-ANGLE       ≥ 15  RECT, WPANE
```

        (f)   *(g)*

```
KY=3       SKY=3       SKY=3          CROSSBAR    CROSSBAR    HANDLEBAR
OOF=5      ROOF=7      ROOF=5         DROPBAR     FRONTFORK   FRONTFORK
/INDOW=7,  DOOR=9,     WINDOW=7,      WHEEL       WHEEL       WHEEL
;USH=4     STOOP=7     BUSH=4
                       ≥ 29→HOUSE, BUILDING                   ≥6  CYCLE, BIKE
```

        (i)   *(j)*

FIGURE 15-2. Some Simple Examples of Transforming Operations. a) Up-oriented horizontal edge. b) Down-oriented horizontal edge. c) NorthWest diagonal. d) Thin vertical and vertical. e) Right-oriented vertical and vertical. f) SouthWest Angle. g) Rectangle, Window pane. i) House and Building (At a Much Higher Level). j) Cycle and Bike (At a Much Higher Level). [These are 2-dimensional masks that are placed over each location in the array being transformed. Each value shown might be multiplied against the value found directly under it in the array, then all values added together; then, if this result achieves a designated threshold, the transform's implications are merged into the designated cell (either in the same array or a directly linked array). For simplicity, assume that the array pixel is either 0 or 1, and often the result of prior operations that get gradients, thin, etc. Thresholds and weights are not always shown.]

has enough memory). Then any transforming process can make use of whatever mixture of information the programmer deems appropriate. For example, an enclosure can be implied by a threshold operator that will succeed from a large variety of different sets of information about interior textures and color, exterior indicants of background, and sections (not necessarily perfect or continuous) of the contour, including some of its curves, angles, and gradients.

The hardware best suited to this kind of pyramid program would probably not be a traditional pyramid. It would need more power—that is, more memory, more processors, more powerful and independent processors, and/or more communication bandwidth—moving up toward the apex. A multi-apex pyramid, or some other structure that diverged as well as converged information might well be preferable.

Some Comments: The Great Complexity and Difficulty of the Perception Problem

No matter what the approach, to date results have been meager. Only a handful of programs have demonstrated an ability to recognize only a few objects in a few carefully chosen images. This should not be surprising, since perception is one of the most difficult problems people have ever tried to attack, with the computer or without.

In most cases, researchers have not even considered the actual physical structure of a system that would execute their programs in real time. The major exceptions are the cone/pyramid systems, which are based on specific underlying models of multi-computers that would execute them directly, and efficiently.

Because of the extreme complexity of the problem, many researchers have decided to concentrate on a specific subproblem. Some are examining how to extract regions, others how to determine 3-dimensional shape aspects of surfaces, others how to detect motion, others how to detect complex textures. These are all given meaning and purpose only when they are used, as diverse sources of relevant information, for the higher level process of perceptual recognition. Indeed, it seems likely that none of these problems can be completely solved. To the contrary, there will be many images from which each type of information can not possibly be got. That is exactly why the full system must make use of many different types of information.

In such a situation it is vitally important to examine the total problem, so that each subsystem plays its appropriate role. The subsystems themselves cannot be meaningfully evaluated in any other way. This places a much greater burden on the computer. Only very large multi-computers can offer researchers the enormous amount of computing power needed to develop and examine perception systems that combine the various subparts into a total system.

MULTI-COMPUTERS FOR PERCEPTION: ARRAYS, PIPES, PYRAMIDS, NETWORKS

There have probably been more multi-computers and specialized architectures proposed and built for perception than for any other AI function.

2-Dimensional Arrays

The parallel arrays (Chapter 8), and the pipeline processors that simulate them (Chapter 7), are to some extent modeled after, and reminiscent of, the retinal array, but with the following simplifications:

Today's systems are much smaller, with 64-by-64 to 256-by-256 processors in the arrays and, at most, 256 in the pipelines. If the retina were a square array its dimensions would be roughly 3,000-by-3,000 cones and 10,000-by-10,000 rods. One of the most important features of the true parallel array multi-computers is that they can be made larger as needed, without any theoretical limit.

Each processor links directly to only a small local window of 4, 6, or 8 near neighbors, whereas in the retina substantially larger numbers are linked to. But arrays can handle larger windows, albeit serially or via a switching network, and more hardware links can be added.

In both living visual systems and multi-computer arrays the likelihood of links is inversely proportional to distance; but in the computer arrays the drop-off is far more abrupt, where the directly connected window ends.

Today's multi-computer arrays are completely regular and without any tolerances for faults, whereas the retinal arrays in living organisms function well despite irregularities and defective cells. However (although little has yet been done), fault tolerance can be built into computer arrays.

An array of processors is ideal for executing the same local window operation everywhere in the image array, or in arrays that contain transformations (e.g., averages, extractions, or abstractions) of the raw image array. An array with N processors can give N-fold speedups (see, for example, Cordella et al., 1978; Uhr et al., 1982) on a wide variety of (but by no means all) algorithms. Arrays can be made even faster, by a factor of n, for example, by building in special convolution or other window operations that fetch and transform n pieces of data (e.g., a 5-by-5 window of 25 pixels, or even a 100-by-100 window, with appropriate strengths assigned to each).

Arrays are general purpose, although they can easily become extremely slow and inefficient. They can be used in reasonably efficient ways for a wide variety of processes other than local window operations—for example, syntactic recognition (Chiang, 1985), relaxation (Marks, 1980), Fourier transforms (Strong, 1985), rotation (Reeves and De Sellas Moura, 1985), segmentation and labeling (Oldfield and Reddaway, 1985).

Pipelines that Serially Simulate Arrays

The pipeline systems (Chapter 7)—such as the Cray vector processor and the Floating Point System for number crunching; and the Cytocomputers, PICAP, Pipe, an Warp for image processing—can all be used to simulate array processors. However, whereas the true array processor executes an operation everywhere in one instruction cycle, a P-computer pipeline takes $P + (NxM/P)$ instruction cycles. To be used efficiently, it should execute a sequence of instructions that is exactly P, or an integer multiple, m, of P. This will need $mP(NxM/P) + mP$—or $m(NxM + P)$—instruction cycles. A true array will need mP instruction cycles.

The longer the pipeline the faster the system, but the harder it becomes to assign a fruitful sequence of instructions to all the processors, and to handle intermediate results with the limited memory in each stage of the pipeline. Some of these problems can be eliminated by a reconfigurable pipeline (see Chapter 13) where each processor has access to a larger random access memory. It is not clear whether the necessary additional costs are justified.

The simulated arrays will inevitably be much slower than the true arrays. On the other hand, careful design can introduce a number of significant speedups when an architecture is specialized to a specific type of problem (e.g., image processing) and a specific array size. For example, iteration and border tests can be built into the hardware—but an operation that takes 1 microsecond on a true 512-by-512 array will take 250,000 microseconds (250 milliseconds) in a scanning array, even if all the overheads for iteration and border tests have been eliminated. Because a scanning array has far fewer processors, each processor can be made much faster, using more expensive hardware. Typically, then, the processors in these arrays take roughly 100 nanoseconds or less per operation, or 25 milliseconds for the whole array.

The basic image processor can be made faster by adding hardware that scans the image array with a longer pipeline or/and an array of processors like the CLIP7 or PIXIE-5000 (see Chapter 8). To achieve the speed of a true array the pipeline would need as many processors as are used in the true array (i.e., 250,000 in our example). It would be quite difficult, if not impossible, to keep such a long pipeline filled.

Therefore it appears that an array of processors will be faster than a pipeline of the same size. On the other hand, a much smaller pipeline can be given much faster (and more expensive), carefully optimized processors. Sometimes, as in the new short-pipeline Cyto-computers and the PIPE, these may approach an array in speed, and may well be more cost-effective. A system like the PIXIE-5000 or CLIP7 that scans a smaller hardware array over a larger image array can combine many of the virtues of pipelines and arrays.

Pseudo-Complete Graphs: Reconfiguring Networks, Rings, Etc.

The shuffle-exchange-based BBN Butterfly (Chapter 6) has been chosen by the Rochester computer vision group as the hardware they will use to implement their vision systems. It appears that these will be of several general types, including "connectionist" nerve network-like models (Feldman, 1982), feature-detecting systems that use Hough (1962) transforms (Ballard, 1981), which extract features and map them into feature space, and hierarchical, roughly pyramid-structured vision systems (Ballard, 1985).

The generality of the reconfiguring network, which gives a pseudo-complete graph, should make these applications feasible. The amount of parallel speedup may well be relatively small. The Rochester Butterfly is roughly a million dollar system, even though it has only 128 computers. Larger reconfiguring networks are likely to be even more expensive per processor, because of the increasingly larger NlogN bank of switches needed.

A general approach that may be well suited to vision is to divide-and-conquer. The raw image array can easily be decomposed into virtually any desired number of subarrays. Each of these can then be assigned to a different processor. The mapping of a large image array into a smaller physical array processor described in Chapter 8 is an example of this.

PASM (Chapter 13) is probably the system most suited to a divide-and-conquer approach. Each of its computers can be given a subarray of the larger image array. All can shift information at interior borders directly to the proper neighbor, via the reconfiguring network, with relatively little delay. After a succession of operations has transformed the image into a set of abstract images (e.g., maps of edges, curves, textures, angles, enclosures, and other simple and compound features), PASM can repartition these images and assign subregions of interest to different subsets of processors. A different controller can be assigned to each of these subsets (or each processor can use its own controller). Therefore, PASM offers a variety of tools that give the programmer a great deal of flexibility in concentrating the appropriate amount of processor power at each region of interest and on each problem of importance.

The array/net could handle the image array in a similar way. It could intersperse simple local and powerful global processes without moving the data at all. It could get appreciable speedups when operating in SIMD mode, and interior border information could be passed with great efficiency. But other types of information could be passed only relatively slowly over the global bus. Nor would it have PASM's flexibility in partitioning an abstracted image array into regions of different sizes, and concentrating just the appropriate amount of processing power on each.

In contrast to PASM, the BBN Butterfly, and the array/net, a system linked via a crossbar, star, bus, or ring (e.g., the S-1, Cm*, Crystal) will usually suffer from two major problems: The number of processors that can be linked together is much smaller, on the order of a few dozen at most. The operating system overhead for message-passing, and the consequent slowdowns, are much greater—at least with today's operating systems. These two problems mean first that the programmer must try to find "large grain" algorithms (i.e., with long periods of processing between messages) and send messages a long time before they are needed. Even then the speedup will almost certainly be too small for real-time perception.

Task/Process/Algorithm-Structured Architectures

This section examines a variety of more or less task, process, algorithm-structured architectures. These can be developed to be extremely specialized and almost optimized to a particular, more or less narrow, specific job or class of jobs—for example, to inspect a carefully designed and handcrafted circuit. Or they can be developed to be as general as possible, as would be the case if true general-purpose data-flow hardware could be achieved. Or, as with pipelines, arrays, pyramids, and augmented pyramids, they can be made more or less general.

SPECIAL-PURPOSE SYSTOLIC AND CUSTOM-DESIGNED PROCESSORS

Special-purpose systolic processors and custom designed chips (Chapter 7), for example, for thresholded convolutions to extract edges, can, where appropriate, give substantial speedups. Today they are simply added to the high-speed bus of a conventional serial computer, to serve as additional special processors when needed, much like special floating point hardware. They should probably be incorporated into efficient larger heterogeneous systems that have an overall process-structured architecture.

SPECIAL-PURPOSE PROCESS-STRUCTURED NETWORKS

The EMMA (Manara and Stringa, 1981) is an architecture that begins to mirror the structure of processes that it must execute. Variant EMMA systems have been developed for the Italian Post Office and the French Post Office. The parallel-serial set of processes devised to recognize the relevant information on the envelope defines and is mapped into an appropriately configured set of computers.

There appears to be a general structure indicated by this kind of multiletter pattern recognition problem. However then the more specific problem posed by the specific language and type of information to be processed for each country's envelopes leads to further specialization. It seems likely that a general-purpose EMMA system could be developed for this type of application, but one that, because it used more computers and more time than absolutely necessary, would not be as cost effective in the actual applied setting.

ARRAYS AND PYRAMIDS

The large arrays, as discussed previously, are strikingly fast at computing local window and other near-neighbor operations, but they slow down drastically when assessing global characteristics—which they must do to recognize complex, highly variable, real-world objects.

Pyramids (Chapter 9) that stack and link successively smaller arrays, and that superimpose a converging tree-like structure over the input array, can handle global communications and global processes with great efficiency so long as root bottlenecks are avoided. They can reduce message-passing from linear to logarithmic time, and can hierarchically compute complex functions. A pyramid can be used to successively transform the successively more abstract image that it is pipelining up from input array to apex, and to handle a continuing stream of such images—that is, moving images. When desired, a pyramid that executes programs that apply T transforming processes at each layer can be given up to T physical processors at each cell at each layer, giving up to T-fold additional speedups.

Pyramid processes can be handled by several of the scanning array systems—in particular PIPE and the Cyto-HSS. The PIXIE-5000 can efficiently handle pyramid convergence in one direction only—the direction of its serial scan.

Both arrays and pyramids can enormously speed processing (see Uhr et al., 1982 and Li and Uhr, 1985, for timing comparisons indicating three to six orders of magnitude speedups of a pyramid over a serial computer). It seems unlikely that such massive speedups can be achieved without appropriately structured, highly parallel architectures of this sort. Indeed they may well be necessary to achieve the perception of complex real-world objects in real time. Whether they can handle all the necessary processes, or need to be augmented with a suitable network, is an open question.

THE CONNECTION MACHINE'S PROCESS-STRUCTURED ARRAY

From the perspective of vision, a Connection Machine is probably best thought of as an array but with the additional global N-cube or reconfiguring network links. As an array it is quite similar to the CLIP, DAP, or MPP arrays. The superimposed global topologies appear to serve much the same purposes of global message-passing as a tree or pyramid. The reconfiguring network is substantially more expensive. It gives a richer set of paths than a pyramid but only to each chip of 64 processors and not, as in the pyramid, to every processor. The N-cube does not appear to give especially appropriate links.

ARRAYS AND PYRAMIDS AUGMENTED INTO HETEROGENEOUS SYSTEMS

An intriguing, and difficult, problem is to invent a complete set of sufficiently parallel algorithms that map into the pyramid (almost certainly, because of its O(N) diameter, an array alone will not suffice). Until this is done, the problem is to discover the other structure(s) needed in a complete heterogeneous system, good topologies for linking them to a pyramid, and good algorithms that can be executed with sufficient speed and power on these heterogeneous systems (Chapter 13).

There are a variety of possibilities for augmenting an array or a pyramid, by:

increasing the power and independence of its individual nodes,

building a multi-apex structure that diverges as well as converging,

linking its nodes to a network of more powerful and more independent processors, or/and embedding the array or pyramid into a larger structure.

These augmentations can also serve to make the system more useful for a variety of other intelligent functions. So we will return to examine augmented pyramids where appropriate in subsequent chapters.

SUMMARY COMMENT

There probably are more promising candidate multi-computers for image processing and perception than for any other intelligent process. These include the pipelines and large arrays that are so effective for massively parallel operations, trees for more global processes, and pyramids for both. There are also a number of attractive asynchronous and/or process-structured architectures. These might serve as the complete system, or to augment arrays or pyramids.

Really powerful robust real-world visual perception in real time needs million-fold speedups, so a relatively small number of processors will not suffice. The massively parallel systems are almost certainly necessary for real-time perception of complex real world objects in motion, at least as components of a larger heterogeneous system.

STRUCTURING AND ACCESSING SYMBOLIC, LINGUISTIC, ICONIC, AND PERCEPTUAL INFORMATION

One of artificial intelligence's key problems is the discovery of good representational structures that allow relevant information to be accessed, retrieved, and processed quickly and efficiently (Amarel, 1968; Bobrow and Collins, 1975; Findler, 1979; Winograd, 1982).

Every intelligent function must be able to find—with great speed and reasonable accuracy—information stored in memory, and then make appropriate use of that information. This means that the memory must be appropriately structured, and also that the attendant processes must be able to access and make effective use of stored information. AI research has treated the memory representation problem for perception as though it were an entirely different problem from the memory representation problems for language processing, reasoning, and problem solving. But almost certainly, the problem is ultimately the same for every cognitive function. It seems likely that in nature these systems developed together and in much the same way during the evolutionary process.

THE GREAT SIMILARITIES BETWEEN PERCEPTUAL AND SEMANTIC INFORMATION

For example, the issues of how objects should be modeled in a system for visual perception are ultimately issues of memory representation, storage, and access. A complex object is composed of a whole hierarchy of successively simpler objects and features. And it is related to a variety of other objects with which it shares characteristics or might be confused.

Indeed, there is already a striking similarity between the structures used by associative semantic memory networks (Quillian, 1968; Anderson and Bower, 1973; Brachman, 1979; see Peirce, 1931-1958, for interesting earlier formulations) and by the "higher" and more abstract levels of the perceptual process. For example, a vision program might have perceptual transforms of the sort exemplified in Figure 16-1. (These are shown in a different format than those used in Chapter 15—both to use one more similar to the typical semantic memory nets' formats, and also to emphasize that different formats can be equivalent—since their behavior is a function of the programs that use them.)

within(wall,windows)——➤ windowed-wall
above(roof,windowed-wall)——➤ house
above(roof,windowless-wall)——➤ barn
next(house,barn,silo)——➤ farm

(a)

linked(wheel[at-center], dropbar[at-bottom])
&(dropbar[at-top],welded,crossbar[at-back])
&(crossbar[at-front],linked,handlebar[at-middle-back])
&(crossbar[at-front],linked,frontfork[at-top])
&(frontfork[at-bottom],linked,wheel[at-center])——➤ cycle

(b)

FIGURE 16-1. Simple Examples of Fragments of High-Level Vision Models. a) This starts at the highest levels of an over-simplified example for the extremely complex and variegated classes of buildings. b) This gives a little more of the detail needed to recognize some of the relatively simpler subparts of members of the class 'cycle.'

Note that the actual transforms needed to recognize a wide variety of buildings and cycles would have many more terms and more complex relations, and almost certainly would use weights and thresholds. A great deal of additional information would be needed to recognize different individual houses and types of house (e.g., colonial, shaker, prairie, Sullivan, Wright) and cycle (e.g., 10-speed, 3-speed, racer, recliner, Harley, BMW, unicycle). Much the same kinds of IF-THEN rules would be entirely appropriate to represent the information in a semantic memory network (although typically much less detail will be needed, except when the program must be able to cope with all possible details—as a general perception program must).

This information, which is necessary for the perception program, can be extremely useful for any intelligent program. For example, a program that tries to describe, answer questions, and talk about these objects could make very powerful use of such information. It would no longer need to store and attempt to analyze and use potentially very long verbal descriptions of all objects; instead it could compute the pertinent information from the object-model that the perception program must have in order to recognize that object.

But AI researchers whose central goal is to develop memory representations have concentrated on memory structures for information stored in associative semantic memory networks of verbal symbolic information. The structure of information stores used for vision, speech, robot motor control, and even problem solving are typically handled differently. A truly intelligent system would almost certainly combine the information needed for all these problems, in a structure that allows each part to make fast, flexible, efficient use of any other relevant part.

ASSOCIATIVE SEMANTIC MEMORY NETWORKS, PROCEDURES, LOGIC, AND GRAPHS

Many systems have been proposed, and a few have been programmed, to handle parsing (e.g., Woods, 1970; Pereira, 1980), question-answering (e.g., Lindsay, 1963; Bobrow, 1968; Simmons, 1970; Woods, 1973; Gallaire and Minker, 1978), translation (e.g., Wilks, 1973), paraphrasing and story telling (e.g., Klein, 1965; Schank, 1975; Schank and Riesbeck, 1981), and various other aspects of "language understanding" (see Simmons, 1973; Findler, 1979). They are often divided into two major types: (1) networks that are described with logical expressions, and (2) networks that are graphs consisting of nodes (pieces of information) and edges (pointers) linking these nodes. Both types must make use of procedures, to make inferences and follow links, and information, which may either be stored in tables or embedded in these procedures.

Since logical expressions are implicitly linked via the elements they have in common—directly via constants, or, when linked by possibly common variables, by searching among possibilities—logic-based networks can also be represented as graphs. Conversely the systems that are structured as graphs must be given procedures that traverse these graphs, searching for and assessing needed information. Essentially these sets of procedures add up to a deductive inference engine. The inference engine in a particular system may even turn out to be a relatively standard logic, or, more likely, a rough and little understood approximation to one.

Therefore it appears that all of these systems have much the same underlying anatomy-like structure. They all link pieces of information to one another, forming a connected graph. The hope is that the system will be able to find appropriate paths between nodes either by procedures that act on this graph as their data (e.g., Raphael, 1968), or by process structures—as in augmented transition networks (Bobrow and Fraser, 1969; Woods, 1970, 1972) that are embedded into and form part of the graph itself.

These systems tend to divide into two major types of graphs. Possibly the most popular in recent years are those that make use of a minimum number of relations, typically 'isa', and 'partof'. Alternately larger numbers of relations are used, for example, 'above', 'like', 'possess', 'member', 'instance', 'colored', 'shaped', ... Figure 16-2 gives some examples.

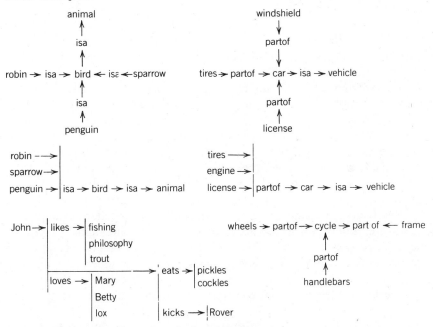

FIGURE 16-2. Simple Examples of Fragments of Semantic Memory Nets.

Figure 16-2 shows stars (that look a bit like arrays) linking four nodes to the center, and different drawings of identical graphs. Alternately these might be drawn as trees, with the center node the root. Any number of things might be linked to the center (root) of the star within the hardware limits on the number of links.

One might want to argue with the way everything must be squashed down into a simple relation like 'isa' and 'partof', or 'like': Is penguin a bird; is the license part of a car? Is it the same to like fishing as to like trout or philosophy?

These figures show only the symbol—for example, 'penguin'—but no strength or probability. That is, they assume 2-valued "yes" or "no" certainty. In fact, many such systems actually use numbers—interpreted variously as weights, confidences, fuzzy values, and so on. This kind of additional information is probably as useful here as anywhere else.

MULTI-COMPUTERS FOR "LANGUAGE UNDERSTANDING" SEMANTIC MEMORIES

The search problem in an associative network, where nodes representing information (including processes) are linked into a very large graph, appears to be parallelizable in any of several different ways.

A hardware network might be constructed whose nodes and links form a graph that is isomorphic to, or similar to, the associative network's software graph. This might include reconfiguring switches that would allow the hardware to accept a variety of different software structures. Alternately the graph might have a general enough structure to handle a variety of networks of associated information with reasonable efficiency. Processing would now fan out in parallel in all directions.

A divide-and-conquer approach might be taken. For example, the software graph might be decomposed into N subgraphs of roughly equivalent size, and each subgraph mapped into a different computer in an N-node network. Now algorithms must be developed that minimize the need to pass information between subgraphs, and multi-computer networks must be used that can pass this information fast enough.

Fifth Generation Logical Inference and Heuristic Search Machines

Logic-based language understanding systems attempt to set up goals that are equivalent to theorems to be proved. Then they apply some standard deductive engine to search for proofs. Thus they use the same kinds of systems—for example, Prolog or a parallelized version of Prolog—discussed in the section on problem solving in Chapter 18.

This suggests using the kind of Fifth Generation computer that is being developed as a specialized logic engine, to execute sequences of Prolog-like logical inferences as fast as possible.

Heuristics are often employed to direct the search through a large semantic memory. This makes attractive networks of the sort discussed in Chapter 18 for heuristic problem solving. However, it may well be that directed heuristic searches are not very good at accessing information in enormously large, human being-sized, semantic networks.

It is certainly the case that today researchers are finding it inordinately difficult to develop heuristics to access pertinent information in other than toy databases. It also appears to be hard to parallelize heuristic searches; therefore they might well turn out to be excessively slow. It is not clear how a hardware network of multi-computers can efficiently execute a heuristic search unless each processor has its own controller. Different heuristics will be indicated at different locations; the system will need to move in different directions through different parts of the total information graph.

But an asynchronous system can easily lead to major degradations in performance due to message-passing overheads. Nor is it clear that a large amount of continuing parallelism can be maintained; therefore many processors may frequently remain idle. (Note that, as in the case of programs for problem-solving and expert production systems, to a great extent this follows from the fact that heuristic searches—since their basic strategy is to gather and assess ever more information, and then attempt to decide what to do next—tend to be structured in a preponderantly serial way.)

An attractive alternative is something closer to the concept of "spreading activation"—which in living brains manifests itself as a relatively rapid fanning out of activity, starting from loci of initial activation, and spreading in all directions. This may best be captured by the very simple (but highly parallel) "breadth-first" search, where the system follows links moving out in all directions.

Fan-Out/Fan-In Networks for Search

It appears that breadth-first spreading activation-like searches will map naturally into, and be handled reasonably efficiently by, an architecture with several links FROM each node (giving divergence) and several links INTO each node (giving convergence).

An especially attractive structure is a network that, at almost any node, locally fanned out (and in) logarithmically in all directions—call this a fan-out/fan-in structure. This would minimize the distance from any node to any other node.

```
machine— | vehicle ——— | car–(ford, honda, gm)
          | tool         | bike–(tandem, 10-speed)
          | appliance    | plane–(jet, propr, concorde)
               |
        (oven, clock, tv, book, paper)
```

FIGURE 16-3. Fragments of a Network that Fans Out and Fans In. NOTE: Different representations are used than in Figure 16-2 ["(...)", "—", "|"] for the same purpose, to indicate how the same network can be drawn in a variety of ways.

ARRAYS FOR FAN-OUT/FAN-IN NETWORKS

Possibly the simplest fan-out/fan-in network structure is a D-dimensional array. For example, a 5-dimensional square array (with only two square links in each dimension) has 10 links to each node; an 8-dimensional array has 16; a 2-dimensional array has 4. Thus the amount of local fan-out can be controlled, but the array's locally dense linkage means that many fan-out paths fan back in to the same node.

Consider an array linked at its edges to form a torus: Each node is now the central root of a fan-out/fan-in tree. For example, in a 3-dimensional array with each node linked to all nodes in the 3-by-3-by-3 cube surrounding it, each node has 26 links. In a 2-dimensional array each node has 8 links to its 3-by-3 surrounding square. Such a system will have N^D nodes (N = length in each dimension, D = number of dimensions), $3^D - 1$ links to each node, and a distance of N-1 links in an array and (N/2)-1 links in a toroidal array between the most distant pair(s) of nodes. Thus, for example, a 100x100x100x100 array will have 100,000,000 nodes, each with 80 links to the near-neighbors that surround it. The path between the most distant pair of nodes will be 99 links in the array, and 49 links in the toroidal array. These are not unreasonably large distances for such a large graph.

GRAPHS THAT HAVE THE DESIRABLE PROPERTY OF LOGARITHMIC FAN-OUT.

Because an array has many local cycles fewer nodes are fanned out to than would be the case if every new link connected to a new node, as in Figure 16-5.

Optimal fan-out can be achieved locally with a graph of the sort shown in Figures 16-5, where each of a degree d node's links goes to a different node. Thus in Figure 16-5's degree 4 graph the center node

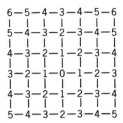

FIGURE 16-4. A (2-Dimensional) Array as a Fan-Out Structure. [Numbers indicate distance from the center—the node being fanned out from.]

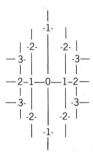

FIGURE 16-5. Logarithmic Fan-Out, Every Link Connecting to a New Node. This figure shows only a small fragment of a very large graph, where a node joined to d links links in S steps to S^d nodes.

(named 0) links to 4 nodes 1 away, 16 nodes 2 away, 64 nodes 3 away, and so on.

A tree is actually such an optimal structure from the point of view of its root, and also of all other interior nodes that are relatively distant from any leaf nodes. Indeed, Figure 16-5 is a standard way of embedding a tree into a VLSI chip. However, since a leaf of a tree has only one link there can be no fan out from it, or from nodes near to it. Since most of a tree's nodes are leaf nodes, most of the nodes in a tree will not be at the center of a fan-out/fan-in structure.

TREES FOR FAN-OUT/FAN-IN NETWORKS

Consider a tree with 8 links to its root and 8 links to each of its interior nodes. We can draw its root and the 8 immediately linked neighbor nodes as shown in Figure 16-6.

To build this into a larger tree, simply replace each numbered node by the root of another 9-node tree-module. Continue this process to

```
1 2 3
4 R 5
6 7 8
```

FIGURE 16-6. A Tree with 8 Leaf Nodes Linked Directly to its Root Node. NOTE: The root node is labeled R, the leaves are labeled 1,2,..8. The 8 links (from the Root to each of the numbered neighbors) are not shown.

generate as large and as deep a tree as desired (each replacement adds 8 nodes to the tree).

AUGMENTED TREES FOR FAN-OUT/FAN-IN STRUCTURES

To turn this into an augmented tree, add links between pairs of nodes that are still numbered (these are the leaves), linking pairs of nodes according to whatever scheme is desired.

A tree is usually thought of as having a root node, and directionality, moving from root to leaves (and from leaves to root). When viewed from above, as though with branches spread wide, it becomes a star of stars; any directionality is destroyed. Such a perspective obscures where the (central) root is located, and emphasizes how uniform the tree is. This is not true at the leaves, until they are linked into an augmented tree (although, except for the Moore graphs, the result will be less than perfect).

Directionality can now be established whenever a node is accessed. This must be done through one of its links; this accessing link therefore becomes the "incoming" link and the d-1 remaining links become the "outgoing" links. Now, for example, when a system to answer questions—or, as we shall see in Chapter 18, to solve problems—is started at several "given" nodes (e.g., axioms, known facts), it can start fanning out (as in a breadth-first search, possibly with some heuristic control) from each of these designated nodes, as though each is the center of a tree.

There is no need to restrict the links that augment the original tree to the leaves only. The leaves are the most reasonable nodes They are on the periphery and hence more distant from other nodes than are interior nodes. They have room for more links, since they have only one whereas the interior nodes have d. But there may well be reasons to link a leaf to an interior node (as is done in the De Bruijn graphs). Or links might be added between pairs of internal nodes (as is done in some of the X-tree constructions).

Indeed one might want to add links between pairs of nodes simply because they are related with respect to the semantic information they contain, from whatever point of view. This suggests that, in general, there should be a physical link, a physical pathway, wherever there might be good reasons for information to move directly from one node to the other. In general that is impossible, since the requirements of whatever hardware we are using will restrict the number of links that can be connected directly to a single node—for today's hardware this is a small number such as 4, 8, or possibly 16.

ATTRACTIVE AUGMENTED TREES AND COMPOUNDS FOR FAN-OUT/FAN-IN NETS

Note that both augmented trees and arrays can (in theory) be constructed with whatever number of links, and therefore whatever fan-out properties, may be desired at each node. The array need simply be made of sufficiently high dimensionality to give the desired number of links to each node. The augmented tree need simply be made of whatever degree desired. Trees are far denser than arrays. Judiciously augmented trees, good compounds, and other dense graphs can be constructed that are far denser still.

When a tree is judiciously augmented with new links at its leaves, to pull specific nodes or regions of the tree closer together, more and more of its interior nodes have increasingly uniform logarithmic fan-outs. A Moore graph is entirely uniform; it has this property everywhere, since every node is the root of an identical tree.

Since the 10-node and 50-node Moore graphs are too small for this purpose, the following structures are attractive candidates (see Chapter 11):

(2550,8,5), which compounds 51 Singleton graphs, each linked to all the others, might be large enough for a small semantic memory network with each node handled by a different computer.

Alternately (2550,8,5) might be used to store a subgraph of a much larger network in each node.

(5000,8,6), which compounds 100 Singleton graphs into a complete bipartite graph with each linked to the 50 graphs in the other set, might be used in either of the two ways just described for (2550,8,5).

A De Bruijn network might be used; now locally each node fans out in all directions, both up and down the tree, and also along one link to more distant nodes.

A Hyper-tree, where leaves are linked to one another via a reconfiguring network, might be used.

Other suitably augmented trees might be constructed, where leaves linked to one another, or back into different parts of the network.

An O(N) Array and O(logN) tree might be judiciously combined (a pyramid is one example), to give whatever mix of local and global properties seemed most appropriate.

A SUMMARY COMMENT

Remembering and understanding language and other symbolic information are in many ways similar to the perceptual understanding of sensed information, and also to the searches and transformations of information that must be carried out when reasoning. A full-blown intelligent system will need to be able to associate (to find), access (remember), and make use of (think about) many thousands, or millions, of shapes, properties, objects, words, concepts, and ideas.

A good fan-out/fan-in structure would appear to be the most appropriate for the multi-computer that handles associative semantic memory networks. This might consist of a very large network of simple processors, into which the actual network of information is mapped, each node to a different physical processor. Or each processor might handle a much larger subgraph, the system taking a divide-and-conquer approach.

Chapter Seventeen

SPEECH AND LANGUAGE: ANALYSIS, RECOGNITION, UNDERSTANDING

Auditory perception involves the recognition of a variety of sounds, for example, bird and mammal calls, whistles, explosions, motors, scrapings, winds and rains, shrieks and screams—but speech is special. Understanding can involve almost anything, whether percepts, gestures, body language, concepts, ideas, techniques, objects. However in our verbal society language is central. Since virtually all AI research on auditory perception and "understanding" has focussed on speech recognition and language understanding this chapter will do the same.

(Auditory) speech recognition and language understanding are typically examined together; the spoken word is the most common, and probably the most natural, vehicle for language, and for symbolic, referential communication. Language understanding entails the use of "semantic" information stored in what AI researchers have named "associative semantic memory networks" of the sort examined in Chapter 16.

RECOGNIZING THE SPOKEN SPEECH AND UNDERSTANDING THE LANGUAGE UTTERANCE

Speech must be recognized and understood in real time, at the speed with which it is produced. Depending on the speaker and the situation, spoken speech might stream into the system at rates from roughly 1 to 4 words (1 to 12 syllables) per second. There are a number of commercial speech recognition systems that use dynamic programming to handle isolated words spoken by a trained speaker (Itakura, 1975). Recognition of continuous speech (Reddy, 1967; Vicens, 1969; Reddy et al., 1973; Lowerre, 1980) is far more difficult, because words often occur with no boundaries between them, and they typically interact in subtle ways.

Research in AI usually treats speech recognition as hierarchical, with several major levels. These appear to have little noticed analogs to successively higher levels of processing in vision, moving from the acoustical (roughly equivalent to the raw image array in visual perception), to the phonemic (equivalent to letters and strokes?), to the syntactic (equivalent to compounds of features?), to the semantic (equivalent to recognizing meaningful objects, and to placing objects into groups, for example, words, phrases, sentences; knife, fork, place-settings, dining room furniture?), to the pragmatic (equivalent to following a perceived command and noting the perceived consequences?), and back and forth between them.

Handling Continuing Speech Utterances (e.g., Stories, Books)

Typical speech contains sequences of sentences that contain words that refer to or interact with one another (e.g., pronouns that refer to previous sentences), occasionally over relatively large distances. Thus a story—or whole book—might begin, "Mary took her cat Bessie to the woods, because they both loved to play fetch. It was a long distance. . . [many sentences or even chapters might intervene, using only 'she']. . . When she dropped a stick in the lake and she (wagged her tail and) jumped in she almost expected to hear a bark."

This example may seem a bit strange. Yet it is only slightly ambiguous so long as words like 'fetch' and 'wag'—even though they may commonly be considered more dog-like than cat-like (and therefore explain why most of us would take the last sentence to mean "Mary expected Bessie to bark")—help to disambiguate sentences that include the pronoun 'she'. But if strings like 'fetch' were changed to 'play' or/and 'wagged her tail' left out, ambiguities would dominate. This example also demonstrates how subtle interactions can dominate at arbitrary distances. The two words 'cat Bessie' completely change the meaning of 'Bessie' in contrast to 'Mary' and determine the relation between these two 'she's' throughout the entire book. (Almost) any reader would assume Mary to be a human being, probably because of a rather subtle inference that the following line of reasoning oversimplifies but roughly captures: 'her cat' refers to a 'her' that owns the cat and only human beings 'own' things. To handle all this properly the system must absorb, and keep readily accessible, a good bit of pertinent semantic information about women, cats, the relation between cats and dogs, and all the other things that must be understood.

And some rather complex and relatively mysterious—or at least not yet programmed—kind of running short-term memory of most-salient information must be abstracted, absorbed and stored, and constantly up-dated. This memory is almost certainly relatively small—far too much space and time would be needed to store and access the pertinent information using a complete recording of the entire corpus.

Language Understanding

To complete the semantic and pragmatic parse, resulting in an "understanding" of the language string (see, for example, Findler, 1979; Schank and Riesbeck, 1981; Winograd, 1982), the system must make full use of its large semantic memory. To some extent this raises the problems of that memory's structure, and of how to search into it, examined in Chapter 16. But it seems plausible that the actual recognition and understanding of the words and phrases can largely be achieved by a relatively simple access of the nodes in that memory—first those that are directly pointed to by the semantic rewrite rules used, and then by following a path of those pointed to by newly accessed nodes. Thus understanding language appears to be similar to perceiving scenes in that in both cases there is a much larger body of information that can serve to deepen that understanding. A successful parse means that the language utterance has, in the limited sense of parsing, been understood.

MULTI-COMPUTERS FOR SPEECH RECOGNITION AND LANGUAGE ANALYSIS

Systems with One Processor, or a Small Number of Processors

The running store of most-salient information might be on the order of a few dozen small pieces when we consider a small corpus like a script extracted from a 3 inch newspaper article of the sort handled by Schank and his associates (see Schank and Riesbeck, 1981). It seems likely that several hundred, or even several thousand, pieces of information might be needed when trying, in any but the most superficial manner, to absorb and understand a whole novel, or a big news story as it unfolds over the weeks or years in newspapers and conversations. A variety of architectures might be used to look for interactions between these and the new text being read and absorbed. If the number of pieces of information is small enough, this might be handled by a single processor that searched for interactions serially—for example, a super-Lisp machine. But such a system would need very fast access to a very large semantic memory network, to compute the needed contextual information.

If the problem proves too large for a single processor to handle in real time, it might be possible to use a modified divide-and-conquer approach, assigning subsets of possible interactions to different processors. Since relatively few processors are probably needed, they might be linked via a bus, ring, or crossbar.

Blackboard Model Star-Based Memory-Linked Systems

A widely publicized alternate possibility is the Hearsay model for speech recognition (Reddy et al., 1973; Erman and Lesser, 1980). The "blackboard" memory model used for the Hearsay speech systems places the different major "knowledge source" levels (e.g., the acoustic, phonetic, syntactic, semantic, and pragmatic) into different computers. These computers then ask one another for needed information, and tell one another their results, by posting and reading messages using the common blackboard.

This kind of system has a slightly different topology from other pseudo-complete graphs (e.g., buses, rings and crossbars)—that of a star, with the common blackboard memory serving as the central node that is linked to each of the other nodes. That means that two processors can communicate only through the memory that serves as the root of the star. This gives a potential bottleneck, unless only a small amount of parallel speedup is needed, and communication demands are very low. [The C.mmp network used to execute the blackboard model actually linked computers via a crossbar virtual star (Chapter 6).]

Note how similar this is to an expert production system's use of a single common memory (see Chapter 18), except that the latter has hundreds or thousands of simple micromodular procedures (the productions) acting on and communicating via that single memory.

It appears that at best a blackboard-linked system can achieve only 5 or 10-fold speedups. Each processor must handle a very large task. There might be possibilities of dividing-to-conquer, assigning a number of processors to work at each level; but even with 4 or 5 processors the relatively poor star design of a shared memory will degrade performance.

Connection Machines, N-Cubes and Reconfiguring Networks

It is not at all clear how today's three most highly publicized multi-computer structures might be used effectively.

A reconfiguring network gives a pseudo-complete graph, and therefore allows for general connectivity. It can probably be made large enough for speech recognition and to handle a limited amount of semantic information for limited language understanding. Processing can probably be divided-and-conquered and thus spread out among all its nodes. But it seems unlikely that its ability to send N messages simultaneously among N processors will often be needed. A system like the BBN Butterfly might well be powerful enough, but it would be over-kill.

The N-cube linkage does not appear to have any especially desirable properties for speech and language. Density is relatively poor, as is the ability to hierarchically combine and transform information. That is, the N-cube is not especially appropriate for operations that fan in and combine, or fan out and broadcast, information.

A Connection Machine that links nodes via reconfiguring networks will have similar strengths and weaknesses, at even greater expense. Nor will the 2-dimensional array links used in Connection Machines be especially appropriate for speech.

Process-Structured Architectures

De Mori (1985) has developed a software structure for multilevel speech recognition, and suggested that this might form the basis for a multi-computer that would execute it in a data-flow, process-structured manner. Bronson and Jamieson (1985) are designing a pipeline where each major function in the speech recognition process is assigned to a special subpipe. Much like the process-structured arrays and scanning arrays for image processing, these kinds of algorithm-structured architectures might well be unusually powerful and efficient for applications where hardware can be dedicated to a continuing stream of inputs to be recognized. Real-time recognition of continuing speech is an especially good application of this sort.

Tree and Pyramid Structures

The successive processing of information, to abstract and extract what is most relevant and most worth storing, as possible context for later processing, suggests a hierachical fan-in structure, where information is extracted and abstracted as it is moved and converged upward, compounded and transformed, used to recognize, and kept around as needed.

Such an approach might use a 2-dimensional tree or pyramid structure to evaluate, moving up from leaves to root, successively higher-level interactions (much as 3-dimensional pyramids can be used for vision). This has the additional advantage of making relatively homogeneous the several different perceptual subsystems in a more complete integrated perceptual system, one that combined vision and speech (as is the case whenever a system watches and listens to a talkie, as opposed to a silent movie, or a radio). The same general structure of transforming procedures would be used for both vision and speech (and sound in general), and between-modality information would be merged and combined in the same ways that within-modality information is combined.

Moving into the larger semantic memory network for language understanding would appear to need good fan-out structures of the sort examined in Chapter 16.

THE SIMILARITY BETWEEN VISION AND SPEECH/LANGUAGE UNDERSTANDING/RECOGNITION

The 2-dimensional visual image (an array of intensities of visible light, or of the intensities of each of the primary colors) must be input by a tv camera or other sensor of 2-dimensional arrays of light intensity. The 1-dimensional speech input (an acoustical signal with different intensities at different frequencies) must be input over the second dimension of the time needed to complete the utterance. Both visual and acoustical signals must be processed at the appropriate succession of successively higher, more abstract, and more global levels.

Finally, the objects in the scene, and the higher-level wholes that they form, are perceived and understood—much as the words, phrases, and meanings of the language utterance are perceived and understood. The similarities become especially apparent when we consider situations where language and objects, sound and sight, are (as is typically the case) processed together—quite possibly in conjunction with still other information from other sense modalities, such as touch, pain, smell—in order to gain a perceptual/symbolic understanding of the external world.

Once the language utterance or the problem to be solved has been "understood," once the scene of objects has been "perceived," the system typically should go on, to respond appropriately, whether to figure out what to do about relevant objects, try to solve the problem or answer the questions, or respond to the issues posed. All of these entail making use of the system's potentially enormously large body of information and abilities to process that information. This appears to entail two major types of processes: those (of the sort examined in Chapter 16) that find stored information, and those (of the sort to be examined next) that deduce, reason and compute.

A SUMMARY COMMENT

Speech recognition and language understanding appear to have much the same structural characteristics as visual perception. Indeed language in the form of written speech—whether letters, billboards, or books—is one of the major types of perceived entity. Therefore, the same types of multi-computers appear to be indicated.

Since the total amount of information that must be input from the environment and then processed is a good bit smaller, other structures, such as reconfiguring network-based pseudo-complete graphs, are also attractive alternatives. For the general problem, which includes recognition and understanding of thousands or millions of things, such a system must be given a very large amount of memory. A good experimental strategy might be to develop relatively small systems on a reconfiguring network-linked multi-computer, then simulate larger process-structured architectures. If and when indicated, a particular process-structured architecture can actually be built.

Chapter Eighteen

PROBLEM-SOLVING, THEOREM-PROVING, DECIDING; "EXPERT SYSTEMS"

Artificial Intelligence has to a great extent concentrated on problems that can be formulated as searches through very large spaces of possibilities, in order to find good paths to goals that have been set for the program in advance. Classic examples are games like checkers, chess and GO, puzzles like crypto-arithmetic and Rubik's cube, arithmetic problems, and theorem proving.

Another closely related type of activity is probably best characterized as everyday reasoning or decision making—just figuring things out and choosing what to do. Here there is an enormous range of behaviors, from choosing a hat to choosing a mate; from finding one's way to the kitchen sink to finding one's way to Mt. Everest, the moon, fame, fortune, success, discovery, happiness.

THE SEVERAL MAJOR APPROACHES TO DEDUCTIVE INFERENCE

Most attempts to develop computer programs for deductive problem solving and everyday reasoning have in common the search and manipulation of complex graphs (typically called list structures) of information, and the use of list processing languages like Lisp, Prolog, and Snobol. The major approaches include: (1) systems that use heuristic tests and heuristic control structures to plan and search for solution paths in complex graph structures; (2) systems that attempt to use logical inference;

and (3) systems that tend to use micromodular productions in a relatively unstructured search.

Systems that Use Heuristics

We typically think of developing an algorithm (i.e., a procedure guaranteed to solve the problem), then coding that algorithm in a programming language and executing that program on a computer, thereby solving that problem. But what is the algorithm that will solve the problem of "recognize all the objects in a tv scene," or "explain what furniture is," or "play championship chess," or "converse intelligently," or "decide how to spend the next year"? When no satisfactory algorithm is known, we can still attempt to handle the problem by using heuristics—that is, a set of more or less bright ideas, partial solutions, and/or stabs in the dark.

No sufficiently powerful and efficient algorithm has yet been formulated for the game of chess, or even for the much simpler games of checkers, gomoku, or backgammon. (Note that since these are all finite problems an algorithm is in fact known—the exhaustive algorithm "try everything, looking ahead to the leaves of the search-tree"; but this is combinatorially explosive and cannot possibly be realized.) Lacking an algorithm that guarantees success, one can develop a program that is a heuristically structured collection of heuristic tests and plans (e.g., Newell, Shaw and Simon, 1963; Nilsson, 1971; Fikes and Nilsson, 1971; Newell and Simon, 1972; Sussman, 1973; Sacerdoti, 1975).

To take a prototypical example, the way most researchers have attempted to program chess (see Frey, 1977) is to follow a procedure first proposed by Claude Shannon (1950): Use a set of heuristics like "take the most valuable piece," "advance pawns as much as possible," "threaten the king," "control the center board"—some simple and easily codable, some complex, vague, and only vaguely realizable. A large set of such heuristics is used. Each results in numbers that are combined in a heuristic evaluation function, and used to choose among alternative moves (or whatever set of alternative possibilities confront the program). The program applies all the heuristics that are appropriate at the particular point in the game, and chooses the move that their combined results imply most strongly.

Higher-level heuristics are usually also used. For example, the program will be coded to look ahead as far as possible in the search tree of moves and countermoves, applying the heuristics at each step, heuristically assuming that the opponent will use the same set of heuristics that the program uses to choose moves. Similar approaches, but each carefully tailored to the particular task, have been programmed for checkers (Samuel, 1959, 1967), backgammon (Berliner, 1980), and other games and problems.

This kind of program can have a very complex and subtle structure. Heuristics are typically embedded in code; they often interact in complex ways. The programmer is constantly trying to improve upon and strengthen the set of heuristics, resulting, over time, in a carefully honed but often rather obscure program. Little is known about how well the program works without thoroughly evaluating it by running it on a definitive set of test cases—something that rarely happens. The program cannot be run on even a slightly different problem.

LOGIC-BASED SYSTEMS

Logic-based systems use a logical engine (like Green's, 1969, QA3; Hewitt's, 1971, PLANNER; Le Faivre's, 1974, FUZZY) or a logic programming language (like Prolog, Warren, 1977; Clocksin and Mellish, 1981) that has a certain amount of logical inferential capabilities built into it. Most systems today use first-order predicate calculus resolution (Robinson, 1965; Kowalski, 1979). One gives such a system its database in the form of valid logical expressions. Then one poses a problem by asserting the goal, stated as an expression, a theorem to be proved. Then the system itself attempts to find a solution-path, using the logical engine that has been built into it.

In theory such a system will be able to prove any provable assertion (i.e., any deducible expression, any theorem in the system). In practice, however, such systems are not very efficient and have relatively little direction in their search for a proof. The logical system itself does not include procedures for efficient, powerful application of that system, just as a parsing system or a production system does not include procedures for applying the rules. Therefore a great deal of research effort goes into devising better, often heuristic, techniques to control the search, and into trying to incorporate these into an expanded logical system.

"Expert" Production Systems

"Expert" production systems, at least in their original pure form, use a) sets of IF-THEN production statements that contain conditions to be looked for in b) a single common memory (Waterman, 1970, 1986;

Newell and Simon, 1972; Rychener, 1976; Forgy and McDermott, 1977; Davis and King, 1977). Programs are therefore extremely micromodular. It is extremely easy to code individual production rules, add new rules, modify and improve old rules, and delete bad or obsolete rules.

First, the system determines which productions would succeed (i.e., for which productions can all the IF-conditions be matched with information stored in the common memory). A "conflict resolution" procedure chooses a single one of the productions that succeed, and "fires" it (usually by making changes in the common memory).

The following are examples of typical productions. (The first two are parenthesised, to make clear what are the basic elements to be matched and actions to be effected. The last three are from Waterman, 1986; they illustrate the kind of simple English-like production that can be handled by a system that has been augmented with "language understanding" procedures.)

IF (face flushed) and (eyes milky) and (state fever)
    THEN (store (patient sick)) and (output (check temperature)).
IF (color white) and (at-root vulva)
    THEN (output (amanita-verna)) and (output ("deadly-don't eat!")).

If a flammable liquid was spilled,
    call the fire department.
If the pH of the spill is less than 6,
    the spill material is acid.
If the spill material is acid, and the spill smells like vinegar,
    the spill material is acetic acid.

The flow of control from procedure to procedure and from statement to statement raises problems. Pure production systems have no control structures (such as the ordering of statements, procedure calls, or gotos) that specify how to move between productions. Instead, they must find candidates for firing by trying to satisfy their conditions in the common memory, then choosing one single production to be fired. This can take a long time. And it is hard to make a program behave correctly in all cases when all of the system's capabilities must be coded as production rules without any explicit, easily understood flow of control.

Therefore most expert systems actually designed to serve a particular practical purpose are given a number of additional capabilities beyond the matching of rules with a common memory of facts, or they make little use of the strict production rule format. For example, the Mycin system (Shortliffe, 1976) for diagnosing and recommending treatments for patients with infectious diseases used weights that allowed it to combine the implications of several rules (rather than the much larger number of boolean rules that would be needed to achieve equivalent results). The Internist/Caduceus system (Pople, 1975), which diagnoses diseases of the internal organs, uses entirely different types of procedures, for example, to make global assessments before moving, in a top-down manner, to specific details.

Although expert systems have been widely publicized, and hundreds have been coded, it is hard to judge how powerful or cost-effective they actually are. Among the few controlled experiments comparing them with human experts that have been published are the following: Yu et al. (1979) in a blind study of diagnoses of 10 patients with infectious meningitis found that Mycin's diagnoses were judged by specialists to be at least as good as those of human specialists. Miller et al. (1982) found that the broader Internist system was judged almost as good as human physicians. The earlier heuristic DENDRAL system (Buchanan et al., 1969; Lindsay et al., 1980) for spectroscopic analysis of unknown molecules has—apparently chiefly because of its systematic search procedures—done better than human experts in some limited domains (Smith et al., 1972, 1973).

It is hard to evaluate these results. In the medical domain one small study of 10 subjects is not considered enough to determine whether to introduce a new drug or diagnostic procedure. One would hope that developers of expert systems, no matter for what purposes, would either carefully evaluate them for their accuracy and cost effectiveness or use them only as advisers to human experts.

It is not clear what special qualities expert production systems have. Are they simply large *ad hoc* systems built to handle a specific job (see Martins, 1984)? Can they be extended by adding more and more productions to handle larger and more general domains of knowledge? Or do they need more general and more powerful types of productions and better control structures? How do they compare in terms of speed and efficiency? To what extent can they be parallelized?

The expert production systems coded today have several hundred, or occasionally up to several thousand, productions. The expectation is that future systems coded for larger and more parallel computers might have many thousands of productions.

Pure production systems with a single set of IF-THEN production rules may well be too slow and inefficient to handle large tasks. When they are given additional capabilities it becomes unclear how they differ from other kinds of AI and of non-AI programs. The production rule format essentially means that they are coded using a language and a style of programming that is more along the lines of Post productions, Comit, and Snobol—rather than the Turing machine (which underlies most assembly languages), the lambda calculus (which underlies Lisp), or some other equivalent underlying model of computation.

Sorting Nets, which are Serial, but with Paths Short Enough to be very Fast

It appears that many (but not all) production systems essentially apply a sorting net of queries—much as in the 20-questions game—to a set of information, in order to arrive at a result. This is a very natural structure to use. We see it in the trees of features biologists use in identifying mushrooms, birds, or other plants and animals. It appears to be equally appropriate for the diagnostician (e.g., physician, electronic repairman, detective) who tries to decide what to do to treat a patient, fix a tv set, or solve a crime. But a sorting net is fastest and most efficient when coded and executed directly.

MULTI-VARIATE PARALLEL PROBABILISTIC STRUCTURES FOR EVERYDAY REASONING

One form of everyday reasoning system makes use of much the same multivariate probabilistic structure that can be used for implying possibilities and combining implications in perception. Such a system takes into account a variety of different pieces of information, combining their various implications into a single set of alternate possibilities, and then choosing the most highly implied possibility or possibilities. This appears to be a natural structure for making everyday decisions and choices—for example, of a restaurant, wine, hat, pet, house, vacation spot, job, mate.

Consider the very large variety of everyday problems that we human beings and other higher animals contend with as we choose and decide among alternative possible actions as a function of a variety of more or less relevant and closely or loosely related sets of information.

We decide what movie to go to, whether to go to a movie or a concert, where to go for a vacation, what hotel to stay at, how to handle meals. If we decide to go to a restaurant we must then decide which and when; what to order; what to eat as the next mouthful; how to extract that from the mess on the plate, and manipulate it safely into the mouth, and chew and otherwise process it down toward the stomach and beyond. If we decide to go on a hike the next day, we must decide when to get up; what to do in the bathroom, for example, whether to brush teeth before or after shaving, which teeth to brush next and how long; what to wear and the order of putting on clothing, which leg to put into which pants leg first; how to get to the starting place for the hike; and so on.

There is an almost endless sequence of still-smaller-detailed decisions and at the same time larger decisions that stretch out into the future. Often these are higher-level decisions that entail the need for new sets of lower-level decisions, and that help to organize them. Thus we decide we need to concentrate on a new project, therefore should take a refreshing vacation first; this in turn entails large numbers of nested decisions, about the most refreshing kind of vacation, where to take it, how to get there, and each step and sub, subsub, ...step of the project.

In all these cases the decision is on the one hand an extremely complex function of a variety of important to unimportant, conscious to unconscious, close to only vaguely related, factors. We decide to go to Cancun for a week because flopping and hiking on the beach is relaxing, several people have mentioned Cancun weather as beautiful, we like Mexican food, there are fast direct flights, swimming and snorkeling sound attractive, the Mayan ruins are nearby, and so on. Also, Mexico has a favorable "feel" from past experiences, and a variety of relatively unconscious, intangible, vague, facts and emotions help to build toward a conclusion that this would be a comfortable, exciting, relaxing, enjoyable thing to do. We choose to go to a Chinese rather than a Mexican restaurant today because we are getting tired of Mexican food, several people have recommended this particular Chinese restaurant, it is crowded and looks attractive, its menu has dishes we can recognize and like, we're tired of looking around and want to decide—and also we have a long-standing liking for Chinese food and a variety of intangibles (typically based on simple past experiences) make for a pleasant feeling about this decision.

Similar sets of factors appear to influence and control decisions as we move successively into the most trivial layers of the situation. At the other extreme, we must decide what to do with our lives. (Of course, this is rarely done as a single conscious decision, one that leads to an irrevocable and never-to-be-modified choice.) Should I be a business-person or scholar, scientist or artist, biophysicist or geophysicist, studying enzymes or monoclonal antibodies, and which, and setting up which particular experiment next, and how? Should I choose this university, city, neighborhood, house, furniture, or that? Should I marry and have children, and whom and how many? It is interesting to consider such a list of small and large choices (and any of us can extend such a list without bounds, since it is the stuff of our existence). For the structures of facts, feelings, and intangibles, and the way they combine into choices, appear to be surprisingly similar, from smallest to largest.

Most striking is the fact that in almost all these cases the decision appears to include at most only a short and shallow serial sequence of inferences. We rarely put our shoes on first and then our socks, even though sometimes only because we notice something wrong the moment shoe hits bare toe. But that is only a 2-step sequence.

When we try to keep a longer sequence of actions straight we often move into a different realm of thinking, more like proving a theorem or playing a game. Here there appears to be an interesting issue—one that may well suggest how the two hemispheres of the brain work together but that AI programs have not so far addressed—of combining an intuitive, metaphorical, freewheeling mode of thinking (which appears to be highly parallel and largely unconscious) with a deductive, highly controlled, serial, conscious mode.

Everyday thinking appears to be handled best by taking into account as many as possible of the relevant factors, trying to assign each its appropriate weight, combining these weights according to the most appropriate combining function, and choosing the most highly implied alternative.

Thus this suggests a rather unusual kind of parallel production system, where repeatedly implications are combined and decisions made, of the following sort:

1. The system has a large number of each relatively simple productions, for example:

    relaxing vacation -> swimming, beach, warm
    heat, sun, sand, beauty -> Mexican beach, Canaries, Riviera
    exciting -> Mexican beach, Paris, Riviera
    Mexican beach -> Cancun, Acapulco . . .

2. These productions are augmented to include weights and thresholds, for example:

    heat = 5,sun = 9,sand = 3,beauty = 7 > 11-> Mexican beach = 23,
        Canaries = 18,Riviera = 6
    exciting -> Mexican beach = 17, Paris = 38, Riviera = 29

3. An initial set of conditions will be input, for example:

    relaxing vacation, exciting, rejuvenating, ...

4. The system will find all productions whose conditions are satisfied, and then will fire ALL of them.

5. The consequences of all the fired productions will be combined. (Thus anything that is implied by several different productions will be implied only once, with the several different weights combined into a single overall weight.)

6. Wherever the programmer chooses, a choice will be made of the most highly weighted implication from among a designated set of possibilities.

7. This process will continue, through a number of cycles.

MULTI-COMPUTERS FOR PROBLEM-SOLVING AND EVERYDAY REASONING

Today a great deal of effort is going into the development of specialized Lisp and Prolog machines for executing list processing and logical operations. The individual processor is carefully designed for the language and types of problems it must handle. However, to achieve major increases in speed and power these processors must be combined together into a larger network. Here the problems are pretty much the same for all multi-computers, no matter what their individual processor nodes may be. The particular language the individual computers are designed to handle can be ignored (except that a language may encourage, or discourage, appropriately parallel programs).

Multi-Computer Structures for Executing Traditional Production Systems

The star topology, with all processors linked via a common "blackboard" memory, would be a direct embodiment of the traditional production system. Such a system cannot be built with more than 4 or 5 processors, so each processor will have to evaluate many productions, and speedups will at best be small. Bus, ring, or (as was done in the case of the C.mmp emulation of a star) crossbar-based systems allow for a few more processors. However, the need for all of them to look at a single memory, and for the system to choose the single production to fire next, would probably result in major degradations from too frequent message-passing. A reconfiguring network like the Butterfly, Ultracomputer, or PASM would probably suffice; but it would be expensive.

One proposal for expert systems on the DADO binary tree multi-computer (Stolfo, 1984) would assign each production to a different computer (Dado's overall tree topology is not taken advantage of except for control, hence it can be ignored), so that all productions can be evaluated at the same time, in parallel. On the surface this seems attractive; but it appears to have several major problems.

First, although today's large expert systems have several hundred or even several thousand productions, and it is conceivable that future systems will have even more, most expert systems are coded so that only a few productions would be expected to fire at one time. More important, it is relatively easy to point directly to those productions that will fire by simply using a discrimination tree-like procedure (e.g., Forgy, 1979) to direct the search. This means that there is no point in having any of the productions evaluated other than the ones directly pointed to by the production that just fired. This suggests modifying the standard production systems, as described in the following, so that the programmer can conveniently designate direct links between productions, thus constructing a discrimination tree that can be used directly.

Second, if each processor is responsible for evaluating a different production, then all processors will need to access the common memory. That would lead to a difficult set of contention problems and bottlenecks if that memory were stored only once, and every processor literally made its own search through that single memory. If that memory is kept sufficiently small this might be handled by storing copies in each processor's memory; but now all these copies must be updated after each change caused by the firing of a production that made changes in the memory—a process that needs a network (like a tree) with good broadcasting capabilities, but that still takes time and can give errors.

It appears, from Gupta (1984) and Gupta and Forgy's (1983) survey of today's expert production systems, that even if all these problems are solved the potential speedups from parallelization are at best discouragingly small. The average production has only 4.9 elements in its condition and 1.9 actions in its consequence. On the average, only 10 productions would fire at each cycle, and must be chosen among. This means that at best 10-fold speedups might be achieved for the subpart of the program that fires productions, and less for the other parts.

Parallel Probabilistic Production Systems

Thus there is very little in present-day systems that can be parallelized. This strongly suggests that the only way to achieve appreciable speedups with parallel networks is to formulate and code much more parallel production systems in the first place. Entirely different formulations, programs, and languages will be needed (Uhr, 1979; Ishida and Stolfo, 1985). We cannot expect much speedup from parallelization by trying to reformulate existing algorithms. That is not surprising, since today's algorithms were formulated to take advantage of the serial computer's positive strengths. Fortunately, good paradigms for such massively parallel formulations already appear to exist, in the multivariate decision-making systems that appear appropriate for everyday inference and are already used in some perceptual recognition programs.

Parallel probabilistic production systems no longer need the conflict-resolution step. (But since conflict resolution is desirable at least some of the time, when serial steps must be taken, a system should give the programmer both options.) The standard production system must be augmented to handle the combining of weights or probabilities (this is often done, as in Mycin), and also the making of intermediate choices. Both of these are, potentially, parallel processes, that can be handled by hardwired logic gates that combine, and that choose, in parallel. Such a system might be coded and executed in the manner of a discrimination tree (as described next).

Another attractive possibility is a fan-out/fan-in net, possibly with specialized coprocessor nodes dedicated to combining weights and evaluating whether thresholds have been achieved.

Tree Structures for Executing Tree-Structured Production Systems

For traditional production systems where parallel structures are not appropriate, a simple serial tree will often fill the gap. Such a system does not process problems in a parallel fashion. Rather, it asks a serial sequence of questions, with each answer taking the indicated branch and thus moving down through the discrimination tree until a leaf node, containing the answer, is achieved. However, if a reasonably good tree of questions can be coded (i.e., where each subsequent question comes close to subdividing the space of possibilities into subspaces of equal size) the series of questions will be logarithmically short, and can be processed in very little time. Thus 20 binary (yes-no) questions are enough to discriminate between a million possibilities—which is enough to make for a satisfying 20-questions game. This kind of tree structure can search through a space of N possibilities in logN (time) steps.

A system to handle such a tree might be implemented in any of the following ways:

A serial computer might simply step through the tree.

A tree-structured MIMD network of computers might be used to handle the problem by having each computer handle a subtree (all subtrees should be as close as possible to equal size).

Each production (i.e., each node on the tree) might be assigned to a different computer in an appropriately structured tree or augmented tree multi-computer. A problem would be input at the root of the tree, where the first computer would decide which path to send the problem down next; this process would continue until the leaf node with the solution was reached.

It would appear that a single traditional serial computer would be the most suitable. It will be extremely fast, since it will take only one step for each ply in the tree. That is, it will need only O(logN) time. There might, however, be situations in which the tree was too big for one computer to store and handle efficiently, in which case a small tree-structured network might be preferable.

A tree-structured network (Chapter 12) with a computer assigned to each node (i.e., to each individual production) might be indicated if long sequences of problems could be batch-pipelined through the tree. Now the system would no longer be using only one node of the tree multi-computer at any time. Rather, it might be using up to P nodes in a P-ply tree. The reason that a tree would be limited to P (which will be a small number, 20 or so at the most) is because only one problem can be input to the root at each moment of time.

Reconfiguring Networks for Batching Tree-Structured Productions

Therefore a reconfiguring network-based N-by-logN structure (see Chapter 9) with N nodes to which problems can be input, might be more appropriate. Such a system would have almost logN times as many nodes; but it might have up to NlogN nodes working in parallel when N problems were input each time. Note that the more different problems were from one another, so that they sorted down different paths, the more the reconfiguring network could handle at each moment. Since that could not be guaranteed, no matter how much care was taken to randomize or in some other way vary the problems, additional hardware (space) and software (time) would have to be dedicated to buffer nodes and to handle contentions.

Fifth Generation Super-Logical Operation Super-Computers

The Japanese Fifth Generation computer effort (see Moto-oka and Stone, 1984), with 1990 as its goal, which has received enormous amounts of funding, and of publicity and imitation by Americans— chiefly the DARPA (Department of Defense Advanced Projects Agency) autonomous land vehicle program—focuses on developing a super-fast computer capable of executing 1,000M LIPS (i.e., one billion logic inferences per second, where each logic inference needs the equivalent of 100 to 1000 ordinary instructions). This is generally envisioned as a gigantic Prolog machine, one that is roughly 1,000 times faster than most that exist today. The Aquarius system being developed at the University of California-Berkeley (Chapter 6) appears to be the most powerful computer of this sort built to date. It presently has only one carefully specialized processor capable of executing up to roughly 300K LIPS. It is estimated that a planned multi-computer extension, which will have 16 processors linked via a crossbar to 32 large memory modules, may be 10 times as fast. Several other systems are being proposed, almost all multi-computers with simple linking topologies, like buses, crossbars, or a reconfiguring network. Prolog, Lisp, and other functional programming languages are neutral with respect to handling serial or parallel constructs. They may well form good bases for parallel programming, but the crucial problem is to develop efficient, highly parallel formulations.

Connection Machines, N-Cubes, and Reconfiguring Networks

It is not at all clear how appropriate are the three types of networks that are today most widely proposed for multi-computers for problem solving.

A reconfiguring network is quite adaptable, since it can be made to give the appearance of a complete graph with a single common memory. However, the cost is high, and the total size of the system limited, hence slow.

N-cubes, although they appear to be appropriate for handling problems of the sort frequently encountered in physics that involve arrays of information, do not appear to have an especially good topology for AI problems. The one possible exception is for image processing of arrays—but this is almost certainly better handled by array multi-computers.

One of the Connection Machines is to be a reconfiguring network, the other an N-cube, so the previous comments apply to them. It is not clear how the additional array topology will help in problem-solving tasks. It would appear that a better design is a heterogeneous system that combined an array with an appropriately structured network, such as an augmented tree, so that both could work simultaneously, but with good communication channels when needed.

Fan-Out/Fan-In Networks for Problem Solving and Everyday Inference

Attractive candidates for architectures for problem solving are 3-dimensional arrays, large trees and augmented trees—that is, fan-out/fan-in systems (Chapter 16). Indeed it appears that the requirements for semantic memory searches are similar to the requirements for search in problem-solving systems. In both cases the system must hunt through a large network for good paths to goals.

In the case of problem solving (at least for most of the relatively well formed problems that AI research has focussed on) the system searches for a path from a set of "given" nodes toward an explicitly stated "goal," or from goal to given(s), or (as in a game like chess) toward a node that satisfies some unambiguous and relatively simple test that a node is the goal.

In the case of memory searches it is not nearly so clear when, or even that, a goal is achieved; rather, a major part of the problem is to assess whether nodes that are achieved can be used to help compose a reasonably satisfactory response. This also means that the search can only be made in the one direction from given(s) toward (possible) goal(s) rather than from given(s) toward goal(s) or/and goal(s) toward given(s). From this it may well follow that heuristically guided search is less useful. In respects other than these major differences the search problem appears to be similar in both domains. From the particular nodes specified the system must fan-out to look for good goal nodes. These searches fan-in to converge at nodes that serve as good candidates for goals. The fact that several paths converge at a node may in itself be a significant criterion in semantic memory searches for choosing that node.

If the problem-solving systems were made more general and broadened to handle the less-well-formed problem of finding "interesting" nodes rather than unambiguous explicitly posed goal nodes, this would hold for them also. That almost certainly would capture more of the essence of everyday reasoning. Rarely do we expect to find the "correct" answer; much more typically we settle for something that "feels right." Even the mathematician's most important task is not to prove already-stated theorems, but rather to explore logistic systems to find theorems worth proving.

A SUMMARY COMMENT

Problem solving has to a great extent been formulated by main line AI researchers as a serial process for conventional single-CPU serial computers. This is evident from the heuristic, often recursive, depth-first, search procedures and serial production systems that are commonly used.

In striking contrast, human everyday reasoning and problem solving are extremely fast and highly parallel. They appear to have much in common with perception, remembering, and language understanding. Similar multi-computer architectures appear to be indicated, and in particular large numbers of small processors linked via carefully augmented trees and other good fan-out/fan-in structures. Networks of relatively powerful computers, each capable of working independently, also appear to be attractive structures—when they have appropriate topologies, along with operating systems and communication channels that can handle the relatively large flows of information that a well integrated cognitive system will need.

Alternately one might attempt to develop a Fifth Generation logical inference or heuristic search machine, possibly a multi-computer. Unless the problem is formulated in a far more parallel way than is typically the case for today's AI programs, it seems unlikely that significant speedups can be obtained, or that realistically large nontoy problems can be handled.

Chapter Nineteen

ROBOT MOTOR CONTROL AND COORDINATION

In sharp contrast to the popular picture of a robot as, essentially, a human being with a stiff neck and a crude sense of humor, the robots one reads about so much today are pretty much sets of motors controlling wheels, and, occasionally, clumsy arm-like or leg-like effectors. These robots are considered to be intelligent AI robots when they are given just enough vision, touch, or problem-solving capabilities to allow them to adapt to slightly changed conditions without making ridiculous mistakes on some carefully chosen, very narrow task.

INDUSTRIAL ROBOTS, AND AI ROBOTS

Today's robots (see Paul, 1981; Beni and Hackwood, 1985) are systems of motors that move wheels, pulleys, or joints, and thus perturb and have an effect upon their outside world. They come in several major flavors:

Robot arms with three to six or more degrees of freedom (for x,y,z direction at each joint) distributed between two or three joints, plus a "hand," welding torch, paint sprayer, gripper, drill, or similar manipulator with one (or even zero) to three more degrees of freedom (Duffy, 1980; Engelberger, 1981; Salisbury, 1982);

Small wheeled carts, with three to a few more degrees of freedom (for x,y direction, speed, turning, acceleration);

Two or three arms arranged to work together at the same manipulative tasks;

A small vehicle on legs—usually six legs working in groups of three—each leg of the complexity of a robot arm (McGhee et al., 1978, 1984; Orin, 1980; Kessis et al., 1983; Raibert and Sutherland, 1983; Messuri and Klein, 1985).

What today is typically called an intelligent robot is, essentially, this robot system of motors driving wheels or limbs, plus distance detectors (e.g., laser range finders) and enough touch sensors (e.g., pressure gauges, either individually placed or in 2-dimensional arrays) to help guide the effectors and keep the system from crashing and jamming into things, and/or tv cameras and analog-digital converters that input and transduce the digitized image into a computer's memory (Nilsson, 1969; Nitzan and Rosen, 1976; Wallace et al., 1985; Beni and Hackwood, 1985). Occasionally they are given some primitive capability to make shallow inferences.

These are today very simple, cut-down versions of the much larger perception and problem-solving systems of the sort examined in the last few chapters. Their recognition and problem-solving processes are relatively primitive—if they exist at all. About all that these added AI procedures do is help the robot exactly locate a few well known simple objects that it has been preprogrammed to find at a particular location, but happen to be misplaced a bit. Unless this kind of basic sensory capability is given the robot, all objects must be positioned so exactly by the the factory's conveyors, and the robot must be preprogrammed so accurately, and be capable of such accurate mechanical motions, that it will always move to exactly the right spot.

There are a variety of industrial jobs for which these AI robots are, potentially, extremely useful.

For example, typical stupid industrial robots have been used for years in factories to paint and to weld, by waving a paint sprayer up and down and around in front of the object to be painted, and by moving from spot to spot to be welded. Such systems are first "programmed" (some people call this "teaching" and say the system has "learned"!) by actually moving the arm through the precise set of motions that it should take when working. This continuous trajectory is periodically sampled, and the samples are recorded as a sequence of exact coordinates in 3-dimensional space. For ever after, the robot will exactly retrace this exact sequence of motions through these coordinates. Thus all its motions are preprogrammed and "ballistic"—in the same sense that a bullet or a baseball pitch is ballistic (except that the robot's sequence of motions can be far more complex). Once the robot has started its sequence of motions it will never make use of new information to modify them.

In sharp contrast to this simple, but limited, technique of programming by showing, an AI robot will be programmed symbolically, by specifying sets of processes in a specialized language that includes constructs for specifying motions. It will be programmed to use its range finders to assess distance, its pressure gauges to "touch" and its tv to "see," for example, to check that a piece of furniture is being spray painted uniformly, or that a welding tool correctly follows the seam, or that fingers properly grasp an object like a cup (Allen and Bajcsy, 1985). It can now be programmed to, for example, check whether more paint is needed in a certain region. It might then even infer the amount of extra paint needed, hence the exact distance and total time for spraying, by computing the discrepancy from the desired intensity and shade. Since such a system is dynamic, rather than ballistic, it is able to correct its behavior as a function of information that its sensors gather and its procedures interpret, and even of simple inferences that its problem solver makes.

Such a system allows the industrial factory to be run without making what can easily become heroic and expensive attempts to achieve 100% perfect placement and movement of objects that are to be processed by robots. The robot becomes capable of handling a much wider variety of tasks. It can more cleanly weld more complex seams and paint more complex objects than can a purely ballistic robot. The robot, assemblyline, and whole factory can much more easily be modified to handle changed procedures and new tasks. The factory can, potentially, become much more flexible in turning out short runs of modified, improved, or different, products.

This kind of robot can even place and turn screws and execute simple manipulations (possibly coordinating two arms) to assemble objects. When given additional vision capabilities it can identify and pick up, and then manipulate, a few simple objects like gears and rods on a moving belt or even in a bin; and it can inspect objects like circuit boards, car doors, and airplane wings.

A really intelligent robot would have a full-blown perception system that could really recognize objects, figure out complex paths and, when needed, deduce alternate, even new, ways of doing things. It would also integrate additional procedures and equipment to input and understand speech, remember information, and, in general, think about what it ought to do. That kind of robot (which does not exist today, and will need major advances in both programs and hardware before it can be developed) will be examined in Chapter 21, on integrated systems.

MULTI-COMPUTERS FOR ROBOT SYSTEMS

The hierarchical characteristic of a robot motor system, where successively higher-level coordination and control must be exercised over separate subsystems that can when necessary act independently, strongly suggests an appropriately augmented tree-structured multi-computer, or one that judiciously combines pyramids and trees. Such a system would need to be specially designed to handle the stringent real time demands of motor coordination and control combined with perceptual processing of potentially extremely complex objects as they move about.

Augmented Tree-Structured Systems that Contain Pyramids

HIERARCHICAL COORDINATION AND CONTROL OF THE MOTOR SYSTEMS

The following assumes that computers, motor systems, and sensing devices will all be designed and built together, with appropriate high-speed interfaces between them.

It seems natural and attractive to assign a computer to each joint, wheel, or other locus of motion—or, possibly (if time constraints dictate this), to each degree of freedom that at the lowest level controls motion. Above these would be a control-coordination computer. For example, the three joints in an arm would each have a computer, and a fourth computer would sit above them. This is what is done in several commercial robots. Alternately, at each joint there might be two or three computers, one for each degree of freedom, plus one extra computer for local control and coordination, giving a three-level system.

Next, a system with two or three arms would have still another level: the computer that controlled and coordinated the several arms. A system with six legs might have one additional computer to control and coordinate each group of three legs, and a still-higher-level computer above them. A system with both arms and legs (and let's throw in several necks for several different visual and auditory sensors) would have several more new subtrees joined at one or two additional higher-level nodes.

This, then, gives a tree structure. Almost certainly it would be desirable to have direct links across the tree, between nodes that would otherwise be able to communicate only much more slowly via the tree's root or other higher-level, potentially bottlenecking nodes. These would handle important interactions among parts that must work together (e.g., 10 fingers on two different hands; or the several legs that must be coordinated in a fluid walk). Therefore a carefully job/algorithm-structured augmented tree might well be preferable.

COMBINING THE TREE STRUCTURED MOTOR SYSTEM WITH TOUCH AND VISION

One interesting and attractive feature of this structure is that we can continue to add higher levels to the tree, to link in additional subsystems for perception and for the other cognitive functions.

For example, a small tree or pyramid might be built whose leaves were microprocessors that analyzed information input by a few judiciously placed touch sensors (e.g., on each finger) associated with a hand. This might link directly to the tree that handles that hand's motor behavior. It might also link into a perceptual tree that combined it with other perceptual processors, for example, for laser range finders and infrared heat sensors. The several touch sensor trees for the several hands might combine into a tree designed to handle touch perception that might have much the same overall structure as the tree for the motor effectors related to those touch sensors.

A potentially more general-purpose 2-dimensional array of touch sensors (Raibert and Tanner, 1982) might be linked by one or several tree/pyramid(s), which analyze their information and then link to the other sensor-trees. In living animals, touch sensors are spread throughout the 2-dimensional skin—although quite unevenly, with great concentrations in sensitive regions like the hand's fingers and palms and the face's cheeks and lips. This specialized, ad hoc arrangement is apparently natural evolution's attempt to cope; it suggests similar concentrations of a robot's sensors at regions of special sensitivity, each with its own processing tree/pyramid.

This sensory-motor system is probably best linked with a similarly structured system for visual perception. A pyramid-structured architecture of the sort that appears to be especially appropriate for vision might well be appropriate for touch as well, since it also has strong tree-like characteristics.

Possible Variations and Augmentations

A number of variants are possible, for example:

Perception and motor control systems might link only at the highest root node, each forming a separate tree under that node.

Local feedback might be integrated with the motor system by building perceptual-motor subtrees. For example, the network (tree or pyramid) for each tactile sensing array might be linked directly to the tree of computers controlling the assembly (e.g., a finger) with which that sensing array is associated. Or, at a somewhat higher level, a tree of the tactile sensors associated with one hand might be cross-linked to the tree of computers that control the motors of that hand.

The tree might naturally be augmented in a process-structured manner, possibly at its leaves but more plausibly at higher-level coordinating nodes, with links that would serve to pass more direct feedback information between the different subsystems.

Alternate Possible Topologies

Other topologies are indeed possible, but they will only be mentioned in this chapter because most do not appear to have as many desirable characteristics. A robot must work at great speed, with a high degree of coordination of its motor processes, intimate perceptual-motor interactions, and rich capabilities to respond extremely quickly to a variety of sources of external feedback. A truly intelligent robot would be the quintessential real time system, since it must not only perceive and track, but also interact with and anticipate, the dynamic real world.

A single Cray, or 16 linked Crays, would not only be far too expensive to be cost effective; it would also almost certainly not have the capability to input and sense all the information from the external world that must be monitored. Entirely different operating systems would be needed, along with attendant additions and changes to hardware, in order to handle real-time processing.

Nor do there seem to be strong reasons to consider a Butterfly or other reconfiguring network-based system. They do not take advantage of the tree-like topology of the motor and perceptual subsystems, yet they are subject to the extra costs of the NlogN switching network, and also the extra time delays it would entail.

The Non-Von and Dado tree-based systems might well be appropriate, especially the former, because of the augmentations built at its leaves to handle array processes. It seems likely that they would need to be augmented substantially, with additional more or less specialized processors and interfaces dedicated to the different motor input and sensory output hardware. They would thus end up looking very much like the structures of augmented trees of trees or/and pyramids suggested earlier.

N-Cubes, Connection Machines, pipelines, arrays, and systolic arrays, along with most other point-to-point topologies that are not carefully chosen to mirror the structures of the robot's motor and sensory-perceptual systems, would similarly appear to have little to recommend them.

Compounds of bus-based clusters, Petersen graphs, or other small basic modules might well be more appropriate. But they, along with many of the simpler bus-based systems and systems with other point-to-point topologies, will not be viable until message-passing is made extremely fast, and not just far faster than it typically is today.

If only because of the economics of a robot, it seems unlikely that a large and expensive super-computer like a Cray, or multi-computer like Cedar or the Connection Machine, would qualify as cost effective. The robot must justify its position by costing less than the human being(s) it replaces. Today this typically means that the entire robot, including its arms, wheels and other effectors, tv cameras, touch sensors and other input devices, and all the attendant computer hardware and software, should cost $30,000 to $80,000, or up to $150,000 at most.

A SUMMARY COMMENT

Each of a robot's subsystems (e.g., wheel, leg, arm, or hand) is typically composed of several motors, each working independently but with some overall coordination. This suggests assigning a physical processor to each motor, and linking the processors for each subsystem, either directly or fanning in via a tree, to a single coordinating/controlling processor. The total robot's collection of such subsystems (e.g., two to six legs or wheels, two arm-linked-to-hand assemblages) is probably best linked in a similar hierarchical manner. This suggests a tree structure, where the overall tree is constructed from subtrees, each in turn constructed from subtrees. When the robot is given sensors and primitive perceptual capabilities these can be linked into the total structure in the same way.

The individual subassemblies in the resulting tree structure can be linked together to reflect the necessary and desirable flows of information between them, giving a process-structured augmented tree.

Chapter Twenty

LEARNING

The standard (but rather black-box-like and uninformative) definition of learning is "a change in performance (for the better, as a function of experience)." A system that learns (by definition) does things differently after it has learned than before. Therefore it must make changes to itself—to its processes or/and to its internal store of information—as a function of information from the external environment (or possibly, depending upon one's definition of experience, of an examination of its internal stores of information that leads to re-structurings).

Many people feel that learning is the vital key to developing intelligent programs. A general, flexible, robust intelligent system needs far too much information to be programmed in advance. The system must be able to adapt to new information, new problems, and changed environments. An ability to learn permeates, and appears to be crucial for, the intelligence of living systems. However, relatively little work has been done on this very important, and very difficult, problem.

TYPES OF LEARNING

Although a major reason for learning is to make the system more general, today's learning programs almost always learn only in a very specific problem domain. A program that plays checkers learns better weights for its preprogrammed heuristics; a program that answers questions about geography learns new facts; a program that recognizes simple objects learns better weights for its preprogrammed features, or learns new features.

Major Approaches: Explicitly Told Advice-Taking; Learning from Experience

Two broad major paradigms are commonly suggested for learning systems:

1. Learning by adding information that has been carefully preformated to fit into appropriate slots in the system's memory.
2. Learning from information sensed and input during experiences with the learner's environment.

There is a wide range of possibilities within each. And there is an ambiguous boundary between them—as when "experiences" are a carefully chosen sequence of examples (e.g., pairs of words or symbol-strings to be associated, like 'apple red' or 'Iowa crop-corn, wheat') in the exact format that the system has been programmed to add to its memory and learn. However, in many cases there appears to be a sharp contrast between explicit perfectly formated advice vs. information that must be extracted and absorbed from raw experiences with the environment. It is helpful to point in these two radically different directions, at least for a preliminary organization.

1. *Advice-taking* (McCarthy, 1958; Zobrist and Carlson, 1973; Davis, 1978; Hayes-Roth et al., 1981; see Michalski et al., 1983, 1986):

The internal representation should be a correctly interlinked structure of correct pieces of information. To use this information, build a program that can input and add new information that is presented to it in the correct prearranged form, by properly positioning and linking new pieces as they are input. Therefore the problem reduces to the demand for the teacher to present information in a correct format, and for the program to add this information and thus learn from this process of "being told."

For example, statements of the following sort might be typed into the system:

John father-of Bill
Bill uncle-of Mary
Bill uncle-of John2.

Alternately, some systems are coded to accept and reformat statements like:

John is Bill's father   {or}   John is the father of Bill

(i.e., statements in one or two agreed-upon grammatical formats, perfectly spelled—and very far from, although superficially appearing to be, unconstrained English).

Unfortunately, it is not clear how much formatting can be done and the system still remain an advice-taking learner. For example, would we want to say that a database management program learns information input to the tables that contain its database? Or that a compiler learns the programs coded in the language that it inputs, compiles, and executes? Or that the very simple operating system procedure that inputs and starts compilers and other utility programs learns all those programs and everything that those programs do? Why should these not be called advice-takers—and especially powerful ones at that?

2.   *Learning from (Raw, Extracted, or Abstracted) Experience* (Uhr and Vossler, 1961; Block et al., 1964; Winston, 1970; Uhr, 1973; Dietterich and Michalski, 1981):

The system learns, attempting to construct a usable model of its world, from its continuing experiences while interacting with its environment, rather than from explicitly formated information. Now the system must extract, abstract, generalize, and approximate. There is not enough space to store all the details, or time to find them. The system must learn from only a small running sample of the enormously larger set of experiences that it should then be able to handle. So the problem becomes one of building a program that can absorb experienced information on the fly, gradually building, refining, and generalizing its internal information as a function of feedback-rich interactions with the environment.

For example, a program for a game like checkers, chess, GO (or, more realistically in terms of the present level of development, tic-tac-toe) might be given the experiences of one or several games, or short sequences of book moves. A vision program might be given a sample of pictures, along with the names of the objects they contain. That is, the system is given raw, or relatively raw, pieces of experience, rather than carefully abstracted and formated symbolic messages.

A major problem arises because of the difficulty in actually embedding the learner into a larger environment. Unless we give the learner good input sensory devices and perception programs and good output effectors and programs to control its actions (i.e., make it into a more powerful robot than can be achieved today), we must abstract and simplify from true real-world "experience." For example, rather than input a whole sequence of hundreds of tv images from which to learn to recognize objects, the system might input only one image, or an image that contained only one object, or a line drawing of one object, or a list of one object's features and attributes. At what point does such extracted, abstracted, and simplified information become "advice?"

COMPARING ADVICE-TAKING AND LEARNING FROM EXPERIENCE

The first alternative might be called "structured learning" or "advice-taking" or "explicit learning."

The second alternative might be called "learning from experience" or "hypothesis formation" or "discovery and induction."

The first relies on a truly omniscient trainer who knows exactly the right format for inputing information, along with an omniscient front-end program that converts information into the correct internal format. It deduces how to add a new piece of information at the correct location in its memory, from information that is explicitly stated or unambiguously implied by the trainer.

The second—to the extent that it does not simplify and abstract from raw experience—has a far more difficult task. It almost certainly must make use of weights (or probabilities, fuzzy values, or other multivalued numbers that attempt to assess such vague things as strength or confidence or importance or value or likelihood). Essentially it can best be thought of as running little experimental evaluations to decide what pieces of information to extract from the large stream of its experiences, how to use this information to learn, and how to modify, adjust, and fine-tune the system. It tries to infer how to incorporate the newly learned information—where to put it, and how to combine it with already-present information. It cannot assume that information is given to it by an all-knowing trainer, and is therefore always properly formated, without errors or misinformation of any sort.

A learning program can either modify the structure of information stored in its memory, or actually change some of the processes it uses. Making changes in procedures is far more dangerous, since one wrong change can, like any bug (no matter how small or obscure) blow up and stop the program. Making changes in descriptions is potentially just as powerful, since a program can always be stored in descriptive form rather than in procedural form—to be interpreted rather than directly executed. It is far simpler to modify descriptive, stored information than to modify actual program code. From this point of view it is preferable to develop programs that learn descriptive information rather than processes that are directly embodied in procedures (code).

Particular Types of Problems Learned

The two broad categories of advice-taking and learning from experience can be broken down into different subtypes and aspects of learning. In addition, the specific learning program is typically coded to handle a specific problem domain. Among the major examples are programs that have been coded to do the following things in the following ways.

INDUCTIVE REWEIGHTING

The system can learn good weights for heuristics (Samuel's checker player, 1959, 1967) and for features (Rosenblatt, 1962; Nilsson, 1965; Flanagan et al., 1980; Nye, 1980).

Thus when a game player wins or loses, makes a good or a bad move, or completes a task successfully or unsuccessfully, it can be given feedback (e.g., "good," or "very good," or "bad"). Or it can infer (e.g., from taking or losing a piece) that it did something good or bad. Or it can be given a book move problem (a board position from which it should achieve, for example, mate in three, or some intermediate goal) and, if it makes the wrong moves, given feedback as to what would have been right. The system must then evaluate this feedback (e.g., "very bad" might mean "drastically lower the weights of the heuristics that led to this bad behavior"), figure out which heuristics actually led to the moves that resulted in this feedback, and reweight each according to its importance.

When a perception program gives an answer it can be given the subsequent input "right" or "wrong" or "wrong—it is [the right answer]." The system must then get the perceptual operations that it used in generating this answer (and, possibly, the perceptual operations that would have led to better performance) and reweight them as suggested by the feedback.

Note that a tv frame input to a vision system is a real slice of perceptual experience (although a continuing sequence of frames would be a much richer and more realistic slice). In contrast, a sequence of moves in a game is a far more abstract and idealized experience.

GENERATION AND DISCOVERY OF NEW FEATURES AND HEURISTICS

The system can attempt to discover good new game-playing heuristics (Koffmann, 1968), features and compounds of features (Uhr and Vossler, 1961a, 1961b; Kamentsky and Liu, 1963), higher-level features (Sauvain and Uhr, 1969; Williams, 1976), and simple examples of metalearning procedures for generating good features (Uhr and Jordan, 1969).

For example, a perception program can attempt to extract from an input image features that it infers would be useful in improving its performance (e.g., when feedback indicates it was wrong, it can generate new feature-detecting transforms by extracting information from the wrongly processed pattern). It can then generalize across similar features (e.g., several instances of a vertical edge or an enclosure, each found useful for a different instance). It can even attempt to find features that good feature-detecting transforms have in common, by comparing sets of good transforms with sets of bad transforms, and try to generate new features that have these good higher-level feature properties.

INDUCTION AND ACQUISITION OF NEW CONCEPTS

The learner can attempt to form good concepts from a sequence of individual example instances. The earliest programs of this sort, developed by Kochen (1961), Hunt (1962), Towster (1970), and others, to form 2-valued boolean conjunctive and disjunctive concepts, were motivated by the experimental studies of human concept formation of Hull (1920), Hovland (1952), and a number of other psychologists.

Such systems are given short abstract encodings of stimuli that, when human beings are used by psychologists as subjects, would be presented as pictures. For example, the human subject might be shown a drawing of a large or small, dotted or solid, edged or filled in, square or circle, then asked to say whether it is a member of the concept class or not, and then told "member" or "nonmember." The problem is to induce the concept from a sequence of such instances. When a computer program is the subject, each instance is encoded and input to it as an extremely simple string of symbols. In this example the set of 4 characteristics of the object can be represented by a string of symbols representing the 4 attributes: (size, [large or small]), (outline, [dotted or solid]), (area, [edged or filled]), (shape [square or circle]), or, equivalently, by a 4-bit string, or array, of 0's and 1's.

For example, from a sequence of instances of the following sort:

"(size, large), (outline, dotted), (area, filled), (shape, circle)"—
   "0011"—member
"(size, small), (outline, solid), (area, edged), (shape, square)"—
   "1100"—member
"(size, large), (outline, solid), (area, edged), (shape, square)"—
   "0100"—member

the learner is expected to induce a concept of the following sort (but note that this is a potentially fallible induction; subsequent inputs might invalidate it and suggest another):

"large square or dotted circle."

Recent work by Michalski (1975), Larson and Michalski (1977), Dietterich and Michalski (1979), Vere (1978), and others (see Michalski et al., 1983, 1986), has investigated the learning of more complex multi-valued and relational concepts, and also the complexity of this type of learning (Valiant, 1985).

For example, an instance of a concept might be presented in either of the equivalent forms:

"(circle a), (square b), (circle c), (small a), (large b), (small c), (ontop(a,b)), (inside(c,b))"
"shape(a, circle), shape(b, square), shape(c, circle), size(a, small), size(b, large), size(c, small), ontop(a,b), inside(b,c)"

Rather than learn—as must be the case for perception—from an image with thousands or millions of multivalued picture elements structured in a 2-dimensional array, where much of this enormous amount of information is noise, redundant, irrelevant, or unnecessary, these systems learn from strings of 2, 5, or 10 binary or n-ary digits, where every speck of information can be crucial. There is an interesting formal similarity between the small 1-dimensional string, or array, of 1-bit or few-bit symbols and the large 2-dimensional array of intensities (typically encoded as 6, 8, or 24-bit symbols). But the kinds of information that each type of system must learn, and the procedures that each must use to learn that information, are very different.

LEARNING FROM EXAMPLES, FOR LANGUAGE, PROBLEM SOLVING, AND VISION

The system can learn new information in associative semantic networks (Quillian, 1969), expert production systems (Buchanan and Mitchell, 1978), or structured vision programs (Winston, 1975; Connell and Brady, 1985).

Here each system uses a standard format (e.g., "robin is-a bird," or set of productions, or graphs that combine structural features like columns supporting a top [to form an arch], or edges linked into shapes), along with special routines that map these inputs into memory. Such systems often have preprogrammed into them complex language understanding procedures that achieve a semantic parse of sentences input to them, and powerful inference programs that try to deduce what should be learned.

These systems benefit greatly from, and indeed depend upon, a very abstract environment from which "experiences" are input that have been very carefully prepared and highly abstracted—for example, inputs that are prefectly spelled words, always perfectly bounded by spaces.

LEARNING NEW PRODUCTIONS, PIECES OF ADVICE, PRINCIPLES, AND PROCEDURES

Several programs have been coded that can input and use relatively simple micromodular pieces of advice. For example, Waterman (1975) has extended standard expert production systems to learn new productions. Zobrist and Carlson (1973) have developed a chess player that uses and can learn heuristics input to it in the form of simple, well formated n-tuples.

Several specialized systems have been developed that attempt to learn new principles in particular problem domains (e.g., Lenat, 1976, 1977; Langley, 1980; Rosenbloom et al., 1985). These programs typically accept only carefully and perfectly formed inputs, are coded to handle a specific problem domain, or/and attempt to do a great deal of heuristic problem solving to decide what particular modifications should be made to their memory networks.

Still other systems have been programmed to learn improved problem-solving procedures (Fikes et al., 1972; Siklossy and Dreussi, 1973; Sussman, 1975). This has chiefly entailed finding a path to a solution and then attempting to generalize it—for example, to replace a particular node on that path with a more general variable node that ranges over a number of particular nodes. As the problem becomes more complex the learning system needs to carry out more and more complex lines of inference.

LEARNING FROM OBSERVATIONS IN EXPLANATION-BASED SYSTEMS

Several interesting and potentially very powerful systems have recently been completed where the program is given a number of powerful functions that can be thought of as providing an (admittedly limited) explanation of symbols (DeJong, 1981; Mitchell, 1983). The system can then be input a sequence of these symbols and, from an analysis of its stored explanations, compose this sequence into a coherent set of actions. Now whenever that sequence is subsequently input the program will be able to execute the implied structure of actions. But this is by no means simply rote learning, since the system is able, because of its built-in explanatory capabilities, adapt the sequence to a great variety of different situations. For example, Segre and DeJong, 1985, are able to tell a robot a sequence of actions for building objects, and the robot will be able to find and manipulate the appropriate parts even though they may have different shapes and be located in different places.

CONNECTIONIST NEURON NETWORK-LIKE LEARNING

A number of programs have been developed during the past few years that modify weights in connectionist systems of relatively large numbers of completely (or densely) connected, each very simple, neuron-like thresholding processors (Feldman, 1982; Hopfield, 1982; Hinton and Anderson, 1981; Hinton, 1984; Ackley et al., 1985; Rumelhart et al., 1986). These are much in the spirit of earlier neuron network-like systems developed to model ideas of researchers like Hebb, 1949; and Rashevsky, 1948; by Rochester et al., 1956; Rosenblatt, 1962; Pitts and McCulloch, 1947; McCulloch, 1965; and a number of others (see Scott, 1977).

Most of these programs handle very simple situations, typically where learning can be effected by successive reweightings that achieve a linear discrimination between possibilities. Actual implementations for more complex problems like object perception where non-linear structures must be assessed (e.g., Sabbah, 1982) tend to put a large amount of structural organization over a number of separate connectionist groups of elements, and they do not yet begin to handle learning.

MULTI-COMPUTER ARCHITECTURES FOR LEARNING PARTICULAR CAPABILITIES

The multi-computer architecture used for a learning program must also be an architecture appropriate for the processes learned. The system must be able to make effective use of the learned structures. This is true no matter what the learned structures are—whether processes, states, or stored (descriptive) items of information.

Augmenting the Structure Necessary for the Capability Learned

In addition, the architecture must be able to handle the flow of feedback information as it is being assigned to the appropriate nodes where learning should occur. However, learning does not typically take place under severe real-time constraints. Although learning can be a function of a continuing sequence of thousands, or even millions, of trials (as when perfecting a motor skill like walking, dancing, or swinging a bat), it is probably the case that each individual step need not be executed at the fastest possible speed. Therefore the additions to the hardware network to expedite learning must be adequate to handle the additional flow and assignment of feedback information; but not necessarily at the fastest possible speed, or with the highest possible accuracy.

Once the necessary structures are learned the system must be able to use them to act appropriately. The system should now be able to perform as closely as possible to an equivalent efficiently structured hardware/software system for that function. So the multi-computer needed to learn a set of capabilities is probably much like the multi-computer needed to execute those abilities. [This is not to say that any group of human beings could ever succeed in programming such structures for nontoy systems that handle complex real-world tasks directly, without learning. To the contrary, that is almost certainly far too large an endeavour; almost certainly powerful, general cognitive systems can be achieved only by getting the system to learn. And the resultant learned structure may at best be less efficient than would be a good (albeit impossible to achieve) directly coded system. Learning, like generality, may well be to some extent *inefficient* although *essential*.]

Architectures for Learning Productions and Other Explicit Information

Production systems that learn are good simple structures to start with when examining architectures for explicit learners. It is not at all clear how best to map production systems into multi-computer networks, but we will examine two major approaches.

EACH PRODUCTION ASSIGNED TO A SEPARATE COMPUTER

First, the production system might be assigned one computer to each production (for maximum speed), or one computer to each subset of productions (through which each computer iterates). Now a learning program would simply assign each new production to a new computer, or to the least busy computer. (This assumes that a larger network is potentially available, possibly because there is actually a much larger multi-computer that is multiprogramming many different jobs, and that is capable of expanding or/and reducing the number of computers assigned to any particular job). For this a system linked via a reconfiguring network, like PASM, the Butterfly, or the Ultracomputer, would probably be the most appropriate structure.

LEARNING IN TREES AND AUGMENTED TREES

Second, a tree or augmented tree multi-computer that executed a production system as a serial discrimination tree would have the new production inserted at whatever point in the tree was indicated by the
trainer. This is a simple matter (basic to coding list structures using
pointers in a language like Pascal or C): To insert node k between
nodes i and j (when i points directly to j), change i's pointer to point to
k, and give k a pointer to j. In an actual physical system with a
different computer for each node the system must either spend time
reorganizing things by moving information down into formerly empty
nodes in the tree, or actually add a new pointer-wire linked to a new
memory that contains the new item, with another wire linking to the
memory that contains the old item.

The ability to grow new wires needs new technologies, but is probably feasible. A bigger problem is simply finding enough physical space
on the chip or in the surrounding computer. Large amounts of empty
space might be incorporated into the original design, to accommodate
future learning (but then why not fill that space with more nodes at the
start?). Or old nodes must be pushed and old links bent to make room;
or long links must be added to link to new nodes that are embedded in
empty-but-distant regions; or old links must be broken, combined, or in
some other way freed.

It seems simpler to develop a system where each of N physical nodes
serially processes the subset of nodes in the subtree that it is responsible
for. Now new nodes can be inserted without problems, as described
above. (The potentially heavy price that must be paid, however, is the
slow-down resulting from the serial processing within each node.) The
system can also periodically attempt to load-balance, evening up the size
of each computer's subtree, either periodically or/and when excessive
waits on an excessively loaded processor begin to occur.

Alternately, a pseudo-complete graph-based structure might be used
(again, a reconfigurable system like PASM, the Butterfly, or the
Ultracomputer would be preferable to a bus or crossbar-based system,
since for nontrivial problems many pieces of information must be
learned).

If we restrict the growth of a tree as a function of learning to take
place only at the tree's leaves, things get much simpler. There is no
need to break links and insert new nodes. There are no problems in
finding empty nearby spaces, or in trying to make space by physically
pushing nodes aside. Such a restriction, to learning at the leaves only,
may be feasible for systems that learn from explicit, carefully ordered
information.

ARCHITECTURES FOR LEARNING FROM EXPERIENCES

But it appears that systems that learn from experience, rather than from carefully ordered and perfectly presented large chunks of predigested information, must be able—in order to form new concepts, generalize, unlearn, and re-structure information as a result of gradual learning—to add and delete new links and nodes, and also to strengthen and weaken connections between nodes. This must probably be done internally as well as on the surface leaves of the tree, since new information might suggest modifications anywhere in the graph.

FAN-OUT/FAN-IN ARRAYS, AUGMENTED TREES, AND PYRAMIDS

The kind of fan-out/fan-in toroidal arrays and augmented trees suggested for semantic memory searches, problem solving, decision making and everyday reasoning, and also the pyramids and augmented pyramids suggested for perceptual processes, and the hierarchical trees for motor control, all appear to be amenable to the same kinds of additions of new nodes and new links, and combinings of nodes, that appear to be required for a number of key types of learning. If links can be ported reasonably cheaply, the fan-out/fan-in networks might be made relatively high-degree graphs, with, for example, 16 or more links to each node.

At the other extreme, a degree 3 graph might be used (basically, a binary tree), where each node fans out over a sequence of processors, or switches, to give 4, 8, 16, and so on, virtual links. To the extent that processors are kept very simple there will be relatively little waste in converting a processor to a fan-out switch.

Very simple micromodular processors may well be appropriate to learning that gradually builds, extends, modifies, cuts down, and in other ways changes the information learned. Ultimately, a brain-like learning network should probably use processors of this sort. Note how a finite state automaton (that can be changed) seems a more realistic substrate than a stored program system.

SYSTEMS THAT CAN ADD NEW HARDWARE LINKS BETWEEN UNCONNECTED NODES

With a physically growable technology, the addition of links between pairs of nodes that (learning) experiences indicate should be brought closer together might well be realizable at some time in the future (although it will probably be harder for the system to implement links between two unconnected, possibly distant, nodes than simply to add new nodes at the leaves).

Semantic nets might best be built by adding links where needed. This might well be the way that the brain itself employs, first growing a basic structure, and then adding links to short-cut paths, as needed. It is also suggestive of learning algorithms that would combine several closely related nodes into one, to form a class, or, alternately, link them to a newly generated common node, over "isa"-like links.

In all these cases it seems attractive to use a learning algorithm that generates both new hardware and new information that this hardware embodies. This might be done as follows: Each node has a potential maximum number of links (wires) joining to it, and each link costs a certain amount. The learning algorithms must decide where to modify the present structure, and what modifications would be desirable. Figure 20-1 shows the only types of modifications that appear to be needed.

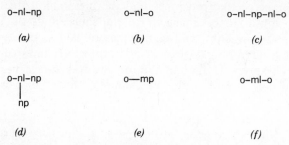

FIGURE 20-1. The Basic Types of Modifications for Learning. [--nl--=new link; np=new processor; —=old link; o=old processor; mp=modified processor; —ml—=modified link.] a) New Leaf Processor. b) New Link. c) New Intervening Processor. d) New Binary Link. e) Modified Processor. f) Modified Link.

Learning in Semantic Networks

Assigning one simple processor node to each semantic memory network node is so appealing that this should be attempted, even though it poses problems in restructuring the physical network. For the hardware use a relatively fat fan-out/fan-in network with 8 or more links to each node, the leaves linked to one another to form a good augmented tree. Then have the system begin learning the semantic network, embedding it to start into the center of the tree, and adding new links and nodes at the leaves. Thus no physical changes are needed to the underlying physical computer. There will probably be an occasional need to restructure the graph, spreading nodes out because too many must be linked directly.

Connectionist Models of Learning Machines

The recent proposals for "connectionist" systems (Kohonen, 1982; Hopfield, 1982; Feldman, 1982; Hinton, 1984; Rumelhart et al., 1986) typically assume thousands of links to each neuron-like node (as indeed is the case in living brains), and often appear to assume complete connectivity, either for the entire system or for large subassemblies. Weights of links are raised and lowered as a function chiefly of simultaneous firings of directly linked units.

The demand for thousands of links to each node and for complete connectivity cannot be realized using VLSI microelectronic technology—especially for the very large networks of millions or billions of (each tiny) neuron-like computer nodes. Optical computers may someday make such networks feasible, for example using networks of computers that communicate via arrays of lasers, sensors, mirrors, and programmable holograms.

However, appropriate point-to-point topologies may well be effective substitutes. The fan-out in an appropriately structured augmented fan-out/fan-in net can be made large enough so that any pair of nodes, even though not directly linked, will have only a short path between them. Thus connectionist systems might be realized with much the same kind of physical network and spreading activation-like searches that appear to be attractive for everyday inference and for remembering.

The chief difference appears to be the much simpler and specialized finite-state automata processors (e.g., threshold operators) that connectionist systems use. For example, Feldman (1982) posits networks of features for object recognition and naming where nodes originally fired by the objects link via several banks of intervening nodes with nodes that are fired by or related to the names. He suggests structures where each node links randomly to several thousand nodes in the next layer. This could be handled by fan-out/fan-in nets with thousands of links per node. Since that is not feasible with today's VLSI technologies, several additional fan-out stages could be added between each pair of banks. For example, with 10 links to each node, 3 stages would give 1,000; 5 stages would give 100,000. Hammerstrom et al. (1986) are beginning to design an architecture of this sort, one that appears to have the overall converging structure of a pyramid or tree.

Learning Gradually from Experiences

A system that learns from experience appears to map well into a fan-out/fan-in network; probably the best is an appropriately augmented tree. The additions resulting from learning need not be actual new physical links in the hardware. If the original hardware structure has a rich enough set of links, the system can build its structure of processes by using more and more of these links (and also by rearranging information, reassigning it as needed to different nodes). The basic capability (to be handled by one node, or a small structure of nodes) would be one that could gradually raise and lower the thresholds for firing information from one node to the next, could store a small amount of information at a node (e.g., one or several name-weight pairs) and could assess and compare weights (values associated with information). This is close to a description of living systems of neurons (serving as wires) that link into synapses (where functions are computed).

Such a system appears to have a much harder set of problems than does a structured advice-taker. It cannot add a new piece of information in one single step; rather, it must in effect set up a little experiment about that piece of information, and collect enough information through subsequent relevant experiences to confirm or deny the validity and the value of that information.

In the simplest case, this process can be of the connectionist sort, where the hypothesis simply entails the firing of one node by another (which signifies "If a then b"), and subsequent experiences raise and lower the weights involved. Essentially the new information leads to the forming of a conjecture, or hypothesis, for subsequent assessment. Then the system must adduce evidence for each such hypothesis from those experiences that are relevant to it. That is, it must abstract information from subsequent experiences (possibly also trying to notice information relevant to the hypotheses that it is presently entertaining) and send the information to the appropriate nodes—those that are testing the hypotheses for which it is relevant.

Such systems may need a large amount of global decision making, coordination, and control, in contrast to connectionist systems, which attempt to make all control local. This may mean that there is a need for a separate global system—to make these decisions and monitor and control the learning process—that must be linked to the nodes in the learning network. That suggests a tree-like structure linked to the behaving/learning system.

A SUMMARY COMMENT

Any multi-computer architecture appropriate for learning must also be appropriate for the capabilities to be learned. So it seems best to start with the architectures that appear to be indicated for the cognitive processes to be learned.

Learning would appear to entail needs for additional information-carrying links. Feedback that can help the learner infer what information is relevant, and what to learn (i.e., how and where to change its own internal structure) must be conveniently accessible, either by broadcasting, selective dissemination, or request.

An attractive long-term possibility is a process-structured system that actually adds, as needed, new hardware nodes, and also new links between old nodes. Since this does not seem feasible, both because the proper structures are not yet known, and existing technologies do not allow the gradual dynamic addition of new nodes and links, a reasonable alternative appears to be a system with sufficiently rich linkages—for example a fan-out/fan-in structure—to contain enough paths for future use. That is, the system might start with many unused or poorly used nodes and links, gradually fill them up and improve their quality, and then gradually move processes around to make room for new processes.

A suitably augmented tree—as described in Chapters 19 and 21 for robots and wholistic systems—possibly combined, where indicated, with specialized structures like pyramids for perception and control subtrees for motor coordination, would appear to be especially appropriate.

Chapter Twenty-One

WHOLISTIC SYSTEMS THAT INTEGRATE SEVERAL INTELLIGENT PROCESSES

Central to a robot is perceptual-motor interaction. Today's "intelligent robots" chiefly add a tv camera, frame-grabbing digitizer, and image memory, and/or pressure gauges and range finders, to motor-driven robot arms, wheels, and/or legs. They use a perception program to identify an object and send its location and probable trajectory to the robot arms', legs', and/or wheels' controller. Sometimes simple procedures that interpret information from tv, pressure gauges, and range finders continue to guide and to correct motion, in a more or less tight perceptual-motor loop. Occasionally very simple problem-solving procedures are added to make a few inferences when needed.

A truly intelligent robot would need not only these, but all the separate intellectual processes, all combined into a smoothly functioning, highly integrated whole. Each such process should be as powerful and as general-purpose as possible, rather than an ad hoc special-purpose system developed for a specific suitably simple and carefully controlled set of tasks. All processes should be integrated as well as possible.

Very little research has been done toward realizing such systems, even though they are the central and ultimate goal of AI. This chapter examines some of the possibilities.

WHOLISTIC INTEGRATED SYSTEMS INTERACTING WITH ENVIRONMENTS

An intelligent robot must continually interact with the larger environment that surrounds it. The real world obviously presents us with an adequate environment, one that contains and confronts the intelligent entity with all the problems—or, as we choose a particular simplified environment, whatever specific problems are of interest, or of practical importance. So it seems best and most natural to think of building a physical robot of the sort examined in Chapter 19, and have it actually move about within and interact with some part of the real world. However it is also possible to replace some, or all, of the robot's hardware parts, including its sensory input and motor output devices, with software programs. That is, we can simulate any—or all—parts of the robot. We can similarly simulate parts of the environment, or all of it.

Such simulations are extremely difficult to accomplish, and almost certainly they simplify the enormous complexity of any but the simplest toy-like environments. It is important to stress that whatever is the most desirable mixture of program procedures and hardware objects (including the "hardware" of the real world—the inanimate objects, animals, and people in the intelligent entity's environment) can be used. What combination of hardware and software is chosen is basically a question of tactical tradeoffs.

Combining Two or Three Intelligent Processes

A truly intelligent robot (call it an intelligent entity) would have problem-solving, speech-handling, and memory-searching capabilities in addition to being able to perceive, make a few shallow inferences, and move about. At a simpler level, there are a number of potentially useful systems that would combine speech recognition and vision, or problem solving and remembering, or a variety of other pairs, triples, or n-tuples of intellectual functions.

As a relatively crude first step, two or three different intellectual processes might be combined by linking together programs for each of these processes taken separately. Much better would be programs that generalize each of these processes in such a way that they could then be integrated into as simple and elegant a total system as possible. This indeed does appear to be the case in living systems. And the problems posed by the real world (e.g., to perceive images where objects and words are intermingled; to attend to the objects that have the greatest import; to manipulate the objects that verbal commands or comments have suggested should be handled) appear to necessitate such highly integrated combinings.

COMBINING SIGHT, SOUND, TOUCH, AND OTHER PERCEPTUAL INFORMATION

Simply sensing and perceiving information from several sensory modalities, and integrating this information into an overall perceptual understanding of the environment, pose major problems of great interest.

For example, two or more tv "eyes" might be used, their images combined into binocular or multiocular vision. These could further be combined with several pressure gauge "fingers" and a laser "bat-like distance detector." All might be used together to gather information for mapping out the terrain that a mobile system is scouting, or for recognizing the objects in a poorly lit room.

An acoustical input device plus sound and speech recognition procedures could gather still more information—not only about the speech itself, but also to help recognize objects that are also perceived visually and/or tactually. For example, "that's a wax banana in front of the robin" plus the characteristic whistle of a robin from the bird with an upraised beak might serve to disambiguate the recognition of ersatz fruit and an almost hidden bird.

Similarly, speech recognition might be combined with vision. This would allow programs to handle the typical scene of a moving picture or television program. Today's vision systems work only as though with silent movies; today's speech recognition systems work only as though with telephones.

COMBINING PERCEPTION AND LANGUAGE PROCESSING

There are a number of other combinations of two or more intelligent subsystems that are, potentially, of great practical and theoretical importance (although virtually no research has been done on them).

Visual perception, language understanding, and remembering might fruitfully be combined. Consider the very common situation when printed words and objects, or pictures of objects, occur interspersed in the same scene. Obvious examples are magazine ads, comics, and streets full of road signs, store fronts, and billboards. Some of the edges, strokes, and other features in such images imply symbols with referential meanings rather than objects. Symbols combine into higher-level symbols (words, phrases, sentences, commands). These symbols can refer to objects, and even to actions to be effected on the objects. For example, an advertisement might say: "write a jingle on this coupon, and mail it," or "eat yogurt [with a picture of yogurt]."

Perception and semantic memory systems might also fruitfully be combined. Now when a system tries to answer questions or converse about objects the actual internal models of those objects that it uses to recognize them could also be used to describe and talk about them. Rather than store long verbal encyclopedic entries on such objects, the system could compute the desired information from the perceptual models. Indeed it seems likely that this is the way a general system will have to work. A symbolic, verbal description of even relatively simple things like 'fruit,' 'apples,' 'chairs,' and so on that was rich enough to describe all their different types and variations would almost certainly have to be far too long to be feasible, and in any case would need an inefficiently large amount of storage space and processing time. The structure of perceptual information needed to recognize these things would also be complex. However, it is absolutely necessary for the perceptual system, and it is almost certainly far smaller than an equivalent verbal description.

COMBINING PERCEPTION AND PROBLEM SOLVING

Problem solving and perception can often be fruitfully combined. For example, procedures to play chess, GO, or a number of other board games where the spatial relations of pieces are important might well benefit from perception procedures that had a good concept of space and objects interacting in space.

Similarly, a system that must figure out how to move from one location to another in a maze or a room crowded with obstacles would benefit from being able to recognize objects, remember pertinent characteristics (e.g., weight), and deduce whether a particular object can be navigated around, or pushed out of the way, or dismembered.

Integrating Cognitive Processes into a Total Intelligent System

The separate areas of artificial intelligence are not really looking at separate problems; they are looking at separate aspects of the single problem of wholistic, integrated intelligence. A simple robot with eyes, ears, touch-sensors, arms, and legs (or wheels) that could recognize objects, understand speech, remember simple facts about where things probably are, figure out what would be best to do, and use perceptual feedback to help it achieve simple goals, comes close to combining all the basic intellectual functions. It would have to do this in a well integrated (and extremely parallel) way in order to have any hope of interacting fast enough with real world objects as they move about.

Such a system could play a variety of useful roles (if it were good enough and cheap enough).

It could patrol the factory, work alongside human beings on a traditional assemblyline, type letters, and keep books. (Note that it might or might not punch word processor or calculator keyboards; the word processor and the calculator might preferably be "in its head"—that is, be programs inside the same computer that the robot was in.)

It could cook meals, regulate the windows and shades, control the lights, dust the furniture, clean the floors, mow the lawn, walk the dog.

These tasks were deliberately stated ambiguously. During the past few years there have been a number of newspaper stories about robots that supposedly do such things. Some have even been sold by mail and by Niemann-Marcus. However, unless the house, sidewalk, lawn and dog are completely reengineered these are extremely difficult problems, far beyond our capabilities today. A robot might be able to walk the dog if we tied the dog's leash to the robot, the sidewalk was smooth and straight enough, no people or other dogs went by, and the dog had been trained and brainwashed never to stop to sniff anything. Similarly, a robot might be able to vacuum a rug if nothing was on it, and if everything fragile had been bolted in place. But a Karel Kapek, Isaac Asimov, Arthur C. Clarke, Stanislaw Lem, or Woody Allen robot is far beyond anything we know how to build. There have been several very primitive simulations of such systems (e.g., Doran, 1968; Uhr and Kochen, 1969; Becker, 1970, 1973; Uhr, 1975); but these are the merest beginnings.

The $600,000,000 DARPA sponsored intelligent autonomous vehicle originally proposed the development of three intelligent entities: a. a robot for the army that can move through unknown terrain at 50 or so miles per hour, collecting information about interesting things it finds; b. a similar device for the navy, that would move in water; c. a pilot's helper for the air force, that would recognize speech in the noisy cockpit, help monitor the plane, give advice, and so on. Each of these needs a full-blown intelligent system to work effectively—especially since each is designed to replace intelligent human beings at a task that taxes all of a human being's skills.

Consider the army robot, whose long term goals have been most clearly stated. What must such a system be able to do in order to be a satisfactory replacement for a human who scouts the enemy's domain? It must be able to avoid rocks, pitfalls, and any other kind of ground so uneven it cannot be traversed. It must be able to figure out how to get around and through tangles of impassable objects such as large boulders, trees, buildings, fences, steep hills, rivers, superhighways. It must be able to recognize complex objects, decide which are "of interest"—whether because expected and being hunted for (e.g., an enemy tank, emplacement, or patrol), or unexpected and surprising (e.g., a strangely shaped object which, because it is not something known, might therefore be something important, possibly in camouflage), or something in-between (e.g., a house with too many lights on, or with people but no lights; a person in a German uniform speaking perfect Russian).

The army robot must play an arbitrary range of games, not only against nature's forces but also against a truly malevolent opponent. It cannot simply decide, "those are two trees with enough space between to go through." It must further decide, "they're not camouflaged enemy soldiers with their lower 'branches' holding a virtually invisible trip-wire that will blow everything up, and a big ditch covered with grass-painted canvas between them." Such a system must do at least as well as a trained soldier on patrol at noticing camouflaged objects, inferring motives, and thinking about what should be recorded and reported. Otherwise it would be national suicide to substitute it for the soldier in a jeep.

Simulated Environments (Ones that Might Include Several Individuals)

There are two major possible approaches to developing robots and wholistic, integrated systems. On the one hand, the hardware robot effectors, whether arms, hands, legs, pulleys or wheels, can be built from metal and plastic, and made to interact with the public "real world." On the other hand, the environment as well as the intelligent system can be simulated inside the computer.

The state of hardware effectors is still so primitive, and the problems of moving and coordinating them are so difficult, that a simulated environment can often be an attractive alternative. It would be a major achievement to develop robot hands that could hold and manipulate arbitrary complex real-world objects (e.g., use a knife and fork to cut and feed a dinner of meat, peas, and potatoes to a baby—at least in polite company—or hand-craft a wooden chair). Simulations would not be able to descend into all the details of interaction between knife, meat, tendon, and bones; or fork-tongs, crumbling potatoes, and rolling peas; or chisel, drill, peg, hammer, screw, screwdriver, and wood. They can, however, serve very useful purposes in developing the first general structure of an integrated wholistic system. We can develop a combination of software/hardware computer structures and external environment structures that best serves our purposes at the present stage of development of our intelligent systems.

MULTI-COMPUTERS FOR WHOLISTIC INTEGRATED SYSTEMS

There appear to be two possible approaches to architectures that would best support integrated cognitive systems: more or less general-purpose networks, either homogeneous or heterogeneous combinations of each specialized parts; and true brain-like data-flow systems.

General Multi-Computer Networks for Wholistic Systems

We might try to achieve a general multi-computer network capable of performing whatever structure of functions a program demands. This would be much like a general-purpose multi-computer in the computing center of the future. Possibly it would not need as wide a range of capabilities, especially with respect to number crunching operations.

UNSTRUCTURED HOMOGENEOUS SYSTEMS

For this approach a system like PASM, the Butterfly, or the Ultracomputer, or an augmented tree or other network with good density or other appropriate topological properties, would seem to be indicated. As Chapter 19 suggests, such a system will have major problems when it must be interfaced to an external environment that contains objects in motion, hence must operate in real time at real world speeds. It becomes more appropriate when the environment is also simulated within the multi-computer.

This would be an extremely expensive beast, and one could hardly expect to keep it busy all the time with wholistic AI programs. To make it more cost-efficient, it might be multiprogrammed, or even given a background stream of jobs that each processor could execute in conventional single-CPU mode.

PARTIALLY STRUCTURED, PARTIALLY HETEROGENEOUS SYSTEMS

To the extent that each separated function is best handled by a particular specialized system, it might be preferable to build a heterogeneous compound of specialized regions—much like the brain appears to be. This might be an extension of the augmented tree of augmented trees and pyramids suggested in Chapter 19. However, additional structures are needed for the central cognitive processes that remember, that solve problems, choose, and figure things out, and that use and understand language. Since a logarithmic pyramid structure seems attractive for perception, a several-level augmented tree for control and coordination, and a fan-out/fan-in structure for problem-solving, everyday reasoning and semantic memory searches, augmented tree-based structures may well be among the most appropriate possibilities.

For example, retina-like arrays, one for each of several tv "eyes," might form the base of several perceptual pyramids; these might merge together, and then flow information into augmenting networks with good global properties, which in turn link to other clusters in the larger system (Uhr, 1986). These might in turn link to the several levels of the control-coordination computers in the robot-motor subsystems. All might be combined with a more general-purpose augmented tree that serves as a fan-out/fan-in network for remembering and problem-solving.

Connection Machines, N-Cubes, and Reconfiguring Networks

(Heterogeneous) Connection Machines and (homogeneous) N-Cubes are today possibly the most commonly considered point-to-point topologies for general-purpose intelligent entities. It is not at all clear, however, how they would be programmed and used, or how fast and efficient they would be. Reconfiguring networks like PASM, the Butterfly and the Ultracomputer may well offer more easily usable power for developing prototype programs, but their completely neutral pseudo-complete graph structure and ultimately limited size appear to keep them from attaining the power and speed needed to achieve really general purpose truly intelligent wholistic systems, which must necessarily be very large and powerful.

True Data-Flow Brain-Like Hardware

It is intriguing to consider trying to design, build, and program true data-flow hardware, such that information could be streamed in through the input transducer(s) (e.g., one or several tv cameras, a number of touch-sensors, a microphone), and also spread out from internal sources (such as lists of "ideas," "needs," or "hypotheses"), with all the flow of processes handled by the structure of the network itself.

That is, the topology of the hardware would mirror the structure of the data-flow graph that describes this whole set of processes. Once again, this appears to mirror the way the brain processes the information, from both external and internal sources, flowing through it.

Today we can begin to design rough approximations (Chapter 13). We might incorporate into hardware specialized substructures of systolic-like data-flow graphs. Such exercises would be extremely instructive, and help us move toward successively better approximations. This may well be one of the best ways to gain experience from which ideas for good general-purpose basic modules might emerge. And it might be attractive to augment such data-flow multi-computers with limited reconfiguring capabilities.

Over the longer term, if general-purpose data-flow hardware structures of the sort suggested in Chapter 13 can be developed, they would be especially appropriate for embodying wholistic systems.

Multi-Computers to Simulate Environments Containing Intelligent Entities

There appear to be two leading candidates for network topologies that could efficiently be used to simulate the environment within which the intelligent cognitive system must reside. This is, potentially, an important application. For it would replace the often very complex, expensive, and fault-prone input and output interfaces and related programs (tv cameras, perception programs; robot arms, legs, wheels, motor programs) between the intelligent system and its environment. It could also serve as a test-bed within which precise, perfectly controlled experiments might be run—to compare different perceptual, cognitive, or motor subsystems by placing each of them in turn in a common larger environment.

N-DIMENSIONAL ARRAYS IN WHICH THE N-DIMENSIONAL ENVIRONMENT RUNS

A 3-dimensional array is in many ways ideal to model a 3-dimensional environment with which a simulated intelligent entity must interact. The "rules" or "laws" of physics of this environment can be specified and carried out to whatever degree of detail the programmer chooses (and has the perseverance to specify and program), and the multi-computer can handle.

These might be approximations to the laws of physics as we know them for our own real physical world; or they might be any other set of rules whereby primitive things and spaces, groupings, compounds, interactions, and changes can be specified. If the rules for interaction are as they essentially are in our real world—that things interact as an inverse function of distance, everything affecting other things by moving through nearby space—then an N-dimensional array can be used to model an N-dimensional space (with time one additional dimension).

ARRAYS, TREES AND APPROPRIATELY AUGMENTED FAN-OUT/FAN-IN TREE STRUCTURES

Alternately an oct-tree might be used. Each node in an oct-tree has 8 children arranged in a 2 by 2 by 2 cube. Essentially, this superimposes a tree over the 3-dimensional array. It allows one to compress the space by eliminating nodes in the tree whose subtree progeny are all identical.

This adds two new capabilities. A. To the extent that the entire array need not be specified (this happens when subregions are homogeneous) the oct-tree gives a smaller, more efficient, representation. B. The different parts of the array can be accessed in O(logN) steps, by moving down the oct-tree, rather than O(N) steps, by moving through the array. This also suggests superimposing a tree over an array, as is being done in the new version of the Non-Von.

COMPARING ARRAYS AND TREES

The array would appear to work reasonably well if the entire program for the intelligent entity could be embedded in one node (or region) of the total array—exactly where that intelligent entity resides. This is probably unrealistic, for several reasons:

This program will be very large. It will therefore take far too long to execute unless a commensurately large subset of computers are assigned to execute it, all in parallel. The array might well be a suitable architecture within which this could be done, but it seems likely that a network with a denser topology would be more powerful.

That suggests modifying the array so that it is a tesselation of dense local networks, for example, Singleton graphs, or has small embedded networks scattered throughout.

Alternately, one network optimized for and dedicated to the execution of programs for intelligent entities (probably an appropriately augmented tree) might be suitably linked to a second network (probably a 3-dimensional array) dedicated to modeling the environment.

It might well be attractive (at least in a few years, when the simulation of large environments becomes economically feasible) to have several intelligent systems embedded within a single environment—for example, models of humans, chimps, dogs, mice, edible grasshoppers, and more than one (and, potentially, a large number) of each. For example, we might want to model a whole community of humans as they cooperate and compete in using other animals and inanimate objects to help sustain themselves and improve their society, at least occasionally at the expense of still other edible or in other ways exploitable animals.

This means that it might be more efficient to have a general program for intelligent entities that called more specific programs and data-banks for information about specific species, animals, and individuals. Otherwise the very large complete program would have to be stored and executed for each instance of each intelligent entity. To handle this successfully, the intelligent organism programs should be executed by a suitably powerful and appropriately structured multi-computer with suitable links that allow it to communicate well with whatever regions of the environment-modeling multi-computer are inhabited by intelligent organisms.

A SUMMARY COMMENT

The whole intelligent AI system obviously needs a very large and powerful, highly parallel, multi-computer network, in order to interact with rich and complex real-world environments in real time. One attractive possibility is a heterogeneous system with large arrays, pipelines, augmented trees, and pyramids assigned as appropriate to different processes. Others are a good pseudo-complete graph (e.g., a crossbar or reconfiguring network), or point-to-point graph (e.g., an augmented tree or other fan-out/fan-in structure) linking together as many powerful computers as feasible. Still another is a very large neuron network-like structure of very simple processors. Indeed, the ultimate system should probably, at a micromodular level, have the properties of a neuron network—if only because the mind/brain has those properties. However, today the connectionist systems and other neuron-like systems are just beginning to handle the simplest problems; they are far from the needed power to attack the whole cognitive system.

To simulate the environment as well as the intelligent system, a large 3-dimensional array may well be the most suitable structure. Such an array should probably also be linked to additional appropriate structures indicated for the intelligent system, in a way that makes possible good interaction between them, as when several examples of the same simulated entity (whether organism or object) must be present in several different regions of the environment.

Modeling the whole integrated intelligent system entails such large and complex problems that we can today only begin to move in the direction of attempting to handle them. For tactical reasons we must successively simplify the problem down to feasible size, whether by simplifying each function, decomposing into separate functions, or relaxing demands for generality, flexibility, robustness, and/or speed. Such simplifications may well make feasible the realization of the resulting program on a much wider variety of architectures. But the art of tactical simplification lies in the ability to successively relax and remove the set of simplifying assumptions, so that steady progress can be made toward the ultimate goal. Therefore the goals of robust, general, flexible systems that work in real time, and also the architecture of the hardware, must be kept in mind.

THE PRESENT STATE; MAJOR PROBLEMS; MOST PROMISING ARCHITECTURES

Chapter Twenty-Two

A CRITICAL LOOK
AT ARCHITECTURES
PROPOPOSED FOR AI

Artificial intelligence is working toward systems that see, hear and touch; think, deduce, and decide; remember, discuss, and understand; speak, move, and manipulate; and learn; and systems that integrate all of these functions. These are distant goals for very difficult problems. It may occasionally be possible to short-circuit robustness and generality, to achieve systems that handle specific relatively narrow problems of practical importance, or appear to give impressive demonstrations for carefully chosen toy domains. Too often such systems are rigid and fragile, and teach us little. Except when they handle practical problems, they frequently turn out to be dead ends.

Large massively parallel software systems, properly embedded into appropriately parallel hardware, appear to be the key to general success over a wide range of problems and conditions. Only such systems would allow and invite the rich and complex range of processes needed to cope successfully with real-world variability at real-time speeds.

SUMMARY OVERVIEW OF TODAY'S STATE OF THE ART, AND TOMORROW'S

A large number of different parallel architectures have been explored during the past few years. An enormously larger number of architectures are possible (essentially, any graph).

Multi-Computers Actually Built to Date

Relatively few multi-computers have actually been built and run. Only a handful of these have more than 50 computers, and almost all (especially the largest) are more or less synchronous machines.

These include the following relatively synchronized systems:

A.   Five synchronized SIMD parallel arrays, which have 4,096 (ICL DAP), 9,216 (University College London CLIP4), 16,384 (NASA-Goddard MPP) 41,104 (Martin-Marietta CAPP), and 65,536 (TMI Connection Machine) computers;

B.   Two synchronized SIMD systems (Goodyear-Aerospace STARAN and ASPRO) that use flip reconfiguring networks to link processors to memories; these have been built with as many as 2,048 processors;

C.   A synchronizing shift-register ring-based system of 128 asynchronous MIMD Z-80 micro-computers (University of Maryland ZMOB);

D.   Two partially synchronized MISD pipelines, of 113 computers (ERIM Cyto-computer) and of 256 (IBM MITE).

The largest of the asynchronous networks actually built and running are:

A.   A cluster of clusters totaling 50 computers (Carnegie-Mellon Cm*);

B.   Networks with 45 to 65 computers that are to some extent algorithm-structured (the different versions of the ELSAG EMMA developed for the Italian and for the French Post Offices);

C.   A reconfiguring network with 128 processors (BBN Butterfly);

D.   An N-Cube with 128 processors (Intel's commercial version of the Cal Tech Cosmic Cube), and one with up to 1,024 (N-Cube's).

In addition to these, several dozen, and probably a hundred or more, prototype systems have been built. These typically have 4, 5, 8 or 16, or a few more, computers. Several more powerful systems now in various stages of construction include new and somewhat larger 2-dimensional SIMD arrays of 1-bit processors (Japanese Telephone), MIMD reconfiguring network-based systems with 512, 1,024 and 4,096 computers (IBM RP3, Purdue PASM, NYU Ultracomputer), trees (Columbia University DADO and Non-Von), Floating Point System's N-Cube of up to 4,096 vector processors, clusters of clusters (University of Illinois Cedar), and an SIMD array of 1-bit processors linked to successively smaller MIMD arrays of successively more powerful processors (University of Massachussetts CAP).

Future Possibilities for Increasing the Number of Computers in the Network

Most of the systems (especially the large number of small MIMD systems) that have actually been built to date are made to appear to the programmer to have the very simple overall topology of a complete graph (as though every processor links to every other processor and to every bank of memory). But only three or five computers can be linked into a true complete graph. For anything larger, such systems are actually implemented as pseudo-complete graphs, using a bus, ring, crossbar switch, or reconfiguring network.

Buses, rings, and crossbars are feasible for 8, 16, or (possibly) 32, or 64 or so computers.

Reconfiguring networks make possible (but at increasingly greater costs) multi-computers with up to several hundred, or even several thousand, computers. Thus they appear to make feasible up to 2 orders of magnitude increases in the number of computers in the network. They exact a certain but relatively small price in loss of generality; but an increasingly greater price in extra hardware for their NlogN banks of switches and extra time to compute paths, and then to re-set and traverse those switches.

The only other topologies that have been widely used are 2-dimensional arrays for synchronized MIMD systems, and N-Cubes, trees, and slightly augmented trees.

Multi-computers with many thousands, or millions, of processors must use point-to-point links, where information passed from one computer to another must often move through a path of intervening computers. They need more complex topologies; these can be chosen from among the enormous variety of all possible graphs.

A number of interesting and potentially very powerful graphs have already been discovered, although they are not widely known among computer architects, and they are virtually unused. These include several small graphs (with 50 or fewer nodes), some of which are optimal on important criteria like density and connectivity. There are also a number of relatively powerful compounding operations that can be used to link these small graphs (and also compounds, recursively) into much larger graphs that often have desirable properties. In addition, there are several global constructions with desirable properties. These include augmented trees, N-dimensional arrays, N-Cubes, pyramids, augmented pyramids, partially reconfigurable true data-flow hardware, and a variety of process-structured and more or less general heterogeneous systems.

Problems with Operating Systems to Handle Communications Between Computers

There are several kinds of synchronized systems, most notably the SIMD arrays and the MISD pipelines, where information is passed from one computer to another with great speed and efficiency—typically at the same speed as information is fetched from and stored into a single-CPU computer's memory by its processor. However, in most of today's asynchronous MIMD networks, no matter what their topology, the operating system used to handle the transfer of information typically slows message-passing to the point where it can be roughly 4 orders of magnitude slower than a basic machine instruction!

This is because the present state of the art for MIMD operating systems makes use of elaborate message-passing protocols that spend several thousand instructions to send a short burst of information (typically from 1 to 2000 words long). This means that, unless one programs these systems to do almost everything within each individual computer and send and share virtually no information at all, the time spent sending messages dominates. Even if each processor sends a message only every 10,000 or so instructions (i.e., virtually never), its productivity will be cut by more than half. Passing of information—which is basically the same operation as a fetch—is over 4 orders of magnitude more expensive than is processing that information!

This is in striking contrast to the synchronous and partially synchronized systems. The SIMD arrays typically take the same amount of time, or even less time, to pass information between neighbor computers as to process it. The reconfiguring networks, crossbars, and ZMOB rings take only a relatively small amount more time. Until operating systems are developed for the bus-based and point-to-point linked topologies that almost eliminate the message-passing overhead needed today, it will be hard to make these networks cost-effective, or offer significant speedups.

There are good reasons to think that message-passing can be speeded up substantially in asynchronous networks. The Occam operating system for Transputer networks already achieves major speedups, essentially by asking the programmer to handle communication as an "output to-input from" process. The reconfiguring networks and the large arrays are faster still.

Problems with Simple Pseudo-Complete Graph Topologies

Since most of the asynchronous networks actually built have been very small, it has been possible to link computers and/or memories using a bus, ring, crossbar, or star, thus giving (more or less approximate) pseudo-complete graphs. Unless a ring or a bus that links large numbers of processors is given enormous bandwidth, it will be plagued with contentions, bottlenecks, and delays. A crossbar needs N^2 B-bit switches to link N computers to one another; this becomes expensive when N = 16, and excessive when N = 64. A star has a severe bottleneck at its center. It may be useful when only 4 or 5 computers are to be linked to a common "blackboard" memory; but limits on ports, pins, and wires into a component, and also contention, will soon overwhelm the system. Therefore these appear to be make-do, interim, and ultimately dead-end techniques suitable for small networks only.

Reconfiguring networks can be used to give a rough approximation to a complete graph. However they need NlogN switches. This becomes expensive with hundreds of computers, and prohibitive with more than a few thousand at most. And the O(logN) time needed to reprogram these switches, and the gate delays as information passes over a sequence of logN switches, can grow to appreciable size.

Possible Point-to-Point Topologies for Large Multi-Computers

A variety of interesting less-than-complete graphs have been proposed as more appropriate for multi-computers. The problems of simultaneously developing (a) good topologies, (b) efficient operating systems, (c) parallel programming languages for asynchronous systems, and (d) suitable parallel algorithms and programs are so great that progress has been slow. Even worse, it may well be that because these problems are difficult and progress is slow, relatively little work is being done—whether because it is difficult to get funding, or because researchers shy away from tough problems, is hard to say. We are therefore in a position where many papers are written about possibilities, but relatively few machines are even designed or simulated in detail.

Even fewer multi-computers have been built and tested—and these systems tend to have the potentially dead-end and less interesting topologies, and to be too small to give much information. Indeed often they might just as well have been simulated on a conventional serial computer. But it is not possible to simulate a network large enough to exhibit the behavior of the larger and more complex topologies. That, very simply, would take much too long. For example, a simulation of 16 computers interfaced to a ring, or linked via a reconfiguring network, is feasible, but it would take far too long to simulate a good compound of good clusters, or a reconfigurable system with PASM's complex 2-level design, or a De Bruijn network large enough to have good global density.

Multi-Computers Actually Designed or Built for Artificial Intelligence

The only multi-computers that have actually been built, or even designed in detail, at least partially for AI problems, are the pipelines, arrays, and pyramids for image processing, computer vision, and pattern perception; the to some extent process-structured EMMAs, each specialized for a slightly different perceptual recognition task; the Aquarius Prolog machine for problem solving and expert systems; and the reconfigurable networks (e.g., TRAC, PASM and the Butterfly), trees (e.g., DADO, Non-Von) and the Connection Machine, for pattern perception, semantic memory searches, and a greater variety of tasks.

There are several architectures that appear to be more appropriate for AI problems than many of the systems designed and built to date. These will be reviewed and examined in more detail in the next chapter.

We are thus in a position where a wide variety of architectures have been proposed for multi-computers. Only a few of these have been proposed for AI applications. Many of those have been described only vaguely, appear to be unrealizable, or seem unmotivated, excessively expensive, and occasionally almost capricious. Only a handful have actually been built or used, and these are preponderantly synchronized pipelines and arrays. For only a few—chiefly the synchronized systems—is it known that substantial increases in speed and power can be achieved. The asynchronous networks pose such severe problems in developing efficient operating systems that today their extremely slow message-passing typically degrades performance by several orders of magnitude.

Chapter Twenty-Three

SUGGESTIONS AS TO THE MOST PROMISING ARCHITECTURES

SUGGESTED ARCHITECTURES FOR ARTIFICIAL INTELLIGENCE

The most promising candidate AI architectures for highly parallel systems appear to be the following:

Process-Structured Array, Pipe, and Pyramid Architectures

Large arrays can enormously speed up local operations that must be applied everywhere, as at the retinal level of vision and, possibly, the acoustical level of sound and speech and the mechanical level of touch.

This comment also applies to the (inevitably?) somewhat smaller pipelines, which typically are used to simulate arrays. Carefully designed and specialized pipelined systems can give very powerful, possibly at times more cost-effective, alternatives to true hardware arrays—especially when speed is not paramount.

Pyramids, while retaining all the virtues of arrays, appear to be able to overcome their major information-passing problems and therefore handle global operations with efficiency. On the one hand, pyramids actually include whole sets of arrays, and can execute processes exactly as though they were arrays. On the other hand, they reduce an N-by-N array's N-step worst case information-passing times to only logN steps.

Pyramids can also be used to pipeline information in a data-flow manner from the retinal input, successively transforming, abstracting, and coalescing information. They can gather, transmit, and broadcast information in logarithmic time.

Pyramids, with their potentially massive parallel speedups, appear to be especially appropriate for vision, including binocular perception and the perception of objects in motion, where two or more pyramids of extracted information are merged together. They are also appropriate for processing and combining information from touch sensors, and for audition, at least at the acoustic and probably at the phonemic and higher levels.

The massively iterated micromodular structures of arrays and pyramids (and to a lesser extent pipes) make them especially suited for implementation in VLSI.

Tree-Based Structures, and Augmented Trees

Tree-based structures, and especially fan-out/fan-in structures and other appropriately augmented trees, appear to be attractive architectures for several purposes:

> Robot motor control and coordination, where a hierarchy of levels is found, as when each joint has several influences and several degrees of freedom; each appendage (e.g., a leg, arm, or hand) has several joints; and each robot has several appendages;
>
> Problem solving and decision making, when information is structured in a reasonably balanced tree form;
>
> Expert systems' diagnoses, at least when they are couched in the form of discrimination trees;
>
> Parsing of language utterances, whether at syntactic or at semantic levels;
>
> Semantic memory networks, for representing and accessing information, using a spreading activation-like fan out from those nodes that are originally accessed (e.g., as the result of perception or language processing);
>
> Systems that learn (since they must have the structure of the information learned).

Pyramids and trees are closely related (a pyramid can be thought of as a tree with lateral links; and several of the variant pyramids are literally trees, or trees linked to arrays at their leaves only). So it seems attractive to consider trees, and especially augmented trees, as basic structures that underlie an integrated wholistic intelligent system.

A large tree gives good local convergence (for processing, extracting, coalescing, abstracting, and reducing information, and for finding global interactions) and divergence (for broadcasting, message-passing, and searching) at all of its interior nodes—since each node is itself the root of a large subtree. A tree also is reasonably dense globally, and quite dense locally, and a tree can be embedded nicely into a VLSI chip.

Appropriately augmented trees, with links added to the leaves until leaves have as many links as the interior nodes, have most of these virtues. In addition, they have much better density and (when augmented for that purpose) a good fan-out/fan-in structure in a much larger subset of the augmented tree, rather than just in the tree's interior. But the augmentations usually will turn the tree, which is a planar graph, into a nonplanar, and often highly nonplanar, graph—one that may be substantially more difficult to embed in and realize with VLSI.

Reconfiguring Switches, Both In Global Networks and Local

Reconfiguring networks, and partial reconfiguring (both local and global), offer several potentially important tools for making multi-computers more general, more powerful, and more adaptable. Consider the following examples:

A relatively general and easily programmable pseudo-complete graph-based system can be built, at least up to several hundred or possibly even several thousand nodes in size.

If a synchronized pyramid is used for vision, and one wants to link it to an asynchronous network—for example a Hyper-tree, De Bruijn net, or Moore graph—a reconfiguring network may serve that purpose best.

The individual computer might be designed to be reconfigurable—for example, to either 64 1-bit, 16 4-bit, 8 8-bit, 4 16-bit, 2 32-bit, or 1 64-bit processors.

A pyramid might be given such a reconfigurable processor at each node, plus the additional capability to reallocate some of the processors to bottom-up and others to top-down flows of processes.

A chip might be designed that uses partial local reconfiguring—for example, so that an array processor might handle either square or hexagonal arrays, or so that the network might be configured either as an array or as a tree.

A learning system might make use of partial reconfiguring to emulate the growing of new links between nodes.

True Data-Flow Systems

True more or less general-purpose data-flow computers—if they could be designed and built—would be extremely attractive. They would allow information to flow in a natural way through the entire structure, much as in a pipeline, systolic system, or pyramid—but with greater flexibility and absolutely no message-passing overheads or delays.

A neuron network-like system, with extremely large numbers of each very small specialized or special-purpose processors, is a particularly appropriate example. Separate regions might be specialized to handle different functions (much as in the brain).

It might be possible to develop a reasonably small number of basic data-flow structures, and to use these as a general-purpose data-flow network's basic building blocks. Such a system might also benefit from limited reconfiguring capabilities, to handle programs with different data-flow graphs.

THE VITAL NEED FOR NEW PARALLEL FORMULATIONS AND APPROACHES

Sources of Parallelism

Perception, especially visual perception, and also remembering, appear to be the two major loci of massively parallel processes, potentially offering orders of magnitude speedups—possibly 1 to 3 (for speech), 2 to 4 (for touch), 6 to 8 (for vision), and 2 to 8 (for remembering).

Motor control and coordination, and perceptual-motor loops, are certainly other sources of significant potential parallelization—but almost certainly less, probably offering at most 1 to 3 orders of magnitude speedups.

Language handling and problem solving are less well understood; but it would appear that it may be possible to parallelize today's traditional serial approaches to give 1 or 2 orders of magnitude speedups. More promising is the development of entirely new parallel approaches—possibly along the lines of perception-like everyday thinking and everyday decision making—to try to achieve substantially greater speedups.

Moving from Traditional Serial to New Parallel Approaches

This suggests that the development of networks for conventional serial "expert" production systems, or the Japanese version of a Fifth Generation computer—one that can make traditional sequences of logical inferences at tremendous speed—might actually slow down, or even HALT, progress in AI. For these would offer possibilities of only very limited parallelizations—those one or two orders of magnitude speedups associated with standard productions and traditional problem solving.

Even worse, enthusiasts might tend to force perception, remembering, and learning into these relatively serial and minimally parallelizable molds. The whole history of the development of heuristic AI programs for problem solving—whether for chess, theorem proving, inference, or expert behavior—has taken a serial (and often recursive) gather-information-and-test one-step-at-a-time approach. Serial and recursive procedures may well be suited to the serial computers and serial programming languages researchers have been using, and even to the serial ways of (conscious) thinking that have been trained and conditioned into us all.

The new parallel(-serial) multi-computers invite an entirely new and far more parallel approach, starting at the level of program formulation. Rather than attempt to parallelize architectures and programs constructed to handle sets of productions used in today's expert systems, where the programmer has chosen and organized these sets to make a serial search, or to emulate a serial decision tree, we should try to uncover and implement the kinds of parallel algorithms that the human brain routinely uses—or if possible other, even better, algorithms. For example, rather than search serially through trees of tests, the system might apply large handfuls of tests in parallel, combine their results, and then, if needed, continue to apply other large sets of tests.

Rather than a super-fast logic engine, or a multi-computer specialized to handle today's production-based expert systems, there are a large number of structures that are more general and more parallel, and have better process-structured architectures.

Among these, several appear to be especially promising. These include:

a. Pipelines, arrays, pyramids, and augmented pyramids (especially for perception-related problems);

b. Augmented trees, fan-out/fan-in structures, Moore graphs, compounds of clusters, and other good graphs (for problem solving, remembering and robot control);

c. Reconfigurable, and partially reconfigurable, systems;

d. True data-flow systems (these we don't yet know how to build, except in a few specialized cases);

e. Heterogeneous systems; for example, augmented pyramids, aug-
    mented trees, and augmented trees linked with and/or containing
    pyramids and other structures.

At least a few of each of these should be built, and thoroughly
explored. Nor does it seem likely that we are close to the point where
most of the efforts should be focusing on implementing a certain type of
system designed to handle particular programming languages, such as
Prolog or Lisp, or a particular approach, like serial production systems.

Chapter Twenty-Four

PARALLEL ARCHITECTURES SUMMARIZED, AND SEVERAL KEY ISSUES

The following attempts to categorize and summarize the major known types of parallel architectures, both those already developed and those that are promising possibilities.

These can be divided roughly into two major classes: systems that simulate a complete graph and those with point-to-point topologies. The simulated (pseudo) complete graphs account for most of the multi-computers built to date. There are an enormous number of possible point-to-point topologies, but only a few have been built. Several others have been suggested that may well turn out to be more powerful and more promising. It seems likely that there are still other, possibly even better, topologies that have not been identified and appreciated as attractive, or even discovered.

PARALLEL MULTI-COMPUTERS: THE MAJOR POSSIBILITIES

1. *Today's super-single-CPU computers* are specialized for numerical problems—for example, the Crays and Cybers with their very fast hardware, pipeline vector processors, and multi-processors. The newer of these are already multi-computers, albeit with a well integrated set of relatively small numbers of relatively powerful processors. Super-computers can be hundreds of times faster than ordinary computers, at least when executing programs for which they are well tailored. Comparable carefully specialized systems might be designed and built for artificial intelligence problems—for

example, image processing, pattern perception, expert systems, semantic memory networks, robot control. (Little of this has been done, and only on a very small scale—chiefly the pipelines that scan arrays, parallel arrays, and projected Prolog, Lisp, and production machines.)

2. *A bus, ring, or crossbar* can be used to link a small number (up to 16, or possibly, in unusual cases, 32 or 64 or so) of conventional computers or super-computers into what appears to the programmer to be a complete graph. But, at least today, communication is usually handled by a message-passing operating system, and can be very costly and time consuming. A single channel shared among all computers will inevitably lead to hardware bottlenecks unless extremely high bandwidth (hence expensive) links are used; but the N^2 crossbar quickly becomes too expensive. In such networks the individual computers should probably be as powerful and cost-effective as possible. They are probably best programmed to take a divide-and-conquer approach. Thus the problems for which they will be most suited will be divide-and-conquerable, with relatively little need to communicate between processors.

3. *A reconfiguring network* can be used to link from 16 to 256—or even 1,024 or possibly 8,192—processors into a pseudo-complete graph. Time is needed to re-configure the switching network and to send information over the logN sequence of switches; but this tends to be on the order of a few microseconds rather than the milliseconds needed in networks with message-passing operating systems. However, it is not clear whether the relatively large NlogN banks of switches needed for the larger systems are cost-effective.

4. *A serial pipeline* of 5, 10, or 20 processors, or possibly even a few hundred, can be used to iteratively execute complex sequences of operations. When each processor repeatedly executes the same instruction and communicates the results directly to the next processor, pipelines can substantially reduce the time needed for instruction decoding and memory access. There is no need for a message-passing operating system; but information must be passed down through the pipe. The processors and the pipeline can be specialized to execute appropriate operations—for example, 64-bit floating-point arithmetic for numerical problems; or 8-bit fixed-point arithmetic and 1-bit logic (when desired over 3 by 3 windows) for image processing. But the longer the pipe the less often

the programmer will be able to fill it completely and use it efficiently. This will often limit the amount of speedup that can be obtained from parallelizations.

5.   *A synchronized array of computers* can be built, potentially to any size, with each computer linked to its near neighbors. Arrays can be specialized for 1-bit logic, 3 by 3 window, 8-bit fixed-point arithmetic, or 64-bit floating-point arithmetic (or whatever other operations are deemed most useful). When a single controller is used, arrays handle local message-passing with great speed and efficiency. However, the O(N) diameter of an N-by-N array (even when its opposite edges are linked to form a torus) makes nonlocal communication slow and expensive. An array of N-by-N processors might be controlled by from 1 to N-by-N controllers. More than a few controllers are relatively too expensive when used for simple processors, and more sophisticated processors are too expensive when the major thrust is to build as many processors as possible into a massively parallel system.

6.   *An asynchronous network of independent computers* can be constructed with potentially any number of computers. After a few dozen (or possibly a few hundred) computers are linked together, a point-to-point topology is usually preferable to a pseudo-complete graph; and after a few thousand it is mandatory. Now the problem becomes one of choosing from the enormous number of possible graphs. Among the more interesting topologies already discovered are N-Cubes, trees, trees with extra links, augmented trees (e.g., Hyper-trees, De Bruijn networks), graphs that are optimal, or near-optimal, with respect to desirable qualities (e.g., density, connectivity), compounds of good structures, heterogeneous networks, partially reconfigurable systems, and true data-flow systems.

7.   *Carefully augmented trees* can have good local and global properties in terms of whatever set of criteria are deemed important. Their good fan-out and fan-in properties are very useful for dispersing and broadcasting information, and for combining, converging, transforming, and searching for information—as done in perception, language processing, problem solving, and remembering.

8.   *An especially important topology is a compound* of clusters or good local structures. Each local structure, and also the global structure, should be appropriately configured, in terms of the structure of algorithms executed and/or formal properties, such as density. The optimal Moore graphs appear to be especially

interesting candidates for local structures. Programs should be written and mapped into such systems so that most communication takes place within a structure. Much still needs to be learned about such structures: What are good topologies for local structures? What are good compounding operations? What are good criteria for evaluating and choosing good structures and good compounding operations? What is the best combination of operating system, programming language, and programmer specifications, in terms of uncovering the most appropriate highly parallel algorithms, mapping them properly into the network, and executing them with speed and efficiency?

9. *A pyramid* (stacked successively smaller arrays, or a tree linked laterally into arrays) can be built that combines the good near-neighbor properties of the array (for local window operations) with the good diverging-converging capabilities of a tree (for combining, for broadcasting, and for effecting global operations). Pyramids are used most efficiently when problems (e.g., images to be processed and recognized) are pipelined through them. Pyramids must either be programmed to execute appropriate parallelizations (which the speed of the human brain/mind indicates are possible, but which AI researchers have to date only partially understood), or they can become slow and inefficient.

10. *A pyramid (or an array) can be augmented internally,* or/and externally with networks of asynchronous computers. This can give the system much more flexibility to do different things in different places. The pyramid can be given more power (e.g., links with more bandwidth, more processors, more powerful processors) moving upward toward the apex. Suitable augmenting networks (e.g., NlogN shuffle networks) can also reduce the potential bottlenecks from the tree fan-in. A wide variety of point-to-point networks can be linked to a pyramid in a variety of potentially interesting ways.

11. *Special-purpose and general-purpose systolic systems* can be used to transform information pipeline flowed through them. Systolic systems can be extremely fast and efficient. They are closely related to linear pipelines (except that they are not always lines, hence look more like assemblylines). The special-purpose systolic arrays are quite similar to (but sometimes slower than) custom chips for special-purpose processes. Like other special-purpose processors, they must be integrated into a larger total system.

When they are made general-purpose, systolic systems look very similar to 1-dimensional pipelines and 2-dimensional arrays.

12. *Partial reconfiguring can be used, globally or/and locally,* to tailor and improve the topology as needed, by restructuring the system from one topology to another. However, much more needs to be known about which useful basic structures can be reconfigured to one another with a reasonably small number of switches.

13. *Very large numbers of micromodular processors* might be combined in topologies other than arrays, giving networks reminiscent of the brain's many synapsing neurons. Such systems may well be especially appropriate for VLSI and WSI technologies, and for perception, remembering, and learning.

14. *True assembly-line-like, data-flow hardware* might be constructed. Such a system would have information flow through the physical computer much as it flows through systolic systems, pyramids, and micromodular brain-like structures. Possibly a system with converging-diverging links everywhere, as in an N-dimensional array, or a tree carefully augmented to serve as a fan-out/fan-in network, might serve this purpose with reasonable efficiency. Or a small general-purpose data-flow network might be scanned over, and execute, the program specified by a large data-flow graph. Or partial reconfiguring capabilities and a set of primitive structures might be used to build and rebuild the appropriate overall data-flow architecture.

15. *Heterogeneous structures of different types of substructures* might be built from special-purpose custom and systolic chips, or from larger structures (like pipes, arrays, trees, pyramids, or N-Cubes). Especially attractive are systems that integrate massively parallel processors for local operations (like arrays), and good global topologies (like trees, De Bruijn networks and Moore graphs). These can in turn be combined with other more or less specialized structures, for example, ones that hierarchically control and coordinate a complex perceptual-cognitive-motor system. Or each might be scattered throughout, or concentrated in different regions. This might also make possible the adding, removing, and changing of substructures as appropriate.

SEVERAL KEY ISSUES

Tradeoffs Between Processor Power and Number

A suitably designed super-computer might be 10^2 to 10^3 times faster than a 10^2 times less expensive ordinary computer; a simple network of super-computers can give an additional significant boost in power. Thus, a system of 16 or 32 super-computers linked via a bus or crossbar (as planned for the Cray-3) would be a very powerful beast. And the 10^3-fold parallel reconfiguring network-linked multi-computer could be given another 10^3-fold boost if each node were a super-computer. The range of power from the weakest micro-computer to the strongest super-computer is roughly 10^3 to 10^4. The range of the feasible numbers of processors in a multi-computer is roughly 10^6 to 10^9, or even more. Thus, there is a very large range of possible trade-offs between numbers of processors and power of each processor.

Global vs. Point-to-Point Links

Probably a link is used most efficiently when it is shared among a number of computers. This will tend to smooth out any peak bursts of message-passing (except when all processors are deliberately synchronized to send messages at once—which the programmer should be instructed, helped, or forced not to do).

However, a shared resource, whether link or memory, invites contention problems, and inevitably becomes a bottleneck. So only a small number of computers can be linked together via a star, bus, or ring. Crossbars and reconfiguring networks become too expensive as the network grows in size.

Therefore (and this will depend heavily on the economics of the particular technologies used) one must build point-to-point topologies.

An attractive intermediate possibility is to build small local structures. Each might be a cluster that shares a common bus or ring with enough bandwidth so that performance is not degraded, and all might be linked via a point-to-point compounding network.

The 10-node and 50-node Moore graphs are very attractive alternatives to bus-linked clusters, since they are optimally dense and symmetric, and have at most one node separating any pair of nodes. It is an interesting question whether a bus or ring, or a Moore graph or other relatively dense graph, would (using what technologies and under what conditions) be preferable as a basic structure.

Globally Dense Graphs vs. Reconfiguring Networks for Message-Passing

The reconfiguring networks were originally designed to permute N pieces of data among N processors. Unless, as in STARAN and the Ultracomputer, processors are programmed to constantly fetch from memory and remap data, they will only occasionally be used for that purpose. Many of their links will effectively remain idle and wasted. A more efficient, denser graph may well be preferable.

Globally dense graphs are best at handling one, or a few, messages passed between distant nodes. If programs are mapped randomly into the multi-computer, then globally dense graphs (those that achieve or approach the Moore bound) appear to be best. To the extent that mappings are achieved where processes that communicate are executed by neighboring processors local density becomes preferable.

Possibly best would be topologies optimized to pass a relatively small handful of messages at a time—far less than N—for example, logN or N/logN (these are probably more realistic numbers in terms of what actual programs will do most of the time). This probably means that most of the network's links will lie idle; but that is not unreasonable when links are kept small, hence cheap. Since computers will continue to decrease in cost, it will not be too important that all their parts are always working. Economics will become increasingly less significant in comparison with speed and power.

Optical Components and Optical Computers

Optical computers and optical communication channels may well open up new possibilities for very large multi-computers, and especially for multi-computers with much richer interconnections. Holograms that serve as crossbars or any desired point-to-point topologies, and programmable holograms that serve to reconfigure from one topology to another, appear to be real possibilities once the components for optical computers begin to be developed vigorously. Large arrays or other ensembles of laser or light-emitting diode output devices, of light-sensitive input devices, and of microminiaturized optical gates configured into special-purpose or general-purpose processors, also appear to be possible.

These would offer a very rich range of new types of computers, including ones where many more links could be joined to each processor. Indeed even large complete graphs might be feasible, using lenses and mirrors to broadcast light-born messages everywhere, or to selected regions. But it will take a while (at least 10 or 20 years) before the extremely exciting range of possibilities that optics appears to offer can be realized. And the software problems, in developing suitable operating systems and suitably parallel algorithms and programs, will remain.

Efficiency and Generality in Different Types of Multi-Computers

SPECIALIZATION, EFFICIENCY, GENERALITY

Building specialized, special-purpose, or carefully customized systems can effect major improvements in speed, but almost always at the cost of decreasing generality.

Consider the following example: A serial computer like a VAX needs from 3 to 30 seconds, or more, to execute a local window operation everywhere in a large array; a pipelined image processor like the VICOM might need 30 milliseconds; a massively parallel array like the MPP might need 1 microsecond, or less. Enlarging the array of processors, adding a pyramid, adding more processors at each cell, and speeding up the hardware can each further increase speed by at least one order of magnitude.

Speed and efficiency can plummet for any of these structures when it must execute processes for which it is unsuited. Potentially, architectures that effectively combine these kinds of tremendously fast, massively parallel specialized systems into larger networks containing still other types of needed resources might gain the advantages of each. Designing and building good heterogeneous architectures of this sort, and using them efficiently, pose major unsolved problems.

USING TRUE DATA-FLOW MULTI-COMPUTERS EFFICIENTLY

Hardware through which data flow, in brain-like fashion, is an intriguing, but little understood, possibility. Is there a common underlying structure for all data transformations that could be built into such a system? Could reasonably economical partial reconfiguring switches change to a suitable topology as needed?

A multi-computer that works in true data-flow fashion, by actually flowing information through the appropriately structured processors that transform these data as they pass through, will make efficient use of the links, and of the processors, only when they are at what might be called the cutting edge of the program, and are actually being used. There appear to be two possible ways of overcoming this inefficiency. First, programs can be continuously pipelined through or mapped into the system, as when a stream of images is input by a tv camera. Second, a much smaller scanning network might be used, one that continues to execute only the leading edge of the program and, if and when necessary, reconfigures itself in order to do this efficiently.

USING LARGE MULTI-COMPUTERS EFFICIENTLY

A possible model for the computing center of the future is one where a large multi-computer handles all the different jobs that the members of a large business, university, or research center might submit—much as is done by today's conventional single-CPU computer. Some jobs will be very large, some small. Some will demand extremely fast real time processing; others can wait minutes, hours, or days. Therefore the multi-computer must be large enough to execute large real-time programs fast enough. It must therefore at other times be multiprogrammed, so that it can execute enough different jobs at the same time to keep the whole system busy.

This poses a new set of problems for the operating system to handle, in allocating and reallocating subgraphs of processors to the different jobs. No matter how well the system handles this problem, there will be idle computers. One possible way to keep all processors busy is to have a background stream of jobs going into each individual computer, to be executed by that computer alone, in conventional single-CPU mode. Another is to assign each node as a workstation to one, or to a few, individual interactive users.

Without such sharings of resources among many different programs, often of radically different types, the hardware will be used very inefficiently. Rarely will a researcher want to run brain simulations, or chess programs, or vision systems, or simulated or real robots, day and night, or even much of the time.

It is difficult to judge the economics of even the near future. Computers are getting cheaper so quickly that all researchers will soon be able to have their own, for only a few hundred or a few thousand dollars, with very little compulsion to use them all the time. Personal computers and workstations are beginning to serve like personal cars, bikes, tvs, and newspapers—cheap enough to almost completely replace such things as the public bus or the communal bulletin board. However, the extremely large multi-computers needed for artificial intelligence will probably remain expensive for a good time to come. They need to be built to be as large and as fast as possible—hence to be used efficiently, and shared.

Developing Multi-Computers; Support for Research and Development

The phenomenal success of the conventional single-CPU serial computer paradoxically makes it harder to develop new kinds of computers. It is almost as though rather than design and build cycles, autos, motor boats, prop planes, jets, and space ships, vehicle designers, enthralled by the great success of the carved out log, were to think only in terms of structures of canoes. The many billions of dollars already invested in painfully developed programs coded in traditional languages for conventional computers is another enormous source of resistance to change. Nobody can stand the thought of ever again having to modify, much less recode, only distantly (mis-) understood programs (coded by people who long ago left the company because they couldn't stand any more bugging about bugs) for yet another computer.

The world is nevertheless moving into the era of parallel multi-computers, simply because there is no other way to get around the speed-of-light barrier and achieve faster, more powerful systems. This move has today too much the flavor of people being pushed and dragged. Too often people who have worked all their lives with traditional computers start designing multi-computers for the wrong reasons: because the company says to, or the granting agency is giving out money for this purpose. They tend to extend and modify traditional serial computers, then slap a number of them together, rather than try to develop new kinds of parallel systems. The result too often can be a flotilla of streamlined canoes with wings.

American for-profit companies do not spend 5 or 10 years developing new products with unknown markets, especially in a rapidly growing field like computers. A company feels daring and innovative simply because it introduces the merest sugar-coating (a faster bus, a mouse)—and indeed it may well be: it may well go bankrupt as a result.

Few universities are in a position to develop new multi-computers. They are just beginning to give courses in parallel architecture. Rarely do they have the facilities, staff, and money to sustain a careful, continuing research and development program. Several university groups have built small prototype multi-computers—almost all too small and too difficult to use. The operating system, programming languages, and programming environment are even harder to develop than is the hardware. Even less is known about them, and almost always the researchers run out of steam and money before completing the tedious finishing touches.

Making the problem even more difficult, there is a vital need for a vigorous group of researchers eager to use the new multi-computer who are involved from the beginning in its design and construction. The needed total group—multi-computer hardware architects, systems programmers, and researchers with a range of appropriate applications—is the sort one might expect to find at a number of good universities. But it is rare that everybody really wants to, and can, work together on a project of this sort. Hardly ever does such a potentially productive group get sufficient funding to design, build, and thoroughly evaluate a system large enough to be used effectively.

One very attractive possibility is to have university and industrial groups work together, each contributing its own unique set of resources. But it is far easier to say that than to establish a stable, continuing effort of this sort.

There is not even one university, or one research organization, planning to (1) examine the alternative possibilities for multi-computers; (2) set up a good architecture lab where people can develop, build, use, evaluate and compare systems; and (3) actually build and evaluate a continuing stream of such systems. There should probably be 5 or 10, serving as regional centers that people with real interests and real ideas could use and visit. Yet such an enterprise would be little more expensive than the large one-shot developments occasionally funded, and less expensive than the new super-computer institutes now being set up to make traditional computers available to more physicists (which may be healthy for physics today, but not necessarily for computer scientists developing new systems for physicists, among others, for tomorrow).

Deciding What Systems to Develop, Build, Use

How can we decide what to do, in the face of all this complexity?

Should we concentrate on building more and more powerful Cray-type super-computers—that is, until they hit their inevitable limits in speed?

Should we link as many Cray-type systems as feasible via a bus, crossbar, or reconfiguring network?

When would linking larger numbers of less powerful computers be more cost effective?

What point-to-point topologies should we choose, and why?

For what classes of jobs and specific algorithms should carefully specialized architectures be developed?

When is massive parallelism needed, and what are the most appropriate topologies and allocations of resources to processor power, memory, switches, controllers?

Should we try to move toward more and more general-purpose or more and more specialized networks, or specialized regions within larger networks?

These are only a few of the questions that we might ask, both for multi-computer architectures in general and for architectures for AI. These are the kinds of questions that should be asked long before we decide what systems to build, or to use. Only if questions of this sort are asked and answered as well as possible will systems that work as well as possible be available at all, to use or to buy.

Clearly there are no simple answers. How else proceed, other than to examine these issues as carefully as possible, attempt constantly to develop and improve upon our criteria for evaluation, and explore as fully as possible what appear to be the most promising directions?

After systems are finally built and running we can benchmark and compare them. Even here there are major unsolved problems in developing adequate sets of benchmarks—especially when new parallel systems are being developed that open up new and largely unknown possibilities for parallelizing formulations and algorithms—and above all for attacking hitherto intractable problems. Ultimately far more important than choosing among the systems already built and available are the choices of which systems to build, to design, to simulate, to examine, to explore, to consider.

Only a small number of the possibilities can even be explored and examined carefully, much less built and benchmarked. Therefore they should be chosen from informed study, thought, and whatever analysis and simulation tools (even if only partially satisfactory) can be used. They should span as wide as possible a range of the most promising approaches, not ten of one, and possibly one or two of all the rest. Searching and objective examinations, evaluations, and comparisons should be made at every step in the development of architectures—and also in the development of a highly parallel artificial intelligence, including algorithms, programs, formulations, and approaches. Gould's (1986) comments about Darwin as a scientist apply equally well to the development of multi-computer architectures and the development of artificial intelligence: "So many people think that an idea becomes true or probable by their very cleverness in devising it....They have missed what any good scientist knows in his bones: that fruitfulness in action, expressed as testability in practice, separates the good idea from the idle speculation."

This may sound like a plea for motherhood, and indeed it basically boils down to the scientific method's continuing cycle of thought and construction, experimental test and evaluation, thought and reconstruction, ... But today's development of both parallel multi-computers and artificial intelligence suffers tremendously from an almost complete absence of attempts to analyze, test, evaluate, compare.

Although the scientific method is an ideal that can only be approximated, the closer we come the more progress we make.

A SUMMARY OVERVIEW AND A FEW FINAL COMMENTS

The best hope for computers capable of the million-fold speedups absolutely necessary to perceive scenes of moving objects in real time, and almost certainly necessary to remember, answer questions, infer and solve problems, and interact with complex environments, appears to lie in developing highly parallel multi-computer networks where many different more or less independent processors work in parallel.

The Most Promising Possibilities for Large Multi-Computers

Very large networks of many thousands or even millions of computers can today be built in the form of an array or pyramid with only one or a few controllers. Smaller numbers of (possibly each much more powerful) computers, each with its own controller, can be linked via a pipeline, bus, ring, crossbar, or reconfiguring network.

Large asynchronous networks of computers, each computer with its own controller, are, potentially, very attractive, but they pose several problems. They typically use much more powerful processors, substantially more memory, and large numbers of inherently expensive controllers. Even more important, today they are very hard to program, and operating system overheads for message-passing, and communication bandwidth problems, can enormously degrade their performance. Much research must be done to develop good operating systems, programming languages, techniques for mapping programs into architectures, and above all parallel algorithms.

A wide variety of point-to-point topologies are possible, including ones with reconfiguring capabilities. Among the most promising are graphs that optimize desirable characteristics (e.g., the Moore Graphs and other dense graphs), good compounds of good basic structures, N-dimensional arrays (including N-Cubes), and judiciously augmented trees. However, the operating system overhead remains so great for most such systems that sending information to another computer typically takes thousands of times longer than does an actual operation.

Heterogeneous systems that efficiently combine subsystems that are each specialized to handle particular frequently occurring problems appear to be among the most promising approaches. The specialized parts might each be a major module, as when a highly parallel array or

Table 24-1. Promising Multi-Computers: Components and Overall Structures

Primitive Modules:
  Points;
  Lines, polygons;
  Meshes, trees;
  Benes networks, Moore graphs.

Basic Structures:
  Buses (lines), rings (polygons), crossbars (meshes);
  Pipelines (lines, polygons);
  Arrays (meshes, including systolic arrays and N-Cubes);
  Trees, fan-out/fan-in networks;
  Good local structures (e.g., Moore graphs and other dense graphs).

Promising Larger Structures:
  Multiple pipelines, augmented arrays;
  De Bruijn graphs, other augmented trees;
  Pyramids, augmented pyramids;
  Compounds of good local structures;
  Heterogeneous systems;
  Partially reconfigurable systems;
  True data-flow hardware.

---

pyramid is combined with an asynchronous network. Or each might be very tiny, as when special-purpose systolic chips are combined with a conventional computer.

True data-flow hardware, through which information moves and is transformed (much as by the brain, and by complex assembly-lines) is still another desirable goal (when and if such systems can be designed and built). Pipelines, systolic systems, arrays, and pyramids are today's first examples of such structures. Future data-flow hardware may well be heterogeneous hybrids, built by interlinking different structures, each chosen because it is most appropriate for some special type of problem or subproblem. Or switches might be used for partial reconfiguring, to build, as needed, a few primitive microstructures into the appropriate macrostructures. Alternately, homogeneous systems might be used; promising possibilities include fan-out/fan-in networks and small scanning graphs.

Parallel Formulations and Massively Parallel Algorithms

The development of massively parallel algorithms may well be the key to the whole enterprise of achieving AI systems that are fast, robust, and flexible enough to succeed at real-world problems in real time. Better programming languages, ones that help the programmer think in a parallel, data-flow manner, would help substantially. Without suitably parallel algorithms even the fastest and most efficient multi-computer will not be able to execute large AI programs fast enough so they can act and interact in real time. But we know that sufficiently parallel algorithms exist—at least in the form that the human brain/mind embodies them with such outstanding speed and success.

We human beings have been trained and conditioned for so long by serial mathematics, serial programming languages, serial speech and language, and serial conscious thought processes that we find it very difficult to think about parallel processes. However, the living mind/brain proves that they exist. It is almost as though we must regain contact with our deeper unconscious selves—actually those parts of our mind that almost certainly do most of our most profound thinking, yet about which we are least aware.

Systems Indicated for the Immediate and the More Distant Future

For today and for the immediate future, the systems that appear to offer the most brute power are probably super-computers like the Crays and, where they are appropriate, arrays like the CLIP, DAP, and MPP; pipelined scanning arrays like the Cytocomputers, PIPE, and Pixie-5000; pyramids; and augmented arrays and pyramids. The existing asynchronous networks are probably not yet large enough to offer the power of a large Cray, because the individual nodes are relatively weak, the total number used is relatively small, and (because of bottlenecks in the hardware communications channels and delays resulting from the software message-passing protocols) they cannot be used effectively enough.

In the short run, linking 2, 4, 8, or 16 Crays (as is planned for the Cray-3) may well continue to give the most power for the next few years. Then probably preferable will be substantially larger numbers of relatively weaker computers, where each chip contains at least one entire CPU plus as much (possibly cache) memory as can be squeezed onto it. Nodes might be linked via a crossbar, bus, or reconfiguring network. Such systems can handle a great variety of programs, and can serve as convenient test-beds for simulating topologies that are not to be treated as though all processors and memories are directly linked via a complete graph. At some point, as such pseudo-complete graph structures grow larger, communications bottlenecks and/or hardware costs will grow unacceptable high.

Point-to-point topologies are necessary once more than a few dozen, or at most a few hundred, or possibly a few thousand, computers must be linked together to gain the needed power and speed. They become increasingly useful to the extent that the structure of the flow of information among the program's processes can be embodied in the hardware architecture. They raise new problems, since when two nodes that are not directly linked must communicate, a whole path of additional nodes between them must be involved. These are problems that are already handled well by the pipelines and arrays that demonstrate so strikingly how powerful and efficient point-to-point topologies can be. Point-to-point connectivity makes possible much larger and denser networks with far fewer communications bottlenecks, and networks that can be configured and used in an algorithm-structured way, where the flow of processes through the physical computer nodes mirrors the program's flow of processes.

It is not clear whether general-purpose homogeneous networks can be developed to be fast, powerful, efficient, and cost-effective over a wide range of problems; or whether heterogeneous systems combining appropriately specialized subsystems will be preferable; or whether it will be best to develop separate, each relatively specialized, often process-structured, systems for different purposes. Very little research has been done to explore how different types of programs might be mapped into and executed by different network structures, or how effective might be judiciously placed switches that partially reconfigure networks to better fit programs.

Today's situation is unusually ripe and fraught with new possibilities for both highly parallel, algorithm-structured multi-computer topologies, and also for new highly parallel artificial intelligence formulations and algorithms that make effective use of this enormous power. We are confronted with the intriguing possibility of developing architectures and algorithms together, in effect building software/hardware information processing systems.

Attractive Possibilities, and The Great Variety Still to be Explored

This book has examined a number of interesting and promising topologies for highly parallel multi-computers, including several little known and only recently discovered constructions. These indicate the range of interesting possibilities that are already known (optimal and near-optimal graphs, good compounds of good basic graphs, pyramids, augmented trees and augmented pyramids, algorithm-structured architectures, heterogeneous systems, and true data-flow hardware), in addition to the most widely used and proposed (bus, ring, crossbar, reconfiguring network, pipeline, array—including N-Cube—and tree). They also serve to suggest the possibly very rich set of additional structures waiting to be discovered and explored during the next few years.

The achievement of really large, powerful, and efficient highly parallel multi-computers, and especially systems appropriate for artificial intelligence, including those whose structure throws light on the anatomy of living intelligent systems, would appear to need the following developments:

Highly parallel yet flexible architectures;

Better job/process/algorithm-structured information-flow hardware/-software architectures;

Operating systems that consider the hardware architecture, map programs properly into its structure, and execute them with efficiency and speed;

Programming languages that encourage and help the programmer formulate and code well-structured, highly parallel AI systems.

A crucial part of the same enterprise is the development of extremely parallel artificial intelligence algorithms and programs that, when executed on appropriate parallel hardware, will handle complex real-world problems in real time.

REFERENCES

Abu-Sufah, W., and Kwok, A. Y. 1985. Performance prediction tools for Cedar: a multiprocessor supercomputer. *12th Int. Symp. Comp. Arch.* 406–413.

Ackley, D. H., Hinton, G. E., and Sejnowski, T. J. 1985. A learning algorithm for Boltzmann machines. *Cognitive Science*, 9: 147–169.

Aho, A. V., Hopcroft, J. E., and Ullman, J. D. 1974. *The design and analysis of computer algorithms*. Reading, MA: Addison-Wesley.

Ahuja, N., and Swami, S. 1984. Multiprocessor pyramid architectures for bottom-up image analysis. *Multiresolution Image Processing and Analysis* (A. Rosenfeld, ed.). Berlin: Springer-Verlag, 38–59.

Allen, P., and Bajcsy, R. 1985. Object recognition using vision and touch. *Proc. Int. Joint Conf. on Artif. Intell.* 9: 1131–1137.

Allman, J. M., and Kaas, J. H. 1974. A crescent-shaped cortical visual area surrounding the middle temporal area (MT) in the owl monkey. *Brain Research* 81: 199–213.

Amarel, S. 1968. On representations of problems of reasoning about actions. *Machine Intelligence 3* (D. Michie, ed.). New York: Elsevier, 131–171.

Anderson, J., and Bower, G. 1973. *Human associative memory*. Washington, DC: Winston.

anon. 1979. *Untitled, unpublished paper on ASPRO*. Goodyear-Aerospace, Akron, OH.

anon. 1984. *ELXSI Multiprocessor Computers*. ELXSI Computers.

anon. 1985. *The Connection Machine supercomputer: A natural fit to applications needs*. Thinking Machines Inc., Cambridge, MA.

Antonsson, D., Gudmundsson, B., Hedblom, T., Kruse, B., Linge, A., Lord, P., and Ohlsson, T. 1982. PICAP—a system approach to image processing. *IEEE Trans. Comput.* 31: 997–1000.

Ballard, D. H. 1981. Generalizing the Hough transform to detect arbitrary shapes. *Pattern Recog.* 13: 111 – 122.

——. 1985. Task frames in visuo-motor coordination. *Proc. 3rd Workshop on Comp. Vision.* IEEE Computer Society Press, 3 – 10.

Barnes, G. H., Brown, R. M., Kato, M., Kuck, D. J., Slotnick, D. L., and Stokes, R. A. 1968. The ILLIAC IV Computer. *IEEE Trans. Computers* 17: 746 – 757.

Bartlett, F. C. 1982. *Remembering, a study in experimental and social psychology.* Cambridge, England: Cambridge University Press.

Batcher, K. E. 1973. STARAN/RADCAP hardware architecture. *Proc. 1973 Sagamore Comp. Conf. on Parallel Process.* 147 – 152.

——. 1974. STARAN parallel processor system hardware. *Proc. AFIPS Nat. Comp. Conf.* 43: 405 – 410.

——. 1976. The flip network in STARAN. *Proc. 1976 Int. Conf. on Parallel Process.* 65 – 71.

——. 1980. Design of a massively parallel processor. *IEEE Trans. Comp.* 29: 836 – 840.

——. 1982. Bit-serial parallel processing systems. *IEEE Trans. Comp.* 31: 377 – 384.

Becker, J. D. 1970. An information processing model of intermediate-level cognition. Ph.D. diss., Department of Computer Science, Stanford University.

——. 1973. A model for the encoding of experiential information. *Computer models of thought and language* (R. Schank and K. Colby, eds.). San Francisco: Freeman, 396 – 446.

Beetem, J., Denneau, M., and Weingarten, D. 1985. The GF11 supercomputer. *12th Ann. Int. Symp. on Comp. Arch.* 108 – 115.

Bell, G. C. 1985. Multis: A new class of multiprocessor computers. *Science* 228: 462 – 467.

Benes, V. E. 1965. *Mathematical theory of connecting networks and telephone traffic.* New York: Academic.

Benevento, L. A., Fallon, J., Davis, B. J., and Rezak, M. 1977. Auditory-visual interaction in single cells in the cortex of the superior temporal sulcus and the orbital frontal cortex of the macaque monkey. *Exp. Neurol.* 57: 849 – 872.

Beni, G., and Hackwood, S. 1985. *Recent advances in robotics.* New York: Wiley.

Bentley, J. L., and Kung, H. T. 1979. A tree machine for searching problems. *Proc. Int. Conf. on Parallel Process.* 257 – 266.

Berliner, H. 1980. Computer backgammon. *Sci. Amer.* 142: June.

Bermond, J-C., Delorme, C., and Quisquater, J-J. 1982. Grands graphes non diriges de degre et diameter fixes. Philips Research Laboratory, Brussels, Belgium, Technical Report.

———. 1983. Strategies for interconnection networks: Some methods from graph theory. Manuscript M58. Brussels, Belgium, Phillips Research Lab., 1964.

Block, H. D., Nilsson, N. J., and Duda, R. O. 1964. Determination and detection of features in patterns. *Computer and information sciences* (J. T. Tou and R. H. Wilcox, eds.). Washington, DC: Spartan, 75–110.

Bobrow, D. G. 1968. Natural language input for a computer problem-solving system. *Semantic information processing* (M. Minsky, ed). Cambridge, MA: MIT press, 146–226.

Bobrow, D. G., and Collins, A., eds. 1975. *Representation and understanding: Studies in cognitive science.* New York: Academic.

Bobrow, D. G., and Fraser, B. 1969. An augmented state transition network analysis procedure. *Proc. Int. Joint Conf. on Artif. Intell.* 1: 557–569.

Bode, A., Fritsch, G., Handler, W., Henning, W., Hofmann, F., and Volkert, J. 1985. Multi-grid oriented computer architecture. *Proc. Int. Conf. Parallel Process.* 89–95.

Bokhari, S. H. 1981. On the mapping problem. *IEEE Trans. Comp.* 30: 207–214.

Bondy, J. A., and Murty, U. S. R. 1976. *Graph theory with applications.* New York: Elsevier.

Brachman, R. J. 1979. On the epistemological status of semantic networks. *Associative networks* (N. V. Findler, ed). New York: Academic, 3–50.

Briggs, F., Fu, K. S., Hwang, K., and Patel, J. 1979. PM4—A reconfigurable multimicroprocessor system for pattern recognition and image processing. *Proc. AFIPS Nat. Comput. Conf.* 225–265.

Bronson, E. C., and Jamieson, L. H. 1985. A distributed parallel architecture for speech understanding. *Algorithmically specialized parallel computers* (L. Snyder, L. H. Jamieson, D. B. Gannon, and H. J. Siegel, eds.). New York: Academic, 139–148.

Brooks, R. A. 1981. Model-based three dimensional interpretations of two dimensional images. *Proc. Int. Joint Conf. on Artif. Intell.* 7: 619–624.

Brown, C. M., Ellis, C. S., Feldman, J. A., LeBlanc, T. J., and Peterson, G. L. 1985. Research with the Butterfly multicomputer. *Univ. of Rochester Computer Sci./Engin. Res. Rev.* 3–23.

Browning, S. A. 1980. The tree machine: A highly concurrent programming environment, Ph.D. diss., Computer Science Department, California Institute of Technology.

Bruce, C., Desimone, R., and Gross, C. G. 1981. Visual properties of neurons in a polysensory area in superior temporal sulcus of the macaque. *J. Neurophysiol.* 46: 369–384.

Buchanan, B. G., and Mitchell, T. M. 1978. Model-directed learning of production rules. *Pattern-directed inference systems* (D. A. Waterman and F. Hayes-Roth, eds.). New York: Academic, 297–312.

Buchanan, B. G., Sutherland, G. L., and Feigenbaum, E. A. 1969. Heuristic DENDRAL: A program for generating explanatory hypotheses in organic chemistry. *Machine intelligence 4* (R. Meltzer and D. Michie, eds.). Edinburgh: Edinburgh University Press, 209–254.

Burks, A., ed. 1966. *Theory of self-reproducing automata.* Urbana: University of Illinois Press.

Burt, P. J. 1984. The pyramid as a structure for efficient computations. *Multiresolution image processing and analysis* (A. Rosenfeld, ed). Berlin: Springer-Verlag, 6–35.

Cantoni, V., Ferretti, S., Levialdi, S., and Maloberti, F. 1985. A pyramid project using integrated technology. *Integrated technology for image processing* (S. Levialdi, ed). London: Academic, 121–133.

Chen, S. S., Dongarra, J. J., and Hsiung, C. 1984. Multiprocessing linear algebra algorithms on the CRAY X-MP-2. *J. Parallel Distributed Comput.* 1: 22–31.

Chiang, Y. P. 1985. Array processing for syntactic pattern recognition. *Proc. Workshop on Comp. Arch. for Pattern Analysis and Image Database Management.* IEEE Computer Society Press, 211–216.

Chomsky, N. 1957. *Syntactic structures.* The Hague, Netherlands: Mouton.

Christman, D. P. 1984. Programming the connection machine. Master's Thesis, Department of Electrical Engineering and Computer Science, Massachusetts Institute of Technology.

Church, A. 1936. The calculi of lambda-conversion. *Annals of Mathematics Studies 6.* Princeton, NJ: Princeton University Press.

Cibulskis, J. M., and Dyer, C. R. 1984. An analysis of node linking in overlapped pyramids. *IEEE Trans. Syst., Man, Cybern.* 14: 424–436.

Clocksin, W. and Mellish, C. 1981. *Programming in Prolog.* New York: Springer-Verlag.

Codd, E. F. 1968. *Cellular automata.* New York: Academic.

Connell, J. H., and Brady, M. 1985. Learning shape descriptions. *Proc. Int. Joint Conf. on Artif. Intell.* 9: 922–925.

Cordella, L. P., Duff, M. J. B., and Levialdi, S. 1978. An analysis of computational cost in image processing: A case study. *IEEE Trans. Comp.* 27: 904–910.

Crowther, W., Goodhue, J., Starr, E., Thomas, R., Milliken, W. and Blackadar, T. 1985. Performance measurements on a 128-node Butterfly parallel processor. *Proc. Int. Conf. on Parallel Process.* 531−540.

Cyre, W. R., Frank, A. A., Redmont, M. J., and Rideout, V. C. 1977. WISPAC: A parallel array computer for large-scale simulation. *Simulation* 30: 165−172.

Davis, R. 1978. Knowledge acquisition in rule-based systems: Knowledge about representations as a basis for system construction and maintenance. *Pattern-directed inference systems* (D. A. Waterman and F. Hayes-Roth, eds.). New York: Academic, 99−134.

Davis, R., and King, J. J. 1977. An overview of production systems. *Machine intelligence* (E. Elcock and D. Michie, eds.). Chichester, England: Ellis Horwood, 300−332.

De Bruijn, D. G. 1946. A combinatorial problem. *Koninklijke Nederlansche Academie van wetenschappen et Amsterdam, Proc. Section of Sciences 49* 7: 758−764.

DeJong, G. 1981. Generalizations based on explanations. *Proc. Int. Joint Conf. on Artif. Intell.* 7: 67−70.

De Mori, R. 1985. Algorithms and architectures for speech understanding. *Algorithmically specialized parallel computers* (L. Snyder, L. H. Jamieson, D. B. Gannon, and H. J. Siegel, eds.). New York: Academic, 149−158.

Deshpande, S. R., Jenevein, R. M. and Lipovski, G. J. 1985. TRAC: An experience with a novel architecture prototype. *Proc. Nat. Comp. Conf.* 54: 247−257.

Despain, A. M. 1985. The architecture of machines for logic programming, Paper presented at Distinguished lecturer series, University of Wisconsin, Computer Sciences Department.

Despain, A. M., and Patterson, D. A. 1978. X-tree: A tree structured multi-processor architecture. *Proc. 5th Ann. Symp. on Comp. Arch.* 144−151.

DeWitt, D. J., Finkel, R., and Solomon, M. 1984. The CRYSTAL multicomputer: Design and implementation experience. Computer Science Department, University of Wisconsin, Technical Report.

Dietterich, T. G., and Michalski, R. S. 1981. Inductive learning of structural descriptions: Evaluation criteria and comparative review of selected methods. *Artif. Intell.* 16: 257−294.

Dobry, T. P., Despain, A. M., and Patt, Y. N. 1985. Performance studies of a Prolog machine architecture. *12th Int. Symp. Comp. Arch.* 180−190.

Dohi, Y., Fisher, A. L., Kung, H. T., and Monier, L. M. 1985. The programmable systolic chip: Project overview. *Algorithmically specialized parallel computers* (L. Snyder, L. H. Jamieson, D. B. Gannon, and H. J. Siegel, eds.). New York: Academic, 47−53.

Doran, J. E. 1968. Experiments with a pleasure seeking automaton. *Machine intelligence 3* (D. Michie, ed). Edinburgh: Edinburgh University Press, 195 – 216.

Douglass, R., Jamieson, L., and Gannon, D., eds. *Characteristics of parallel programs and parallel algorithms* (in preparation).

Doyle, W. 1960. Recognition of sloppy, handprinted characters. *Proc. West. Joint Comput. Conf.* 17: 133 – 142.

Dreyfus, H., and Dreyfus, S. January 1986. Why computers may never think like people. *Tech. Rev.* 89: 42 – 61.

Duda, R. O., and Hart, P. E. 1973. *Pattern classification and scene analysis.* New York: Wiley.

Duff, M. J. B. 1976. CLIP4: A large scale integrated circuit array parallel processor. *Proc. IJCPR-3* 4: 728 – 733.

———. 1978. Review of the CLIP image processing system. *Proc. AFIPS Nat. Comp. Conf.* 1055 – 1060.

———. 1982. Parallel algorithms and their influence on the specification of application problems. *Multi-computer algorithms and image processing* (K. Preston, Jr. and L. Uhr, eds.). New York: Academic.

Duff, M. J. B., and Levialdi, S., eds. 1981. *Languages and architectures for image processing.* London: Academic.

Duffy, J. 1980. *Analysis of mechanisms and robot manipulators.* New York: Wiley.

Dyer, C. R. 1981. A quadtree machine for parallel image processing. *Information Engineering Department,* University of Illinois at Chicago Circle, Technical Report KSL51.

Dyer, C. R. 1982. Pyramid algorithms and machines. *Multicomputers and image processing* (K. Preston, Jr. and L. Uhr, eds.). New York: Academic, 409 – 420.

Engelberger, J. F. 1981. *Robotics in practice.* American Management Association.

Erman, L. D., and Lesser, V. R. 1980. The Hearsay-II speech understanding system: A tutorial. *Trends in speech recognition* (W. A. Lea, ed.). Englewood Cliffs, NJ: Prentice-Hall, 361 – 381.

Etchells, R. D., Grinberg, J., and Nudd, G. R. 1981. The development of a novel three-dimensional microelectronic processor with ultra-high performance. *Proc. Soc. Photo-Optical Instrumentation Engin.*

Fahlman, S. E. 1979. *NETL: A system for representing and using real-world knowledge.* Cambridge, MA: MIT Press.

———. 1980. Preliminary design for a million-element NETL machine. Computer Science Department, Carnegie-Mellon University, Technical Report.

Fahrat, N., and Psaltis, D. March 1985. Optical implementations of the Hopfield model. *Proc. of the Topical Meeting on Opt. Comp.* Optical Society of America.

Farber, D. J., Griswold, R. E., and Polonsky, I. P. 1964. SNOBOL, a string manipulation language. *J. Assoc. Comput. Mach.* 11: 21–30.

Farber, D. J., and Larson, K. C. April 1972. The system architecture of the distributed computer system—The communications system. *Symposium on computer networks.* Polytechnic Institute of Brooklyn.

Feldman, J. A. 1982. Dynamic connections in neural networks. *Biolog. Cybern.* 46: 27–39.

Fiat, A., and Shamir, A. 1984. Polymorphic arrays: A novel VLSI layout for systolic computers. *Proc. 25th Symp. on Foundations of Comp. Sci.* 37–45.

Fikes, R. E., and Nilsson, N. J. 1971. STRIPS: A new approach to the application of theorem proving to problem solving. *Artif. Intell.* 2: 189–208.

Findler, N., ed. 1979. *Associative networks: Representation and use of knowledge by computer.* New York: Academic.

Finkel, R. A., and Solomon, M. H. 1977. Processor interconnection strategies. Computer Science Department, University of Wisconsin, Technical Report 301.

———. 1980a. The Arachne kernel. Computer Science Department, University of Wisconsin, Technical Report 380.

———. 1980b. The Lens interconnection strategy. Computer Science Department, University of Wisconsin, Technical Report 387.

Finkel, R. A., Solomon, M. H., DeWitt, D. and Landweber, L. 1983. The Charlotte distributed operating system: Part IV of the first report on the Crystal project. Computer Science Department, University of Wisconsin, Technical Report 502.

Fisher, A. D., Giles, C. L., and Lee, J. N. March 1985. An adaptive associative optical computing element. *Proceedings of the Topical Meeting on Optical Computing.* Optical Society of America.

Fisher, A. L., Kung, H. T., Monier, L. M., and Dohi, Y. 1984. The architecture of a programmable systolic chip. *J. VLSI and Computer Systems* 1: 153–169.

Flanagan, J. L., Levinson, S. E., Rabiner, L. R., and Rosenberg, A. E. 1980. Techniques for expanding the capabilities of practical speech recognizers. *Trends in speech recognition* (W. A. Lea, ed.). Englewood Cliffs, NJ: Prentice-Hall, 425–444.

Flynn, A. M. 1982. The connection machine RAM chip. AI Laboratory, Massachusetts Institute of Technology, Working Paper 242.

Flynn, M. 1972. Some computer organizations and their effectiveness. *IEEE Trans. Comput.* 21: 948–960.

Forgy, C. 1979. On the efficient implementation of production systems. Ph.D. Diss., Department of Computer Science, Carnegie-Mellon University.

Forgy, C., Gupta, A., Newell, A., and Wedig, R. 1984. Initial assessment of architectures for production systems. *Proc. Nat. Conf. on Artif. Intell.*

Forgy, C., and McDermott, J. 1977. OPS, a domain-independent production system language. *Proc. Int. Joint Conf. on Artif. Intell.* 5: 933 – 939.

Fountain, T. J. 1983. The development of the CLIP7 image processing system. *Pattern Recog. Letters* 1: 331 – 339.

———. 1985. Plans for the CLIP7 chip. *Integrated technology for image processing* (S. Levialdi, ed.). London: Academic 199 – 214.

Fox, G. C., and Otto, S. W. May 1984. Algorithms for concurrent processors. *Physics Today,* AR-370, 13 – 20.

Frey, P. W., ed. 1977. *Chess skill in man and machine.* New York: Springer-Verlag.

Fritsch, G., Kleinoder, W., Linster, C. U., and Volkert, J. 1983. EMSY85—The Erlangen multiprocessor system for a broad spectrum of applications. *Proc. Int. Conf. Parallel Process.* 325 – 330.

Fu, K. S. 1974. *Syntactic methods in pattern recognition.* New York: Academic.

———. 1978. Special computer architectures for pattern recognition and image processing—An overview. *Proc. AFIPS Nat. Comput. Conf.* 1003 – 1013.

Gallaire, H., and Minker, J. 1978. *Logic and databases.* New York: Plenum.

Garcia-Molina, H., Lipton, R. J., and Valdes, J. 1984. A massive memory machine. *IEEE Trans. Comput.* 33: 391 – 399.

Gemmar, P. 1982. Image correlation: Processing requirements and implementation structures on a flexible image processing system (FLIP). *Multi-computer algorithms and image processing* (K. Preston, Jr. and L. Uhr, ed.). New York: Academic.

Gerstein, G., Aertsen, A., Bloom M., Espinosa, E., Evanczuk, S., and Turner, M. 1985. Multi-neuron experiments: Observation of state in neural nets. *Complex systems-operational approaches* (H. Haken, ed.). Berlin: Springer-Verlag, 58 – 70.

Gilbert. B. K., Kenue, S. K., Robb, R. A., Chu, A., Lent, A. H., and Swartzlander, E. E., Jr. 1981. Rapid execution of fan beam image reconstruction algorithms using efficient computational techniques and special purpose processors. *IEEE Trans. Biomed. Engin.* 28: 98 – 115.

Golay, M. J. E. 1969. Hexagonal parallel pattern transformations. *IEEE Trans. Comput.* 18: 733 – 740.

Goodman, J. R. 1983. Using cache memory to reduce processor-memory traffic. *10th Symp. on Comput. Arch.* 124 – 131.

Goodman, J. R., and Sequin, C. H. 1981. Hypertree: A multiprocessor interconnection topology. *IEEE Trans. Comp.* C-30: 923 – 933.

Gottlieb, A. B., Grishman, R., Kruskal, C. P., McAuliffe, K. P., Rudolph, L., and Snir, M. 1983. The NYU ultra-computer—Designing an MIMD shared memory parallel computer. *IEEE Trans. Comp.* C-32: 175 – 189.

Gould, S. J. 1986. This view of life: Soapy Sam's logic. *Nat. Hist.* 95: 16 – 26.

Graham, M. D. 1983. The diff4: A second-generation slide analyzer. *Computing structures for image processing* (M. Duff, ed). London, Academic, 179 – 194.

Granlund, G. H. 1981. GOP: A fast and flexible processor for image analysis. *Languages and architectures for image processing* (M. J. B. Duff and S. Levialdi, eds.). London: Academic.

Green, C. 1969. The application of theorem proving to question answering systems. Ph.D. Diss., Department of Computer Science, Stanford University.

Gregory, J., and McReynolds, M. 1963. The SOLOMON computer. *IEEE Trans. Comp.* 12: 774 – 780.

Grimsdale, R. L., Sumner, F. H., Tuni, C. J., and Kilburn, T. 1959. A system for the automatic recognition of patterns. *Proc. IEE,* 106(B): 210 – 221.

Gross, C. G. 1973. Inferotemporal cortex and vision. *Progress in physiological psychology, Vol. 5* (E. Stellar and J. Sprague, eds.). New York: Academic, 77 – 123.

Gross, C. G., Schiller, P. H., Wells, C., and Gerstein, G. L. 1967. Single-unit activity in temporal association cortex of the monkey. *J. Neurophysiol.* 30: 833 – 843.

Gupta, A. 1984. Parallelism in production systems: The sources and the expected speed-up. Computer Science Department, Carnegie-Mellon University, Technical Report 84 – 169.

Gupta, A., and Forgy, C. L. 1983. Measurements on production systems. Computer Science Department, Carnegie-Mellon University, Technical Report 83 – 167.

Hammerstrom, D., Maier, D., and Thakkar, S. 1986. The cognitive architecture project. *Comp. Arch. News* 14: 9 – 21.

Hanaki, S., and Temma, T. 1982. Template-controlled image processor (TIP) project. *Multi-computer algorithms and image processing* (K. Preston, Jr. and L. Uhr, eds.). New York: Academic.

Handler, W. 1975. A unified associative and Von-Neumann processor—EGPP and EGPP array. *Lectures notes in Computer Science, Vol. 24—Parallel processing, 97 – 99.* Berlin: Springer-Verlag.

———. 1977. Aspects of parallelism in computer architecture. *Parallel computers—Parallel mathematics* (M. Feilmeier, ed). International Association for Mathematics and Computers in Simulation.

Handler, W., Schreiber, H., and Sigmund, V. 1979. Computation structures reflected in general purpose and special purpose multi-microprocessor systems. *Proc. 1979 Int. Conf. on Parallel Process.* 95 – 102.

Hanson, A. R., and Riseman, E. M. 1974. Pre-processing cones: A computational structure for scene analysis. Department of Computer Science, University of Massachusetts, COINS Technical Report 74C – 7.

———. 1976. A progress report report on VISIONS. Department of Computer Science, University of Massachusetts, COINS Technical Report 76 – 9.

———. 1978. Visions: A computer system for interpreting scenes. *Computer vision systems* (A. R. Hanson and E. M. Riseman, eds.). New York: Academic, 303 – 334.

———. 1980. Processing cones: A computational structure for image analysis. *Structured computer vision* (S. L. Tanimoto and A. Klinger, eds.). New York: Academic, 101 – 131.

Harris, Z. 1951. *Methods in structural linguistics.* Chicago: University of Chicago Press.

Hayes-Roth, R., Klahr, P., and Mostow, D. 1981. Advice-taking and knowledge refinement: An iterative view of skill acquisition. *Cognitive skills and their acquisition* (J. R. Anderson, ed). Hillsdale, NJ: Erlbaum, 231 – 253.

Hebb, D. O. 1949. *Organization of behavior.* New York: Wiley.

Hewitt, C. 1971. PLANNER: A language for proving theorems in robots. *Proc. Int. Joint Conf. on Artif. Intell.* 2: 167 – 182.

Hillis, W. D. 1981. The connection machine. MIT AI Laboratory, Massachusetts Institute of Technology, A. I. Memo 646.

———. 1985. *The connection machine.* Cambridge: MIT Press.

Hillyer, B. K., and Shaw, D. E. 1986. Execution of production systems on a massively parallel machine, *J. Parallel and Distributed Computing.* 3.

Hillyer, B. K., Shaw, D. E., and Nigam, A. 1985. NON-VON's performance on certain database benchmarks. Computer Science Department, Columbia University, Technical Report.

Hinton, G. E. 1984. Distributed representations. Computer Science Department, Carnegie-Mellon University, Technical Report 84 – 157.

Hinton, G. E., and Anderson, J. A. 1981. *Parallel models of associative memory.* Hillsdale, NJ: Erlbaum.

Hinton, G. E., Sejnowski, T. J., and Ackley, D. H. 1981. Boltzann machines: Constraint satisfaction networks that learn. Computer Science Department, Carnegie-Mellon University, Technical Report 84 – 119.

Hoffman, A. J. and Singleton, R. R. 1960. On Moore graphs with diameter 2 and 3. *IBM J. Res. Devel.* 4: 497 – 504.

Hopfield, J. J. 1982. Neural networks and physical systems with emergent collective computational abilities. *Proc. Nat. Acad. Sci.* 79: 2554 – 2558.

Horn, B. K. P., and Sjoberg, R. W. November 1978. Calculating the reflectance map. *Proc. DARPA IU Workshop* 115 – 126.

Hough. P. V. C. 1962. *Method and means for recognizing complex patterns.* U. S. Patent 3,069,654.

Hovland, C. I. 1952. A communication analysis of concept learning. *Psychol. Rev.* 59: 461 – 472.

Hubel, D. H., and Wiesel, T. N. 1959. Receptive fields of single neurons in the cat's striate cortex. *J. Physiol.* 148: 574 – 591.

———. 1962. Receptive fields, binocular interaction and functional architecture in the cat's visual cortex. *J. Physiol.* 160: 106 – 154.

———. 1965. Receptive fields and functional architecture in two non-striate visual areas (18 and 19) of the cat. *J. Neurophysiol.* 28: 229 – 289.

———. 1977. Ferrier Lecture: Functional architecture of macaque monkey visual cortex. *Proc. Royal Soc. London B Biol. Sci.* 198: 1 – 59.

Hull, C. L. 1920. Quantitative aspects of the evolution of concepts; an experimental study. *Psycol. Monographs 28*, No. 123.

Hunt, E. B. 1962. *Concept formation: An information processing problem.* New York: Wiley.

Hwang, K., and Briggs, F. A. 1984. *Computer architecture and parallel processing.* New York: McGraw-Hill.

Hwang, K., and Xu, Z. 1985. Remps: A reconfigurable multiprocessor for scientific supercomputing. *Proc. Int. Conf. Parallel Process.* 102 – 111.

Ibrahim, H. A. H. 1984. Image understanding algorithms on fine-grained tree-structured SIMD machines. Ph.D. Diss., Department of Computer Science, Columbia University, New York.

Imase, M., and Itoh, M. 1981. Design to minimize diameter on building-block network. *IEEE Trans. Comp.* 30: 439 – 442.

INMOS Limited. 1984. *Occam programming manual.* London: Prentice-Hall.

Ishida, T., and Stolfo, S. J. 1985. Toward the parallel execution of rules in production system programs. *Proc. Int. Conf. Parallel Process.* 568 – 575.

Itakura, F. 1975. Minimum prediction residual principle applied to speech recognition. *IEEE Trans. Acoustics, Speech and Signal Proc.* 23: 67 – 72.

Jenkins, B. K., Sawchuck, A. A., Strand, T. C., Forchheimer, R., and Soffer, B. H. 1984. Sequential optical logic implementation. *Applied Optics* 23: 3455 – 3464.

Kahle, B. L. 1982. Design and implementation of a micro-micro processor for a highly distributed computer. B.S. thesis, Department of Electrical Engineering and Computer Science, Massachusetts Institute of Technology, Cambridge, MA.

Kandel, E. R., and Schwartz, J. H. 1981. *Principles of neuroscience.* Amsterdam: Elsevier/North-Holland.

Kamentsky, L. A., and Liu, C. N. 1976. Computer-automated design of multi-font print recognition logic. *IBM J. of Research and Devel.* 7: 2 – 13.

Kazmierczak, H. 1960. The potential field as an aid to character recognition. *Information processing.* Paris: UNESCO, 244 – 247.

Kapauan, A., Field, J. T., and Gannon, D. B. 1984. The Pringle parallel computer. *11th Ann. Int. Symp. Comp. Arch.* 12 – 20.

Kelly, M. D. 1971. Edge detection in pictures by computers using planning. *Machine intelligence 6* (R. Meltzer and D. Michie, eds.). New York: Elsevier, 379 – 409.

Kent, E. W., Shneier, M., and Lumia, R. 1985. PIPE—Pipelined image processing engine. *J. Parallel and Distrib. Comp.* 2: 50 – 78.

Kent, E. W., and Tanimoto, S. L. 1985. Hierarchical cellular logic and the PIPE processor: Structural and functional correspondence. *Proc. Workshop on Comp. Arch. for Pattern Analysis and Image Database Management.* IEEE Computer Society Press, 311 – 319.

Kessis, J. J., Rambaut, J. P., and Penne, J. 1983. Walking robot multi-level architecture and implementation. *Proc. 4th Symp. Theory and Practice of Robots and Manipulators,* 297.

Kimmel, M. J., Jaffe, R. S., Mandeville, J. R., and Lavin, M. A. 1985. MITE: Morphic image transform engine an architecture for reconfigurable pipelines of neighborhood processors. *Proc. Workshop on Comp. Arch. for Pattern Analysis and Image Database Management.* IEEE Computer Society Press, 483 – 500.

Kleene, S. C. 1936. General recursive functions of natural numbers. *Math. Annalen* 12: 340 – 353.

Klein, S. 1965. Automatic paraphrasing in essay format. *Mech. Translat.* 7: 50 – 61.

Kochen, M. 1961. An experimental program for the selection of disjunctive hypotheses. *Proc. West. Joint Comp. Conf.* 19: 571 – 578.

Koffman, E. B. 1968. Learning games through pattern recognition. *IEEE Trans. Systems Science and Cybernetics 4*: 12 – 16.

Kohonen, T. 1982. Clustering, taxonomy and topological maps of patterns. *Proc. Int. Joint Conf. on Pattern Recog.* 6: 114 – 128.

Kondo, T., Nakashima, T., Aoki, M., and Sudo, T. 1983. An LSI adaptive array processor. *IEEE J. Solid-State Circ.* 18: 147−155.

Kowalski, R. A. 1979. *Logic for problem solving.* Amsterdam: North-Holland.

Kozdrowicki, E. W., and Thies, D. J. November 1983. Second generation of vector supercomputers. *Computers* 13: 71−83.

Krüger, J. 1985. Investigation of a small volume of neocortex with multiple electrodes. *Complex systems-operational approaches* (H. Haken, ed.). Berlin: Springer-Verlag, 71−80.

Kruse, B. A parallel picture processing machine 1973. *IEEE Trans. Comp.* 22, 1075−1087.

———. 1976. The PICAP picture processing laboratory. *Proc. IJCPR-3* 4: 875−881.

———. 1978. Experience with a picture processor in pattern recognition processing. *Proc. AFIPS Nat. Comp. Conf.* 1015−1022.

———. 1980. System architecture for image analysis. *Structured computer vision: Machine perception through hierarchical computation structures* (S. Tanimoto and A. Klinger, eds.). New York: Academic, 169−212.

Kruse, B., Danielsson, P. E., and Gudmundsson, B. 1980. From PICAP I to PICAP II. *Special computer architectures for pattern processing* (K. S. Fu and T. Ichikawa, eds.). New York: CPR Press.

Kuck, D. J. 1978. *The structure of computers and computation: Vol. 1.* New York: Wiley.

Kuck, D. J., Lawrie, D., Cytron, R., Sameh, A., and Gajski, D. 1983. The architecture and programming of the Cedar system. *Proc. 1983 LASL Workshop on Vector and Parallel Processing.*

Kuehn, J. T., Siegel, H. J., Tuomenoksa, D. L., and Adams, G. B., III. 1985. The use and design of PASM. *Integrated technology for image processing* (S. Levialdi, ed.). London: Academic, 133−152.

Kuffler, S. W., Nicholls, J. G., and Martin, A. R. 1984. *From neuron to brain.* Sunderland, MA: Sinauer.

Kumar, V. K. P., and Raghavendra, C. S. 1985. Image processing on enhanced mesh connected computers. *Proc. Workshop on Comp. Arch. for Pattern Analysis and Image Database Management.* IEEE Computer Society Press, 243−247.

Kumar, V. K. P., and Tsai, Y. C. 1985. Geometric algorithms for digitized pictures on the mesh of trees organization. Electrical Engineering Department, University of Southern California. Technical Report.

Kung, H. T. 1980. Special-purpose devices for signal and image processing: An opportunity in VLSI. Computer Science Department, Carnegie-Mellon University, Technical Report 80−132.

————. 1982. Why systolic architectures? *Computer Magazine* 15: 37 – 46.

Kung, H. T., and Song, S. W. 1982. A systolic 2-d convolution chip. *Multi-computers and image processing* (K. Preston, Jr. and L. Uhr, eds.). New York: Academic.

Kung, H. T., and Lam, M. S. 1984. Wafer-scale integration and two-level pipelined implementations of systolic arrays. *J. Parallel and Distributed Comput.* 1: 32 – 63.

Kung, H. T., and Menzilcioglu, O. 1984. Warp: A programmable systolic array processor. *Proc. SPIE Symp. Real-Time Signal Process. VII.* Society of Photo-Optical Instumentation Engineering.

Kung, S. Y., and Gal-Ezer, R. J. 1985. Eigenvalue, singular value and least square solvers via the wavefront array processor. *Algorithmically specialized parallel computers* (L. Snyder, L. H. Jamieson, D. B. Gannon, and H. J. Siegel, eds.). New York: Academic, 201 – 212.

Langley, P. W. 1977. Rediscovering physics with BACON.3. *Proc. Int. Joint Conf. on Artif. Intell.* 6: 505 – 507.

Larson, J., and Michalski, R. S. 1977. Inductive inference of VL decision rules. *SIGART Newsletter* 63: 38 – 44.

Lawrie, D. H. 1975. Access and alignment of data in an array processor. *IEEE Trans. Comp.* 31: 435 – 442.

Le Faivre, R. 1974. FUZZY Problem-Solving. Ph.D. diss., Department of Computer Science, University of Wisconsin.

Leighton, T., and Leiserson, C. E. 1985. Wafer-scale integration of systolic arrays. *IEEE Trans. Comp.* C-34: 448 – 461.

Leiserson, C. E. 1985. FAT-TREES: Universal networks for hardware-efficient supercomputing. *IEEE Trans Comp.* 34: 892 – 901.

Lenat, D. B. 1976. AM: An artificial intelligence approach to discovery in mathematics as heuristic search. Ph.D. diss., Department of Computer Science, Stanford University.

————. On automated scientific theory formation: A case study using the AM program 1978. *Machine intelligence 9* (J. E. Hayes, D. Michie, and L. I Mikulich, eds.). New York: Halsted, 251 – 286.

Levine, M. D. 1969. Feature extraction: A survey. *Proc. IEEE,* 57: 1391 – 1407.

————. 1978. A knowledge-based computer vision system. *Computer vision systems* (A. Hanson and E. Riseman, eds.). New York: Academic, 335 – 352.

————. 1980. Region analysis with a pyramid data structure. *Structured computer vision* (S. L. Tanimoto and A. Klinger, eds.). New York: Academic, 57 – 100.

Li, H., Wang, C.-C., and Lavin, M. 1985. Structured process: A new language attribute for better interaction of parallel architecture and algorithm. *Proc. Int. Conf. Parallel Process.* 247 – 251.

Li, Z. N., and Uhr, L. 1985. Comparative timings for a neuron recognition program on serial and pyramid computers. *Proc. Workshop on Comp. Arch. for Pattern Analysis and Image Database Management.* IEEE Computer Society Press, 99 – 106.

———. 1986. A pyramidal approach for the recognition of neurons using key features. *Pattern Recog.* 19: 55 – 62.

Lindsay, R. K. 1963. Inferential memory as the basis of machines which understand natural language. *Computers and thought* (E. A. Feigenbaum and J. Feldman, eds.). New York: McGraw-Hill, 217 – 233.

Lindsay, R. K., Buchanan, B. G., Feigenbaum, E. A., and Lederberg, J. 1980. *DENDRAL.* New York: McGraw-Hill.

Lipovsky, G. J. 1977. On a varistructured array of microprocessors. *IEEE Trans. Comp.* 26: 125 – 138.

Lipovsky, G. J., and Tripathi, A. 1977. A reconfigurable varistructure array processor. *Proc. 1977 Int. Conf. on Parallel Process.* 165 – 174.

Lohmann, A. March 1985. What optics can do for the digital optical computer. *Proc. of the Topical Meeting on Opt. Comp.* Optical Society of America.

Lougheed, R. M., and McCubbrey, D. L. 1985. Multi-processor architectures for machine vision and image analysis. *Proc. Int. Conf. Parallel Process.* 493 – 497.

Lowerre, B., and Reddy, R. 1980. The Harpy speech understanding system. *Trends in speech recognition* (W. A. Lea, ed.). Englewood Cliffs, NJ: Prentice-Hall, 340 – 360.

Lubeck, O., Moore, J., and Mendez, R. 1985. A benchmark comparison of three supercomputers: Fujitsu VP-200, Hitachi S810/20 and Cray X-MP/2. *IEEE Comp.* 18: 10 – 23.

Mago, G. A. 1980. A cellular computer architecture for functional programming. *Proc. COMPCON Spring 1980,* 179 – 187.

Manara, R., and Stringa, L. 1981. The EMMA system: An industrial experience on a multi-processor. *Languages and architectures for image processing* (M. J. B. Duff and S. Levialdi, eds.). London: Academic.

Maples, C. 1985. Pyramids, crossbars and thousands of processors. *Proc. Int. Conf. Parallel Process.* 681 – 688.

Maples, C., Rathburn, W., Weaver, D., and Meng, J. 1981. The design of MIDAS—A modular interactive data analysis system. *IEEE Trans Nuclear Sci.* 28: 3746 – 3751.

Marill, T., Harley, A. K., Evans, T. G., Bloom, B. H., Park, D. M. R., Hart, T. P., and Darley, D. L. 1963. Cyclops-I: A second generation recognition system. *Proc. AFIPS Comp. Conf.* 24: 27 – 34.

Marks, P. 1980. Low-level vision using an array processor. *Comp. graph. image process.* 14: 281–292.

Marr, D. 1983. *Vision.* San Francisco: Freeman.

Martins, G. R. November 1, 1984. The overselling of expert systems. *Datamation,* 76–80.

May, D., and Shepherd, R. 1984. Occam and transputer. INMOS Limited, Bristol England, Technical Note No. 1.

McCarthy, J. 1958. Programs with common sense. *Proc. Symp. Mechaniz. of Thought Processes.* London: National Physical Lab., 77–84.

———. 1978. History of LISP. *Assoc. for Comp. Machinery SIGPLAN Notices* 13: 217–223.

McCarthy, J., Abrahams, P. W., Edwards, D. J., Hart, T. P., and Levin, M. I. 1962. *LISP 1.5 programmer's manual.* Cambridge, MA: MIT Press.

McCormick, B. H. 1963. The Illinois pattern recognition computer ILLIAC III. *IEEE Trans. Comp.* 12: 791–813.

McCubbrey, D. L., and Lougheed, R. M. 1985. Morphological image analysis using a raster pipeline processor. *Proc. Workshop on Comp. Arch. for Pattern Analysis and Image Database Management.* IEEE Computer Society Press, 444–452.

McCulloch, W. S. 1965. *Embodiments of mind.* Cambridge, MA: MIT Press.

McCulloch, W. S., and Pitts, W. 1943. A logical calculus if the ideas immanent in nervous activity. *Bull. of Math. Biophys.* 5: 115–133.

McGhee, R. B., Chao, C. G., Jaswa, V. C., and Orin, D. E. 1978. Real time computer control of a hexapod vehicle. *Proc. 3rd Int. Symp. Robots and Manipulators,* 23.

McGhee, R. B., Orin, D. E., Pugh, D. R., and Patterson, M. R. 1984. A hierarchically structured system for computer control of a hexapod walking system. *Proc. 5th Symp. Robots and Manipulator Systems,* 5.

Mead, C. March 1985. Potential limitations of vlsi. *Proc. of the Topical Meeting on Opt. Comp.* Optical Society of America.

Messuri, D. A., and Klein, C. A. 1985. Automatic body regulation for maintaining stability of a legged vehicle during rough-terrain locomotion. *IEEE J. Robotics and Automation,* 1: 132–141.

Michalski, R. S. 1975. Variable-valued logic and its application to pattern recognition and machine learning. *Computer science and multiple-valued logic theory and applications* (D. C. Rine, ed). Amsterdam: North Holland, 506–534.

———. 1983. A theory and methodology of inductive learning. *Machine learning: An artificial intelligence approach* (R. Michalski, J. G. Carbonell, and T. M. Mitchell, eds.). Palo Alto: Tioga, 83–134.

Michalski, R., Carbonell, J. G., and Mitchell, T. M., eds. 1983. *Machine learning: An artificial intelligence approach.* Palo Alto: Tioga.

——. 1986. *Machine learning: An artificial intelligence approach, Vol. II.* Palo Alto: Tioga.

Miller, J. S., Lickley, D. J., Kosmala, A. L., and Saponaro, J. A. 1970. *Multiprocessor computer system study—Final report.* Cambridge, MA: Intermetrics, Inc.

Miller, R. 1984. *Pyramid computer algorithms.* Ph.D. diss., Department of Mathematics, SUNY Binghamton.

Miller, R., Pople, H., and Myers, J. 1982. Internist-I, an experimental computer-based diagnostic consultant for general internal medicine. *New England J. Of Med.* 307: 468–476.

Miller, R. and Stout, Q. F. 1984. The pyramid computer for image processing. *Proc. 7th Int. Conf. on Pattern Recog.*

——. 1985. Varying diameter size in mesh-connected computers. *Proc. Int. Conf. Parallel Process.* 697–699.

Miller, W. F., and Shaw, A. C. 1968. Linguistic methods in picture processing—A survey. *Proc. AFIPS Nat. Comput Conf.* 33: 279–290.

Minnick, R. C. 1966. Cellular arrays for logic and storage. *SRI Project 5087 Final Rept.*, 197–215.

——. 1967. A survey of microcellular research. *J. Assoc. Comput. Mach.* 14: 203–241.

Minsky, M. 1963. Steps toward artificial intelligence. *Computers and thought* (E. A. Feigenbaum and J. Feldman, eds.). New York: McGraw-Hill, 406–450.

——. 1975. A framework for representing knowledge. *The psychology of computer vision* (P. H. Winston, ed). New York: McGraw-Hill, 211–277.

Minsky, M., and Papert, S. 1971. On some associative parallel and analog computations. *Associative information techniques* (E. J. Jacks, ed.). New York: Elsevier.

Mishkin, M., Ungerleider, L. G., and Macko, K. A. 1983. Object vision and spatial vision: Two cortical pathways. *Trends in Neurosci.* 6–21.

Mitchell, T. 1983. Learning and problem-solving. *Proc. Int. Joint Conf. on Artif. Intell.* 8: 1139–1151.

Moore, E. F. Gedanken experiments on sequential machines. *Automata Studies* (C. E. Shannon and J. McCarthy, eds.). Princeton Univ. Press: 129–153.

Moto-oka, T., and Stone, H. S. March 1984. Fifth generation computer systems: A Japanese project. *Computer,* 17: 6–13.

Mountcastle, V. B. 1978. An organizing principle for cerebral function: The unit module and the distributed system. *The mindful brain* (G. M. Edelman and V. B. Mountcastle, eds.). Cambridge, MA: MIT Press.

Mudge, T. N. 1985. Vision algorithms for hypercube machines. *Proc. Workshop on Computer Architecture for Pattern Analysis and Image Database Management.* IEEE Computer Society Press: 225 – 230.

Mukhopadhyay, A., and Stone, H. S. 1971. Cellular logic. *Recent developments in switching theory* (A. Mukhopadhyay, ed.). New York: Academic, 256 – 313.

Narasimhan, R. 1966. Syntax-directed interpretation of classes of pictures. *Comm. Assoc. for Comp. Mach.* 9: 279 – 290.

Nazarathy, M., and Goodman, J. W. March 1985. Systolic signal processing with integrated optical coupled-wave device arrays. *Proc. of the Topical Meeting on Opt. Comp.* Optical Society of America.

Neveu, C. F., Dyer, C. R., and Chin, R. T. 1985. Object recognition using Hough Pyramids. *Proc. IEEE Conf. Computer Vision and Pattern Recognition.* 328 – 333.

Newell, A., Shaw, J. C., and Simon, H. A. 1963. Empirical explorations with the logic theory machine: A case history in heuristics. *Computers and thought* (E. A. Feigenbaum and J. Feldman, eds.). New York: McGraw-Hill, 109 – 133.

Newell, A., and Simon, H. A. 1956. The logic theory machine. *IRE Trans. Info. Theory* 2: 61 – 79.

——. 1961. GPS, a program that simulates human thought. *Lernende automaton* (H. Billing, ed.). Munich: Oldenbourg, 109 – 124.

——. 1973. *Human problem solving.* Englewood Cliffs, NJ: Prentice-Hall.

Nilsson, N. J. 1969. A mobile automaton: An application of A.I. techniques. *Proc. Int. Joint Conf. on Artif. Intell.* 1: 509 – 520.

Nitzan, D., and Rosen, C. A. 1976. Programmable industrial automation. *IEEE Trans. Comp.* 25: 1259 – 1270.

Nudd, G. R., Grinberg, J., Etchells, R. D., and Little, M. 1985. The application of three-dimensional microelectronics to image analysis. *Integrated technology for image processing* (S. Levialdi, ed.). London: Academic, 167 – 185.

Nye, J. M. 1980. The expanding market for commercial speech recognizers. *Trends in speech recognition* (W. A. Lea, ed.). Englewood Cliffs, NJ: Prentice-Hall, 461 – 468.

Oldfield, D. E., and Reddaway, S. F. 1985. An image understanding performance study on the ICL Distributed Array Processor. *Proc. Workshop on Comp. Arch. for Pattern Analysis and Image Database Management.* IEEE Computer Society Press, 256 – 264.

Onoe, M., Preston, K., Jr., and Rosenfield, A., eds. 1981. *Real-time parallel computing: Image analysis.* New York: Plenum.

Orin, D. E. 1982. Supervisory control of a multilegged robot. *Int. J. Robotics Res.* 1: 79 – 91.

Patel, J. H. 1978. Design and analysis of processor-memory interconnections for multi-processors. School of Electrical Engineering, Purdue University, Technical Report EE-78-40.

Patton, P. C. 1972. Estimated performance loss of 7600 multiprocessors due to LCS memory conflicts. *AIC Tech. Note 1687-C-3.* Analysts International Corporation.

Paul, R. P. 1981. *Robot manipulators: Mathematics, programming, control.* Cambridge, MA: MIT Press.

Pease, M. C. 1977. The indirect binary n-cube microprocessor array. *IEEE Trans. Comp.* 26: 458 – 473.

Peirce, C. S. 1931 – 1958. *Collected Papers.* Cambridge, MA: Harvard University Press.

Pemberton, W. 1985. The Martin-Marietta array processor. Paper presented at the Workshop on Multi-Computer Architectures for Image Processing, Bonas, France, 1985.

Pereira, F., and Warren, D. 1980. Definite clause grammar for language analysis—A survey of the formalism and a comparison with augmented transition networks. *Artif. Intell.* 13: 231 – 278.

Perrett, D. I., Rolls, E. T., and Caan, W. 1979. Temporal lobe cells of the monkey with visual responses selective for faces. *Neurosci. Letters Suppl.* 2: 340.

Perrett, D. I., Smith, P. A. J., Potter, D. D., Mishkin, A. J., Mead, A. S., Milner, A. D., and Jeeves, M. A. 1984. Neurons responsive to faces in the temporal cortex, Human Neurobiology, 3: 197 – 208.

Petersen, J. 1891. Die Theorie der regularen Graphen. *Acta Math.* 15: 193 – 220.

Peterson, J. C., Tuazon, J. O., Lieberman, D. and Pniel, M. 1985. The Mark III Hypercube-ensemble concurrent computer. *Proc. Int. Conf. Parallel Process.* 71 – 73.

Petri, C. A. 1962. Fundamentals of a theory of asynchronous information flow. *Proc. IFIP Congress 62.*

———. 1979. Introduction to general net theory. *Net theory and applications* (W. Brauer, ed). Berlin: Springer-Verlag, 1 – 19.

Pfeiffer, J. J., Jr. 1985. Integrating low level and high level computer vision. *Proc. Workshop on Comp. Arch. for Pattern Analysis and Image Database Management.* IEEE Computer Society Press, 119 – 125.

Pfister, G. F., Brantley, W. C., George, D. A., Harvey, S. L., Kleinfelder, W. J., McAuliffe, K. P., Melton, E. A., Norton, V. A., and Weiss, J. 1985. The IBM research parallel processor prototype (RP3). *Proc. Int. Conf. Parallel Process.* 764 – 771.

Pietikainen, M., and Rosenfeld, A. 1981. Image segmentation by texture using pyramid node linking. *IEEE. Trans. Syst., Man, Cyber.* 11, 822 – 825.

Pigarev, I. N., Rizzolatti, G., and Scandolara, C. 1979. Neurons responding to visual stimuli in the frontal lobe of macaque monkeys. Neurosci. Lett. 12: 207 – 212.

Pitts, W., and McCulloch, W. S. 1947. How we know universals: The perception of auditory and visual forms. *Bull. Math. Biophysics.* 9: 127 – 147.

Pople, H. 1977. DIALOG: A model of diagnostic logic for internal medicine. *Proc. Int. Joint Conf. on Artif. Intell.* 5: 848 – 855.

Post, E. L. 1936. Finite combinatory processes. *J. Symb. Logic.* 1: 103 – 105.

———. 1943. Formal reductions of the general combinatorial decision problem. *Am. J. Math,* 65: 197 – 268.

Preparata, F. P., and Vuillemin, J. 1979. The cube-connected-cycles: A versatile network for parallel computation. *Proc. Twentieth Ann. Symp. on Foundations of Comp. Sci.* 140 – 147.

Preston, K., Jr. 1971. Feature extraction by Golay hexagonal pattern transforms. *IEEE Trans. Comp.* 20: 1007 – 1014.

Preston, K., Jr., and Uhr. L., eds. 1981. *Multi-computers and image processing.* New York: Academic.

Psaltis, D., and Farhat, N. March 1985. Optical computing and the Hopfield model. *Proc. of the Topical Meeting on Opt. Comp.* Optical Society of America.

Quillan, M. R. 1968. Semantic memory. *Semantic information processing* (M. Minsky, ed.). Cambridge: MIT Press, 227 – 270.

———. 1969. The teachable language comprehender: A simulation program and theory of language. *Comm. Assoc. for Comp. Mach.* 12: 459 – 476.

Rabinow, J. 1968. The present state of the art of reading machines. *Pattern recognition* (L. Kanal, ed.). Washington: Thompson, 3 – 26.

Raibert, M. H., and Sutherland, I. E. January 1983. Machines that walk. *Sci. Amer.,* 248: 44 – 53.

Raibert, M. H., and Tanner, J. E. 1982. Design and implementation of a VLSI tactile sensing computer. *Int. J. Robotics Res.* 3: 3 – 18.

Randell, B. 1973. *The origins of digital computers: Selected papers.* New York: Springer.

Raphael, B. 1968. SIR: A computer program for semantic information retrieval. *Semantic information processing* (M. Minsky, ed.). Cambridge: MIT Press, 33 – 145.

Rashevsky, N. 1938. *Mathematical biophysics.* Chicago: University of Chicago Press. (3rd Edition, 1960)

Reddaway, S. F. 1978. DAP—A flexible number cruncher. *Proc. 1978 LASL Workshop on Vector and Parallel Processors,* Los Alamos, 233 – 234.

———. 1980. Revolutionary array processors. *Electronics to microelectronics* (W. A. Kaiser and W. E. Proebster, eds.). Amsterdam: North-Holland. 730 – 734.

Reddy, D. R. 1967. Computer recognition of continuous speech. *J. Acoust. Soc. Amer.* 42: 329 – 347.

Reddy, D. R., Erman, L. D., Fennell, R. D., and Neely, R. B. 1973. The Hearsay speech understanding system: An example of the recognition process. *Proc. Int. Joint Conf. on Artif. Intell.* 3: 185 – 193.

Retberg, R., Mann, B., Goodhue, J., and Hoffman, M. 1983. *The chrysalis operating system.* Cambridge, MA: Bolt, Beranek and Newman.

Reeves, A. P., and De Solla Moura, C. H. 1985. Data mapping and rotation functions for the massively parallel processor. *Proc. Workshop on Comp. Arch. for Pattern Analysis and Image Database Management.* IEEE Computer Society Press, 412 – 419.

Rieger, C., Bane, J., and Trigg, R. 1980. A highly parallel multiprocessor. *Proc. IEEE Workshop on Picture Data Description and Management,* 298 – 304.

Riganati, J. P., and Schneck, P. B., 1984. Supercomputing. *Computer* 17: 97 – 113.

Robinson, J. A. 1965. A machine-oriented logic based on the resolution principle. *J. Assoc. Comp. Mach.* 12: 23 – 41.

Rochester, H., Holland, J. H., Haibt, L. H., and Duda, W. L. 1956. Tests on a cell assembly theory of the action of the brain, using a large digital computer. *IRE Trans. Info. Theory* 2: 80 – 89.

Rosenblatt, F., *Principles of Neurodynamics,* Washington, DC: Spartan, 1962.

Rosenbloom, P. S., Laird, J. E., Newell, A., Golding, A., and Unruh, A. 1985. Current research on learning in SOAR, *Proc. 3rd Int. Machine Learning Workshop,* 163 – 172.

Rosenfeld, A. November 1983. Parallel image processing using cellular arrays. *IEEE Computer* 16: 14 – 21.

———. ed. 1984. *Multi-resolution systems for image processing.* Amsterdam: North-Holland.

———. 1986. The prism machine: An alternative to the pyramid, *J. Par. Distr. Computing* 3: 404 – 411.

Rosenfeld, A., and Kak, A. C. 1982. *Digital picture processing.* 2nd ed. New York: Academic.

Rumelhart, D. E., Hinton, G. E., and Williams, R. J. 1986. Learning internal representations by error propagation. *Parallel distributed processing: Explorations in the microstructure of cognition. Vol. 1: Foundations* (D. E. Rumelhart and J. L. McClelland, eds.). Cambridge: MIT Press. 318–365

Rumelhart, D. E., McClelland, J. L., and the PDP Research Group 1986. *Parallel distributed processing: Explorations in the microstructure of cognition. Vol. 1: Foundations.* Cambridge: MIT Press.

Russell, R. M. 1978. The Cray-1 computer system. *Comm. Assoc. Comp. Mach.* 21: 63–72.

Rychener, M. D. 1976. Production systems as a programming language for artificial intelligence applications. Ph.D. diss., Department of Computer Science, Carnegie-Mellon University, Pittsburgh, PA.

Sabbah, D. 1982. A connectionist approach to visual perception. Ph.D. diss., Department of Computer Science, University of Rochester, Rochester, NY.

Sacerdoti, E. D. 1973. A structure for plans and behavior. Ph.D. diss., Department of Computer Science, Stanford University, Stanford, CA.

Sakai, T., Kanade, T., and Ohta, Y. 1976. Model-based interpretation of outdoor scenes. *Proc. Int. Joint Conf. on Pattern Recog.* 4: 581–585.

Salisbury, J. K. 1982. Kinematic and force analysis of articulated hands. Ph.D. diss., Department of Computer Science, Stanford University, Stanford, CA.

Samatham, M. R., and Pradhan, D. K. 1984. A multi-processor network suitable for single-chip VLSI implementation. *11th Ann. Int. Symp. Comp. Arch.* 328–337.

Samuel, A. L. 1959. Some studies in machine learning using the game of checkers. *IBM J. Res. and Devel.* 3: 210–229.

———. 1967. Some studies in machine learning using the game of checkers, II: Recent progress. *IBM J. Res. and Devel.* 11: 601–617.

Sandon, P. A. 1985. A pyramid implementation using a reconfigurable array of processors. *Proc. Workshop on Comp. Arch. for Pattern Analysis and Image Database Management.* IEEE Computer Society Press, 112–118.

Sauvain, R., and Uhr, L. 1969. A teachable pattern describing and recognizing program. *Pattern Recog.* 1: 219–232.

Sawchuk, A. A., and Jenkins, B. K. March 1985. Algorithms for digital optical processors. *Proc. of the Topical Meeting on Opt. Comp.* Optical Society of America.

Sawchuck, A. A., and Strand, T. C. 1984. Digital optical computing. *Proc IEEE* 72: 758–779.

Schaefer, D. H. 1979. Massively parallel information processing systems for space applications. *AIAA 2nd Conf. on Comp. in Aerospace*, 284–286.

——. 1985. A pyramid of MPP processing elements—Experiences and plans. *Proc. 18th Int. Conf. on System Sciences.*

Schaefer, D. H., Fischer, J. R., and Wallgren, K. R. 1982. The massively parallel processor. *J. Guid. Control and Dynam.* 5.

Schaefer, D. H., and Strong, J. P. 1977. TSE computers. *Proc. IEEE* 65: 129 – 38.

Schank, R. C. 1975. *Conceptual information processing.* Amsterdam: North-Holland.

Schank, R. C., and Riesbeck, C. K., eds. 1981. *Inside computer understanding: Five programs plus miniatures.* Hillsdale, NJ, Erlbaum.

Schwartz, J. T. 1980. Ultra-computers. *Assoc. Comp. Mach. Trans. Programming Languages and Systems,* 2: 484 – 521.

Scott, A. C. 1977. *Neuro-physics.* New York: Wiley.

Sebestyen, G. S. 1961. Recognition of membership in classes. *IRE Trans. Info. Theory.* 7: 44 – 50.

Segre, A. M., and DeJong, G. 1985. Explanation-based manipulator learning: Acquisition of planning ability through observation. *Int. Conf. on Robotics and Automation* 555 – 560.

Seitz, C. L. 1985. The cosmic cube. *Comm. Assoc. Comp. Mach.* 28: 22 – 33.

Sejnowski, M. C., Upchurch, E. T., Kapur, R. N., Charlu, D. P. S., and Lipovski, G. J. 1980. An overview of the Texas reconfigurable array computer. *Proc. Nat. Computer Conf.* 49: 631 – 641.

Sequin, C. H. 1981. Doubly twisted torus networks for VLSI processor arrays. *Proc. 8th Ann. Symp. on Comp. Arch.* 471 – 480.

Shannon, C. E. 1950. Programming a computer to play chess. *Philosophy Magazine,* 41: 256 – 275.

Sharma, M., Patel, J. H., and Ahuja, N. 1985. NETRA: An architecture for a large scale multiprocessor vision system. *Proc. Workshop on Comp. Arch. for Pattern Analysis and Image Database Management.* IEEE Computer Society Press, 92 – 98.

Shaw, D. W. 1982. The NON-VON supercomputer. Computer Science Department, Columbia University, Technical Report.

——. 1984. SIMD and MSIMD variants of the NON-VON supercomputer. *COMPCON Spring 84.*

——. 1985. NON-VON's applicability to three AI task areas. *Proc. Int. Joint Conf. on Artif. Intell.* 9: 61 – 72.

——. 1986. Organization and operation of a massively parallel machine. *Computers and technology* (G. Rabat, ed.). Amsterdam: North-Holland.

Shirai, Y. 1978. Recognition of real-world objects using edge cues. *Computer vision systems* (A. R. Hanson and E. M. Riseman, eds.). New York: Academic, 353 – 362.

Shortliffe, E. H. 1976. *Computer-based medical consultations.* New York: Elsevier.

Siegel, H. J. 1979. A model of SIMD machines and a comparison of various interconnection networks. *IEEE Trans. Comp.* 28: 907 – 917.

———. 1981. PASM: A reconfigurable multimicrocomputer system for image processing. *Languages and architectures for image processing* (M. J. B. Duff and S. Levialdi, eds.). London: Academic.

———. 1984. *Interconnection networks for large scale parallel processing.* Lexington, MA: Lexington Books.

Siegel, H. J., Siegel, L. J., Kemmerer, F. C., Mueller, P. T. Jr., Smalley, H. E., and Smith, S. D. 1981. PASM: A partitionable SIMD/MIMD system for image processing and pattern recognition. *IEEE Trans. Comp.* C-30: 934 – 947.

Siklossy, L., and Dreussi, J. 1973. An efficient robot planner which generates its own procedures. *Proc. Int. Joint Conf. on Artif. Intell.* 3: 423 – 430.

Simmons, R. F. 1970. Natural language question-answering systems: 1969. *Comm. Assoc. Comp. Mach.* 9: 211 – 214.

———. 1973. Semantic networks: Their computation and use for understanding English sentences. *Computer models of thought and language* (R. C. Schank and K. M. Colby, eds.). San Francisco: Freeman, 63 – 113.

Slotnick, D. L., Borck, W. C., and McReynolds, R. C. 1962. The Solomon computer. *Proc. AFIPS Nat. Comput. Conf.* 97 – 107.

Smith, D. H., Buchanan, B. G., Englemore, R. S., Adlercreutz, H., and Djerassi, C. 1973. Applications of artificial intelligence for chemical inference IX: Analysis of mixtures without prior separation as illustrated for estrogens. *J. Amer. Chem. Soc.* 95: 6078.

Smith, D. H., Buchanan, B. G., Englemore, R. S., Duffield, A. M., Yeo, A. M., Feigenbaum, E. A., Lederberg, J., and Djerassi, C. 1972. Applications of artificial intelligence for chemical inference VIII: An approach to the computer interpretation of the high resolution mass spectra of complex molecules. Structure elucidation of estrogenic steroids. *J. Amer. Chem. Soc.* 94: 5962.

Smith, S. D., Walker, A. C., and Wherrett, B. S. March 1985. Cascadable digital optical logic circuit elements in the visible and infrared: prospects for fast array processors. *Proc. of the Topical Meeting on Opt. Comp.* Optical Society of America.

Snyder, L. 1982. Introduction to the configurable, highly parallel computer. *IEEE Comp.* 15: 47 – 56.

———. 1984. Supercomputers and VLSI: The effect of large-scale integration on computer architecture. *Advances in Comp.* 23: 1 – 33.

———. 1985. An inquiry into the benefits of multigauge parallel computations. *Proc. Int. Conf. Parallel Process.* 488–492.

Sternberg, S. R. 1978. Cytocomputer real-time pattern recognition. Paper presented at the Eighth Pattern Recognition Symposium, National Bureau of Standards.

———. 1980. Language and architecture for parallel image processing. *Proceedings of the Conference on Pattern Recognition in Practice* (E. S. Gelsema and L. N. Kanal, eds.). Amsterdam: North-Holland.

Stolfo, S. J. 1984. Five parallel algorithms for production system execution on the DADO machine. *Proc. Nat. Conf. on Artif. Intell.*

Stolfo, S. J., and Shaw, D. E. 1982. DADO: a tree structured machine architecture for production systems. *Proc. Nat. Conf. on Artif. Intell.*

Stone, D., Dreher, B., and Leventhal, A. 1979. Hierarchical and parallel mechanisms in the organization of visual cortex. *Brain Res. Rev.* 1: 345–394.

Stone, H. S. 1971. Parallel processing with the perfect shuffle. *IEEE Trans. Comp.* 20: 153–161.

———. 1980. *Introduction to computer architecture.* Chicago: SRA.

Storwick, R. M. 1970. Improved construction for (d,k) graphs. *IEEE Trans. Comp.* 19: 1214–1216.

Stout, Q. F. 1983. Sorting, merging, selecting, and filtering on tree and pyramid machines. *Proc. Int. Conf. on Parallel Process.* 214–221.

———. 1985a. An algorithmic comparison of arrays and pyramids. *Evaluation of multicomputers for image processing* (L. Uhr, K. Preston, S. Levialdi, and M. J. B. Duff, eds.). London: Academic.

———. 1985b. Tree-based graph algorithms for some parallel computers. *Proc. Int. Conf. Parallel Process.* 727–730.

———. 1985c. Mesh and pyramid computers inspired by geometric algorithms. Electrical Engineering and Computer Science Department, University of Michigan, Ann Arbor, Technical Report.

Strong, J. P. 1985. The Fourier transform on mesh connected processing arrays such as the massively parallel processor. *Proc. Workshop on Comp. Arch. for Pattern Analysis and Image Database Management.* IEEE Computer Society Press, 190–196.

Sullivan, H., Bashkov, T., and Klappholz, D. 1977. A large scale, homogenous, fully distributed parallel machine. *Proc. 4th Ann. Symp. on Comp. Arch.* 105–124.

Sussman, G. J. 1975. *A computer model of skill acquisition.* New York: Elsevier.

Swan, R. J., Fuller, S. H., and Siewiorek, D. P. 1977. Cm*—A modular, multi-microprocessor. *Proc. AFIPS Nat. Comp. Conf.* 637–663. Conf. *637–663.*

Szentagothai, J. 1978. The local neuronal apparatus of the cerebral cortex. *Cerebral correlates of conscious experience* (P. A. Buser and A Roguel-Buser, eds.). Amsterdam: North-Holland.

Tanimoto, S. L. 1976. Pictorial feature distortion in a pyramid. *Comp. Graphics Image Proc.* 5: 333–352.

————. 1978. Regular hierarchical image and processing structures in machine vision. *Computer vision systems* (A. R. Hanson and E. M. Riseman, eds.). New York: Academic, 165–174.

————. 1981. Towards hierarchical cellular logic: Design considerations for pyramid machines. Computer Science Department, University of Washington, Seattle.

————. 1982. Programming techniques for hierarchical image processors. *Multicomputers and image processing* (K. Preston, Jr. and L. Uhr, eds.). New York: Academic.

————. 1983a. A pyramidal approach to parallel processing. *Proc. 10th Annual Int. Symposium on Comp. Arch.* Stockholm, 372–378.

————. 1983b. Algorithms for median filtering of images on a pyramid machine. *Computing structures for image processing,* (M. J. B. Duff, ed.). London: Academic, 123–141.

————. 1984. A hierarchical cellular logic for pyramid computers. *J. Parallel and Distrib. Comp.* 1: 105–132.

————. 1985. An approach to the iconic/sybolic interface. *Integrated technology for image processing* (S. Levialdi, ed.). London: Academic, 31–38.

Tanimoto, S., and Klinger, A., eds. 1980. *Structured computer vision.* New York: Academic.

Thurber, K. J. 1976. *Large scale computer architecture.* Rochelle Park, NJ: Hayden.

Towster, E. 1970. Studies in concept formation. Ph.D. diss., Department of Computer Science. University of Wisconsin.

Tuazan, J., Peterson, J., Pniel, M., and Liberman, D. 1985. Caltech/JPL Mark II hypercube concurrent processor. *Proc. Int. Conf. on Parallel Process.* 666–673.

Turing, A. M. 1936. On computable numbers, with an application to the Entscheidungsproblem. *Proc. London Math. Soc., Ser. 2* 42: 230–265.

————. 1950. Computing machinery and intelligence. *Mind* 59: 433–460.

Uhr, L. 1972. Layered "recognition cone" networks that preprocess, classify and describe. *IEEE Trans Comp.* 21: 758–768.

————. 1973. *Pattern recognition, learning, and thought.* Englewood Cliffs, NJ: Prentice-Hall.

——. 1975. Toward integrated cognitive systems, which must make fuzzy decisions about fuzzy problems. *Fuzzy Sets* (L. Zadeh et al., eds.). New York: Academic, 353–393.

——. 1976. "Recognition cones" that perceive and describe scenes that move and change over time. *Proc. Int. Joint Conf. on Pattern Recog.* 4: 287–293.

——. 1978. "Recognition cones" and some test results. *Computer vision systems* (A. Hanson and E. Riseman, eds.). New York: Academic, 363–372.

——. 1979. Parallel-serial production systems with many working memories. *Proc. Int. Joint Conf. on Artif. Intell.* 6.

——. 1981. Converging pyramids of array. *Proc. Workshop on Comp. Arch. for Pattern Analysis and Image Database Management.* IEEE Computer Society Press, 31–34.

——. 1982. Comparing serial computers, arrays and networks using measures of "Active resources." *IEEE Trans. Comp.* 30: 1022–1025.

——. 1983a Pyramid multi-computer structures, and augmented pyramids. *Computing structures for image processing* (M. J. B. Duff, ed). London: Academic, 95–112.

——. 1983b. Augmenting pyramids and arrays by compounding them with networks. *Proc. Workshop on Comp. Arch. for Pattern Analysis and Image Database Management.* IEEE Computer Society Press, 162–169.

——. 1984. *Algorithm-structures computer arrays and networks: Architectures and processes for images, precepts, models, information.* New York: Academic.

——. 1985a. Augmenting pyramids and arrays by embossing them into optimal graphs to build multicomputer networks. *Integrated technology for image processing* (S. Levialdi, ed.). London: Academic, 19–30.

——. 1985b. Pyramid multi-computers, and extensions and augmentations. *Algorithmically specialized parallel computers* (L. Snyder, L. H. Jamieson, D. B. Gannon, and H. J. Siegel, eds.). New York: Academic, 177–186.

——. 1986. Multiple-image and multimodal augmented pyramid computers. *Intermediate level image processing* (M. Duff, ed.). London: Academic, 127–145.

Uhr, L., and Douglass, R. 1979. A parallel-serial recognition cone system for perception. *Pattern Recog.* 11: 29–40.

Uhr, L., and Jordan, S. 1969. The learning of parameters for generating compound characterizers for pattern recognition. *Proc. Int. Joint Conf. on Artif. Intell.* 1: 381–415.

Uhr, L., and Kochen, M. 1969. MIKROKOSMs and robots. *Proc. Int. Joint Conf. on Artif. Intell.* 1: 541–556.

Uhr, L., Schmitt, L., and Hanrahan, P. 1982. Cone/pyramid perception programs for arrays and networks. *Multi-computers and image processing* (K. Preston, Jr. and L. Uhr, eds.). New York: Academic, 180–191.

Uhr, L., Thompson, M., and Lackey, J. 1981. A 2-layered SIMD/MIMD parallel pyramidal "Array/Net." *Proc. Workshop on Comp. Arch. for Pattern Analysis and Image Data Base Management.* IEEE Computer Society Press, 209–216.

Uhr, L., and Vossler, C. 1961a. A pattern recognition program that generates, evaluates and adjusts its own operators. *Proc. West. Joint Comp. Conf.* 19: 555–569.

———. 1961b. Recognition of speech by a computer program that simulates a model for human visual pattern recognition. *J. Acoustical Soc. of Amer.* 33: 1426.

Ullman, S. 1979. *The interpretation of visual motion.* Cambridge: MIT Press.

Unger, S. H. 1958. A computer oriented toward spatial problems. *Proc. IRE,* 46: 1744–1754.

———. 1959. Pattern detection and recognition. *Proc. IRE,* 47: 1732–1752.

Valiant, L. G. 1984. Learning disjunctions of conjunctions. *Proc. Int. Joint Conf. on Artif. Intell.* 9: 560–566.

Van Essen, D. C. 1985. Functional organization of primate visual cortex. Cerebral Cortex: Vol. 3 Visual Cortex (A. Peters and E. G. Jones, eds.). New York: Plenum, 259–329.

Van Essen, D. C., and Maunsell, J. H. R. 1983. Hierarchical organization and functional streams in the visual cortex. *Trends in Neurosci.* 6 570–575.

Vere, S. 1978. Inductive learning of relational productions. *Pattern-directed inference systems* (D. A. Waterman and F. Hayes-Roth, eds.). New York: Academic, 281–295.

Vicens, P. 1967. Aspects of speech recognition by computer. Ph.D. diss., Department of Computer Science, Stanford University, Stanford, CA.

Von Neumann, J. 1945. *First Draft of a Report on the EDVAC.* Moore School of Electrical Engineering, University of Pennsylvania. (Reprinted in part in Randell, 1973.)

———. 1966. *Theory of self-reproducing automata* (A. Burks, ed.). Urbana: University of Illinois Press.

Wah, B. W., Shang, W., and Aboelaze, M. 1985. Buffering in macropipelines of systolic arrays. *Proc. Workshop on Comp. Arch. for Pattern Analysis and Image Database Management.* IEEE Computer Society Press, 2–8.

Wallace, R., Stentz, A., Thorpe, C., Moravec, H., Whittaker, W., and Kanade, T. 1985. First results on robot road-following. *Proc. Int. Joint Conf. on Artif. Intell.* 9: 1089–1095.

Warner, B. 1985. *The Intel concurrent computer.* Portland, OR. Intel.

Warren, D. H. D., Pereira, L. M., and Pereira, F. 1977. PROLOG—The language and its implementation compared with LISP. *Sigplan Notices* 12.

Waterman, D. A. 1970. Generalization learning techniques for automating the learning of heuristics. *Artif. Intell.* 1: 121–170.

———. 1975. Adaptive production systems. *Proc. Int. Joint Conf. on Artif. Intell.* 4: 296–303.

———. 1986. *A guide to expert systems.* Reading, MA: Addison-Wesley.

Weems, C. 1984. Image processing with a content addressable array parallel processor. Ph.D. diss., Computer and Information Science Department, University of Massachusetts.

Weems, C., Levitan, S., and Foster, C. 1982. Titanic: A VLSI-based content addressable parallel array processor. *Proc. IEEE Int. Conf. on Circuits and Computers*, 236–239.

Wiezenbaum, J. 1976. *Computer power and human reasoning: From judgment to calculation.* San Francisco: Freeman.

Whitby-Stevens, C. 1985. The transputer. *12th Ann. Int. Symp. on Comp. Arch.* 292–300.

Widdoes, L. C. 1980. The S-1 project: Developing high-speed digital computers. *Proc. Compcon 80,* 282–291.

Wilks, Y. A. 1973. An artificial intelligence approach to machine translation. *Computer models of thought and language* (R. C. Schank and K. M. Colby, eds.). San Francisco: Freeman, 114–151.

Williams, H. A. 1976. A net-structure learning system for pattern description. *Pattern Recog.* 8: 261–272.

Wilson, S. S. 1985. The PIXIE-5000—A systolic array process. *Proc. Workshop on Comp. Arch. for Pattern Analysis and Image Database Management.* IEEE Computer Society Press, 477–483.

Winograd, T. 1982. *Language as a cognitive process.* Reading, MA: Addison-Wesley.

Winston, P. H. 1975. Learning structural descriptions from examples. *The psychology of computer vision* (P. H. Winson, ed.). New York: McGraw-Hill, 157–209.

Wittie, L. D. 1976. Efficient message routing in mega-micro-computer networks. *Proc. 3d Ann. Symp. on Comp. Arch.* New York: IEEE.

———. 1978. MICRONET: A reconfigurable microcomputer network for distributed systems research. *Simulation* 31: 145–153.

Wittie, L. D., and van Tilborg, A. M. 1980. MICROS, a distributed operating system for MICRONET, a reconfigurable network computer. *IEEE Trans. Comp.* 29: 1133 – 1144.

Woods, W. A. 1970. Transition network grammars for natural language analysis. *Comm. Assoc. Comp. Mach.* 13: 591 – 606.

———. 1972. An experimental parsing system for transition network grammars. *Natural language processing* (R. Rustin, ed). New York: Algorithmics Press.

———. 1973. Progress in natural language understanding: An application to lunar geology. *Proc. AFIPS Nat. Comp. Conf.* 42: 441 – 450.

———. 1975. An experimental parsing system for transition network grammars. *Natural language processing* (R. Rustin, ed.). New York: Algorithmics Press, 113 – 154.

Woolsey, C. N. ed., 1981. *Cortical sensory organization, Vol. 2: Multiple visual areas.* Clifton, NJ: Humana.

Wu, C.-L., and Feng, T.-Y. 1981. The universality of the shuffle-exchange network. *IEEE Trans. Comp.* 30: 324 – 332.

Wulf, W. A., and Bell, C. G. 1972. C.mmp—A multi-mini processor. *Proc. AFIPS Nat. Comp. Conf.* 41: 765 – 777.

Wulf, W. A., Cohen, E., Corwin, W., Jones, A., Levin, R., Pierson, C., and Pollack, F. 1974. HYDRA: The kernel of a multiprocessor operating system. *Comm. Assoc. for Comp. Mach.* 17: 337 – 345.

Wulf, W. A., Levin, R., and Harbison, S. P. 1981. HYDRA/C.mmp: An experimental computer system. New York: McGraw-Hill.

Yalamanchili, S., and Aggarwal, J. K. December 1985. Reconfiguration strategies for parallel architectures. *Computer* 18: 44 – 60.

Yngve, V. H. 1957. A framework for syntactic translation. *Mech.Translation* 4: 59 – 65.

———. 1963. COMIT. *Comm. Assoc. for Comp. Mach.* 6: 83 – 84.

Yu, V. L., Fagan, L. M., Wraith, S. M., Clancy, W. J., Scott, A. C., Hannigan, J., Blum, R. L., Buchanan, B. G., and Cohen, S. N. 1979. Antimicrobial selection by a computer. *J. Amer. Med. Assoc.* 242: 1279 – 1282.

Zeki, S. M. 1978. Uniformity and diversity of structure and function in rhesus monkey prestriate visual cortex. *J. Physiol.* 277: 273 – 290.

Zimmer, H. 1951. *Philosophies of India.* New York: Bollingen.

Zobrist, A. L., and Carlson, F. R., Jr. January 1973. An advice-taking chess computer. *Sci. Amer.* 228: 93 – 105.

AUTHOR INDEX

Note: Numbers in *italics* indicate pages on which full references appear.

SUBJECT INDEX